CANADIAN NURSING

Issues and Perspectives

CANADIAN NURSING

Issues and Perspectives

Janet Ross Kerr, RN, PhD
Professor, Faculty of Nursing
University of Alberta
Edmonton, Alberta

Jannetta MacPhail, MSN, PhD, FAAN, LLD (Hon)
Professor Emeritus, Faculty of Nursing
University of Alberta
Edmonton, Alberta

Illustrated

Mosby
Year Book

St. Louis Baltimore Boston Chicago London Philadelphia Sydney Toronto

Mosby
Year Book
Dedicated to Publishing Excellence

Editor: Linda L. Duncan
Project Manager: Carol Sullivan Wiseman
Production Editors: Lisa Cohen and Diana Lyn Laulainen
Design: Liz Fett

Printed in Canada

Mosby-Year Book
11830 Westline Industrial Drive, St. Louis, Missouri, 63146

The C.V. Mosby Company ltd.
5240 Finch Avenue East, Scarborough, Ontario M1S 5A2, Canada

Canadian Cataloguing in Publication Data

Kerr, Janet C.
  Canadian nursing

2nd ed.
Includes bibliographical references.
ISBN 0-8016-6274-5

1. Nursing—Canada. 2. Nursing—Study and
teaching—Canada. I. MacPhail, Jannetta.
II. Title.

RT6.A1K4   1990   610.73'0971   C90-095605-4

GW/BP   9   8   7   6   5   4   3   2   1

To the University of Alberta nursing students whose enthusiasm and desire for knowledge about professional issues and trends in nursing inspired us to write this book. Also to nursing educators who value the history and philosophy of the profession and who have helped make opportunities available for students to study nursing issues and trends at the undergraduate and graduate levels.

Preface

It is sometimes difficult to see progress and feel a sense of pride or satisfaction with the events in a profession when you are in the middle of the action. Every nurse is a part of that action, since each one of us contributes in a unique way to the development of the profession. Although things may not always go as we would want and progress often seems to be slow and uneven, the pursuit of our goals is important to us, and in working for them individually and collectively, we can and do make a difference in the course of events over time.

The publication of the second edition of our book 2½ years after the first has allowed us to take stock of developments in the profession and has given us the opportunity to measure the extent of progress over this time. Despite the fact that we would want things to move faster in some areas, it is evident that there has been steady and measurable progress in a relatively short period. Movement toward the entry-to-practice goal of the profession has been considerable in some areas of the country, and the realization of a doctoral program in nursing seems more certain at this time. Nurses are asserting their needs and are using political skills and labor relations processes to their advantage. Our issues are being taken more seriously by politicians, employers, and institutions. In some cases, governments have literally been brought to their knees by the voices of nurses. The primary health care movement in Canada is being nurtured and led by nurses, and there have been positive steps forward in this area. It is also evident that nursing research has been enhanced by the quality of work done by an increasing number of nurses with research preparation. Questions about workforce supply have also been raised. These and other developments have been explored in the second edition. The addition of a new chapter on nursing theory compliments the other chapters in the section on the development of nursing knowledge. The historical basis of developments in nursing is an integral part of each chapter, and an entirely new chapter on the history of diploma education in nursing has been added.

The success of the first edition confirmed our view that the need for a resource book on issues and trends in contemporary Canadian nursing was real. It was intended for all practising nurses, including those involved in direct care, educating nurses, doing research, and administering nursing systems, as well as for nursing students. It is our hope that this book will inspire our colleagues to consider issues that will positively influence the health care of Canadians. This opportunity to step back and identify and evaluate what has happened has given us satisfaction and pleasure. It is our hope that readers will be able to share with us a renewed appreciation of the accomplishments of nurses and the rewards of being involved in professional developments.

Janet Ross Kerr
Janetta MacPhail

Acknowledgments

We are indebted to the following authors who contributed chapters to this book:

Marion N. Allen, RN, BN, MScN, MN, PhD
Associate Professor,
Faculty of Nursing, The University of Alberta,
Edmonton, Alberta

Heather F. Clarke, RN, BNSc, MN, PhD
Nursing Research Consultant,
Registered Nurses Association of British Columbia,
Vancouver, British Columbia

Louise A. Jensen, RN, BScN, MN, PhD
Associate Professor,
Faculty of Nursing, The University of Alberta,
Edmonton, Alberta

Eleanor Ross, RN, BScN, MScN
Clinical Nurse Specialist,
Sunnybrook Health Science Centre, and
Doctoral Candidate, University of Toronto,
Toronto, Ontario

Richard Splane, MA, MSW, PhD, LLD (Hon)
Professor Emeritus, School of Social Work, University of
British Columbia, and Consultant in Social Policy, Splane Associates,
Vancouver, British Columbia

Verna Huffman Splane, RN, MPH, LLD (Hon)
Associate Professor (Associate Faculty), Faculty of Nursing, University of Alberta,
and Nursing Consultant (International Health Policy), Splane Associates,
Vancouver, British Columbia

Contents

PART I

The Profession in Canada

CHAPTER ONE

Early Nursing in Canada, 1600-1760: A Legacy For The Future

JANET ROSS KERR

As a result of Jacques Cartier's numerous voyages across the Atlantic, including his 1535 landing on Newfoundland, France laid claim to the vast area
along the St. Lawrence River, later to become Canada. Exploration and establishment of the first French settlement in the new land occurred over the next
century. Samuel de Champlain, who made his first voyage to the new territory
in 1603, was well qualified for his prominent role as explorer and leader, for he
had already attained the rank of royal geographer in France before setting off
for New France (Repplier, 1931). In 1608, he selected Quebec as the site for a
colony of settlers because this sheltered and beautiful spot would serve as an
ideal trading centre for the growing fur trade.

The story of the early colonization of New France parallels the development
of nursing because the establishment of hospitals and a system of health care
preceded the general settlement of the colony. The development of health care
in the new land was considered to be of prime importance in the civilization of
the colony. At the outset, and for many years thereafter, human services, including health care, education, and social welfare, focused on the indigenous peoples—the numerous Indian tribes populating the region. Spurred on by religious
fervour and zeal, nuns and priests made great efforts to befriend and subsequently convert natives to Christianity. They and other early settlers endured
considerable hardship and were subject to hazardous living conditions in the
early years; these first colonists in the new land had to provide their own health
care, as had the native peoples before them. Abbott reports that the first
physician-surgeons in this part of New France were:

> Jehan de Brouet, who sailed up the St. Lawrence to Tadousac in A.D. 1600 as
> surgeon of Chauvin's fleet; one Bonnerme, who, in 1608 accompanied Champlain to
> Quebec and thus became its first surgeon, but who died the following year from
> either scurvy or dysentery (Abbott, 1931, p. 15).

THE FIRST NURSES IN NEW FRANCE

The first nurses in New France have received considerable attention as a result of their courage, sacrifice, and altruism, as well as their skill. It should be noted at the outset, though, that the several thousand Indians living in the region before the immigration of colonists from France had developed a system of health care characterized by numerous herbal remedies for particular ailments. Although the concept of nurse was somewhat different from that of today in this new and struggling colony, the first nurses to tend the sick were male attendants at a "sick bay" established at the French garrison in Port Royal in Acadia in 1629 (Gibbon and Mathewson, 1947). In addition, the Jesuit priests who were missionary immigrants to New France found themselves caring for the sick in the course of their primary mission, the conversion of the natives to Christianity: "The Jesuits singly or in pairs travelled in the depth of winter from village to village, ministering to the sick and seeking to commend their religious teachings by their efforts to relieve bodily distress" (Parkman, 1897, p. 176).

MARIE ROLLET HÉBERT

The first lay woman who regularly cared for the sick, both in her home and in other homes in the community, was Marie Rollet; she was married to the surgeon-apothecary, Louis Hébert. The Hébert family emigrated to Quebec, at the request of Champlain, in 1617. Louis Hébert had had previous experience in the new world, having made journeys to Île St. Croix in 1604 to 1605, and in 1606 to 1607 and 1610 to 1613 to Port Royal. On his fourth journey, he embarked from Honfleur in 1617 accompanied by Mme Hébert and their three children. Mme Marie Hébert thus became the first woman to emigrate to the new colony from France in what was to become Canada (Brown, 1966). It is reported that in Quebec, Louis Hébert's apothecary skill and his small store of grain were a godsend to the sick and starving winterers. In spite of the company's demands on his and his servant's time, he succeeded in clearing and planting some land (Brown, 1966, p. 368).

Louis Hébert's wife, "Marie Rollet aided her husband in caring for the sick and shared his interest in the savages" (Brown, 1966, p. 578). This was quite natural, as it was common practice for French wives of the early seventeenth century to collaborate with their husbands in their work. Of special attention was Mme Hébert's genuine concern for the indigenous people as intelligent human beings. Her efforts, as well as those of her husband, to care for them and share knowledge about health with them appear to have been welcomed and appreciated by the native people (Thwaites, 1959).

A CALL FOR NURSES

The people of France learned about the new colony through the *Jesuit Relations,* informative reports written regularly by the Jesuit missionary priests to spread word about life in the new world and to stimulate needed support. These were written over a 72-year period and provide a marvellous account of life in early Canada. According to Parkman, "It was clear to the fathers that their ministrations were valued solely because their religion was supposed by many to be a 'medicine' or charm, efficacious against disease and death" (Parkman, 1897, p. 179). Thus, they sent urgent requests for nurses to come to the colony to assist with their work. In 1634, Father LeJeune wrote in his *Relation*:

> If we had a hospital here, all the sick people of the country, and all the old people, would be there. As to the men, we will take care of them according to our means; but, in regard to the women, it is not becoming for us to receive them into our houses (Kenton, 1925, p. 49).

Evidently questions of propriety, undoubtedly an important part of the culture of the times, made it a problem for the Jesuit priests on missionary premises to care for native women who were ill. This then presented another pressing reason for female members of a nursing order to come to Canada to assist with the work. It is somewhat curious to reflect on the fact that "Quebec, as we have seen, had a seminary, a hospital, and a convent, before it had a population" (Parkman, 1897, p. 259).

HOSPITALIÈRES DE LA MISÉRICORDE DE JÉSUS

The Duchesse d'Aiguillon, a niece of Cardinal Richelieu, read and was moved by the *Relations* and developed a plan to build the Hôtel Dieu at Quebec. She used her influence to obtain a grant of land and arranged for the careful selection of three nuns of the Hospitalières de la Miséricorde de Jésus to go to Canada to establish the hospital. The three nuns, who all came from good families, were Marie Guenet de St. Ignace (later Mère de St. Ignace), Anne Lecointre de St. Bernard, and Marie Forestier de St. Bonaventure de Jésus. Aboard ship at Dieppe, the "hospital nuns" encountered three Ursuline nuns, whose mission was to teach the natives, and Madame de la Peltrie, who intended to help establish a convent school for the native children. The voyage was perilous, lasting from May to August 1639 (Juchereau & Duplessis, 1939), and upon their arrival the women began work immediately:

> The Hospital Nuns arrived at Kebec on the first day of August of last year. Scarcely had they disembarked before they found themselves overwhelmed with patients. The hall of the hospital being too small, it was necessary to erect some cabins, fashioned like those of the savages, in their garden. Not having furniture for so many people, they had to cut in two or three pieces part of the blankets and sheets they had brought for these poor sick people. (Kenton, 1925, p. 157)

As there was no time to make any preparations, the nuns had to throw themselves into their work from the first day and:

> ...in a word, instead of taking a little rest and refreshing themselves after the great discomforts they had suffered upon the sea, they found themselves so burdened and occupied that we had fear of losing them and their hospital at its very birth. The sick came from all directions in such numbers, their stench was so insup-

portable, the heat so great, the fresh food so scarce and so poor, in a country so new and strange, that I do not know how these good sisters, who almost had not even leisure in which to take a little sleep, endured all these hardships (Kenton, 1925, p. 157).

The smallpox epidemic, which was raging on their arrival and for a considerable length of time thereafter, also required the labours of the Ursuline nuns, whose school convent became a hospital: "and they found themselves nursing instead of teaching" (Millman, 1965, p. 424). Jamieson has commented on the fact that the Ursulines used native Indian women for assistance in their hospitals, and that "their teacher training was instrumental in providing the earliest instruction and supervision of nurses in America" (Jamieson, Sewall, and Gjertson, 1959, p. 196).

New recruits from Dieppe were sought and the first two sisters arrived the following summer. The nuns also moved their base of operations to Sillery, a settlement outside Quebec, in a more convenient location for the Indians. The structure in which they had spent the first winter had proven woefully inadequate to withstand the winter elements, and a new building was constructed in Sillery. Soon the hospital was inundated with Indian patients, and many had to be cared for in adjacent cabins. With considerable regret, the nuns had to abandon their white habits for a more serviceable brown. It is reported, too, that the sisters applied themselves to learning the language of the Hurons and Algonquins for whom they cared (Gibbon and Mathewson, 1947).

In 1644, Governor De Montmagny implored the sisters to return to the safety of Quebec, as the Iroquois were reported to be on the warpath and the sisters would be in danger by staying in Sillery. They returned and were lodged in temporary quarters while a new hospital was constructed. The latter was not completed until two years later and, during the smallpox epidemic of 1650, the number of patients received was so great that they could not all be accommodated in the hospital. The sisters also considered it their duty to assist new settling families in Quebec as much as they could. The archives of the Hôtel Dieu of Quebec contain a letter from Vincent de Paul written in April, 1652, in which he states: "I consider this enterprise as one of the greatest accomplished within fifteen hundred years" (Gibbon and Mathewson, 1947, p. 15).

Another addition to their hospital, begun in 1654, was completed four years later. A series of epidemics started in the year after the addition's completion, beginning with typhus and followed by smallpox. This was to be an unending series of epidemics that had started with the sisters' arrival and would continue over the years. Danger from the Iroquois Indians was a serious concern at some periods; because of this danger, for three weeks in 1660, the Governor ordered that only three or four sisters should stay overnight in their hospital convent and the rest would stay in the safer Jesuit monastery. By 1671, the nuns were obtaining sufficient recruits to the order from the local area so that they no longer depended on assistance from France.

In 1690, hostilities broke out once more between the British and the French, and the sisters of the Hôtel Dieu of Quebec found themselves in the middle of the conflict. It is reported that 26 cannonballs hit the hospital on one day of heavy fighting. The siege was over in four days and the British withdrew. Epidemics followed from time to time, but the worst appears to have been one of smallpox in 1703, when more than a quarter of the nuns died:

> Our sisters fell ill in such numbers from the very first that there were not enough of those who were well to look after the infected cases in our rooms and wards. We accepted the offer of service from several good widows (Gibbon and Mathewson, 1947, p. 35).

JEANNE MANCE

La Société de Notre Dame de Jésus was composed of a group of philanthropists who wanted to establish a colony of a religious character to work with the Indians on the Island of Montreal. This was no easy matter, as they had to secure the charter for the land and raise sufficient funds to send a carefully selected group of people to create the society they had in mind. The hospital, however, might, they thought, be begun at once. Jeanne Mance had read the *Jesuit Relations* regularly and believed she had been called to serve in the New World. Through the wealth of Mme de Bullion, Jeanne Mance was asked to take charge of building a hospital in the settlement which was to be established at Montreal. Thus, she sailed from La Rochelle, along with 3 women and 40 men, under the leadership of Paul de Chomédy, Sieur de Maisonneuve (Canadian Nurses Association [CNA], 1968). Their two ships arrived in Quebec, but their reception was not a welcoming one. They

> ... arrived too late in the season to ascend to Montreal before winter. They encountered distrust, jealousy, and opposition. The agents of the Company of the Hundred Associates looked on them askance; and the Governor of Quebec, Montmagny, saw a rival governor in Maisonneuve. Every means was used to persuade the adventurers to abandon their project, and settle at Quebec (Parkman, 1897, p. 296).

Steadfast in his resolve to accomplish the mission to establish a settlement at Montreal, Maisonneuve "expressed his surprise that they should assume to direct his affairs. 'I have not come here,' he said, 'to deliberate, but to act. It is my duty and my honour to found a colony at Montreal; and I would go, if every tree were an Iroquois!'" (Parkman, 1897, pp. 296-297). The group had difficulty finding housing for the winter, but through the generosity of one colonist, they were housed at St. Michel, and Jeanne Mance found that her neighbours were the hospital nuns, who lived in their mission at Sillery, not far from Quebec. Here, Jeanne Mance spent a good deal of her time assisting in the work of the hospital, and this undoubtedly served her well as she ventured to Montreal as the only person with health care knowledge.

When on May 17, 1642, Maisonneuve and his followers landed at Montreal, the Associates of Montreal took possession of the land which "Champlain, thirty-one years before, had chosen as the fit site of a settlement" (Parkman, 1897, p. 302). They gave thanks, then proceeded to establish their settlement. The hospital was one of the first buildings constructed in the colony, although there were apparently some misgivings.

It is true that the hospital was not wanted as no one was sick at Ville Marie and one or two chambers would have sufficed for every prospective necessity; but it will be remembered that the colony had been established in order that a hospital might be built . . . Instead then of tilling the land to supply their own pressing needs, all labourers of the settlement were set at this pious though superfluous task (Parkman, 1897, p. 362).

The hospital was about 46 by 18.5 m and contained a kitchen, living quarters for Jeanne Mance and for the servants, and two large areas for the patients: "It was amply provided with furniture, linen, medicine and all necessaries and had two oxen, three cows and 20 sheep. A small oratory of stone was built adjoining it" (Parkman, 1897, pp. 362-363). As there was considerable danger of Iroquois attacks, a palisade was constructed around it, and "here Mlle Mance took up her abode and waited the day when wounds or disease should bring patients to her empty wards" (Parkman, 1897, p. 363). All of the new settlers were committed to the objective of converting the Indians to Christianity, and sought to gain their favour in whatever way they could: "If they could persuade them to be nursed, they were consigned to the tender care of Mlle Mance" (Parkman, 1897, p. 364). A year after its founding Montreal became the target of the Iroquois, and Jeanne Mance had

. . . her hands full attending to men wounded by their arrows. She dressed wounds of all kinds. Chilblains and frost-bite frequently required her attention. According to the Clerk of the Court, she had mortar, scales, a syringe with ivory tube, razors and lances. She had sufficient skill to compound her own medicines, and also had experience in blood letting (Gibbon and Mathewson, 1947, pp. 25-26).

As she was soon in need of more help than the one young girl who had come with her, she enlisted the assistance of two others to cope with the load. Jeanne Mance made three trips back to France, one four years after her arrival, one in 1657, and one in 1663; all of these trips were made primarily for the purpose of meeting with members of the Associates of Notre Dame of Montreal and other benefactors to generate resources for her hospital. She managed to arrange for assistance from a nursing order in France in 1659; thus, three nuns of St. Joseph de la Flèche arrived to assist in nursing the sick in her hospital, of which she remained the administrator. By 1663, the Associates were bankrupt and could no longer continue their assistance to the colony and the hospital; accordingly they transferred their interests to the Gentlemen of Saint Sulpice, and Jeanne Mance witnessed the transfer of ownership to this group. When she died in 1673, she was "universally respected and beloved by the Colony which she had helped to found" (Gibbon and Mathewson, 1947, p. 30).

THE GREY NUNS OF MONTREAL

Considered the first visiting nurses in Canada, this uniquely Canadian order of nuns was formed in 1738 by Marguerite d'Youville, a widow who was a niece of the explorer, La Vérendrye. Les Soeurs Grises were also the first noncloistered order to be established in Canada, patterned after the model initiated by St. Vincent de Paul. Madame d'Youville organized a group of women with charitable intentions, and they "agreed to combine their possessions in a house of refuge chiefly for the poor, taking the names of Soeurs Grises or Grey Nuns" (Gibbon and Mathewson, 1947, p. 45).

Life was by no means easy for them as they had to raise funds to subsist and carry on their work with the sick and the poor. For the purpose of raising money, wealthy paying guests were taken in, and the sisters did handiwork that they sold. Because the order was not cloistered and because it took up the nursing of patients in their homes, something not previously done in Canada, there was some mistrust of its work and intentions from the outset: "Though they usually did their visiting in pairs for self-protection, the Grey Nuns were innovators and subject to misunderstanding" (Gibbon and Mathewson, 1947, p. 46). It is important to recognize that the other orders of nuns working in Canada, the Augustinians in Quebec and the St. Joseph's Hospitallers of Montreal, were cloistered and were not permitted to venture into the community except in an emergency by special permission of the Bishop.

A fire in 1745 destroyed their house, and the Grey Nuns were forced to move from one place to another for the next two years to carry on their work. Then, the Gentlemen of Saint Sulpice gave permission for Madame d'Youville and the Grey Nuns to take over the General Hospital under a charter as the Soeurs de la Charité de l'Hôpital Général de Montréal. Their debts were so great that they had to resort to all sorts of new fund-raising activities, including making military garments and tents, establishing a brewery as well as a tobacco plant, and operating a freight and cartage business. Patients who regained health as the result of the nuns' charitable efforts were put to work to aid in the fund-raising effort (Gibbon and Mathewson, 1947, p. 47).

When war broke out between the British and the French in 1756, a section of the hospital called the Ward of the English, was opened to care for the wounded English soldiers. It is also reported that the sisters were sufficiently generous of spirit that they provided refuge to escaped English soldiers fleeing from the Indians and that "one of these English showed his gratitude, in 1760, by saving the hospital from the artillery fire of the army of invasion" (Gibbon and Mathewson, 1947, p. 48). The transfer of authority for Montreal to the British in 1760 brought with it statements testifying to the respect in which the sisters were held, and General Amherst stated:

> Of the goodwill I have to a Society so worthy of respect as that of the Monastery of St. Joseph de l'Hôtel Dieu de Montreal, which can count so far as the British Nation is concerned on the same protection that it has enjoyed under French rule (Gibbon and Mathewson, 1947, p. 48).

Although French nursing orders extended invitations of welcome to the Canadian sisters after the war and a Canadian philanthropist offered to pay all expenses of the voyage, only two sisters accepted the offer. Most were thoroughly Canadian by now and did not wish to leave; however, abject poverty ensued after the war because communication with wealthy citizens resident in France who had provided donations before the war became difficult or impossible and the sisters were dependent on charity for some time.

THE STATUS OF NURSING IN CANADA IN THE SEVENTEENTH AND EIGHTEENTH CENTURIES

There was a marked contrast between Canada and Britain in the status of nursing and the quality of care provided at this time. Nursing in Britain had fallen into disrepute after Henry VIII's renunciation of the Catholic Church. The nursing orders of nuns, which had previously provided the nursing service in the large London hospitals, were expelled and replaced by those of the "Sairey Gamp" ilk. Gibbon and Mathewson (1947) recount a number of descriptions of such nurses in England, noting the negative impact on hospitals of incompetent staff who were more concerned about personal pleasure than the welfare of patients.

These conditions did not occur to any great extent in early Canada because of the historical fact that the first settlement at Quebec developed as a colony of France from the outset. In France, nursing did not undergo the regressive period that occurred in England. Young women of good character, who came from reputable families, were recruited to nursing in France—primarily under the auspices of the Catholic Church—throughout this period of time. As Gibbon and Mathewson have observed:

> If the settlements along the St. Lawrence River had been colonized in the seventeenth century by the English instead of by the French, the history of nursing in Canada might have been very different. Fate, however, decided in favour of the French, and that was fortunate both for the Huron and Algonquin Indians and for the white pioneers, since in the wake of the fur traders and coureurs de bois, came the Augustinian Hospitallers or Nursing Sisters of Dieppe to Quebec and the St. Joseph Hospitallers of La Fleche to Montreal on their missions of healing and of mercy—missions which had no counterpart in the colonizing efforts of the Protestant English in North America (1947, p. 1).

The health care system was firmly established and in operation when the English defeated the French in the battle of the Plains of Abraham in 1759. Undoubtedly, geographic separation from England ensured the continuation of the French traditions of good nursing in Canada.

Voluntarism, philanthropy, and a concern for others figured prominently in the values of both lay and religious French citizens who came to New France to provide health and social services. As such, the basis of the new society that developed over the next three and a half centuries was, from the outset, inherently Christian in its character based on Roman Catholicism, and outwardly focused on the health, well-being, and religious life of the inhabitants of the new land. Such a heritage would prove to be an enduring strength that would persist through clashes with the aboriginal peoples, war with Britain and, later, with the Americans to the development of a new and independent Canada in the nineteenth and twentieth centuries.

REFERENCES

Abbott, M.E. (1931). *History of medicine in the province of Quebec.* Montreal: McGill University.

Brown, G. (Ed.). (1966). *Dictionary of Canadian biography: 1000 to 1700* (Vol. 1). Toronto: University of Toronto Press.

Canadian Nurses Association. (1968). *The leaf and the lamp.* Ottawa: Author.

Gibbon, J.M. and Mathewson M.S. (1947). *Three centuries of Canadian nursing.* Toronto: The Macmillan Co.

Jamieson, E., Sewall, M., and Gjertson, L. (1959). *Trends in nursing history.* Philadelphia: W.B. Saunders.

Juchereau, J-F., and Duplessis, M-A. (1939). *Les annales de l'Hôtel Dieu de Québec: 1636 - 1716.* Québec: l'Hôtel Dieu de Québec.

Kenton, E. (1925). *The Jesuit relations and allied documents.* New York: The Vanguard Press.

Millman, M.B. (1965). In G. Griffin and J. Griffin (Eds.), *Jensen's history and trends of professional nursing* (pp. 423-439). St. Louis: The C.V. Mosby Co.

Parkman, F. (1897). *The Jesuits in North America in the seventeenth century.* Boston: Little, Brown & Co.

Repplier, A. (1931). *Mère Marie of the Ursulines.* New York: Sheed & Ward.

Thwaites, R.G. (1959). *The Jesuit relations and allied documents: Travels and explorations of the Jesuit missionaries in New France* (Vols. I to XII). New York: Pageant Book Co.

CHAPTER TWO

Nursing in Canada From 1760 to the Present: The Transition to Modern Nursing

JANET ROSS KERR

After the war of 1756 to 1763, the transition to British rule was difficult for the nursing orders, which were now firmly established in Quebec. The nuns received little or no financial support because their wealthy benefactors had returned to France, and donations from those who had previously supported the establishment of health services in the New World were cut off. Without a regular income on which they could rely, the nuns were impoverished at the outset of the new regime. However, William Pitt, Prime Minister of Great Britain, in correspondence with the Duchesse d'Aiguillon, niece of the woman who had founded the Hôtel Dieu of Quebec, stated that: "He has the satisfaction to be able to state that our officers, who are very strong in their praises of the charitable care of our sick and wounded by these nuns, have paid them every attention required by piety and misfortune" (Gibbon and Mathewson, 1947, p. 52).

In addition there is a record of some financial assistance from the British for the sisters: "By instruction of Pitt, General Murray relieved the Hôtel Dieu of a debt of taxes to the extent of 3,389 livres, which had reverted to the British at the change of the regime, and also paid £808 for rent of lodgings to the troops, and £3,085 for the use of furniture, laundry and utensils of the hospital (Gibbon and Mathewson, 1947, pp. 52-53). Nevertheless, all of the hospital systems remained in place at the transfer of power; the nuns were thoroughly Canadian by this time and most had no desire to return to France.

During the American War of Independence from 1775 to 1776, the American attack on the Canadian border brought patients from each side of the battle to the Hôtel Dieu, where all were cared for with warmth and humanity. An American Lieutenant recorded the following in his diary on March 10, 1776:

12

Was removed to the Hotel Dieu, sick of the scarlet fever, and placed under the care of the Mother Abbess, where I had fresh provisions and good attendance. For several nights the nuns sat up with me, four at a time, every two hours. Here I feigned myself sick after I had recovered, for fear of being sent back to the Seminary to join my fellow-officers, and was not discharged until I acknowledged that I was well. When I think of my captivity, I shall never forget the time spent among the nuns who treated me with so much humanity (Gibbon and Mathewson, 1947, p. 55).

Among other hospitals that also cared for the sick and wounded were the Hôtel Dieu at Trois Rivières, which had been established in 1697. In 1778, another hospital was built at Sorel, L'Hôtel des Invalides; and, in 1781, La Samaritaine was opened across the Richelieu River. However, the tradition of caring for all, regardless of race, nationality, or creed, stayed with these nursing sisters from the beginning of their tenure in Canada in the seventeenth century. Preservation of human life and nourishment of the spirit through religious beliefs and practices remained central characteristics of their work.

EFFECTS OF IMMIGRATION ON NURSING

After the defeat of the French forces at the Plains of Abraham, the Treaty of Paris of 1763 established certain rules for the government of the colony; its thrust was anglicisation in order to attract the English-speaking settlers to help rebuild the shattered economy after the war. Although the British had imagined that a flood of settlement would soon help anglicise Quebec, "in fact few people came" (Morton, 1983, p. 23). Soon, the people of Quebec were recognized as Canadians, and the Quebec Act of 1774 restored many of their former freedoms and rights. The Act was also designed to win the support of these Canadians in the upcoming conflict with the Americans. With some difficulty, the British were able to hold Quebec in the conflict.

After the war, those United Empire Loyalists who wanted to remain loyal to Britain immigrated to Canadian territory. Their numbers eventually totalled 50,000. These settlers were joined by large numbers of immigrants from Britain and Ireland. "Late Loyalists" followed during the early nineteenth century. There was also a sizeable increase in the French Canadian population, from 60,000 in 1760 to 110,000 by 1784 and 330,000 by 1860. The Act of 1791 divided Quebec into Upper and Lower Canada, each with its own system of government, and confirmed the rights for French colonists as laid down earlier in the Quebec Act.

The devastating effects of the Napoleonic wars on trade in England led many in the British Isles to emigrate to new areas, where there might be some hope of overcoming poverty: "Factory folk, miners, and farmers became equally distressed, and the British Government could do little more than divert the resulting emigration to countries where the British flag still flew" (Gibbon and Mathewson, 1947, p. 71).

This meant that a majority of these immigrants were poorly nourished and travelled in "vessels which were overcrowded and unsanitary," so disease found easy prey among the new settlers. The United Empire Loyalists did not have to travel in disease-infested vehicles or under unsanitary conditions, and thus escaped the devastation that followed the voyages of the Europeans. Nevertheless, diseases brought by new arrivals spread rapidly among residents of the new colony. Dramatic increases in the population gave epidemic diseases more scope, and these epidemics seriously affected the colony. Immigrants and travellers brought with them cholera, typhus, smallpox, and trachoma. It is reported that, in 1832, an epidemic of cholera wiped out one-seventh of the population of Montreal, or 4,000 people (Gibbon & Mathewson, 1947). The necessity of health examinations for new immigrants to protect the Canadian population was recognized, and a quarantine station and hospital were established at Grosse Isle in the St. Lawrence.

Because of the rapid increase in the population in English-speaking Canada in the late eighteenth and early nineteenth centuries, it was difficult to keep up with the need for health-care facilities. The persistent waves of epidemics, however, made them a necessity. The rather dismal state of nursing in Britain was parallelled in new areas of the country that were opened up by the English and not served by the French nursing orders. It is noted that "nursing in English-speaking Canada remained primitive for many years" (Canadian Nurses Association [CNA], 1968, p. 30). Lay women attempted to do nursing in the hospitals that were established, but they were largely without the proper training and skill to do what was needed. The established French-speaking sisterhoods expanded and the new English-speaking orders were formed to try to fill the need.

Because so many of the arriving settlers were destitute as well as ill, they needed a great deal of assistance. The Female Benevolent Society was organized in Montreal in 1816 to assist the immigrants and was responsible for the establishment of what would be called the Montreal General Hospital. In Kingston, the Kingston Compassionate Society secured a grant of land from the government and constructed the first version of what would become the Kingston General Hospital. Likewise in York, the Toronto General Hospital was founded by a philanthropic group with funds designated to buy medals of the War of 1812 (Gibbon and Mathewson, 1947). The introduction of lay nurses in areas previously served by nursing sisterhoods met with some opposition at first, but the needs of the sick and the poor had to be met. Meanwhile, the Grey Nuns continued to visit the sick in their homes and "had accommodation for incurables and the insane" (Gibbon and Mathewson, 1947, p. 74).

THE INFLUENCE OF FLORENCE NIGHTINGALE ON NURSING IN CANADA

In 1854, Florence Nightingale set off with her small band of 38 carefully selected nurses to tend the British soldiers in the Crimea. Up to that time, British military hospitals had been staffed exclusively by male attendants. It had not been easy to secure permission to nurse the sick and wounded military personnel during the Crimean War. However, Florence Nightingale came from a prominent and wealthy family and had many connections with powerful people. She managed not only to obtain permission to go to the Crimea, but also to stir the British consciousness in relation to the need for good nursing for the sick. It has been reported that: "her onslaught on the appalling lack of sanitation in the wards of the General and the Barrack hospitals at Scutari contributed greatly to the reduction in the deaths of cases treated from 315 per thousand to 22 per thousand" (Gibbon & Mathewson, 1947, pp. 109-110).

The outpouring of public support for Florence Nightingale's cause was over-whelming, and a fund was established, even before she returned from the Crimea, to allow her to organize a training school for nurses (Nutting & Dock, 1937). At last, nursing was to become a suitable occupation for women.

> Mark what by breaking through customs and prejudices Miss Nightingale has effected for her sex. She has opened to them a new profession, a new sphere of usefulness...a claim for more extended freedom of action, based on proved public usefulness in the highest sense of the word (Gibbon and Mathewson, 1947, p. 110).

Florence Nightingale's influence was worldwide and reached Canada by way of both Britain and even the United States when, during the American Civil War, there was an attempt to establish Nightingale's standard of nursing to minimize suffering. After the war, training schools on the Nightingale model were opened in three American hospitals in 1873; at Bellevue in New York, Massachusetts General, and New Haven (Gibbon and Mathewson, 1947). Cana-dian hospitals, particularly the secular hospitals in English-speaking settlements, considered educating nurses to raise the standards of care; this was a direct result of Nightingale's influence. The establishment of schools of nursing is discussed in some detail in Chapter 22; however, it is important to recognize the profound influence that Florence Nightingale had on the initiation of an orga-nized system of nursing education for lay nurses throughout the world.

OPENING UP OF THE WEST AND THE GREY NUNS

On April 24, 1844, four nuns set out in long canoes bound for St. Boniface, Manitoba. The measure of courage required for the strenuous journey is difficult to appreciate in an age where superhighways are commonplace. A description of the two-month trip, by one of these nursing pioneers, who had twisted her ankle en route, draws attention to the rigours involved:

> Most of the portages are frightful, above all those which are after the Great Lakes. One has to climb mountains, clamber over rocks, descend precipitous slopes, do four or five miles in the Savannas and by unblazed trails — you understand what I must suffer, being obliged to be carried over difficult roads (Gibbon and Mathewson, 1947, p. 86).

The onslaught of a series of epidemics, beginning in 1846, was the first big challenge facing the nuns after their arrival. These were extremely serious and the death toll was high. Sister Laurent has described how they coped with the load:

> Each of us was appointed to do that which she was best fitted for. Some of us went into the houses where sick people were. They used to have measles and dysentery and inflammatory rheumatism, and smallpox sometimes. We had medicines from

Montreal, but we also learned the uses of herbs that grew in this country, and how to help the sick people so as to ease their pain and aid them to get better (Gibbon and Mathewson, 1947, p. 89).

In Saskatchewan and Alberta, the Grey Nuns were again the pioneers who trekked west to establish health-care facilities and systems for the populace. In 1860, three nuns of this order from St. Boniface arrived at Île-à-la-Crosse, an Indian settlement 200 miles north of Prince Albert. In Alberta, the Grey Nuns established the first hospital, in 1881, at the St. Albert Mission near Edmonton. Arriving before most of the settlers, the sisters established systems of quality health care that were available to people who needed assistance. A great deal of visiting nursing was performed by the Grey Nuns, who regularly visited the sick in their homes as they had since the founding of their order.

ESTABLISHMENT OF NATIONAL PROFESSIONAL NURSING ORGANIZATIONS

A leading figure in British nursing was Mrs. Bedford Fenwick, who was influential in the formation of nursing organizations and editor of the forerunner of the *British Journal of Nursing*. Attending the Congress of Charities, Corrections, and Philanthropy in Chicago in 1893, Mrs. Fenwick met the leaders in American nursing at the time: Isabel Hampton, Adelaide Nutting, and Lavinia Dock. It is of interest to note that of these three American leaders, two were Canadians living and working in the United States—Isabel Hampton and Adelaide Nutting. They discussed the need for concerted effort to secure legislation for the registration of nurses to raise the standard of professional nursing and to ensure that those practising were qualified and able. Mrs. Fenwick had been struggling to achieve this in Britain at the time and became convinced that, to have any hope of achieving their goals, nurses had to band together and form professional organizations. The three American leaders were so impressed with the case Mrs. Fenwick made for organizations that they immediately organized the American Society of Superintendents of Training Schools for Nurses of the United States and Canada, of which Isabel Hampton became the first President. Although this was to become the National League for Nursing in 1912, the major thrust of the organization never strayed from the original goal "to work for higher standards of nurse preparation" (CNA, 1968, p. 35).

Alumnae associations began soon after at the large schools of nursing in the United States. In 1896, under the leadership of its first President, Isabel Hampton Robb, The Nurses' Associated Alumnae of the United States and Canada was formed. The criterion for membership for alumnae was that they must have graduated from a school associated with a hospital over 100 beds in size, and the training program must have been at least two years long. The organization directed its efforts at first to improving the quality in educational programs, but this proved to be too difficult for a voluntary organization. Instead, they directed their efforts toward working for legislation to ensure the registration of nurses. This organization was the forerunner of the American Nurses Association that began in 1911. The *American Journal of Nursing* began to publish in 1900 and provided a vehicle for information to assist with the development of the organization (CNA, 1968).

One of Mrs. Bedford Fenwick's major goals was the formation of an international organization of nurses. She had initiated discussions about such an organization with American nursing leaders in 1893 in Chicago. Because it was decided that the first step was the formation of national groups, these became a matter of priority. Although the North American organization had initially included both Canada and the United States, it was necessary to separate the organizations because of the concept of membership by country in an international organization. In addition, the responsibility for health was vested at provincial and state levels; thus, the fight for registration of nurses was decentralized. A structure involving separate national organizations seemed more useful to pursue the goal of registering nurses. The International Council of Nurses (ICN) was accordingly formed in 1899 with Britain, the United States, and Germany as charter members. Canada was represented at this meeting by five nurses, and Mary Agnes Snively became the first honorary treasurer of the fledgling organization.

In Canada, the Canadian Society of Superintendents of Training Schools for Nurses was the first completely Canadian national organization of nurses; it was formed in 1907 with Mary Agnes Snively as President. The next year, the society invited representatives from all nursing organizations in Canada to meet to establish a national association of nurses. The result of the meeting was the inception of the Provisional Society of the Canadian National Association of Trained Nurses (CNATN), and Mary Agnes Snively was inducted as founding President. Initially, membership took place through member societies composed primarily of graduate nurse and alumnae associations. It is reported that the first alumnae association in Canada had been founded in 1894, at the Toronto General Hospital (Gibbon and Mathewson, 1947). Nearly every school formed such an organization shortly thereafter. Many of these amalgamated with other groups regionally, and eventually, provincially. The CNATN applied for membership in the ICN in 1908, with formal admission taking place the next year at the meeting in London.

As the CNATN had been organized somewhat hastily for the purpose of joining the ICN, a structure that would be suitable for the national organization and would recognize the historical division of powers between the provincial and federal governments had yet to be considered. According to Mrs. E.G. Fournier, who studied the question for the CNATN:

> It should be the object of the national Association to organize the unorganized provinces, to strengthen the weak ones, to encourage the disheartened, bind all together, inform all of the nursing achievements, and suggest work to be taken up (CNA, 1968, p. 37).

A full-time executive secretary, Miss Jean Wilson, was appointed in 1923, and the first national office was opened in Winnipeg. Later, it was moved to Montreal and then to Ottawa. In the meantime, *The Canadian Nurse* had begun publication in 1905. Membership of affiliated organizations in the CNATN went from 28 in 1911 to 52 in 1924 when the association changed its name to the Canadian Nurses Association (CNA). In 1930, the organization became a federation of the provincial nurses associations that "made the provincial association the official representative of registered nurses in each province and automatically ensured that all members of the CNA were registered nurses" (CNA, 1968, p. 39).

The Provisional Council of the Canadian Association of University Schools and Departments of Nursing held its first meeting in 1942; representatives from eight university schools and departments of nursing met to consider how university schools might respond to a proposed program of federal financial assistance for university schools of nursing (J. Bouchard, personal communication, 1987).

The organization was a small one for a considerable period of time after its founding, due to a relatively low membership, the sector of the nursing population falling within its purview being rather small. The work of the organization was accomplished on a totally volunteer basis until 1970 when a part-time executive secretary was hired for the first time; also at that time, the name of the organization became the Canadian Association of University Schools of Nursing (CAUSN). It was not until 1984 that the position of executive secretary became full-time. An ongoing discrepancy in the way the organization collects fees to finance its operations has continued to be a problem. At the national level, fees are paid by member schools. At the regional level, Ontario and Quebec collect fees from institutions, but in the Atlantic provinces and in the West, individual faculty members of university schools of nursing pay fees on an individual and voluntary basis. The total fees collected, however, tend to be rather small; and it is difficult to finance committee travel, projects, and other programs the organization might desire to undertake. The organization has provided a vehicle for communication between faculty members in university schools of nursing and has addressed some important questions about university education for nursing.

In 1962, the Canadian Nurses Foundation (CNF) was incorporated as an organization separate from the CNA in order to provide scholarships, bursaries, and fellowships for graduate study in nursing. As a charitable organization, donations could be accepted on a tax-exempt basis, thus facilitating the collection of funds for scholarship. A grant of $150,000 from the W.K. Kellogg Foundation in 1962 helped build up the fund at its inception; memberships, collected on a voluntary basis, provided the financial base for operations. However, the Foundation has had some difficulty in soliciting the number of memberships needed to maintain a solid financial base for the organization. It continues to seek memberships from affiliates of provincial nurses associations to support a national program of scholarships and fellowships for university-level study in nursing and for research.

At the outset, the CNA and the CNF operated quite autonomously. However, when it became clear that the financial structure of the CNF was not strong, closer links were developed between the two organizations. The executive director of the CNA is the secretary-treasurer of the CNF; the CNF is housed in

CNA House in Ottawa, and annual meetings of the CNF in the years of CNA biennial conventions are held in association with the CNA meeting. In recent years, CNF has broadened its activities to work closely with the CNA on matters of importance to both organizations. "Operation Bootstrap" involved seeking funds for a doctoral program in nursing, doctoral fellowships for nurses pursuing PhD preparation in nursing, and other supportive activities; although the effort was not successful in achieving external funding for these projects, CNA, CNF, and CAUSN participated in the effort as equal partners.

Although it is reported that provision was made in 1966 to include assistance for study at the baccalaureate level (CNA, 1968, p. 11), in practice, fellowships were awarded almost exclusively for master's and doctoral study until a resolution, passed at the 1982 annual meeting in St. John's, Newfoundland, provided a mandate for the awarding of one scholarship for study at the baccalaureate level in each province or territory each year.

NURSING DURING THE WORLD WARS

Nurses have played pivotal roles during military conflicts throughout Canadian history. Reference has already been made to the important, bipartisan role played by the nursing sisters of the Hôtel Dieu hospitals in Quebec and Montreal during the hostilities between the French and English from 1756 to 1763. During the Northwest Rebellion of 1885, a military request for nursing services shows the influence of Florence Nightingale and the experience gained during the American Civil War: "No volunteer nurses. If you can send an organized body under a trained head, they will be welcome" (CNA, 1968, p. 63). Two groups of nurses responded to the call, one headed by Mother Hannah Grier from the Anglican order of St. John the Divine in Toronto; the other by Miss Miller, a head nurse at the Winnipeg General Hospital (CNA, 1968). In 1898, nurses with the Victorian Order of Nurses (VON) were attached to the Yukon Military Force and accorded considerable praise for their efforts (Gibbon and Mathewson, 1947).

In 1899, an offer of a Canadian contingent of nurses for the Boer War was made by the Canadian government to Mr. Joseph Chamberlain. The first group of four nurses was sent to assist in South Africa under the leadership of Georgina Fane Pope, a Bellevue Hospital–educated nurse from Prince Edward Island. She described the conditions under which nursing took place as follows:

> We nursed in huts and found the work at times very heavy, often times having our dinner between nine and ten p.m. We received our first convoy of wounded a few days after the Battle of Maggersfontein and Modder River when the beds were filled with men of the Highland Brigade. We remained at Wynberg for nearly a month, when No. 3 General Hospital of 600 beds was pitched under canvas at Rondesbosch, a few miles away—Here we arrived on Christmas Day and remained almost six months, having at times very active service; sometimes covered with sand during a "Cape South-Easter"; at others delayed with a fore-runner of the coming rainy season, and at all times in terror of scorpions and snakes as bed-fellows (Gibbon and Mathewson, 1947, pp. 290-291).

The South African nursing experience was sufficient to persuade the Canadian Army Medical Corps that an army nursing service ought to be an integral part of the permanent corps. Georgina Pope and Margaret Macdonald thus were appointed to the staff on a permanent basis in 1906. When World War I broke out, the Army Nursing Corps consisted of five nurses. However, within three weeks of the declaration of war, thousands of nurses had volunteered for service overseas. Margaret Macdonald, who was appointed Matron-in-Chief of the Army Nursing Corps, described the first group of volunteers:

> The selection, from coast to coast, of over one hundred nurses from thousands of applicants, the vast majority of whom were entirely unacquainted with Army Life and regulations, constituted somewhat of a problem. However, when all the formalities incident to the appointment of these as Nursing Sisters were concluded, it was astonishing how quickly and naturally in becoming military minded they fell into place. Their example and esprit de corps became the pattern for the many hundreds that followed (Gibbon and Mathewson, 1947, p. 296).

There are many accounts of the nature of service rendered by Canadian nurses during the war, all of which make note of the flexibility and devotion to duty that was required. Matron Macdonald described the introduction of the first group of nursing sisters to field nursing as follows:

> Their first introduction to Field Nursing began at Salisbury Plain in 1914; patients, many seriously ill, poured into huts that were ill-equipped to receive them. Cold, damp weather with continuous rain prevailed, adding much to the general discomfort. The sisters literally ploughed their way through mud and water from hut to hut; their living quarters left much to be desired. In the matter of rations, assuredly, vitamins were not the order of the day (Gibbon and Mathewson, 1947, p. 297).

Margaret Macdonald, who was given the rank of major, was succeeded by Edith Rayside as Matron-in-Chief of the nursing service. In all, approximately 1,800 nurses saw service during this war, 47 losing their lives as a result of the conflict. Fourteen nurses perished in the sinking of the Canadian hospital ship, Llandovery Castle (CNA, 1968).

The number of nurses who saw service during World War II was approximately double that in World War I, at 4,000. Matron-in-Chief of the nursing service of the Army Medical Corps from 1940 to 1944 was Elizabeth Smellie. In civilian life, Miss Smellie had been chief superintendent of the (VON); she became the first Canadian woman to achieve the rank of colonel. The significant service provided by nursing sisters during World War I led to the establishment of a permanent corps of nursing sisters by the Royal Canadian Army Medical Corps (RCAMC), as well as a registry of nurses who could be available for active service in the event of war. Twenty-four Canadian general hospitals were established to care for the wounded during World War II, compared with sixteen during World War I. In addition, there was a convalescent hospital in France, a neurologic and plastic surgery hospital in England, and casualty clearing stations, totalling 34 overseas hospitals. Sixty hospitals were maintained in Canada, as well as two hospital ships. All were staffed with nurses (Gibbon and

Mathewson, 1947). In response to a request from South Africa, nurses under the leadership of Matron-in-Chief Gladys Sharpe were sent to care for wounded British soldiers.

For the major part of the war, Canadian nurses staffed the military hospitals in England and Canada and did not see service under battle conditions in Europe until 1943, when they were sent to assist after the invasion of Italy:

> Canadian nurses were the first to reach Sicily after the invasion . . . The unit was recruited largely from Winnipeg, and other Western cities, but the first girl ashore was Lieutenant Elizabeth Lawson of St. John, New Brunswick . . . Lieutenant Trennie Hunter, of Winnipeg, was a close second. The Matron of this hospital is Miss Agnes J. MacLeod, of Edmonton. They were described as a 'group of grimy, tin-hatted girls, perspiring in the terrific heat and burdened with cumbersome equipment' (Gibbon and Mathewson, 1947, p. 465).

Conditions were described by one Red Cross officer: "Comfort was a rarity to them that first winter. Often casualties were heavy, and they were on duty in the wards night and day" (Gibbon and Mathewson, 1947, p. 467). Gladys Sharpe, describing conditions in South Africa and the response to the arrival of Canadian nurses, stated:

> Our beds filled rapidly, the first convoy via hospital train brought casualties from Burma, Madagascar, the Middle East and Singapore, at the rate of 257 admitted in just two hours — the highlight was the official opening ceremony at which Field Marshall Smuts took the opportunity of publicly thanking 'Canada' for sending nurses (Gibbon and Mathewson, 1947, p. 462).

It is reported that, up to this point, nurses in military service held the relative rank of officers, but did not actually have the official status of officers or the authority that accompanied the rank. This was changed, about half-way through the war, by order of the privy council, who granted nurses commissions equivalent to those of other commissioned officers. By contrast, nurses in Britain and the United States did not achieve this until the end of the war (CNA, 1968, p. 65).

THE EMERGENCE OF PUBLIC HEALTH NURSING

The development of public health nursing as both an area of specialization in nursing and an integral part of nursing in all settings is largely a process that occurred in the twentieth century. The idea of prevention of illness and spread of disease by educating people about beneficial health practices and life-style modifications facilitating health was not recognized until the twentieth century. Further, it was realized that good nutritional practices were important for all, but essential for the health of young children and pregnant women. Some of the first public health nursing was performed by visiting tuberculosis patients and teaching preventive measures in the home. The first school nurses were appointed in Hamilton, Ontario, in 1909, and then in Toronto in 1910. Lina Rogers, a Canadian nurse who had graduated from the Hospital for Sick Children, had achieved international fame for her work that correlated the absence of children from school with lack of medical care. Her appointment to the School Nursing Service of the Toronto Board of Education led to the recruitment of a staff of nurses and dentists and emphasis on teaching children and their families hygienic practices to prevent disease. The Nursing Service was transferred to the Health Department several years later; its work provided a model for the rest of the country to gradually initiate a system of public health nursing in each province (Gibbon and Mathewson, 1947).

After World War I, the Canadian Red Cross Society facilitated the development of public health nursing by providing grants for the establishment of certificate courses in public health nursing at six universities across the country (The Canadian Red Cross Society, 1962). The VON also encouraged nurses to study public health nursing at the universities by initiating a program of bursaries for advanced study in 1921. These programs continue to the present day and have been very important in encouraging the study of public health nursing.

The development of public health nursing throughout the twentieth century has been a gradual process. The entrenchment of a hospital-based system of health care, encouraged by Canadian federal health legislation since 1948, has undoubtedly retarded recognition of the need for preventive services, home-based services, and consumer involvement in health care. The Lalonde Report (1975) provided the first evidence of concern about prevention of disease and maintenance of health at the federal level. However, skyrocketing costs of care in hospitals have, at last, focused attention on the need to care for people in different ways. Day surgery services, ambulatory care, outpatient services, and home care are now being used as substitutes for hospital-based care; and the nurse is playing a prominent role in all of these areas. Even though many of these services can be described as "illness care," the need to teach health practices for prevention of disease and maintenance of health is an important facet of nursing care in all of these areas.

Public health nursing was also the driving force behind the establishment of nursing courses at universities in Canada, beginning with certificate courses in public health nursing, initiated at six universities with financial support from the Canadian Red Cross Society. Gradually, these certificate programs were phased into baccalaureate degree programs, and preparation in public health nursing became an essential component of the basic curriculum. Notwithstanding its essential role in the development of university education for nursing in Canada, the fact remains that public health services are only just beginning to be recognized as critical to the health of Canadians. Acute care has, for years, usurped much of the attention and most of the funds designated for health. There is now renewed public interest in community health services, however, and their development is an important step in maximizing the investment of Canadians in health.

The history of nursing in Canada is long and distinguished. Nurses have been caring for people from the time of the earliest French settlements on the shores of the St. Lawrence. Over time, they have adapted to changing health-care needs of society. In the beginning, the primary health-care needs centred around care of those with infectious diseases, which often became epidemics.

Nurses also distinguished themselves in caring for the wounded in various conflicts. As time went on, cures were found for many of the most troublesome infectious diseases, leading to a dramatic extension of life span, which added a new dimension to health care. Nurses have been at the heart of new developments in high technology acute care, and they have pressed for more emphasis on encouraging the populace to adopt behaviour that is beneficial to health. Altruism has characterized nursing and nurses from the outset, and a review of the deliberations of organized nursing over time reveals that commitment to the public good has been a firmly entrenched principle guiding professional activities. The future is likely to hold many new and difficult challenges for the nursing profession. With such a historical record, nurses will likely continue to distinguish themselves in meeting the challenges ahead.

REFERENCES

Canadian Nurses Association. (1968). *The leaf and the lamp.* Ottawa: Author.

Canadian Red Cross Society. (1962). *The role of one voluntary organization in Canada's health services: A brief presented to the Royal Commission on Health Services on behalf of the Central Council of the Canadian Red Cross Society.* Toronto: The Canadian Red Cross Society.

Gibbon, J.M., and Mathewson, M.S. (1947). *Three centuries of Canadian nursing.* Toronto: The Macmillan Co.

Lalonde, M. (1975). *A new perspective on the health of Canadians.* Ottawa: Health and Welfare Canada.

Morton, D. (1983). *A short history of Canada.* Edmonton: Hurtig Publishers Ltd.

Nutting, M.A., & Dock, L. (1937). *A history of nursing. vols I and II.* New York: Putnam's.

CHAPTER THREE

Professionalization in Canadian Nursing

JANET ROSS KERR

T he advancement of nursing as a profession has occurred gradually over the 350 years of nursing history in Canada, which began when three Augustinian nuns from France arrived to provide nursing care to the small population at Quebec . From this humble beginning, nursing evolved as an essential service in the New World at a time when knowledge of disease was in a primitive state, technology was virtually nonexistent, and a few herbal remedies were the only drug therapies available.

Over the centuries the practice of nursing was refined and perceived as important to the health and well-being of the community. In the twentieth century, a concerted effort was made to develop educational standards and programs to prepare nurses for practice. Efforts were also made to gain control over the practice of nursing through registration of nurses and development of professional standards. The process of professionalization, or the evolution of an occupation as a profession, can be clearly seen and identified; however, there is considerable diversity of opinion about the characteristics of a profession and the extent to which particular occupational groups may meet these characteristics.

DEVELOPMENT OF PROFESSIONS

The categorization of an occupation as a profession has traditionally been based on fairly standard criteria, developed by persons with expertise in the study of professions. The occupation of nursing has generated controversy and conflict, and much time has been spent debating whether nursing is a profession; some have termed it a semiprofession. With the passage of time and the phenomenal changes in the nature and scope of nursing practice over the past two decades, this debate has seemed less relevant. Moloney (1986) has noted: "The significant question to ask about occupations, however, is not whether or not they are professions but to what extent they exhibit characteristics of professions."

The debate began shortly after the turn of the century, when Abraham Flexner identified six characteristics of a profession based on his observations of the traditional professions of law, medicine, and theology:

1. It is basically intellectual, carrying with it high responsibility.
2. It is learned in nature, because it is based on a body of knowledge.
3. It is practical rather than theoretical.
4. Its technique can be taught through educational discipline.
5. It is well organized internally.
6. It is motivated by altruism (1915, pp. 578-581).

These characteristics were presented to address the question of whether social work was a profession. Flexner (1915) observed that nursing did not appear to be a profession because "... the responsibility of the trained nurse is neither original nor final" (1915, p. 581). It should be noted that his assessment of how nursing met the stated criteria was made before the passage of laws regulating the practice of nursing in most provinces and before nursing education first appeared in a university prospectus in Canada.

Quinn and Smith pointed out that "Although the term 'profession' is sometimes used in a purely descriptive way, a careful analysis of the nature of a profession will show that the idea of a profession carries with it some important ethical implications"(1987, p. 3). The ethical dimension may be the critical one in determining the esteem in which members of a profession are held by the public. Further,

> ... the idea of a profession can be examined sociologically, which results in a descriptive account of the professions. The sociologist would first identify those occupations usually called professions and then determine what characteristics they have that nonprofessional occupations do not have. That list of characteristics is sometimes used as a way of classifying other occupations as either professions or nonprofessions. This is a descriptive approach and does not entitle us to draw any conclusions about what one's own occupation ought to be (Quinn and Smith, 1987, p. 3).

In arriving at a definition of a profession, Quinn and Smith have melded the descriptive and ethical models of professionalism:

> The professions are those forms of employment that require an uncommonly complex knowledge base, used by persons committed to the direct benefit of human beings, with minimal societal control placed on their practice, and organized among themselves to ensure that they continue to provide those benefits (1987).

Moloney (1986) has referred to the "natural history of professionalization" as a description of the milestones in the development of professions. Some of these include when the profession first became a full-time occupation, the date of the first educational program to prepare practitioners of the profession, and the date the first university school was established. Also included as significant events were the date the first national professional association was formed, the date of the enactment of the first provincial registration act, and the development and adoption of a formal code of ethics. Although these events are static and finite in terms of time, they allow for comparisons between professions and assessment of where a particular group is in terms of the process of professionalization (Moloney, 1986).

Flexner saw knowledge, the first criterion, as the most central for professions. It appears that others concur, as knowledge is common to the vast majority of categorizations of professions. The knowledge needed to practise a profession is complex and cannot be mastered by the ordinary person. Practitioners require a lengthy period of preparation and supervised practice before they can function competently on an independent basis. The educational process is considered important and complex enough that programs are offered within universities, and the first professional degree often follows a four-year university arts or science degree. The knowledge base of a profession is continually upgraded through research performed by some members, to expand and update knowledge for practice. Members of the profession also maintain control over educational standards for the admission of new practitioners to the profession. The "direct benefit" idea, referred to by Quinn and Smith (1987), is a key element in the definition of a profession that places emphasis on the ethical dimension. The knowledge of the professional practitioner must be used for the direct benefit of the public.

Since the professions are inherently important to the public, some form of licensing or registration of those qualified to practise is necessary. Control of this process, while vested in legislation, is normally left to the profession. Professions are organized for the purpose of regulating practice; their associations seek to improve standards of practice and education, register members, monitor professional conduct, and judge practice of professionals where disputes have arisen. Thus, professions retain the authority to remove those who are incompetent from practice.

Professional commitment to the public is demonstrated by the development of a code of ethics, or statement of moral or ethical duty. A code of ethics has been described as "a set of principles to guide the individual practitioner" and as addressing "some of the most common temptations that professionals might experience in the course of their practice, temptations to take advantage of the special power that their expertise gives them over clients" (Quinn and Smith, 1987, pp. 9-10). Storch commented: "Codes are an essential characteristic of a profession, and are a statement of the acceptance of the trust and responsibility the public has placed in a profession" (1982, p. 20). Although codes of ethics are important for the health professions, they are limited by their purpose to guide professional practice, and they may not "include all issues of importance to the patient" (Storch, 1982, p. 20).

EVOLUTION OF NURSING AS A PROFESSION

In Canada, the nursing profession has been prominent in the life of society since the first nurses were encouraged to emigrate to the shores of New France. Later, in the nineteenth century, members of the Order of the Sisters of

Charity of Montreal (Grey Nuns) bravely set out, without benefit of reliable transportation, to remote parts of the country where small settlements were opening up to provide needed health care. Around the turn of the twentieth century, there was a movement to secure legislation to regulate nursing practice to differentiate qualified from unqualified practitioners. The first provincial statute governing the practice of nursing was passed in Nova Scotia in 1910; by 1922, with the passage of legislation in Ontario, there were statutes governing nursing in all provinces. The development of stronger legislation, which would differentiate the actual practice of nursing from title only (the designation R.N.), occurred later, with the initial passage of legislation in Newfoundland in 1953. Eight provinces today have mandatory acts, leaving only two to achieve this goal. Achieving exclusive right to practise embodied in law is an important step in professionalizing nursing; the profession in Canada is well on its way to uniform acceptance of the need for this legislation.

Nursing education in Canada began in 1874, in St. Catharines, Ontario, after worldwide recognition of Florence Nightingale's efforts in nursing education. Nightingale believed that nurses needed to be educated to care for patients properly; she demonstrated her point by dramatically lowering mortality and morbidity rates of soldiers in the Crimea in 1856, when she and a small group of nurses provided care for wounded soldiers. Nursing education moved into the universities in 1919 with the inception of a degree program in nursing at the University of British Columbia under the direction of Ethel Johns. In 1959, master's degree education in nursing was initiated at the University of Western Ontario, and nursing research development began in earnest. Although initial preparation is still largely based in community colleges and hospitals across the country, the adoption and active promotion of entry to practice position by the Canadian Nurses Association (CNA) and various professional associations is significant. The position seeks to ensure that those entering the practice of nursing in the year 2000 and thereafter qualify at the baccalaureate level. Doctoral-level preparation in nursing has not yet been initiated in a Canadian university, but it is likely that this will occur in the near future.

According to Wilensky, the development of a code of ethics for a profession normally occurs relatively late in the process of professionalization: "Toward the end, legal protection appears; at the end, a formal code of ethics is adopted" (1964, pp. 143-144). A historical review indicates that this was the case for the nursing profession in Canada. The first North American Code of Ethics for nursing was published by the American Nurses Association in 1950; in 1953, the International Council of Nurses (ICN) approved a Code of Ethics. The latter was generally accepted and used by professional associations until 1980, when the first CNA Code was developed. Disagreement about the wording of the initial Code resulted in the development of a new Code, adopted in 1985. Recently, the CNA has taken the position that the Code should be reviewed every five years; an ad hoc committee of four persons and an ethics consultant have been appointed to undertake this review in 1990 (CNA Connection, 1990).

EMERGENCE OF A SCIENTIFIC KNOWLEDGE BASE FOR NURSING

Recognition of the need for research to create and extend the knowledge base in nursing, although a relatively recent development, has been enhanced by the establishment of graduate programs in nursing at the master's level since 1959. There are now eleven master's programs in nursing and one in health sciences with a nursing major. Many of these programs have a strong research thrust, and graduates of such programs are engaged in advancing the scientific basis of nursing. The movement to prepare nursing scholars who have the skills to undertake research has been inhibited by the failure to establish a doctoral-level program in nursing in this country, a development that has been discussed publicly since the 1979 Kellogg National Seminar on Doctoral Education in Nursing (Zilm, 1979). Several attempts to establish doctoral programs were thwarted because external funding was not forthcoming or because of failure to gain approval by university program approval committees; however, four universities currently have active proposals for doctoral programs.

The importance of studying nursing questions has been emphazised by leaders in the profession, who have stressed scientific testing of traditional nursing care practices. As Quinn and Smith have observed:

> For members of the professions, being expert is more than a matter of personal pride; it becomes a matter of professional ethics. Clients come to a professional expecting and trusting that the professional has knowledge and expertise that the client needs but does not have. The implicit promise that the professional makes in accepting a client or patient involves their mutual understanding that the professional has a special knowledge and will use it for the benefit of the client (1987, p. 103).

There is a scientific knowledge base for nursing, and a review of the chapters in Part 2 will help the reader gain an appreciation of this basis of professional nursing practice.

PROFESSIONAL EDUCATION FOR NURSING: ISSUES OF STATUS AND CONTROL

Nursing education has been the subject of considerable controversy; however, the entry to practice proposal has possibly engendered more heated debate than other issues in recent decades. Initially proposed by a government-appointed committee in Alberta, the proposal that all nurses entering the profession be qualified at the baccalaureate level by the turn of the century has been ratified by the CNA and provincial associations. Implementation of the position is a much more difficult matter, requiring public consent because nursing education is funded under federal-provincial programs for post-secondary education. Although universities, colleges, and hospital schools of nursing operate under boards of governors, independent of governments, difficulties may arise if special funding or funding increases are required to support baccalaureate-level education in a period of retrenchment of higher education. The CNA has advised that assuming the entry to practice proposal will result in higher costs is unwise:

> Contrary to the popular assumption we suggest that the institutional costs of educating nurses through universities are very likely to be overstated relative to those of other post-secondary institutions . . . costs . . . may well be lower in universities than in other institutions and that in any case, the assumption that a baccalaureate program is necessarily costlier is unwarranted. (1986, p. 1)

It is becoming increasingly evident in parts of the country that arrangements are being made to facilitate the baccalaureate entry to practice standard. The School of Nursing of the Vancouver General Hospital and the School of Nursing of the University of British Columbia initiated a collaborative degree program in 1989. The University of Alberta Hospitals and the Faculty of Nursing at the University of Alberta plan on implementing a collaborative basic degree program in 1991.

The professional association monitors standards in initial programs of nursing education in all provinces except Alberta, Ontario and Quebec; this is discussed in Chapter 26. Nursing remains different from most other professions in terms of this process. The difference is that the majority of nurses graduating from educational programs are prepared in non-university programs, whereas in law, medicine, theology, pharmacy, engineering, architecture, and other professions, all educational preparation is centred in the universities. When the profession's goal of having all practitioners enter the field of nursing as graduates from university programs in nursing, the monitoring function will no longer be necessary.

The nursing profession is bound to be preoccupied for some time to come with establishing educational programs within universities. This process is likely to extend over several decades, since the majority of new graduates are still prepared in diploma programs. However, a more immediate concern is establishing doctoral programs in nursing to provide nurse researchers with the expertise to undertake theory-building and theory-testing research. An issue likely to arise after the establishment of initial programs of nursing education at the university level centres on the placement of the professional program. Whether some university-level study in the liberal arts and sciences will be required before admission to the program remains to be seen.

CONTROL OF PROFESSIONAL NURSING PRACTICE

The first phase of the drive by nurses to gain control of professional nursing practice extended from the enactment of the first provincial legislation regulating nursing, in Nova Scotia in 1910, to the conclusion of the process, in Ontario in 1922. Prowse drew attention to the importance of "aspects of nursing legislation which (a) expedite effective utilization of nursing knowledge and expertise, (b) influence the supply of qualified competent nurses, and (c) ensure regulation and monitoring of both practice and practitioners" (1983, p. 33).

The second phase of this process was the development of mandatory acts regulating nursing in each province; this ensured that the practice and practitioners would be more strictly regulated. Legislation incorporating mandatory registration requires a definition of nursing and a description of the scope of nursing practice. The first mandatory nursing legislation in Canada was enacted in 1953 in Newfoundland. Other provinces did not follow suit until Prince Edward Island passed such legislation in 1972, followed by Quebec in 1973 (with significant amendments in 1974). Although the Manitoba statute, passed in 1980, is permissive and protects only the title of registered nurse, it requires employers to demonstrate that those employed as registered nurses are registered. Alberta passed a mandatory Nursing Profession Act in 1983, followed by New Brunswick in 1984, Nova Scotia in 1985, and Saskatchewan and British Columbia in 1988. Thus, only two provinces have not developed mandatory legislation to regulate nursing practice: Manitoba and Ontario. These issues are discussed in more detail in Chapter 27.

The tremendous change in nursing roles over the past 25 years has altered the nature and scope of practice extensively. Specialization is almost a requirement because of changes in the knowledge required to practise in a specific area. Certification of practitioners in specialty areas is a concern; the way in which the CNA has addressed this issue is described in Chapter 27. The trend toward increased specialization can be expected to continue as health care knowledge and technology continue to develop.

FACILITATING PROFESSIONALIZATION

It is likely that changes in nursing will continue as society becomes more aware of the benefits of health promotion and the need to develop healthier life-styles to prevent disease. Alternatives to hospitalization for tertiary and long-term care, in the form of home care and ambulatory care, appear attractive at both the personal and societal levels. Nurses have been preparing for their new roles in community and long-term care settings and have the knowledge and the communication and interactional skills to assist consumers in meeting health goals.

The development of doctoral education is important to the profession, preparing nurses to contribute to the discovery of nursing knowledge through theory and research, and will lead to improved care. Increased availability of baccalaureate programs in nursing will provide a stronger basis for the practice of nursing. The profession will need a great deal of political expertise to surmount the obstacles that will arise while implementing the entry to practice proposal. Dynamic leadership will be required to provide direction to new generations of skilled practitioners and to ensure that their talents are used to the fullest extent for the benefit of the public.

REFERENCES

Canadian Nurses Association. (1986). *Entry to Practice Newsletter*, 2(1).

Flexner, A. (1915). Is social work a profession? In *Proceedings of the National Conference of Charities and Corrections* (pp. 578-581), Chicago: Heldermann Printing Co.

Moloney, M.M. (1986). *Professionalization of nursing: Current issues and trends.* Philadelphia: J.B. Lippincott Co.

Prowse, A.J. (1983). *Nursing legislation in Canada: An overview for health services administrators.* Edmonton: Department of Health Services

Administration and Community Medicine, The University of Alberta.

Quinn, C.A., and Smith, M.D. (1987). *The professional commitment: Issues and ethics in nursing.* Philadelphia: W.B. Saunders.

Storch, J. (1982). *Patients' rights: Ethical and legal issues in health care and nursing.* Toronto: McGraw-Hill Ryerson Ltd.

Wilensky, H.L. (1964). The professionalization of everyone? *American Journal of Sociology, 70*(2), 143-144.

Zilm, G., LaRose, O., and Stinson, S. (1979). *Proceedings of the Kellogg National Seminar on Doctoral Education for Canadian Nurses.* Ottawa: Canadian Nurses Association.

CHAPTER FOUR

The Role of the Canadian Nurses Association in the Development of Nursing in Canada

JANNETTA MacPHAIL

T he Canadian Nurses Association (CNA) has played a key role in the development of nursing in Canada since its establishment in 1924, as did its
forerunner, the Canadian National Association of Trained Nurses (CNATN),
which was initiated in 1908. The CNATN comprised affiliated member societies,
including alumni associations of hospital schools of nursing and local and regional groups of nurses, with a total of 28 such groups by 1911 (Canadian Nurses
Association [CNA], 1968). By 1924, each of the nine provinces "had a provincial
nurses' organization with membership in the CNATN, and in that year the
national group changed its name to the Canadian Nurses' Association" (CNA,
1968, p. 38). Fifty-two nursing organizations were affiliated with the CNA; some
nurses had multiple memberships and some organizations had members who
were nonregistered nurses, so it was decided in 1930 that the CNA would
become a federation of the nine provincial nurses' associations. This change
established the current policy that the provincial/territorial nurses' association is
the official representative of registered nurses in each province/territory and that
all members of the Canadian Nurses Association are registered nurses (CNA,
1968).

Membership in the CNA has increased dramatically, from about 8000 in 1930
to approximately 100,000 members of nine provincial and two territorial nurses'
associations in 1988. This excludes 55,000 potential members from Quebec; in
1985, the Order of Nurses of Quebec disaffiliated itself from the CNA. The
100,000 membership figure also takes into account the decrease in memberships

from Ontario in 1987 as a result of the decision made by the nurses' union, the Ontario Nurses Association (ONA), to terminate the arrangement for block memberships of 40,000 in the Registered Nurses Association of Ontario (RNAO). Many Ontario nurses who were thus excluded from the RNAO joined, as individual members, through other provinces/territories.

The Board of Directors of the CNA consists of a President; a President-Elect; a Vice-President; five members-at-large representing nursing administration, nursing education, nursing practice, nursing research, and socioeconomic welfare; one representative of the CNA Advisory Council; three public members, appointed by the Board from nominees from the provinces; and the presidents of the provincial/territorial nurses' associations. The CNA Advisory Council was established in 1985 and held its first meeting on June 21, 1986. It includes representatives from recognized CNA Interest Groups and the Executive Committee of the Board of Directors. The Council's function is to provide information and advice to the Board of Directors on selected nursing and health-care issues; the first issue identified was certification.

From its inception, the CNA has focused on the needs of the profession and the needs of Canadians served by professional nurses. Priorities, established by the Board of Directors at the beginning of each biennium, are responsive to changes in society, the health-care system, and the educational system for the preparation of nurses. In her inaugural address in June 1986, CNA President Helen Evans stated:

> I believe that we can achieve our goals . . . health care for all, baccalaureate education, certification for specialization, reforms to our health care system, strong nursing leadership, theory-based practice, more funds for nursing research and 'completeness' as an association . . . through reaching out and touching others of like beliefs, keeping in touch with consumers and colleagues. Together, with common purpose, we can make our beliefs become realities (CNA Connection, 1986d, p. 19).

In her inaugural address in 1988 and in a subsequent message to the membership, CNA President Judith Ritchie conveyed clearly that, in the 1988 to 1990 biennium, priority would be given to nursing practice and that all nursing issues should be addressed from the perspective of how they affect or are affected by nursing practice (Ritchie, 1988).

The role of the CNA in the development of nursing in Canada will be presented here in relation to CNA's corporate objectives and the biennial priorities established for the last two bienniums, along with some historical perspective in relation to each priority.

THE IMAGE OF NURSES AND NURSING

Improving the image of nurses and nursing was deemed by the CNA Board of Directors as the top priority for the 1986 to 1988 biennium and is still a priority. The image has become a cause for increasing concern among nurses in provincial/territorial nurses' associations, as well as at the national level. Nurses and the professional associations are concerned about how nurses and nursing are perceived by the public because this influences who is attracted to and retained in nursing. The outcomes of the recruiting process have a great effect on the growth of the profession and the quality of care that can be delivered. Perceptions of nurses and nursing also affect resource allocation for education and service, the influence that nurses have in shaping health policy, and the structure and functioning of the health-care system.

A description of the way in which nurses and nursing are perceived by the public and by nurses themselves is included in Chapter 5. It is sufficient at this point to state that the efforts of the CNA are directed at communicating with the public to produce a more positive image. CNA's President Ritchie stated:

> We must find better ways of describing [our] practice so that the complexity of our assessments and judgments are understood. With such understanding, others will value the visible and the invisible aspects of our work. Such value will lead to adequate remuneration and working conditions, and the assumption that such complex work requires solid educational preparation and continuing education (Ritchie, 1988, p. 3).

NURSING PRACTICE

The involvement of the CNA in nursing practice centres on efforts to develop standards for nursing care, the issue of the expanded role of the nurse, statements pertaining to primary health care and health promotion, statements addressing major issues in health and illness care, the issue of specialization in nursing, certification for specialty nursing practice, and development of a code of ethics. Because of the emphasis on functional aspects of nursing, education, and administration, one finds limited reference to practice issues in the early development of the CNA. In 1967, the CNA endorsed a statement by the Canadian Public Health Association (CPHA) of functions and qualifications for the practice of public health nursing in Canada. In 1970, the CNA issued position statements on the delivery of health services, delivery of nursing care, transfer of functions, and health services to the poor. This was followed by a CNA "Statement on the Expanded Role of the Nurse — the Physician Assistant," which reinforced the strong belief that the professional nurse was best qualified to assume the functions and responsibilities that have been suggested for the proposed category of physician's assistant. At a subsequent conference on the physician's assistant, held jointly by the CNA and the Canadian Medical Association (CMA) in 1971, it was agreed that the physician's assistant would not be introduced in Canada (CNA, 1981).

In 1971, the CNA issued statements on family planning programs and nurses' rights relative to nursing care of patients having therapeutic abortions. To assist in developing standards for nursing care, the CNA published *Guidelines for Developing Standards of Nursing Care* in 1972. In support of the CNA's emphasis on health promotion and maintenance, a statement, "The Expanded Role of the Nurse — Part 3: The Nurse in Primary Care", was issued in 1973. This was followed by statements on nurses in health promotion in 1975 and a survey of the expanded role of the nurse in 1976 (CNA, 1981).

A Special Committee on Health Issues, appointed by the CNA Board of Directors in 1986, includes nurses from all areas of practice and each member jurisdiction. The Committee meets twice yearly to identify and discuss nursing and health care issues from a national perspective, which is one of CNA's corporate objectives. To date, the issues addressed include: "biomedical technology and its impact on home care, quality of life, nursing care and financial demands on the health care system" (CNA Connection, 1989b, p. 7); the use of tobacco as a hazard to health; the habits and attitudes of nurses and nursing students about smoking; acquired immune deficiency syndrome (AIDS) as a major health problem and implications for nursing practice; and the pervasive and complex problems of sexual abuse among children and family violence. Position statements have been developed, some by the CNA alone and others collaboratively with other health disciplines and other members of the community. For example, CNA developed a position statement on mandatory drug screening in which "CNA goes on record as opposing mandatory pre-employment or random drug screening in the workplace" (CNA Connection, 1989b, p. 7). CNA "supports the development and maintenance of prevention programs and Employee Assistance Programs in the workplace . . . which are designed to identify problems early and provide a confidential method for employees to seek assistance" (CNA Connection, 1989f, p. 10). On the other hand, CNA took both an individual and a collaborative approach in addressing the vexing problem of AIDS. A five-year strategic plan, designed by CNA, pertains to educating nurses and the public, to research stimulation, and to policy formulation (CNA Connection, 1989b). In addition, a workshop was given in collaboration with the CPHA and a resource kit for health professionals was developed in collaboration with Health and Welfare Canada. An interdisciplinary approach has been chosen to address the complex societal problem of family violence in conjunction with physicians, psychologists, teachers, social workers, lawyers, and the police (H. Cousineau, personal communication, August 1989).

CNA has made many health promotion efforts, including a strategic plan to reduce tobacco use and promote a smoke-free society over the years. The CNA banned smoking at meetings of the Board of Directors in 1973; issued a statement on smoking in 1975 and another on smoking and health in 1989; and made its headquarters in Ottawa, CNA House, a smoke-free environment in 1987 (CNA Connection, 1986b, 1986c, 1986e). Smoking was banned at all CNA functions, including social gatherings, and another Statement on Tobacco and Health, published in 1987, communicates clearly that CNA "actively supports efforts to reduce, discourage and eradicate the use of tobacco . . . and actions leading to a smoke-free society" (CNA Connection, 1988b, p. 10). Although some health care agencies have taken steps to ensure a smoke-free environment, CNA recommended to the Canadian Council on Accreditation in 1987 "that consideration for hospital accreditation include the availability of smoking cessation resources for staff and establishment of a goal to move toward a smoke-free environment" (CNA Board of Directors' Minutes, February 18-20, 1987). In 1989, CNA sought and was awarded a research grant for more than $72,000, from Health and Welfare Canada's Health Promotion Directorate, to conduct a study to assess smoking prevention and cessation needs of Canadian nurses and nursing students. "There are no national data on Canadian nurses' rates and patterns of tobacco use and their current smoking cessation and prevention needs. However, American and British studies indicate that many nurses start smoking in nursing school and smokers entering nursing school increase their consumption" (CNA Connection, 1989o, p. 10). Although registered nurses' rates of smoking have declined over the past decade, the decline has occurred at a much slower rate than that of other health professionals. Moreover, nurses who smoke are likely to have attitudes and beliefs that reduce their efficacy in helping others to stop smoking. The study is the "first step in a strategic plan to reduce tobacco use among nurses by 50%, and to enhance the position of nurses as nonsmoking role models" and health educators (CNA Connection, 1989o, p. 10).

A code of ethics is very much a part of nursing practice. Although the CNA adopted the International Council of Nurses (ICN) Code of Ethics as its official code of ethics in 1966 (CNA, 1968), a code of ethics project was undertaken in 1979. This resulted in the publication of a paper, *CNA Code of Ethics: Ethical Basis for Nursing in Canada,* in 1980. This was followed by the appointment of another ad hoc committee on ethics, which culminated in the approval and publication of the *CNA Code of Ethics* in 1985. As the official code of the CNA, it was distributed to all members of the CNA through *The Canadian Nurse* journal. Most provincial/territorial nursing associations have now adopted the CNA Code as the standard for professional conduct in their jurisdictions.

WORK-LIFE AFFAIRS

Closely related to nursing practice are the environment in which nurses practise and issues pertaining to the working lives of nurses. In 1985, severe budgetary constraints caused a number of CNA staff positions to become part-time, including Manager of Work-Life Affairs. However, this position was restored to full-time in 1988 because of the importance of work-life affairs; the need to systematically collect information on the working environment of nurses; and the need for more attention in occupational health and safety (CNA Connection, 1989e). Funds have been allocated to collect background information on the subject of nursing personnel in the direct delivery of care, in view of the increasing attention given by government to the study of the nursing care system and the assessment of productivity (CNA Connection, 1989m).

Attracting and retaining nurses have presented major problems, particularly in hospitals. Much is spent on advertising and other recruitment strategies; however, much less attention is given to the even more perplexing problem of retention. CNA and the Canadian Hospital Association (CHA) have undertaken an extensive review of the literature on nurse retention as a first step in preparing a project proposal for further investigation of factors that help to retain nurses in places of employment. The CNA is matching CHA's contribution of

$5000 by providing the services of the CNA Research Manager (CNA Connection, 1989a).

In late 1989 and early 1990, two conferences were sponsored by CNA, one in the West and one in the East, to involve practising nurses in "identifying work-life issues in the nursing environment; examining strategies to increase recognition within nursing practice; exploring avenues to provide nurses with a more meaningful voice in work-life issues; and addressing the impact of work-life issues on caring" (CNA Connection, 1989k, p. 8). The nurses' input will be used to develop addtional strategies and programs that address the important issue of work-life affairs.

CNA's Work-life Affairs Department analyzed recent reports, from across Canada, pertaining to human resources in nursing and the recruitment and retention of nurses. The findings and recommendations are strikingly similar, with a recurring theme about the quality of nurses' working lives. Nurses are concerned about the feasibility of providing quality care with existing staffing; the need for more support staff; the need for more input in decision making; and the need to foster staffing innovations, such as job sharing, flexible scheduling, and self-scheduling. They emphasize the importance of strong and supportive leadership in nursing administration, including the head nurse level. Concern is also expressed about compensation issues, such as appropriate salaries and benefits and much broader salary scales; and about opportunities for advancement and recognition of clinical expertise by such means as the clinical ladder (CNA Connection, 1989l). These issues are not new; they have been addressed in the literature and by some health care agencies. They need to be addressed in individual hospitals and other health care agencies, where changes can be made, and by the governments who fund the health care system.

On January 1, 1988, CNA established a vitally important service to fill the gap that resulted from changes in the liability protective insurance available to nurses in Canada. The Canadian Nurses Protective Fund (CNPF) is managed by nurses for nurses and "is designed to protect nurses from professional liability claims and to address inequities in the present insurance system". It "will provide protection for any nurse who is, or was, a member in good standing or a permit holder of a subscribing provincial association" (CNA Connection, 1988a, p. 17). At the outset, the subscribing associations were Alberta, Manitoba, Newfoundland, Nova Scotia, and Saskatchewan. Policy-making and fund administration is the responsibility of the CNPF Committee, which reports directly to the CNA Board of Directors. Requests for assistance are considered by the Adjudicating Committee, which has available the expert services of the largest independent claims adjusting company in Canada and legal counsel CNA has retained to investigate occurrences and advise on settlement and defence of claims. CNA has also engaged a nurse lawyer as Coordinator of the Professional Liability Project to provide support, advice, and help with documentation to eligible nurses who report a claim or occurrence that might give rise to a claim (CNA Connection, 1988a).

CERTIFICATION

Certification is also closely linked to nursing practice in that the program is designed to recognize the clinical expertise of nurses in specialty practice. The question of specialization in nursing has been the discussed for a number of years. In 1973, the CNA published a discussion paper on specialization in nursing, written by Dr. Alice Baumgart, which is "a summary of collected views on specialization in hospital and community nursing practice in Canada" (CNA, 1981, p. 21). In the 1970s and 1980s, increasing specialization in nursing led to the creation of specialty practice groups interested in gaining recognition and eager to have a certification program in Canada. Many nurses wishing to obtain recognition of their level of competence in a specialty area of practice were seeking certification through certification programs in the United States, offered by the American Nurses Association and a variety of specialty nursing organizations. In an effort to avoid multiple certification bodies in Canada, the CNA has focused on establishing a certification program, under the auspices of the CNA, to serve nurses practising in a variety of specialty areas.

The first Ad Hoc Committee on Certification, established in 1980, developed basic principles and guidelines for establishing a certification system. This was followed by the appointment of two other committees and, finally, a third committee, which proposed a system for certification that was approved by the CNA Board of Directors in 1986. A mechanism for establishing certification in a given nursing specialty is now available through the CNA. "The three-part certification program involves designation of a specialty area of certification, development of a certification examination and certification of individuals" (CNA Connection, 1987, p. 7). To become involved in the certification process, a group of nurses must demonstrate that their specific areas of nursing should be recognized as specialties. Once specialty designation is achieved, the nurses may continue, to the development as an examination and, finally, to certification. Criteria for designation of a nursing specialty and the other steps in the process are described in the CNA publication *Certification Program: An Information Booklet*. A Special Committee on Certification was established in 1986 to review requests for specialty designation and to make recommendations to the CNA Board of Directors.

Since the certification program was approved by the CNA Board of Directors in 1986, two areas of specialty practice have qualified for specialty designation: neuroscience nursing and occupational health nursing. A Department of Certification has been established within the CNA organizational structure with a designated manager. No certification examinations have been developed to date; however, the first one is in process. Since 1987 the CNA Testing Service has had a contract with the Canadian Council of Occupational Health Nurses (CCOHN), Inc., to develop and administer their certification examination. In 1989 the CNA reached an agreement with representatives of two occupational health nursing groups to incorporate the existing occupational health nursing certification process into CNA's new certification program beginning in 1990 (CNA Connection, 1989g). However, subsequently the CCOHN decided they "would like more time to consider integration criteria, and suggested waiting until at least 1991 to begin the process. This gives CCOHN an opportunity to watch other groups move through the CNA certification process" (CNA Connection, 1990, p. 14). The CNA Board agreed to continue to provide consultation for CCOHN examination development and administration for another year. In lieu of this change in plans and the work that had been scheduled for the CCOHN integration, the CNA will accomodate other groups waiting to enter the certification program. The first is the neuroscience nursing certification examination whose development had been delayed because of fiscal constraints within the CNA and the need to seek additional funding for what is known to be a costly process, based on CNA's long experience in developing and administering the registration/licensure examinations for both registered nurses and registered nursing assistants in Canada (CNA Connection, 1989a).

It is important to understand that the process of certification, of which designation as a nursing specialty practice is the first step, differs from special interest groups in Canadian Nursing. To date, twelve specialty practice groups that are organized outside CNA have met the criteria to become a CNA Interest Group and a member of the CNA Advisory Council, established in 1986 "to provide a formal liaison structure to strengthen CNA's relationship with the national nursing groups and to promote unity and enhance interorganizational communication in a spirit of cooperation and collaboration" (CNA Advisory Council Minutes, June 21, 1986). In addition to having a representative of each of the national nursing groups who have met CNA's criteria serve on the Advisory Council, CNA welcomes representatives from other groups as observers at Advisory Council meetings; many who do not meet the criteria for membership have chosen to send a representative. Thus the Advisory Council is representative of special interest groups and not of specialty practice. Further, "certification does not require the establishment of a specialty organization prior to designation as a specialty practice" (CNA Connection, 1989, p. 10).

NURSING EDUCATION

In the past two bienniums, high priority has been given to the goal of requiring a baccalaureate degree in nursing for entry to practice by the year 2000. Nonetheless, CNA has supported and promoted the enhancement and expansion of graduate education in nursing and, more recently, increasing opportunities for continuing education for all nurses.

Although nursing education is a provincial matter, the CNA has prepared background materials on the issue and goal of entry to practice to be used by the provincial nursing associations and by individuals to communicate the goal and educate a variety of audiences. Background material prepared by the CNA, entitled *Entry to the Practice of Nursing: A Background Paper* (1982), provides an excellent historical perspective that clearly describes the rationale for the position taken for entry to practice. The CNA publishes an Entry to Practice Newsletter on a bimonthly basis so the provincial nurses' associations will not have to expend funds on this task. The contents are very useful in educating others and in lobbying. Newsletters are available to individuals and provincial associations and educational institutions.

The position on entry to practice originated with the Weir Report, *Survey of Nursing Education in Canada,* published by the CNA in 1932. "Among the major recommendations was one suggesting that schools of nursing should be incorporated into the general education system of the country and be subsidized by government funds" (CNA, 1968, p. 86). The first professional nursing organization to endorse requiring a baccalaureate degree for entry to practice by new graduates by the year 2000 was the Alberta Association of Registered Nurses (AARN, 1976). The position was adopted by the Board of the CNA and affirmed by delegates to the biennial convention in 1982. At this time, the background paper cited previously was published to explain the rationale for the CNA Board's policy stance on entry to practice.

Throughout the CNA's history there are references to efforts to upgrade the preparation of nurses. In 1957, a statement was made that preparation for nursing should be an educational experience. In 1960,

> . . . the Director of Special Studies for the CNA was appointed as the CNA liaison member to the Canadian Conference of University Schools of Nursing, which marked one of the first major moves to link the CNA with progress in higher education for nurses and to establish close working relationships with the university schools of nursing (CNA, 1968, pp. 92-93).

The establishment of the Canadian Nurses Foundation (CNF) in 1962 was additional evidence of support for nursing education. The CNF provided "scholarships, bursaries and fellowships for postgraduate study in nursing. Provision was made in 1966 to include assistance for study at the baccalaureate level" (CNA, 1968, p. 93). In 1978, the CNA published *Standards for Nursing Education* — a first in education in Canada — and urged universities with baccalaureate programs to include preparation for primary care nursing as an integral part of basic nursing education as soon as possible (CNA, 1981). In the same year, the CNA sponsored a national forum on nursing education that was attended by 350 nurses. The focus was to identify concerns and priorities in relation to nursing education. The forum was financed in part by the W.K. Kellogg Foundation.

Entry to practice continues to be a high priority for CNA and the provinces. Progress is being made in the design and implementation of collaborative efforts between university and diploma programs to attain the goal. All provincial nursing associations have now accepted the goal; New Brunswick was the last to make the decision in 1988. A variety of models can be expected to evolve. Reference is made in Chapter 26 to the decisions made in Prince Edward Island and British Columbia to phase out a diploma program and either replace or integrate it into a baccalaureate degree program (CNA Connection, 1989h; CNA News, 1989).

In Alberta in early 1990, the University of Alberta Faculty of Nursing and Red Deer College Department of Nursing announced their plan to provide an option for diploma students to earn a baccalaureate degree while remaining on the Red Deer campus. The first two years of the University's baccalaureate degree program will be offered by Red Deer College as a university transfer program, and students can elect to take third year University courses taught by College faculty. In the fourth year, courses will be taught by university faculty, using teleconferencing, self-learning modules, and on-site lectures. Clinical practice will take place in Red Deer clinical agencies, supervised by University faculty. For students who elect not to take the baccalaureate option at the end of two years, Red Deer College will offer a diploma program of 23 weeks. The collaborative endeavour was designed over a five-year period and is being implemented as a five-year pilot project, approved and funded by Alberta Advanced Education, with a joint evaluation (University of Alberta, January 18, 1990). Collaborative ventures such as these will be monitored with great interest by the CNA and the entire Canadian nursing community. Other models are being explored, and many will be tested to facilitate progress toward the goal of a baccalaureate degree as a minimal requirement for entry to the profession, as it is for other professions.

The CNA has also been a strong proponent of graduate education, and urged the development of master's programs. As described in Chapter 31, the first master's program in nursing was established at the University of Western Ontario in 1959. There are now 11 master's programs in nursing in Canada and efforts have been ongoing since 1978 to establish a doctoral program in nursing. In 1978, the CNA sponsored a national Seminar on Doctoral Preparation for Canadian Nurses and published the Proceedings (Zilm, Larose, and Stinson, 1979). An outgrowth of this seminar was the development, by CNA, CNF, and Canadian Association of University Schools of Nursing (CAUSN), of a proposal, "Operation Bootstrap," seeking $5.2 million from the W.K. Kellogg Foundation. Its purpose was to obtain establishment grants for PhD in Nursing programs, two nursing research consortia, emergency fellowships for doctoral preparation, and funding for communicating nursing research and maintaining an inventory of nurses with doctoral preparation. Unfortunately, the funding was not granted; by 1990, a doctoral program in nursing had not yet been established.

Between 1978 and 1988, several universities initiated efforts to establish a PhD in Nursing program. In 1980, the nursing faculties at McGill University and l'Université de Montréal proposed a joint, bilingual program, but it was not approved. In the same year, the University of Toronto approved in principle the development of a PhD in Nursing program, but a proposal has not been approved to date. Meanwhile, the faculty of nursing at that university obtained input into the PhD program offered by its Institute of Medicine so selected nurses could study in a program more closely related to their own discipline than to doctoral programs in such disciplines as sociology, anthropology, and education. L'Université de Montréal is continuing to work toward approval of a PhD in Nursing program. In 1986, a proposal for a PhD in Nursing program was approved by the Board of Governors at the University of Alberta. When the Alberta government had still not provided funding by 1988, the Faculty of Nursing decided to admit three predoctoral students on a "special case" basis, an option available, on a very limited basis, in the absence of program funding. However, no further admissions were made and the Alberta government had still not provided funding by 1990 to implement the program because of severe financial constraints. It is hoped that the program will be funded in the near future. Nonetheless, the CNA has continued to promote doctoral education and provide a strong lobbying force for this important goal for nursing in Canada.

NURSING RESEARCH

In addition to promoting graduate education in nursing, the CNA has been a very strong proponent of nursing research. Until 1969, its only involvement in relation to research was emphasis on making the CNA Library the most outstanding collection of nursing literature in Canada. In 1969, the CNA submitted a brief to the Special Senate Committee on Science Policy, which included a statement "that research in nursing practice and more prepared nurse researchers are vital to the provision of health care for Canadians" (CNA, 1981, p. 18).

Additional evidence of support for research and education was the CNA's allocation of $10,000 to support the CNF, which was established in 1962 to provide financial support for nurses enroled in baccalaureate and graduate programs, and finally for small nursing research project grants in 1984. The CNA's Board of Directors appointed a special committee on nursing research in 1971. In 1978, this committee became a standing committee of the Association, one of only two in the organization. The other is the Committee on Testing, which is advisory to the CNA Testing Service. The CNA Committee on Research has continued as a standing committee. In 1976, the CNA's bylaws were amended to include a member-at-large for nursing research on the Board of Directors.

The CNA has strongly supported the series of 10 national nursing research conferences held between 1971 and 1985, as described in Chapter 12. It sponsored the 1977 conference on Research Methodology in Nursing Care in cooperation with the University of Ottawa, with the aid of a grant from Health and Welfare Canada (CNA, 1981). The CNA has published research abstracts and a few research articles in *The Canadian Nurse* journal. Reference has been made to the "Operation Bootstrap" proposal, which sought funding for both nursing research and doctoral education.

In 1980, the CNA published the first inventory of Canadian nursing doctoral statistics, reporting 81 nurses with an earned doctorate and 72 nurses enroled in doctoral study (Larsen and Stinson, 1980). An update in 1982 reported 124 with an earned doctorate and 121 enroled in doctoral study (Stinson, Larsen, & MacPhail, 1984). A second update in 1986 reported 193 nurses with an earned doctorate and 224 enroled in doctoral study (Stinson, MacPhail, & Larsen, 1988). The statistics reflect a notable increase in the number of nurses prepared at the doctoral level and the number of nurses engaged in doctoral study; however, they also emphasize the urgent need for more nurses prepared at this educational level and for establishing one or two PhD in Nursing programs in Canada.

One of the major accomplishments of the CNA's Committee on Nursing Research in the 1980s was the CNA's publication in 1984 of *The Research Imperative*, a 10-year plan for nursing research in Canada. It included recommendations for establishing at least one, and preferably several, PhD in Nursing programs, and increased funding for nursing research. A major problem continues to be a dearth of funding for nursing research. Although Medical Research Council (MRC) funds are supposed to be available to nurses, very few have been able to obtain funding from this source because preference is given to medical research and to investigators with a track record. Although a nurse was appointed to the MRC in 1971, it was for a 1-year term only and did not result in increased funding for nursing research. A special nursing committee, appointed by the MRC, presented a proposal to the Council in 1985, recommending separate funding for nursing research and the establishment of a doctoral program in nursing. However, the MRC failed to produce a response after the report was tabled. Active lobbying efforts were finally effective in obtaining the appointment of another nurse, the Executive Director of the CNA, to the MRC in 1986 for a three-year term. It was hoped that having nursing representation on the MRC would be effective in accomplishing the goals for funding of nursing research and doctoral education in nursing; however, this has not happened.

In 1987 the MRC, in collaboration with the National Health Research and Development Program (NHRDP) of the Health Promotion Directorate, Health and Welfare Canada, announced a new competitive research funding program to support programmatic research in nursing. Universities were invited to submit letters of intent to develop a research program around a central theme. Seventeen letters of intent were submitted from the 27 university nursing faculties/schools; six were invited to submit full proposals (Alberta, McGill, McMaster, Montreal, Ottawa and Toronto). All took advantage of the opportunity and expended a great deal of time and effort in the process; however, the outcome was very disappointing, with no proposals approved. Three career awards were made instead, to individuals in different universities, to support research that was part of the total research program proposals. Once again, efforts by nurses to gain access to MRC research funds failed. Nursing still has less than 1% of the health sciences research funding in Canada (M. Harrison, personal communication, August 1989). Moreover, when the term of the nurse appointee to the MRC expired in 1989, she was replaced by a physiotherapist. Nonetheless, the CNA President and Executive Director continue to lobby for a nurse representative on the MRC (CNA Connection, 1989q).

CNA's Nursing Research Committee has continued to work on new approaches to increase nursing research endeavours and research funding. During the 1986 to 1988 biennium the committee presented a proposal to develop a Canadian Centre for Nursing Research to the CNA Board of Directors; the intent was to design this centre to stimulate and coordinate research in nursing across Canada through programmatic and multisite research of national relevance. The board of the proposed centre was to include representatives from the CNA, CNF, CAUSN, the Canadian Nursing Research Interest Group, major funding bodies and the public (CNA Connection, 1988d). Although the Boards of CNA and CNF and the Canadian Nursing Research Interest Group supported the proposal, CAUSN's Board did not. Since their support was considered essential for the project to succeed, no further action was taken on the proposal (CNA Connection, 1989n). Nonetheless, CNA's Nursing Research Committee is continuing to explore possibilities to increase research funding and nursing participation in funding agencies' decision-making, and to facilitate research utilization in clinical agencies. The committee is also examining the structure within the CNA for the continuing advancement of nursing research (CNA Connection, 1989d).

NURSING ADMINISTRATION

Because of the general focus on functional nursing in the early years of the development of nursing, it is logical that the CNA attended to issues and needs pertaining to nursing administration. This is reflected in the historical record of CNA actions in this domain. The first reference found was a "Report on Nursing Service," submitted by the CNA in 1926 at the request of the federal Department of Health. The report "contained statistical data; statement of issues and trends in nursing; the increasing difficulties of recruitment and the large number of drop-outs; the need to reduce wastage and conserve nurse power" (CNA, 1968, p. 85). In 1943, the CNA cooperated with the National Selective Service and the Canadian Medical Procurement and Assignment Board in conducting a survey of nursing service in Canada. The study disclosed a shortage of general duty nurses and recommended improved salaries and working conditions, comparable to other occupations requiring equivalent preparation, to alleviate the shortage and attract the quality of student desired (CNA, 1968).

Concern about the role of the nurse administrator and the lack of preparation for administrative positions was reflected at mid-century. In 1953, the CNA conducted a study of the functions and activities of head nurses in a general hospital, which led to publication of a manual for head nurses in 1960. In the early 1960s, nurses could obtain 1-year certificate preparation in nursing administration, designed to provide them with better preparation for assuming administrative responsibilities. With elimination of these certificate programs and increased emphasis on post–RN baccalaureate preparation, there was continued concern about the preparation of nurses for administrative roles. The problem centred on the fact that few courses on management were included in baccalaureate programs, which emphasized clinical preparation. As a result, other alternatives were developed. An example is the collaboration of the CNA and the CHA in 1961 to develop an extension course in nursing unit administration, which resulted in the Nursing Unit Administration Program: a home-study, distance-education program that still exists.

Because of continued concern about problems in nursing service and the preparation of nurses for administrative roles, in 1963 the CNA became a member of the Canadian Joint Committee on Nursing, as did the CMA and the CHA. Each organization had equal representation, a pattern that continues today. In the same year, a brief presented to the Royal Commission on Health Services by the CNA made 25 recommendations for the improvement of nursing service within the health services of Canada (CNA, 1968).

In 1966, the CNA published three major studies that had been initiated in 1960. One was an evaluation of the quality of nursing service. As a means of promoting improvement, the CNA sought opportunities for involvement in the Canadian Council on Hospital Accreditation. Thus, a CNA representative was appointed to the Canadian Council on Hospital Accreditation Standards Committee in 1969, and the CNA obtained a seat on the Canadian Council on Hospital Accreditation in 1973 and a second seat in 1976. Such involvement in policy making and decision making about accreditation allowed nurses' views to be heard. Nurse surveyors have been included on the hospital accreditation teams since 1974. In 1969, the CNA published *"Standards for Nursing Service in Health Care Facilities, A Self-Evaluation Guide* to help nursing personnel evaluate their service in the light of established philosophy and objectives"* (CNA, 1981, p. 18).

In 1980, at the CNA Biennial Convention, the membership asked that the CNA study the education of nurses for nursing administration (CNA, 1981). The CNA commissioned a paper, to delineate issues and make recommendations on the education of nurses for nursing administration, by Leatt (1981). The publication, *Education for Nursing Administration in Canada: A Discussion Paper,* "described the state of the art of education for nursing administration in Canada, identified some of the critical issues related to preparation for nursing administrative positions in nursing, and outlined some possible strategies for the future" (CNA, 1985, p. 1).

After this paper was published, the CNA Board established an ad hoc committee to clarify the role of the nurse administrator at various levels in health-care organizations, to develop standards for nursing administration, and to critically review the quality and availability of existing educational programs in nursing administration. The committee produced a publication (CNA, 1983), *Position Paper on the Role of the Nurse Administrator and Standards for Nursing Administration,* that was widely circulated because of the urgent need for change and the significance of the area, at a time when the entire Canadian health-care system was undergoing review. The CNA Board of Directors decided to give priority to nursing administration in the 1984 to 1986 biennium; another Ad Hoc Committee on Nursing Administration was established and charged with responsibility for developing a national plan for nursing administration. Lorine Besel, President of the CNA, stated: "Our profession urgently needs politically and economically astute leaders who have a solid background in management, a broad philosophical perspective on health services and a clear vision of the type of health care system we ultimately want to see in place" (CNA, 1985, p. 1).

A National Plan for Nursing Administration in Canada, recommended by the committee and approved by the Board of Directors in 1985, included objectives, strategies for attaining them, target dates and designated involved groups. One of the objectives was to enhance educational opportunities for nurse administrators, a continuing major inadequacy in the nursing education system and a concern for nurse administrators (CNA Connection, 1986a). The Ad Hoc Committee also recommended to the CNA Board regular monitoring of the

National Plan at the beginning of each biennium to ensure continued attention to implementation of the plan. The national plan is still monitored and some progress has been made in its implementation. In December 1987, a joint meeting was held for representatives from CNA, CAUSN, CHA, CPHA and the Canadian Council of Health Service Executives (CCHSE). The main topic of discussion was continuing education for nurse administrators. Priorities established were to promote support to universities to develop continuing education programs and to increase access to educational opportunities for nursing administrators who do not have access to university programs (CNA Board of Directors Minutes, February 18 to 19, 1988). In 1989, representatives from the same five organizations collaborated again to develop a strategic plan for the education of nurse administrators. "It includes objectives of increasing the number of graduate degree programs to prepare nurse administrators, providing additional continuing education opportunities and working to increase the understanding of issues faced by nurse administrators" (CNA Connection, 1989j, p. 10).

During the 1986 to 1988 biennium, nursing groups which discussed the National Plan for Nursing Administration and other national association groups identified the need to update the 1983 position paper on the Role of the Nurse Administrator and Standards for Nursing Administration. The new document (CNA, 1988) "attempted to balance the professional and corporate aspects of current nursing administration and to address the complex issues faced by nursing administrators today" (Evans, 1988, p. v). It should serve as an excellent resource to practising and potential nurse administrators, to teachers in nursing administration, and to other administrators in all types of health care agencies whose support is vital to achieving the goals of nurse administrators and the nursing staff to whom they provide leadership.

HEALTH-CARE REFORM

One of the CNA's long-term objectives has been to promote changes in the health-care system to use nurses' abilities more fully; another objective is to place more emphasis on health promotion and maintenance and less emphasis on illness care in use of funds and priorities in programming. In 1984, the CNA had a major influence on development of the Canada Health Act. CNA members lobbied vigorously against extra billing and user fees, and were successful in obtaining an amendment to the Canada Health Act to include "other health professionals" as potentially qualifying for reimbursement for services by the federal government. This meant that health-care providers other than physicians and dentists could be named as entry points to the health-care system in provincial health-care plans. This was a notable achievement, as it was the only amendment made in the Canada Health Act, and it provided an example of the potential power of lobbying efforts when nurses remain unified. As a result of this change, the CNA is promoting reform of the health-care system to enable nurses to assume greater responsibility and function more effectively in the system. Such a change has implications for health-care costs, because nurses can deliver quality care at decreased cost, particularly in health promotion and health maintenance.

In the 1988 to 1990 biennium, CNA published a major paper on health-care reform, which calls for the creation of a primary health-care infrastructure in Canada by restructuring and reforming the present health-care system. This comprehensive document mandates a health-care system that is accessible, provides equal emphasis on promotion and prevention with curative care, encompasses lay participation, promotes cooperation with other disciplines and government departments, and uses appropriate technology. The CNA confirms a strong commitment to "continue to work within nursing and with other disciplines, consumers and politicians to ensure that a primary health care system is implemented" (CNA, 1988, p. 30; CNA Connection, 1989i).

In keeping with the CNA's firm belief in the need for health-care reform, the CNA published "Health care reform for seniors" in 1990. The major assumption in this document is that "the current organization of the health-care system presents barriers for seniors in Canada and therefore requires reform. Other assumptions are: (1) seniors wish to maintain their independence for as long as possible, and (2) the present health care system is bureaucratic and crisis-oriented and it is, therefore, difficult for seniors to access appropriate services" (CNA 1990, p. 1). The strategies set forth are based on the five principles of primary health care. The role of the nurse in the proposed reformed system is described as "direct care provider, teacher/educator of health personnel and the public, the supervisor and manager of primary health-care services, and researcher and evaluator of health care" (CNA, Position statement on the nurses' role in primary health care, March, 1989).

CONCLUSION

The CNA clearly recognizes the importance of collaboration with other health professionals and their professional organizations in addressing problems and in endeavouring to reform the health-care system. The CNA has endorsed the formation of a Canada Health Council, which has had input from 11 national professional associations. The proposed Canada Health Council would have a primary purpose of providing a national and independent perspective on health and health-related issues. It would identify important issues in maintenance and enhancement of health and health-care delivery in Canada, and through research and analysis, seek ways to improve the health of Canadians. It would also provide objective information on the costs and benefits of existing services and new technologies (CNA Connection, 1986d).

Involvement in the development of this council and in other joint endeavours reflects the goals of the CNA for collaborating with others, being an integral part of future-oriented projects that have important implications for the health-care system of the future in Canada, and the meaningful involvement of nurses in that system.

REFERENCES

Alberta Association of Registered Nurses. (1976). Response to the Alberta Task Force on Nursing Education. Edmonton, Alberta: Author.

Canadian Nurses Association. (1968). *The leaf and the lamp*. Ottawa: Author.

Canadian Nurses Association. (1981). *The seventh decade 1969-1980.* Ottawa: Author.

Canadian Nurses Association. (1982). *Entry to the practice of nursing: A background paper.* Ottawa: Author.

Canadian Nurses Association. (1982). *Position paper on the role of the nurse administrator and standards for nursing administration.* Ottawa: Author.

Canadian Nurses Association. (1984). *The research imperative,* Ottawa: Author.

Canadian Nurses Association. (1985). *A national plan for nursing administration in Canada.* Ottawa: Author.

Canadian Nurses Association. (1988). *Health for all Canadians: A call for health care reform.* Ottawa: Author.

Canadian Nurses Association. (1988). *The role of the nurse administrator and standards for nursing administration.* Ottawa: Author.

Canadian Nurses Association. (1990). *Health care reform for seniors.* Ottawa: Author.

Canadian Nurses Association Advisory Council Minutes, June 21, 1986.

Canadian Nurses Association Board of Directors' Minutes, February 18-20, 1987.

CNA Connection. (1986a). New national plan unveiled for nursing administration. *The Canadian Nurse, 82*(1), 11.

CNA Connection. (1986b). Smoking and health. *The Canadian Nurse, 82*(3), 12.

CNA Connection. (1986c). Committee on health issues: smoking. *The Canadian Nurse, 82*(4), 9-10.

CNA Connection. (1986d). 1986 Biennial convention report. *The Canadian Nurse, 82*(9), 16-20.

CNA Connection. (1986e). CNA position on smoking and health. *The Canadian Nurse, 82*(10), 8.

CNA Connection. (1987). Certification project now complete. *The Canadian Nurse, 83*(1), 7.

CNA Connection. (1989a). CNA initiates protective liability plan. *The Canadian Nurse, 84*(2), 7.

CNA Connection. (1988b). CNA statement on tobacco and health. *The Canadian Nurse, 84*(4), 10.

CNA Connection. (1988c). Health care reform. *The Canadian Nurse, 84*(8), 18.

CNA Connection. (1988d). Nursing research. *The Canadian Nurse, 84*(8), 18.

CNA Connection. (1988e). Tobacco strategies. *The Canadian Nurse, 84*(8), 18.

CNA Connection. (1989a). Certification. *The Canadian Nurse, 85*(1), 7-8.

CNA Connection. (1989b). Despite deficit, practice issues prevail. *The Canadian Nurse, 85*(1), 7.

CNA Connection. (1989c). Nurse retention study. *The Canadian Nurse, 85*(1), 8.

CNA Connection. (1989d). Research committee receives direction. *The Canadian Nurse, 85*(1), 9.

CNA Connection. (1989e). Work-life affairs position reaffirmed. *The Canadian Nurse, 85*(1), 8.

CNA Connection. (1989f). Mandatory drug screening. *The Canadian Nurse, 85*(2), 10.

CNA Connection. (1989g). OHNs find common ground with CNA. *The Canadian Nurse, 85*(2), 10.

CNA Connection. (1989h). Baccalaureate comes to PEI. *The Canadian Nurse, 85*(3), 10.

CNA Connection. (1989i). CNA endorses primary health care. *The Canadian Nurse, 85*(5), 8.

CNA Connection. (1989j). Strategic plan for administrators. *The Canadian Nurse, 85*(5), 10.

CNA Connection. (1989k). Work-life focus of conference. *The Canadian Nurse, 85*(5), 8.

CNA Connection. (1989l). Work-life issues. *The Canadian Nurse, 85*(6), 10.

CNA Connection. (1989m). Focus: Nursing practice. *The Canadian Nurse, 85*(8), 10.

CNA Connection. (1989n). Nursing research. *The Canadian Nurse, 85*(8), 10.

CNA Connection. (1989o). Smoking cessation project funded. *The Canadian Nurse, 85*(9), 10.

CNA Connection. (1989p). Specialization stimulates debate. *The Canadian Nurse, 85*(9), 10.

CNA Connection. (1989q). September 15 meeting with the Minister of Health and Welfare re: MRC. *The Canadian Nurse, 85*(10), 8.

CNA Connection. (1990). Occupational health nurses. *The Canadian Nurse, 86*(1),14.

CNA News. (1989b). VGH school joins UBC. *The Canadian Nurse, 85*(2), 12.

Larsen, J., and Stinson, S.M. (1980). *Canadian nursing doctoral statistics 1980.* Ottawa: Canadian Nurses Association.

Leatt, P. (1981). Education for nursing administration in Canada: A discusssion paper. Ottawa: Canadian Nurses Association.

Ritchie, Judith A. (1988). Editorial. On becoming president. *The Canadian Nurse, 84*(8), 13.

Stinson, S.M., Larsen, J., and MacPhail, J: (1984). *Canadian nursing doctoral statistics: 1982 update.* Ottawa: Canadian Nurses Association.

Stinson, S.M., MacPhail, J., and Larsen, J. *Canadian nursing doctoral statistics: 1986 update.* Ottawa: Canadian Nurses Association.

University of Alberta. Collaborative nursing program with Red Deer College approved. *Folio.* January 18, 1990, p.3.

Zilm, G., Larose, O., and Stinson, S. (1979). Proceedings of the Kellogg National Seminar on Doctoral Education for Canadian Nurses. Ottawa: Canadian Nurses Association.

CHAPTER FIVE

The Professional Image: Impact and Strategies For Change

JANNETTA MacPHAIL

In the 1980s, the image of nursing became the centre of much attention in nursing literature and in deliberations of professional associations. It is also of concern to nurse educators seeking to attract the best students into nursing, to nurse administrators endeavouring to staff healthcare agencies, to nurse researchers who encounter difficulty in explaining nursing research to others, and to all nurses who encounter negative or indifferent responses when identifying themselves as nurses in social situations. The Canadian Nurses Association's Board of Directors made the nursing image a top priority for the 1986 to 1988 and 1988 to 1990 bienniums. Their goal is "to develop a plan of strategic actions to enhance the image of nurses and nursing" (CNA Connection, 1987, p. 7).

In addressing the issue of the image of nursing, it is important to reflect on historical and current factors that influence the image of nurses and nursing. Such a perspective is needed to determine what can be done to enhance the image and who might or should be involved in addressing this important issue.

EXTERNAL AND INTERNAL IMAGES

One often hears or reads about the image of nursing as if there were only one image. Nursing actually has many images, because nurses relate to a variety of audiences. For example, the image presented to attract students or to recruit nurses in health-care agencies is different from the image presented to legislators whose main concern is cost-effectiveness. These are external images; internal images are the views that nurses have of themselves as individuals and of the profession.

In examining studies of nursing images conducted through 1964, Simmons and Henderson (1964) found:

> ... two popular and competing images of the nurse ... At one pole is the image of the humanitarian and altruistic person, more or less competent and endowed with

49

sympathy, compassion, and exceptional capacities for establishing rapport—one who gives of herself. At the other pole is the image of the professional, well-trained, technically efficient and cool-headed individual who can be relied upon for able performance within her specialty, and relatively independent of feeling components—one who may seem to keep herself out of her work.

Probably few nurses can be classified at the two extremes; most fit at various points between the two poles.

Emanating from the time of the Romans, the first persons identified with the nurse role were wealthy Roman matrons who gave nurturance, self-sacrifice, and mothering. Nursing continues to be sex stereotyped even though those who cared for the injured during the Crusades were men and men today have entered nursing. The proportion of men in nursing in Canada and the United States continues to be very limited, at 3.0% (Statistics Canada, 1990) and 3.3% (US Public Health Service [USPHS], 1988), respectively. The proportion in the United Kingdom is considerably higher at approximately 10% (Gaze, 1987; Nursing Times, 1986; Skevington and Dawkes, 1988).

Images of any profession or work group are influenced by the values and orientations learned from family and friends and by individuals' experiences with particular members of a profession. Images are also influenced by the mass media, particularly with today's variety of media. Two recent studies of the public's perception of nurses and nursing (Lippman and Ponton, 1989; Payne, Cook, and Associates, 1990; Giovannetti, 1990), found that respondents' views were strongly influenced by personal contact with nurses or the experiences of others. Hence, observational learning is an important means of developing images of various professions, including nursing; such learning promotes a concept a particular profession. This has great impact on how a profession is regarded by members of society and on how attractive the profession is to individuals.

THE MASS MEDIA AND THE IMAGE OF NURSES AND NURSING

Kalisch and Kalisch surveyed mass media products, pertaining to nursing, from the past century and a half. These included: "the print media (200 novels, 143 magazine short stories, poems and articles and 20,000 newspaper clippings), as well as the newer non-print media (204 motion pictures, 122 radio programs, and 320 television episodes)" (1982, p. 5).

From these products, they classified the image into five dominant types, characterizing five successive time periods.

The "Angel of Mercy" image of the nurse was portrayed "as noble, moral, religious, virginal, ritualistic and self-sacrificing" (Kalisch and Kalisch, 1982, p. 7). Although it has been said that Florence Nightingale epitomized this image, she was a scholar and has been termed the first nurse researcher. Nightingale's achievements were astounding: She saved the lives of many wounded soldiers during the Crimean War; she restored order from chaos by assuming responsibility for the soldiers' environment as well as nursing care, despite strong resistance from the physicians in charge; and she brought innovation and advancement to the fields of nursing, health, and hospital planning. Nightingale was of high social class, well educated, and a true scholar. If her model for nursing had been followed, the nursing profession would be in a much more advantageous position today. The "Angel of Mercy" image, as identified by Kalisch and Kalisch, existed from 1854 to 1919. It continued through World War I, when nurses were presented by the media as noble and heroic. A typical film from that time period portrayed the nurse enlisting in the service to be near her sweetheart, finding him wounded, and restoring him to health (Kalisch and Kalisch, 1982, p. 11).

The next image, "Girl Friday," existed from 1920 to 1929; it was very different and reflected considerable deterioration. The nurse was portrayed as "subservient, cooperative, methodical, dedicated, modest, and loyal" (Kalisch and Kalisch, 1982). In essence, she served as a handmaiden, an image that grew out of the deprofessionalization of nursing that occurred in the 1920s with declining standards of nursing education. The decline was the result of a proliferation of hospitals, accompanied by schools of nursing to staff them, as well as ruthless exploitation of students and poor working conditions. Some of these conditions continued into the 1940s, although the image of the nurse as portrayed by the media changed.

The third image, "The Heroine," existed from 1930 to 1945, when the media portrayed the nurse as "brave, rational, dedicated, decisive, humanistic, and autonomous" (Kalisch and Kalisch, 1982, p. 11). Motion pictures in the 1930s and 1940s depicted this image. Biographies were written about heroines such as Florence Nightingale; Edith Cavell, who was shot by a German firing squad during World War I for helping wounded soldiers to escape; and Sister Kenney, whose treatment of poliomyelitis victims enabled many to recover muscle function at a time when the victims were being kept immobilized by the medical profession. Adventure dramas about air or sea travel involved nurse heroines. Airlines required flight attendants to be graduate nurses; delivering babies, assisting in emergency surgery, and even landing the plane safely when pilots were disabled were among the heroic acts of flight attendants portrayed in movies and other media (Kalisch and Kalisch, 1982). World War II intensified the "Heroine" image; nurses were portrayed very positively on recruitment posters. Many volunteered for military service and were highly regarded by society. When television became available in the mid-1950s, the "Heroine" image was portrayed to a larger audience.

The fourth image, the "Mother Image," existed from 1945 to 1965. It seems almost incredible that women went home to function as wives and mothers after enduring the hardships of war, but they did. At that time, the place for married women was perceived to be in the home, and society frowned on working mothers. Although nursing remained a high status occupation for women, nurse characters were portrayed by the media as "maternal, nurturing, sympathetic, passive, expressive, and domestic" (Kalisch and Kalisch, 1982, p. 15).

As this image faded in the mid-1960s, the most negative media image of the nurse since Dickens' imbibing Sairey Gamp developed—the nurse as a "Sex Object." This negative image of the nurse as "a sensual, romantic, hedonistic, frivolous, irresponsible, promiscuous individual" (Kalisch and Kalisch, 1982, p. 17) continues today on television and particularly in movies. This image is readily identified in such television programs as "M*A*S*H" and "Trapper John"; the nurse is depicted as a sex object with no evidence of being intellectual or professional. The nurse is also depicted as a sex object on greeting cards and in advertisements.

The ideal image, proposed by Kalisch and Kalisch, is "The Careerist"; "an intelligent, logical, progressive, sophisticated, empathic, and assertive woman or man who is committed to attaining higher and higher standards of health care" (1982. p. 21). To what extent has such an image been achieved? Do nurses perceive themselves in this image? What can be done to promote such an image?

PUBLIC'S PERCEPTION OF NURSES AND NURSING

During the past decade, nurses have become increasingly concerned about their image and its effect on recruitment into nursing programs and the retention of nurses in the workforce, and about the shortage of nurses in Canada and the United States. One way to address these concerns is to conduct studies to ascertain the public's perceptions of nurses and nursing as a career to obtain data for formulating plans of action.

Lippman and Ponton (1989) conducted a survey of faculty in all disciplines in 19 northeastern United States universities with accredited baccalaureate degree programs in nursing. They obtained perceptions of nurses and nursing from a random sample of 535 faculty members, 11% of whom were nursing faculty. The 42-item questionnaire, developed by the investigators from literature and their experience, focused on three categories: images of nursing practice, attitudes about nursing education, and sex symbol. Most of the respondents, as indicated by the demographic data collected, had nurse friends or colleagues or had been cared for by a nurse. The findings reflected a different and more positive view of nursing than that presented by the media. Nurses were perceived as "educated, autonomous and compassionate individuals whose role is vital to health care" (Lippman & Ponton, 1989, p. 27). They were viewed as knowledgeable about good health and as good sources of information about health and its promotion. The majority did not perceive nurses as handmaidens to physicians and believed nurses should be treated as equals to physicians. Most were not averse to their daughters entering nursing, although 18% stated that "bright young women should study medicine rather than nursing". The investigators indicated that the responses may have been influenced by the personal contact the respondents had had with nurses. It is also possible that nursing faculty had communicated effectively about nursing and nursing education within the 19 universities from which the sample was drawn.

Because of concerns about the nursing shortage and how to attract more people to nursing, a survey was conducted in Indiana to ascertain the public's attitudes, values and beliefs about nursing as a career. Subjects included college freshmen (27.1%), students in grades 6 through 12 (29.6%), and "enablers" (those who had potential to influence career selection). The "enablers" included parents (19.3%), teachers and counsellors (7.3%), and school nurses (6.8%). The subjects were selected at random from these categories. Questionnaire items were designed to determine attitudes about ideal career and nursing as a career, and were derived from literature on careers and nursing. The findings indicated that, for these respondents, nursing and ideal career were similar in "opportunities for employment, use of intellectual abilities, caring for people as a career attribute, need for academic achievement, and scholastic achievement as a prerequisite for career development" (May, Austin, and Champion, 1988, p. 7). However, an ideal career was viewed as "more financially rewarding, more respected, more appreciated, and more powerful"; providing "more opportunities for leadership, more safety in the workplace, more opportunities for making decisions, and more opportunities for obtaining and applying knowledge"; and involving "less emphasis on manual skills, less utilization of high technology, lighter workload, and easier work" (May et al., 1988, p. 7). Differences were noted in the respondent subgroups: "school-age students had more positive attitudes toward nursing as a career than other groups, and parents and school-age students valued nursing more than other groups" (May et al., 1988, p. 26). Based on the findings, a number of recommendations were made to enhance the positive attitudes and improve the negative perceptions, including ways to increase respect and appreciation for nurses, reduce workloads, promote more autonomy in practice and more safety in the workplace; to achieve more competitive salaries; to increase leadership opportunities and empowerment of nurses; and to place less emphasis on manual skills and high technology in publicity materials. Many of the recommendations reiterate strategies that nurses have advocated for years, both as individuals and as members of study commissions established to address the problems of recruitment and retention in nursing.

Another study was part of a "Public Image of Nursing Campaign" undertaken by nurses in the United Kingdom in 1984. A company skilled in survey techniques was engaged to conduct a survey to determine what the public thinks of nurses and nursing, interviewing a representative sample of 1963 persons aged 15 and over in 172 sampling points (Rayner, 1984). A split sample technique was used; approximately one half of the respondents were asked to state their ideas and impressions of what nurses are like and the other half to delineate what ideal nurses would be like. Although the survey indicated that the public's image of nurses closely matched their ideal, some of the findings need to be examined to create the ideal image of nursing. For example, whereas nurses were perceived as hard working by 82% of the respondents, 70% said they should be (Rayner, 1984). It is doubtful that this image would attract young people into nursing, as reflected in the previous study. Another cause for concern was that only 27% of the respondents believed that nurses are given the opportunity to use initiative in their work; but 39% perceived this opportunity as ideal. This perception needs to be examined in relation to another response: 42% of the respondents indicated that nurses obey physicians' orders without question, and 34% believed they should (Rayner, 1984). Another interesting finding was that younger persons had more positive views than older persons about nurses using their initiative and the extent to which they should obey. Whereas 81% of the respondents believed that nurses are caring and understanding; 86% thought they should be. Only 42% thought nurses are well educated and only 47% believed they should be (Rayner, 1984). This result indicates a lack of understanding of what nursing involves, and should be a cause of concern to all nurses.

A study conducted in Canada in 1988 was commissioned by the Alberta Association of Registered Nurses (AARN) to assess public attitudes about nursing in Alberta. A telephone survey, using a structured interview guide and trained interviewers, was conducted by a company skilled in survey techniques (Payne, Cook & Associates, Inc). A computerized random digit dialing procedure was used, accessing unlisted and listed numbers and ensuring confidentiality; the interviewers had no identifiable information. The instrument was reviewed by a committee of representatives of AARN, with background knowledge and experience in nursing and some expertise in questionnaire design (Payne, Cook, and Associates, 1990). The instrument was also pretested using a small sample of South Edmonton residents. The study sample included 1087 adults, randomly selected from all regions of Alberta. Respondents were asked to describe, in their own words, their perception of the nursing profession. Over 87% of the responses were positive, using descriptors such as caring, compassionate, knowledgeable, intelligent, helpful, devoted, dedicated, professional, responsible, and hard-working. The few negative images pertained to nursing being a hard, tough, and demanding job and nurses being overworked and underpaid. Although the media influenced about 60% of the respondents' images of nursing, more than 80% formed their opinions through personal contact with nurses or experiences of others with nurses. Response to items rated on a 5-point Likert scale indicated that respondents viewed nursing as mentally and physically demanding and as requiring special people. Most also viewed it as challenging and interesting and, for the most part, nursing was highly respected. "Despite the fact that 91% of the respondents believed nursing is a highly respected profession, only 76% would recommend nursing as a career" (Giovannetti, 1990, p. 7). Support for nursing as a career was found to be lowest among persons under age 25 and persons with some postsecondary education, two groups from which potential nursing students could be recruited and who are likely to have strong peer influence. As level of income of respondents increased, positive views of nursing as challenging and interesting decreased and strong support for nursing as a career decreased. Also disconcerting was that 79% of the respondents believed that nurses should always consult a physician before administering patient care, and 72% perceived physicians as having total authority over patient care. These attitudes were less prevalent among the younger persons, the more highly educated, and those with higher incomes. On a more positive note, most respondents perceived nurses as accountable for their own practice and conduct and as having a role in patient education. Moreover, the majority supported nurses' involvement in research to improve practice and believed that nurses should be required to upgrade their education continually. On the controversial issue of nurses being allowed to strike, 47% were firmly opposed, although almost 70% conceded that strike action might be necessary to keep nurses' salaries on a par with those of other professions (Payne, Cook, and Associates, 1990). This is interesting because the province of Alberta has experienced four nurses' strikes since 1977. Because of these study findings the AARN has undertaken a province-wide public education campaign to enhance the image of nurses and nursing (Giovannetti, 1990).

Some of the findings of the AARN public opinion survey are corroborated by another study; Reichelt (1988) conducted a telephone survey of a stratified sample of 1686 American adults to determine their perceptions of nursing. Reichelt found that the public perceived nurses "more as demonstrating care and concern than as providing unique services or utilizing cognitive skills" (1988, p. 475). As in Alberta, the youngest age group held a more negative view of nursing than other age groups and respondents in higher income brackets held more positive views than others. The youngest age group (18 to 24 years) was the least likely to perceive nurses as thinking for themselves and as having their own distinctive practice domain. On the other hand, respondents with high incomes were most likely to view nurses as providing unique services and making independent decisions in providing patient care.

Not all of the public perceives the need for nurses to continue their education, as found in two of the studies. Nurses prepared at the diploma level who earn a baccalaureate degree in nursing have reported that they are asked by family, friends, or patients, why they wish to continue their formal education. These reports reflect the misconception that a registered nurse has all the education needed. They also indicate that the individuals responding in this manner have no concept of the pattern of nursing education or of why nurses need to be knowledgeable and continue to learn. Describing nursing and nursing education to the public is not easy, but it is the responsibility of the profession and of individual nurses to use the findings of research to clarify misunderstandings and communicate clearly and concisely the role and potential of nursing in providing health care and improving the health care system. The communication must be adapted for a variety of publics—patients, students, prospective applicants to nursing programs, colleagues in medicine and other health professions and disciplines, legislators, and the public in general.

SELF-IMAGE OF NURSING

Nurses' view of themselves may be referred to as self-image or internal image. Self-image is vitally important because the public's perception of nurses and nursing is influenced by their interactions and experiences with nurses. The studies cited indicated that these interactions were considerably more influential in shaping images of nursing than were the media.

Nurses have been criticized in the literature for having low self-esteem. This may be reflected in appearance, approach to patients, relationships with other health care professionals, and behaviour in the community. Many factors contribute to the development of self-image, including the values and attitudes one brings to a profession. These values and attitudes are influenced by life experiences before entering the educational system to prepare for the profession; then the educational system influences the learner's concept of nursing practice, of the role of the nurse, of relationships with other health professionals, and of professional responsibilities as a member of the profession and the community.

Nurse educators can help change the self-image of nursing through their teaching and role-modelling. They may also contribute unknowingly to some negative aspects of image development. The importance that they attach to the individual nurse and to the work of nursing can have a major effect on how the students view themselves for many years. Students are also strongly influenced by the nurses—practitioners, administrators, researchers—with whom they interact in clinical practice settings and by the relationships they observe between nurses and other health professionals.

Nurses have the opportunity to effect changes now and assume responsibility for the future of nursing. Individuals can affect the image of nursing through their daily performance in nursing practice and their reactions to various publics— patients, family members, friends, students, potential recruits, other professionals, legislators, policy makers, or colleagues. As indicated by the studies cited, these interactions contribute to other people's views of nursing. Moreover, one's personal experiences as a nurse and one's own perception of nursing have a great impact on daily encounters with the public. Styles (1982) points out that we must view nursing with a sense of collegiality and collectivity, thus sharing responsibility and authority for nursing and working together to preserve the wholeness of the profession. Achieving unified action is difficult, however, because of the disparity in nursing over issues such as educational preparation for nursing; preparation for specialty practice; unionism; research to improve practice; and allocation of funds among practice, education and research. It is well known that others can use such disparity to deter or defeat efforts to make constructive and desirable changes that will help achieve unity.

Nursing is more complex than most people think. Developing the knowledge, skills, attitudes, and values needed to practise nursing is a very complicated undertaking. The list of knowledge and skills needed is endless. Differentiating nursing from medicine, nurses often cite the focus of nursing as "care", as opposed to "cure" as the focus and end goal of medicine. Perhaps the essence of nursing practice is caring, and caring is not easy. Diers (1984, p. 24-25) points out that:

> . . . it is not easy to care for people—any people—anytime, anywhere. It is especially difficult when there are no ties of blood or common interest that bind the nurse and the patient. In nursing, caring requires authentic altruism that must be titrated precisely so as not to overwhelm on the one hand, nor be lost on the other. Caring takes enormous energy, even when genuine liking is present, for it is impossible to care equally for and about everyone. Yet that is precisely nursing's assignment.

The self-image of nursing affects how nurses think students should be educated; whether they encourage others to enter nursing, particularly daughters or sons; the importance they attach to nursing research; how they think nursing services should be organized; how they view nurses' strikes'; the importance they attach to helping people take responsibility for their own health; and how much influence they think people should have in decisions about their own care. Although nurses do not have to agree on everything, they should agree on basic goals and have sound rationale to support their positions. Too much internal disparity weakens the profession and undermines the power of nurses, which is potentially great because the number of persons in the nursing profession far exceeds that of any other health profession.

STRATEGIES FOR CHANGING THE IMAGE

Because of the negative image of nurses and nursing that continues to exist, it is important to identify strategies that may be undertaken by individuals and the profession, through professional associations, to help enhance the image.

A basic requirement is to change the self-image held by a nurse if it is a deterrent to developing the positive image nurses wish to portray. A change in the self-image would logically begin with nursing education promoting the "Careerist" image projected by Kalisch and Kalisch (1982). While this is presumably the objective of all nursing programs, particularly those in universities, in view of the entry to practice goal, nurse educators need to examine their teaching strategies to ensure that they promote the "Careerist" image of nursing.

In discussing nursing education's responsibility for developing nursing's self-image, Hammer and Toughs (1985, p. 280) state that any sustained change will emanate from educational programs in nursing, which will develop a positive self-concept encompassing both self-image and self-esteem. Hammer and Toughs (1985) point out that:

> . . . self-concept is learned. It is derived from all life experiences, from successes, failures and humiliations. It is also derived from feedback from others, particularly those in authority or those most respected . . . Individuals with a positive self-concept are more likely to reach their aspirations and are generally healthier and more productive than those with a more negative concept.

Hammer and Toughs (1985) perceive nurse educators as having the opportunity to help change the image of nursing in a very positive way by providing a supportive and challenging learning environment that engenders a positive self-concept. They emphasize the importance of providing constructive feedback on a consistent basis, particularly in the clinical setting. They believe that faculty convey the importance they attach to nursing practice through their own actions and underscore the need for mutual respect between faculty and staff nurses.

Other methods of changing the image of nursing during the process of education pertain to the attributes or characteristics of a profession that students learn during their basic education. Probably the characteristic of a profession that is least often conveyed to students is that it has its own body of knowledge, defined through research. Research is not emphasized in diploma programs because it is not a component of the programs, but it is important that students know about research development and recognize its importance in advancing nursing knowledge and improving nursing practice. Educators can help students develop research awareness and understand the importance of applying valid and reliable research findings in practice. This inadequacy will be eliminated when all nurses are required to earn a baccalaureate degree to enter practice.

Since mass media influence the public's image of nursing, it is important that nurses be alert and educated to assess the media for the images portrayed. Kalisch and Kalisch advocate a deliberate process of intervention that "involves four key steps: (1) getting organized; (2) monitoring the media; (3) reacting to the media; and (4) fostering an improved image" (1987, p. 187). The "media watch" has been promoted and implemented by professional nursing associations in Canada and the United States. Nurses are encouraged to assess the media for the portrayal of undesirable images and take action by identifying the inadequacies to the producers (Evans, Fitzpatrick and Howard-Ruben, 1983; Kalisch and Kalisch, 1983; Kalisch and Kalisch, 1987). An example of a positive result from "media watch" is the organized protest by many nurses and the professional organizations in 1989 to National Broadcasting Corporation's television series "Nightingales". The series portrayed an extremely demeaning and grossly outdated image of nurses and nursing students. The result of a mass letter-writing campaign organized by professional nursing associations and of meetings with the producers was a victory for nursing; the series was cancelled and the producers and the public became keenly aware of the reasons for nursing's protest. They also became aware of the image that nursing wishes to convey and its importance in attracting and retaining nurses to provide quality health care.

Porter, Porter, and Lower (1989) describe a comprehensive strategy, developed by a task force in a teaching hospital, that is designed to enhance the image of nursing in the hospital and the community. The task force started with a review of literature and developed specific recommendations and strategies, giving first priority to internal enhancement of the image, then addressing the community. The internal changes recommended included: increasing staff participation within the nursing department, empowering nurses, developing a system of reward and recognition, and improving communications. An administrative position was established to implement and coordinate the task force's suggestions, and a survey was conducted to determine nurses' perceptions of nursing in this hospital. A follow-up survey in one year is planned to determine the extent of change in self-image among the nursing staff. The administration's financial investment in this endeavour and their strong support reflect the priority level of enhancing the image of nursing in this institution. Many of these ideas could be implemented by other health care agencies.

Another approach that has been used with considerable success by professional organizations is presenting awards for media presentations that portray the most positive images of nursing. This strategy was implemented by the Canadian Nurses Association (CNA) in 1988, when three awards and five certificates of merit, in the areas of television, radio and journalism, were presented by the Minister of Health and Welfare at a dinner organized by CNA (CNA

Connection, 1988). In 1989, five award recipients and five certificate-of-merit recipients were selected from 29 entries, including national newspapers and magazines, private and public radio and television, and individual publications (CNA Connection, 1989). CNA's media awards have become an annual event during Nurses' Week in May and are having a positive effect on the image of nurses and nursing.

Public opinion surveys are important to enhancing the image of nursing. The samples used must be random and of sufficient size to allow generalization and instruments must be tested for validity and reliability. The results of such surveys should be used in marketing the nursing profession to the public as the AARN has done. The younger age groups should be targeted, not only to increase recruitment into nursing, but also to ensure favourable public opinion in the future. Reichelt (1988) emphasizes the importance of regular assessment of public opinion of nursing, both to formulate marketing strategies and to assess the results of the strategies that are implemented.

Recruitment materials, both to attract persons into nursing and to attract nurses into positions in health-care agencies, must be scrutinized carefully for the image presented. They should apply to both men and women. To attract staff in times of scarce resources, health-care agencies often use gimmicks that promote a negative and sexually oriented image by emphasizing nonprofessional aspects of the place of employment. An example is advertisements emphasizing the advantages of social life in a particular setting rather than the challenges of professional practice.

Another means of promoting the positive and careerist image of nursing is to eliminate some of the traditions and rituals of graduation ceremonies. The graduation ceremony for nursing students in university and college programs should be the same as for other students; not set apart for long-standing rituals. Similarly, the language used in educational programs and among nurses themselves must be changed to eliminate sexist and paternalistic phrases, such as "the girls."

The practice of nursing should be envisioned and interpreted by students as primarily independent and interdependent, with some dependent aspects pertaining to the prescription of therapies. The focus of practice should be on promotion and maintenance of health, not illness care, with the goal of helping people attain, maintain, and regain their optimal levels of health and function. Nurses should be portrayed in interdependent practice, where they have an important role in collaborative decision making and in making independent decisions related to nursing care. They should also be depicted as playing an active role in making policies that pertain to health care and financing of health care; not merely serving in a reactive manner.

Nurses can play a key role in explaining the image of nurses and nursing to society in general and to the other health professionals they work with on a daily basis. The image of nursing held by practitioners themselves is of vital importance, as is their skill at communicating that image to others. Unless nurses have a concept of the "Careerist" image, as proposed by Kalisch and Kalisch (1982), nursing will not succeed in changing the image and developing a cadre of intelligent, sophisticated, assertive, competent, empathic, and supportive individuals whose major goal is to assist persons in assuming increased responsibility for their own health.

The concept of nurses marketing their services in an increasingly competitive health-care system, as proposed by Krampitz and Coleman (1985), is a strategy that would help change the image. This approach is needed in the United States, where physicians organize to protect their practices and work to limit nursing practise and competition from nonphysician providers, and because nursing services are eligible for third-party reimbursement in some states. Some physicians in Canada have voiced similar fears as nurses continue toward their goal of a baccalaureate degree for entry to nursing practice and as some nurses venture into independent practice. Krampitz and Coleman (1985) believe that nurses must identify services unique to their profession and market them to succeed in a competitive marketplace.

CONCLUSION

Although the image of nurses and nursing may be changing to overcome the "Sex Object" image that still exists in the mass media, the challenge for nurses is to change both the internal and external images of nursing to promote the "Careerist" image. Only nurses can change the image, and change will be effected only by commitment on the part of individuals and the profession as a whole. The priority given to enhancing the image of nurses and nursing by professional associations needs to be continued. In addition, individual nurses need to accept the challenge of promoting the ideal "Careerist" image of nurses, which will help attract the kind of person needed to develop the potential of nurses to advance knowledge and improve practice, and to be known as persons committed to knowing and especially to doing. This will require changes in the nursing educational system, in keeping with the profession's goal for entry to nursing practice. Kelly (1989, p. 17) states:

> . . . If enough nurses practice professionally with competence and caring, if they create, direct and/or practice in innovative settings that provide needed care to patients, if they are risk-takers not afraid to develop or assume "different" roles in health care, if with research they find answers to better patient care, if they look beyond the crisis-centred here and now to anticipate and search out ways to meet the public's health care needs, if they simply demonstrate the existing diversity in nursing, there will be like-minded men and women who will see nursing as a worthwhile career opportunity.

REFERENCES

Anatomy of a profession. (1986). *Nursing Times, 82*(13): 24, 1986.

CNA Connection. (1987). Staggering agenda set by directors for 1987. *The Canadian Nurse, 83*(1), 7.

CNA Connection. (1988). CNA media awards a hit. *The Canadian Nurse, 84*(7), 6.

CNA Connection. (1989). Media excellence. *The Canadian Nurse, 85*(7), 9.

Diers, D. (1984). To profess — to be a professional. *Journal of the New York State Nurses' Association, 15*(4), 22-29.

Evans, D., Fitzpatrick, T., and Howard-Ruben, J. (1983). A district takes action. *American Journal of Nursing, 83*(1), 52-59.

Gaze, H. (1987). Men in nursing: Man appeal. *Nursing Times, 83*(20), 24-27.

Giovannetti, Phyllis. (1990). News release. *AARN Newsletter, 46*(1), 7.

Hammer, R.M., and Toughs, M.A. (1985). Nursing's self-image—nursing education's responsibility. *Journal of Nursing Education, 24*(7), 280-283.

Kalisch, B., and Kalisch, P. (1982). Anatomy of the image of the nurse: Dissonant and ideal models. In C. Williams (Ed.), *Image-making in nursing* (pp. 3-23). Kansas City: American Academy of Nursing.

Kalisch, B., and Kalisch, P. (1983). Improving the image of nursing. *American Journal of Nursing, 83*(1), 48-52.

Kalisch, P., and Kalisch, B. (1987). *The changing image of the nurse.* Don Mills, Ontario: Addison-Wesley Publishing Company.

Kelly, L.S. (1989). Editorial: Updating nursing's image. *Nursing Outlook, 37*(1), 17.

Krampitz, S.D., and Coleman, J.R. (1985). Marketing, a must in a competitive health care system. *Nursing Economics, 3*(4), 286-289.

Lippman, D.T., and Ponton, K.S. (1989). Nursing's image on the university campus. *Nursing Outlook, 37*(1), 24-27.

May, F., Austin, J.K., and Champion, V. (1988). *Attitudes, values and beliefs of the public in Indiana toward nursing as a career: A study to enhance recruitment into nursing.* Indianapolis: Sigma Theta Tau International Honour Society of Nursing, Inc.

Payne, Cook and Associates, Inc. (1990). *Insight: the 1989 provincial public opinion study of nursing in Alberta.* (Available from the Alberta Association of Registered Nurses, 11620-168th Street, Edmonton, Alberta, T5M 4A6.

Porter, R.T., Porter, M.J., and Lower, M.S. (1989). Enhancing the image of nursing. *Journal of Nursing Administration, 19*(2), 36-40.

Rayner, C. (1984). Images of nursing: What do the public think of nurses? *Nursing Times, 80*(35), 28-31.

Reichelt, P.A. (1988). Public perceptions of nursing and strategy formulation. *Western Journal of Nursing Research, 10*(4), 472-476.

Simmons, L.W., and Henderson, V. (1964). *Nursing research: A survey and assessment.* New York: Appleton-Century-Crofts.

Skevington, S. and Dawkes, D. (1988). Fred Nightingale. *Nursing Times, 84*(21), 49-51.

Statistics Canada. (1990). *Nursing in Canada: 1988.* Ottawa: Statistics Canada.

Styles, M.M. (1982). *On nursing: Toward a new endowment.* Toronto: The C.V. Mosby Company.

U.S. Public Health Service, Department of Health and Human Services, Division of Nursing. (1988). Registered nurse population: Findings from national survey of registered nurses. Washington, DC: (NTIS Publication #HRP0906938).

CHAPTER SIX

Nursing and Feminism

JANET ROSS KERR

F eminism is an outgrowth of reactions to forms of social organization in which
women are not valued as highly as men; the norms of such a system condone
systematic bias toward women. Although feminism is commonly thought of as a
movement which grew out of the 1960s, feminist ideas are reflected in writing by
women in the seventeenth century (Spender, 1982). In more recent history, the
suffragette movement of the late nineteenth and early twentieth centuries had a
powerful impact on society and resulted in important changes in the treatment of
women. Nightingale's work in this era is "recognized by feminist scholars as
reflecting remarkable feminist insight" (Chinn and Wheeler, 1985, p. 74).

Nurses were profoundly influenced by the thinking of the suffragettes and
were in an important position to demonstrate women's capabilities. Nursing had
recently become a respected profession and was one of few careers open to
women. Nursing leaders who were political activists were able to accomplish
critical professional goals that would allow the profession remarkable development throughout the twentieth century. The entrenchment of registration for
nurses in legislation in Canada and other countries during this time period was
a victory that was an important step forward for the status of women.

Chinn and Wheeler (1985) have documented four philosophic views of feminism. The liberal feminist stance derives its tenets from the belief that women
are an oppressed group, and suggests that the solution is to equalize opportunities for women. In Marxist feminist thinking, capitalism and the acquisition of
property has created a class system that favours men; resolution of the inequal-
ity is seen as an important consequence in a society in which materialism and
capitalism are rejected for a system of collective organization and ownership.
Socialist feminist ideas derive from analyses of sociocultural phenomena and
institutions where "the oppression of women and socioeconomic class oppression are equally fundamental and mutually reinforcing" (1985, p. 75). In contrast,
radical feminist theory emphasizes the importance of defining issues from a
female approach to the world. In this stance, attention is not focused on the
relation of women to men, as in some other perspectives, but on "discovering,
analyzing, and valuing women's experience without the imposed standards of
male ideology or systems" (1985, p. 75).

The ideology of feminism is threatening to some, undoubtedly because its framework is one that is a radical departure from traditional thinking. Although it may be seen as against men and traditional institutions, its fundamental ideas espouse valuing both women and men. However, systems and institutions favouring one sex over the other are targets of feminist criticism. Feminists also model behaviour that may not be thought of as feminine, undoubtedly unsettling to some. In this respect, modern feminists are like the suffragettes in the way their ideas are presented. Independent thought and action, straightforward and hard-hitting commentary on issues of concern, and generally assertive behaviour characterize the feminist modus operandi. McHale (quoted in Eisler) suggested that it will be necessary to:

> ... leave behind the hard, conquest-oriented values traditionally associated with "masculinity." For is not the need for a "spirit of truly global cooperation, shaped in free partnership," "a balancing of individualism with love," and the normative goal of "harmony with rather than conquest of nature," the reassertion of a more "feminine ethos"? And to what end could "drastic changes in the norm stratum" or a "metamorphosis in basic cultural premises and all aspects of social institutions" relate if not to the replacement of a dominator with a partnership society (1988, p. 106)?

THE RELATIONSHIP BETWEEN FEMINISM AND NURSING

The relationship between feminism and nursing has been described as uneasy, but this was not always the case. Although nursing was at the forefront of the women's movement early in the century, predominantly male professions have been the focus of recent feminist concern. This has largely been a successful thrust as women are entering nontraditional professions in greater proportions than ever. Sex stereotyped views of nursing emphasize subservience, lack of assertiveness, and domination of nurses, who are primarily female, by physicians, who are primarily male. The real status of modern nursing may be difficult to appreciate from a view outside the profession. Technologic advances and increases in health-care knowledge heightened performance expectations and had a phenomenal impact on nursing, leading to new and independent roles in many areas. As Vance, Talbott, McBride, and Mason have noted:

> ... nursing has not been valued for its autonomous social contributions, independent decision-making, scholarly productivity, or collective striving for recognition, power and legitimization in professional policy-making and community circles. Feminists have sometimes failed to look beyond the inaccurate sexist stereotypes of nurses and to acknowledge the multiple dimensions of professional nursing (1985, p. 281).

Chinn and Wheeler assert that "a major contribution of feminist thinking in relation to nursing is the basic tenet of feminist theory—that women are oppressed" (1985, p. 76). Persuasive arguments suggesting that nurses can be categorized as an oppressed group are provided by Roberts (1983). The discussion is an illuminating one, and provides some intriguing explanations for characteristic behaviour observed in nurses. Of some interest is how low value placed on participation in professional organizations is explained from this perspective. Emanating from a low degree of esteem for the profession, such behaviour is thought to be based on fear that associating with others who are oppressed may not be in one's best interest. Another example can be found in the struggle to legitimize midwifery in Canada, where many nurse midwives have supported a professional structure completely separate from nursing. Arguments put forward to support this have tended to focus on the fact that nurse midwives do not wish to be associated with a profession perceived as having low status, despite its related phenomena of interest. The extension of this thinking explains the lack of attention to the history and accomplishments of the profession: "A feminist perspective would encourage us to embrace our rich cultural heritage within nursing and value our predecessors, who made brave and courageous strides in developing the foundation upon which nursing is built" (Chinn and Wheeler, 1985, p. 76).

The implications of a feminist view of practice, education, and research in nursing are important, and require a shift in thinking and new approaches to care. The challenge to traditional patriarchal family structures represents an inherent challenge to nursing theories/conceptual frameworks as well because many of these have "underlying patriarchal assumptions about human experience" (Chinn and Wheeler, 1985). By advocating the same treatment for men and women in society, feminist consciousness raising has been tremendously successful in challenging traditional roles of men and women in society. In health care, as in other areas, new approaches to care and treatment and to education in the health-care professions are resulting in a total restructuring because of the influence of new ideas from the women's movement. The change that is occurring is nothing short of revolutionary; the system that results will look very different from that which existed before feminist ideas were widely known and appreciated.

A FEMINIST APPROACH TO WOMEN'S HEALTH

The women's movement has had considerable impact on the ways that nurses have conceptualized health. This has been particularly true for women's health. Baumgart noted that:

> . . . the health problems emphasized in most nursing curriculums are male-biased. We pay a great deal of attention to cardiac disease in our society. It's certainly important for women, but it's a major male medical problem. Why couldn't we concentrate as much on depression in women? What about elderly women? . . . We give a lot of time to the uterus and very little to the head. The implicit message is that cardiac disease is "normal" while depression is "deviant" (Allen, 1985, p. 21).

The areas of focus in health have arisen as an issue largely because of the women's movement. There is new attention to the overall health problems of women (as opposed to reproductive health only) such as osteoporosis, depression, rape, premenstrual syndrome, and menopausal difficulties. The women's movement and the consumers' movement have jointly influenced the role of the health-care client and have legitimized an active role. Delineation of patients' rights in health care (see Chapter 19) has led to consensus that a client has a right to information and should participate in decision making about care because there are often a number of options for treatment. Consumers, including women, are asking for clear statements of these options so they can be informed participants in the decision making.

It has been observed that "nurses are particularly well prepared to meet the health needs of women. Nurses have been schooled to build their assessments on clients' perceptions of their experience and to promote self-help, and that is exactly what women are demanding" (McBride, 1984, p. 66). For many years nursing curriculums have emphasized the importance of communication, interpersonal skills, and health assessment skills. Nurses "are health care providers best suited to meet consumer demands for self-determination, because their professional mandate has long been expressed in terms of helping the client" (McBride, 1984, p. 66), in the words of Virginia Henderson, "to gain independence as rapidly as possible" (Henderson, 1961, p. 42). Thus many of the directions the women's movement is taking coincide with those being taken by the nursing profession; women's health stands to benefit.

Radical changes in the structure of nursing practice in the United States have been taking place during the last decade. Because national health insurance does not exist in that country, nurses have been able to establish clinics or health collectives to serve the public. Vance (1985) referred to the Loeb Center for Nursing and Rehabilitation in New York, the Erie Family Health Center in Chicago, and the Pennsylvania State Consultation Nursing Center as agencies doing important work with consumers, particularly those who have been "unserved and underserved" (Vance et al, 1985, p. 285). Also, nurses have been pushing for legislation that permits independent practice by nurses. "They want to promote the idea that the authority for nursing is based on a social contract, not on doctors' orders" (Vance et al, 1985, p. 285). Securing the authority to practise autonomously as a professional nurse has been a difficult struggle, and is one that is only beginning in Canada. The issues surrounding midwifery are at the forefront of the movement in Canada; however, there is no turning back, and nurses will gain the right to practise independently, as well as to access federal funding through provincial health-care plans. The machinery for direct federal funding for nursing services is in place with the provision for funding for "health practitioners" contained in Canada Health Act of 1984. Provincial health plans may now include direct reimbursement for nursing services among those that can be funded under their plans. As Vance noted, "today the women's movement has helped nurses to realize that their proper place includes not only protecting their right to practice, but reclaiming lost rights to work as independent professionals with consumers" (Vance et al, 1985, p. 285).

RESEARCH AND FEMINISM

MacPherson (1983) has pointed out that nursing research that focuses on women's issues may or may not take a feminist stance. A paradigm shift is necessary because previous theories and conceptual frameworks used in research did not view women's health from a female perspective, and were, therefore, incomplete:

> ... These theories have a dual function: they offer descriptions of women's oppression and prescriptions for eliminating it. They are empirical insofar as they examine women's experience in the world, but they are political insofar as they characterize certain features of that experience as oppressive and offer new visions of justice and freedom for women (MacPherson, 1983, p. 19).

Feminist research is characterized more frequently as qualitative than quantitative. The emphasis on describing the meaning of women's health experiences leads frequently to the use of qualitative approaches. Such research tends to be exploratory and may encompass field studies. Qualitative approaches need to be used to gather basic data that has been unavailable in areas that have received little attention. Undoubtedly, both approaches are likely to be useful in the long run. The problem for women's health is that there has been little exploratory work in some areas. Over the past decade, nursing researchers have become increasingly conversant with qualitative methods, and many studies reported in journals use qualitative methods. Health problems of concern to women are receiving considerable attention from nursing researchers, as evidenced by publications in the nursing research journals (Chiarelli and Wheeler, 1985).

The interpretation of results in research investigations has been the focus of attention by feminists. There is a concern that feminist values may bias the interpretation, just as male values have historically biased the interpretation. "There needs to be an ongoing struggle to conduct research without allowing feminist values to become prisms that distort or bend the truth, or blinders that hide the truth entirely" (MacPherson, 1983, p. 24). Thus open and truly objective approaches are desirable for scholarly work. Undoubtedly, when the framework through which the data are viewed is broader and encompasses human values, the possibility that new interpretations will be derived is enhanced.

Concerns have been expressed about results of previous research investigations. Many studies have used only men as research subjects; results, therefore, are generalizable only to men. There is a need to broaden the subject base for investigations in general, and to use women as well as men in a number of areas. There is also a need to communicate results of studies to consumers. As MacPherson has noted, "A feminist perspective also emphasizes the need to publish these future research findings in both professional and popular journals so that all women can benefit" (1983, p. 24). Nursing research has much to offer in the area of women's health, and a feminist perspective can be very useful to nursing researchers to investigate "methods to get beyond the sex biases characterizing the existing research on women's health issues such as, for example, much of the biomedical research on menopause"(MacPherson, 1983, p. 24). There is much to be learned from research in the area of women's health. Nurses have just begun to recognize the challenges and to make a commitment to carry out meaningful work in these areas. Answers to some of the common and universal questions that concern women's health are vitally important to women. Approaches that incorporate a feminist perspective are essential in studying these problems, and nurses have leading roles to play in investigating topics of concern to women.

REFERENCES

Allen, M. (1985). Women, nursing and feminism: An interview with Alice J. Baumgart. *The Canadian Nurse, 81*(1), 20-22.

Chiarelli, M., and Nadon, F. (1985). Women and mental health: A feminist view. *The Canadian Nurse, 81*(1), 23.

Chinn, P., and Wheeler, C.E. (1985). Feminism and nursing: Can nursing afford to remain aloof from the women's movement? *Nursing Outlook, 33*(2), 74-77.

Eisler, Riane. (1988). *The Chalice and the blade.* San Francisco: Harper & Row.

Henderson, V. (1961). *Basic principles of nursing care.* London: International Council of Nurses.

MacPherson, K.I. (1983). Feminist methods: A new paradigm for nursing research. *Advances in Nursing Science, 5*(2), 17-25.

McBride, A.B. (1984). Nursing and the women's movement, *Image, 16*(3), 66.

Roberts, S.J. (1983). Oppressed group behaviour: Implications for nursing. *Advances in Nursing Science, 5*(4), 21-30.

Spender, D. (1982). *Women of ideas and what men have done to them.* Boston: Routledge & Kegan Paul.

Vance, C. Talbott, S., McBride, A., and Mason, D. (1985). An uneasy alliance: nursing and the women's movement. *Nursing Outlook, 33*(6), 281-285.

Vance, C., Talbott, S., McBride, A., and Mason, D. (1985). Coming of age: The women's movement and nursing. In D.J. Mason and S.W. Talbott (Eds.), *Political action handbook for nurses* (pp. 23-37). Menlo Park, CA: Addison-Wesley.

CHAPTER SEVEN

Men in Nursing

JANNETTA MacPHAIL

D espite an increase in the number of men in nursing over the past two decades, men still constitute an insignificant proportion of the registered nurse population in Canada. This is remarkable at a time when the proportion of women in traditionally male-dominated professions has increased at a phenomenal rate. Areas opened to women include business, dentistry, law, medicine, and pharmacy because of pressure from women's groups, whose allegations of sexism have led to changes in recruitment policies and affirmative action; thus as many as one half of the admission placements in these disciplines are available to women. At the same time, there have been notable increases in the number of men entering other traditionally female-dominated professions, such as teaching and librarianship. Why has the proportion of men in nursing increased so slowly? What factors have influenced the entry of men into nursing? Will these factors continue to exert the same influence? What are the advantages of having more men in nursing? What has the nursing profession done, or not done, to change the proportion of men entering its ranks? What are the implications of the Charter of Rights for the continuation of a predominance of women or men in any profession? These questions will be addressed in this chapter.

HISTORICAL PERSPECTIVE

Historically, nursing had its roots in the Roman matrons, such as Fabiola, who provided care and nurturance for the sick poor in their own homes. This was possible because of the matrons' wealth and arose from their desire to do "good" for others. Care of the sick continued to be female-dominated with the advent of female religious orders in Europe that assumed nursing as one of their responsibilities.

On the other hand, only men were allowed to tend the injured and sick during the Crusades in the eleventh century. This pattern was repeated when Canada was first explored and settled as New France by Jacques Cartier and Samuel de Champlain. As mentioned in Chapter 1, the first nurses were male attendants and Jesuit priests who were missionary immigrants. However, the impropriety of male priests caring for sick women soon brought about change, and three nuns were brought from France in 1639 to establish the first hospital at Quebec. This helped establish a pattern in Canada that continued for four centuries, whereby female religious orders, as one of their major missions, provided hospitals to care for the sick, prevent disease, and promote health. Later, they took on the added responsibility of training nurses to staff the hospitals. After the middle of the twentieth century, religious orders began to withdraw from nursing education and management of hospitals, although today some orders, such as the Grey Nuns, continue to own hospitals that they influence as owners and members of the Board.

Wars had a great influence on who attended the injured and sick men and who was recruited into nursing. Kus (1985) refers to antimale sexism as a major factor, influencing attitudes in society that permitted only men to go to war and not only considered it appropriate but also rewarded men for killing others and being killed in defense of their country. This was apparent in the battles against native peoples when Canada was first settled and in all subsequent wars, including World War I from 1914 to 1918 and World War II, in which Canada was involved from the outset, from 1939 to 1945. During World War I, only men were permitted to join the Medical Corps to serve as stretcher bearers on the battlefield and to help the female nurses who staffed Canadian base hospitals prepare to care for the wounded. In this war and in World War II, women were recruited in great numbers to staff civilian hospitals because many nurses left to enter the Nurse Corps of the three armed services divisions and many men volunteered for, or were conscripted into, the services. This increased the number of women entering nursing even more and decreased the possibility of more men entering nursing because they had to fight. Many men died or were injured.

During the Crimean War, the attitude of having only male attendants care for the injured and sick prevailed until Florence Nightingale was asked by the British government to go to the Crimea with the small group of nurses she recruited. There, she worked to improve the care provided for the soldiers and to decrease the loss of lives. Although Miss Nightingale was not easily accepted by the heads of the army, through her strong determination, expert knowledge, and nursing skill the lives of many men were saved and environmental conditions were vastly improved. She overcame barriers to women tending the wounded and sick during war and later, Victorian barriers to women working outside the home. When she established the first nursing school at St. Thomas' Hospital in London in 1860, all applicants were limited to women. The school was organized separately from the hospital, thus creating an opportunity for women to work outside the home and promoting "a measure of independence from men in the medical/hospital bureaucracy" (Halloran, 1985, p. 970). While overcoming societal pressures for women to conform to Victorian beliefs and customs, Nightingale also excluded men from nursing.

PROPORTION OF MEN IN NURSING

The proportion of men in nursing in Canada has increased very slowly over the past twenty-two years, as shown in Table 7.1.

TABLE 7.1 Comparison of female and male nurses employed in Canada, 1966 to 1988

Year	Total Number of RNs	Total Employed in Nursing	Female		Male	
			Number	(%)	Number	(%)
1966	Data not available	82,917	82,545	99.5	372	0.45
1975	182,828	144,193*	142,095	98.55	2,098	1.45
1986	236,993	204,571*	199,085	97.31	5,486	2.68
1988	249,673	210,506*	204,261	97.00	6,245	3.00

*Remainder employed in other than nursing, not employed or not stated. From Statistics Canada: Nursing in Canada: 1988, Ottawa, 1990, Statistics Canada.

Although the proportion increased by 546% from 1966 to 1975 and another 298% by 1988, the number of men employed in nursing still represents only 3.0% of the total nurse population, a slight increase over the 2.6% in 1986. If segregated by sex and compared with other health care groups, the male registered nurse population is one of the smallest professional groups in the health-care system (Health Manpower Directorate, 1983). Okrainec (1986) reported that the four provinces with the highest number of male nurses are Quebec, Ontario, British Columbia, and Alberta. In 1988, male nurses in Quebec accounted for nearly 7.0% of Quebec's registered nurse workforce and represented slightly more than half of the male nurses employed in Canada (CNA Connection, 1990).

A 1988 study of nurses in Canada, as shown in Table 7.2, indicates that of a total of 249,673 registered nurses, 90% of the men and 84% of the women were employed in nursing. Both represent a 2% decrease, from 92% and 86%, respectively, in 1986. The data also show that a similar proportion of both groups were employed in fields other than nursing and that 6.11% of the female nurses and 2.01% of the male nurses were not employed. In 1986, the latter proportions were 8.60% for female nurses and 2.58% for male nurses. Although from these data it appears that fewer nurses are unemployed, there was a considerable increase in the proportions of both male (from 3.05% to 6.24%) and female (from 3.05% to 7.98%) nurses who failed to provide information about their employment status. The higher percentage of women not employed may reflect those temporarily out of the work force for childbearing purposes, as well as the probability of a larger number of women retired because of their greater life expectancy. To consider gender differences in nursing, one must examine factors that influence the entry of men into a traditionally female-dominated profession.

BARRIERS TO MEN ENTERING NURSING

One of the major barriers to men entering the profession of nursing is societal attitudes about occupations appropriate for boys and girls. In general,

TABLE 7.2 Comparison of female and male nurses in Canada

	Female		Male		Total
	Number	%	Number	%	number
Number of RNs	242,770	100.00	6,903	100.00	249,673
Employed in nursing	204,261	84.14	6,245	90.47	210,506
Employed in other than nursing	4,300	1.77	88	1.28	4,388
Not employed	14,822	6.11	139	2.01	14,961
Not stated	19,387	7.98	431	6.24	19,818

From Statistics Canada: *Nursing in Canada:* 1988, Ottawa, 1990, Statistics Canada.

nursing has not been considered an appropriate career choice for boys because of its characteristics of nurturance, gentleness, and caring; boys are supposed to be strong and powerful and not show emotions. Negative and discouraging reactions from others, including family members, have been reported by male nurses. Undoubtedly, these young men had to be very determined and committed to persist in their efforts to pursue a career in nursing. They also reported implications that they might be "sissies" or "gay." Similar reactions from other health professionals, particularly physicians, have been encountered in years when medicine was predominantly male. Indeed, such reactions were not uncommon within the profession of nursing itself; some women nurses tended to regard men who selected nursing as not "real men."

Men were not accepted readily in nursing schools for many years. Initially, most of those accepted entered schools of nursing connected with mental hospitals, where they were accepted because of the belief that men were better able physically to deal with violence. Strength was considered so important in psychiatric nursing that this specialty did not become a required part of basic nursing education in Canada until the 1950s, and even the 1960s in some schools. Until the 1960s and 1970s, male nursing students were not permitted to study theory and practice in obstetric and gynecologic nursing; they devoted that time to urologic nursing, caring for male patients only.

Other evidence of resistance within nursing included the tendency of female instructors to assign male students to care primarily for male patients; negative reactions of female nursing staff to having male students in maternity and gynecologic nursing when these became a required part of their programs; resistance of female nursing staff to hiring male nurses, particularly for maternity nursing (although the majority of the obstetricians at that time were male); the tendency to assign male nurses primarily to psychiatry and critical care units; and the tendency of nurse educators and nursing staff, even today, to refer to nursing students as "girls," a sexist label. When men began to enter nursing schools where students were housed in dormitories there was no place for them, because the buildings had been designed for women only.

For many years, another barrier to men entering nursing was an economic one; nurses were paid poorly. As a result, men who may have been interested in

TABLE 7.3 Male nurses in management/administrative compared with female nurses

Position	Male (%)	Female (%)
Director/Assistant Director	4.2	2.5
Supervisor/Coordinator	7.1	5.2
Head Nurse	14.2	7.5

From Statistics Canada: *Nursing in Canada*: 1988, Ottawa, 1990, Statistics Canada.

nursing chose not to enter because of the societal expectation that they should be the "breadwinners." Male nurses have sometimes been criticized for aspiring to high positions as administrators in order to earn enough to support a family. In a study of British nursing, which has traditionally had a larger proportion of men than Canada or the United States, Nuttal (1983) reported that male nurses held half of the top nursing posts in the National Health Service, although they represented less than 10% of the state registered nurse population. In Canada "about 26% of male nurses held management/administrative positions in 1988 while just 15% of female nurses worked in this category" (Statistics Canada, 1990, p. 13). The percentage of male nurses compared with female nurses for three such positions are in Table 7.3.

With the advent of unionism in Canada in the 1960s, nursing salaries began to improve. Today they are much more adequate; in fact, staff nurses' salaries in general are higher in Canada than in the United States, although one must consider differences in the cost of living when making comparisons. In his study of male nurses in Alberta, Okrainec (1986, p. 17) reported that the respondents were satisfied with their salaries and that "married men, who represented 71% of the sample, were generally more dissatisfied with their income as compared to single men." To have sufficient income to support a family in the style many desire today requires moving to higher level positions, which requires more education and therefore, more investment of time and money. Male nurses who have such needs and aspirations will have to make such a commitment and investment, but the same requirements apply to female nurses who aspire to leadership positions.

EFFORTS TO SUPPORT MEN IN NURSING

Since there have been very few studies of men in nursing, little data exist to assess men's interest in and satisfaction with nursing. It is known that the number and proportion of men has increased, albeit very slowly. Okrainec (1986) reported that the majority of the 163 respondents who represented 62% of the male nurse population in Alberta "were either satisfied or very satisfied with their choice of nursing as a career . . ." and that "only a small percentage

(4.3%) expressed dissatisfaction with nursing" (1986, p. 17). The three highest ranked areas of satisfaction were "the attitude of male patients toward male nurses, acceptance as a nurse by female co-workers, and the attitude of female patients toward men in nursing" (Okrainec, 1986, p. 17). Although it appears from these findings that attitudes toward male nurses are changing for the better, Okrainec cautions against generalizing his findings to the total population of male nurses because the sample was not a random one and was limited to one province. In addition, there is no evidence that the instrument developed by the investigator was pretested or that the validity and reliability of the instrument were established.

In the United States, where the proportion of male nurses is only slightly greater than in Canada, formalized mechanisms have been implemented to promote the integration of men into the total nursing population and to provide support for them in the process. These included the establishment of a Male Nurses Section within the American Nurses Association from 1941 to 1952 and legislation enacted in 1955 through the efforts of the Honourable Frances Payne Bolton, the first woman in Congress, to permit male nurses to be commissioned as officers in the armed services. As a result, nearly one third of the Army Nurse Corps were men, including medics and corpsmen from the Vietnam conflict who chose to enter nursing. Others chose to become physician's assistants, but found limited opportunity for advancement, as assistants have no mobility beyond a specific physician. The physician's assistant concept did not develop in Canada; there was a deliberate decision against it by the medical and nursing professions.

Men interested in nursing in the United States became attracted to nursing programs designed specifically for university graduates, as offered at Yale University, leading to an MN degree, and at Case Western Reserve University, which offered the first, and to date the only, Doctor of Nursing (ND) Program in 1979. In the first three years of the ND Program, the proportion of men averaged 17% (MacPhail, 1979-1982). In addition, the Nurse Corps in the three US Armed Services divisions began to require a baccalaureate degree in nursing as an entrance requirement in the mid-1970s and offered generous support to nursing students to enroll in such programs. These students had to commit to a specific period of service after graduation.

Another formalized mechanism designed to provide support to men in nursing in the United States was the National Male Nurses Association, established in 1971; the name was changed in 1981 to the American Assembly of Men in Nursing. The objectives of the organization were to encourage men to enter nursing programs, to support male nurses in their efforts to continue their education and professional development, and to assist them in demonstrating the contributions made by men to nursing and to society (Halloran, 1985). The organization also established an annual award, the Luther Christman Award, for outstanding leadership in nursing, which was not limited to men and was in fact given primarily to female nurses in the first five years of its existence.

Although no similar mechanisms for recognition and encouragement of men in nursing have been developed in Canada, there has been an increase in the number of men attracted to and retained in nursing. In fact, the percentage of men in the total nurse population in Canada is only slightly less than that in the United States. Some speculate that the increase in Canada is related to the economy and unemployment. An increase in enrollment in postsecondary educational institutions can be expected, as Canada offers such generous subsidization of education. While some might decry admission under these circumstances, many excellent nurses, male and female, have chosen nursing, as a second or third choice, under such economic circumstances.

RESEARCH ON MEN IN NURSING

In his review of research on men, Christman (1988) found a dearth of studies and, moreover, identified many inadequacies in the methods of investigation used and interpretation of results. The research he reviewed included six survey studies, two studies using focused interview, and five studies using standardized test batteries to assess personality, intelligence, and attitudes. The questionnaires used in the survey research had not been tested adequately for validity and reliability. In general, study samples were small and not representative of the population being studied, which may "result in sampling bias and incomplete knowledge of the phenomenon under study" (Christman, 1988, p. 198).

Christman concludes: "If clarification of the male role in the nursing profession was a goal of the research done so far, then there are major shortcomings in both the research and the outcomes of research" (1988, p. 202). He questions the utility of studies that elicit opinion and does not support doing more of them. He suggests building on the beginnings of two studies by Brown and Stones (1972) and Holtzclaw (1981), both of which used standardized test batteries, and emphasizes obtaining much larger samples, from more than one site, that are representative of the population being studied. Other suggestions are:

> ... (a) cohort studies over time; (b) controlled field experiments assessing competence in both academic and practice settings; (c) comparative studies of settings in which the presence of men nurses is noticeable with settings with none or only a few men; and (d) the nature and quality of interaction of male nurses with patients as well as physicians as compared with female nurses to ascertain whether or not any differences exist (Christman, 1988, p. 203-204).

CONCLUSION

There is no doubt that many factors have deterred men from entering and remaining in nursing, and that some of the negative influences in society are finally beginning to change. Factors, such as cultural influences, may serve to attract or discourage young persons, particularly men, from choosing nursing as a career. The increasing number of Canadian immigrants, coming from Oriental and Hispanic countries where men have not been a part of nursing, is one such factor.

Another factor to be considered is that many fields, such as medicine, dentistry, business, law, and pharmacy, are now available to women. As more women are attracted to these fields, there may well be a reverse effect of attracting more men to nursing, particularly since there is increasing evidence that they are becoming better accepted.

There is little evidence that nursing programs have ever sought to attract and retain men in nursing. In contrast, efforts have been made by some traditionally male-dominated health professions to attract or at least encourage women. To attract more men to nursing, educators and administrators must work together to correct the myths and overcome barriers that deter them. Hospitals and other health care agencies and nursing schools need to portray men in the role of nurse in their publicity materials, to help change the public's perception of nursing. In addition, there has been no systematic effort to study the extent to which attitudes have changed in nursing or society about the acceptability of men as members of the nursing profession. To what extent have the advantages of having men in nursing been considered and propounded, advantages such as increasing stability and continuity in practice settings, increasing longevity of service and commitment to a career in nursing, and perhaps to conducting research to improve practice and the care of patients? Men and women can offer such potential benefits if they are committed to and well prepared for a lifetime of service in the profession of nursing.

REFERENCES

Brown, R.G.S., and Stones, R.H.W. (1972). Personality and intelligence characteristics of male nurses. *International Journal of Nursing Studies, 9*(8). 167-177.

Christman, L.P. (1988). Men in nursing. In J.J. Fitzpatrick, R.L. Taunton, and J.Q. Benoliel (Eds.), *Annual Review of Nursing Research, Vol. 6.* (pp. 193-205). New York: Springer Publishing Co. Inc.

CNA Connection. (1990). Nursing in Canada. *The Canadian Nurse, 86*(2), 4.

Halloran, E.J. (1985). Men in nursing. In J. McCloskey and H. Grace (Eds.), *Current issues in nursing* (2nd ed.) (pp. 969-978). London: Blackwell Scientific Publications.

Health Manpower Directorate. (1983). *Canada Health manpower inventory.* Ottawa: Health and Welfare Canada.

Holtzclaw, B.J. (1981). The man in nursing: Relations between sex-type perceptions and locus of control. *Dissertation Abstracts International, 4202A.* (University Microfilms No. 81-16, 752).

Kus, R.J. (1985). A challenge to nursing: Eliminating anti-male sexism in American society. In J. McCloskey and H. Grace (Eds.), *Current issues in nursing* (2nd ed.) (pp. 979-989). London: Blackwell Scientific Publications.

MacPhail, J. (1979-1982). *Personal experience with ND Program, Case Western Reserve University.*

Nuttal, P. (1983). British nursing: beginning of a power struggle. *Nursing Outlook, 31*(3), 184-187.

Okrainec, G.D. (1986). Nursing: A rewarding career for men? *AARN Newsletter, 42*(5), 21.

Okrainec, G.D. (1986). Trends in nursing for Alberta male nurses. *AARN Newsletter, 42*(5), 13-14.

Okrainec, G.D. (1986). Men in nursing. *The Canadian Nurse, 82*(7), 16-18.

Statistics Canada. (1990). *Nursing in Canada: 1988.* Ottawa: Author. (Catalogue No. 83-226).

PART II

Nursing
Knowledge

CHAPTER EIGHT

Nursing Knowledge: A Foundation for Nursing Practice

MARION N. ALLEN
JANET ROSS KERR
LOUISE A. JENSEN

T he essence of professions or disciplines is the knowledge required for their pursuit. The primary and distinguishing characteristics of a profession embrace extensive and abstract knowledge, requiring a period of concentrated training as well as the service or practice component (Goode, 1960). Disciplines are centred primarily around knowledge development, where emphasis is placed on describing, extending and/or modifying knowledge to reach a higher level of development. Since nursing is a professional rather than academic discipline, it incorporates a clinical practice component as an integral part of its activities. The professional practice of nursing entails providing health care to clients, educating new practitioners, carrying out research and ensuring that the significance of nursing to society is maintained and appropriately interpreted to the public (Shaver, 1978). Underlying professional practice is nursing knowledge that is the foundation of that practice.

Since Florence Nightingales's time, nurses have been discussing and investigating the nature of knowing in nursing. That is, what do nurses need to know and what type of knowing is involved? Many nursing leaders, such as Harmer and Henderson, thought that the way to answer these questions was to analyze the work or tasks that nurses do. Others felt that the way to answer the questions was to identify the concepts and phenomena that are of interest to nurses. Regardless of the answer, it was recognized that the knowledge needed in nursing was different from that of other health professions. In this chapter, the organization and development of nursing knowledge will be addressed. The various issues that have emerged as nurses have discussed how this organization and development has or should take place will be outlined.

Drs. Marion Allen and Louise A. Jensen are Associate Professors in the Faculty of Nursing, University of Alberta, Edmonton. A professor in the Faculty of Nursing, University of Alberta, Dr. Janet Ross Kerr is also co-author of *Canadian Nursing: Issues and Perspectives*.

WAYS OF KNOWING IN NURSING

Since the importance of formal education for nurses was recognized, nursing has depended on formal knowledge as a basis for practice. The type of knowledge used in practice has changed over the years, with a general trend toward increasing the scientific knowledge base (Chinn and Jacobs, 1987). Debates have occurred, however, as to whether the only knowledge needed was scientific. The nature of knowledge required for nursing is closely related to and largely determined by the purpose and goals of nursing practice and the kinds of problems the discipline seeks to address (Carper, 1978). In reviewing nursing literature, Carper stated that the nature of nursing evokes four different ways of knowing, which have been valued and used in practice by nursing. These ways of knowing include empirics, esthetics, ethics, and personal knowledge. Each way of knowing has a different purpose, expression, and process for development and evaluation (Chinn and Jacobs, 1987).

Empirics, the science of nursing, was originally based on the traditional notions of science where reality is viewed as objective verifiable phenomena (Chinn and Jacobs, 1987). However, the traditional approach to empiricism as the only way to acquire knowledge has been questioned. Nurses began to recognize the limitations of this view: the lack of tools to measure phenomena that concern nursing and the need for more than empirical facts when caring for people. As a result, the view of what constitutes science has broadened to include evidence generated from naive inquiry (Reason & Rowan, 1981), such as phenomenology and other inductive methods. The credibility of empirics is determined by methods of validation. Through validation one seeks to answer the question "what is it and how does it function" (Chinn and Jacobs, 1987).

Esthetics refers to the art of nursing. It is knowing unique particulars as opposed to universals (Carper, 1978) and comprehending the meaning that underlies an encounter with another person. This understanding of meaning not only influences the action that the nurse takes but is reflected in the action itself (for example, a hug to a person who is upset). Empathy serves as the main mode of this way of knowing. The truthfulness of this kind of knowledge is determined through criticism. Criticism seeks the relative truth in relation to the present and the foreseeable future and asks "what does this mean?" (Chinn and Jacobs, 1987).

The third way of knowing, ethics, focuses on obligation or what should be done. It involves understanding the different philosophical positions of what is right, what is good, and what should be desired. It is more than just knowledge, however, as it also involves making judgements and carrying out actions that are deliberate and subject to interpretation of right and wrong. The method of determining the credibility of this kind of knowledge is justification; that is, determination of whether the particular theory, standard, or code is just and responsible.

Personal knowledge, the final way of knowing, is knowing the self. This knowing is a "standing in relation to another human being and confronting that human being as a person . . . The relation is one of reciprocity, a state of being that cannot be described or even experienced—it can only be actualized" (Carper, 1978, p. 16). Reflection is the method for determining the credibility of personal knowledge. As Chinn and Jacobs (1987) comment, the important question to ask in reflection is "do I know what I do and do what I know?"

ORIGINS OF THEORY AND KNOWLEDGE IN NURSING

As nurses began to question the nature of the knowledge required for nursing, the debate arose as to whether the required knowledge and theory would be borrowed or unique. Borrowed theory was knowledge developed by other disciplines and drawn on by nursing (Johnson, 1968), and unique theory was knowledge derived from observations of phenomena and asking questions unlike those that characterize other disciplines (Johnson, 1968). As Johnson and others point out, there may be no sense in this issue. Knowledge is part of the public domain and is not owned. Donaldson and Crowley (1978) make the point that knowledge cannot be borrowed from other disciplines because each discipline's perspective is different and the knowledge cannot be understood if it is removed from the context in which it was generated. When one uses borrowed concepts or theories they are redefined and synthesized according to the perspective of the borrowing discipline.

The confusion surrounding this issue arose, in part, from the use of terms. At the outset of the debate, the issue centred around borrowed versus unique theory, but over time the discussion changed to a debate over borrowed versus unique knowledge. R.E. Ellis (personal communication, 1982) commented that there may not necessarily be a need for uniqueness in talking about theory of a phenomenon. In talking about a body of knowledge, uniqueness or distinctiveness might be important. The uniqueness arises from the content and the way the knowledge is organized.

The other major debate around the origins of nursing knowledge concerned the source of that knowledge. The concepts of nursing practice have influenced the subject matter of research, and, therefore, knowledge development since Nightingale (Gortner, 1983). Should practice continue to be the major source of nursing knowledge? Various authors, such as Wald and Leonard (1964), declared that it should and called for theories to be formulated from concepts developed from the realities of practice rather than from the perspective of other fields or disciplines. Although this debate extended to the kinds of theory needed for nursing, it is generally agreed that nursing practice should not be the exclusive source. As Donaldson and Crowley (1978) point out, clinical practice deals with the person requiring immediate action. In contrast, the discipline encompasses a knowledge base relevant to all areas of practice and links the past, present, and future. Its breadth goes beyond that required for nursing practice.

As discussion of the kinds and sources of knowledge in nursing progressed, dialogue also took place about whether nursing was a discipline. The structure of disciplines has been studied by Schwab (1962), who asserts that a discipline has two major components—a substantive structure and a syntax. The substantive structure of a discipline consists of the body of ideas or concepts circumscribing the central subject matter and delineates boundaries about areas of interest. The substantive structure thus gives direction to the search for data to build knowledge in the field. The syntax involves establishing the methods used to seek knowledge in the discipline, as well as specifying standards for verifying and interpreting results of investigations (Schwab, 1962). Thus disciplines evolve when a certain group of concepts are applied to the study of phenomena of interest and there are established ways of discovering and verifying new knowledge.

The evolution of professional disciplines is of interest, as most professions began as vocations and followed a similar pattern in terms of the sequence of events in their development. In most instances, learning occurred through apprenticeship at the outset, then structured training related to practice. Dissatisfaction with standards and the increasing depth of knowledge in the field led to the need for more substantial and rigorous training and inevitably to movement into the universities, where education and research were principal and fundamental missions. In the evolution of medicine, the change from freestanding schools of medicine to schools and faculties within the universities took place in North America in the early part of the twentieth century after a castigating report about conditions in the existing schools by Abraham Flexner (1910). Historical development has been similar in nursing. Although nursing became a full-time occupation in the seventeenth century, as did law, medicine and teaching, it has been slow to move through the established steps in the process of professionalization; for example, the first training school in medicine was established about 100 years before the first formally recognized school of nursing; medicine adopted a formal code of ethics in 1912; and the International Council of Nurses, in the forefront of this movement in nursing, developed its first code in 1950 (Wilensky, 1964). With the growth and acceptance of the entry to practise movement, nursing education is gradually becoming the exclusive domain of the universities through programs leading to the conferring of degrees.

In exploring the disciplinary status of nursing, one encounters the difficulties of defining the boundaries between nursing and other disciplines: "We take for granted the nursing perspective as generally accepted and understood, until explanation of the particulars is required." (Donaldson & Crowley, 1978, p. 113). Presumably, it is somewhat inevitable that members of particular disciplines continually justify the existence of the field in a particular form to themselves, their colleagues and society. However, in nursing, "authors tend to emphasize speculative formulations and theoretical reflections aimed at deriving the nature of nursing rather than explicating the structure of the body of knowledge that constitutes the discipline of nursing (Donaldson and Crowley, 1978, p. 113)." These authors have suggested that nurses should "seek relationships and commonalities in the ideas of writers whose work has influenced (and continues to influence) tacit knowledge of the scope of the field (Donaldson and Crowley, 1978, p. 113)."

Academic disciplines have been characterized as meeting the following criteria (Shermis, 1962):

1. An impressive body of time-tested works
2. Suitable techniques for studying the concepts of the discipline
3. Creation of a link between human activities and aspirations
4. A connection past and present that inspires and sustains future inquiry
5. Achievements of revered scholarship

It can be concluded that there has been a period of great growth and development of the knowledge base in nursing in the recent past. Also, there seems to be a developing consensus about the phenomena of interest in the discipline. Chinn and Jacobs have noted that "Since disciplines do not simply come to exist but are created by the generation of knowledge, including theory, the gains made by early nursing leaders are remarkable and significant (1983, p. 40)." The growth in nursing research over the past three decades alone is astounding; evidence of this can be found in the rapidly expanding number of serial publications that focus upon nursing research and the significant increase in nursing research funding.

Three categories for classifying the general areas of inquiry have emerged from the work done by Donaldson and Crowley:

1. Concern with principles and laws that govern the life processes, well-being, and optimum functioning of human beings—sick or well . . .
2. Concern with the patterning of human behavior in interaction with the environment in critical life situations . . .
3. Concern with the processes by which positive changes in health status are affected. (1978, pp. 113-114).

Chinn and Jacobs have referred to some of the enduring dilemmas relative to the primary concepts of the discipline, one of which is "how to know and how to judge the adequacy of knowledge, including theory (1983, p. 40)." The concepts of the metaparadigm of nursing, generally described as person, health, environment, and nursing, have been debated at length in terms of the focus provided for research and theory development in the discipline. Other concepts may also be viewed as primary in terms of the direction provided for education, practice, and research. For example, the idea of holism has been raised, which "dictates that no phenomena can be analyzed without residue into the sum of its parts or reduced to discrete elements" (Chinn and Jacobs, 1983, p. 41). If the intent is to view the whole person in terms of the phenomena to be studied, research studies would be structured differently if this idea were not valued or considered important. Similarly, practice might be conducted differently if the person is viewed from a holistic perspective.

CONCEPTUAL MODELS IN NURSING

As the debate over the origin and nature of nursing knowledge continued, abstractions representing the structure of the subject matter of nursing began to emerge formally. Models provide a frame of reference; they organize our thinking, observing, and interpreting. Their value lies in their ability to increase understanding or give us a sense of what is going on and why, and to explain phenomena (Lancaster & Lancaster, 1981). Models are not new to nursing. Although not always labelled as such, they have existed since Nightingale advanced her ideas about the knowledge nurses needed that was distinct from medicine. It was not until the 1950s that Peplau developed the first articulated concept of nursing as an interpersonal relationship. Since then, various conceptual models of nursing have been developed as individual nurses have attempted to demonstrate nursing, but they were not labelled conceptual models until the 1970's (Nursing Development Conference Group, 1973; Johnson, 1974; Riehl and Roy, 1974; Reilly, 1975).

Conceptual models in nursing, as in any discipline, are derived from the metaparadigm or world view of the discipline. Besides indicating the theorists' views of the metaparadigm concepts, nursing models also reflect the nursing interests and social and cultural milieu of the day and the educational background of the model developer (Meleis, 1985). The various models can also be grouped according to the central question about nursing they attempt to answer (Meleis, 1985). One group of theorists developed their models in response to the question "What is it that nurses do?" (Meleis, 1985). Theorists such as Henderson, Abdellah, and Orem focused on a description of the functions and roles of the nurse. Clients were considered in terms of a hierarchy of needs; when they were unable to meet their needs nursing was needed. These early theorists were among the first to address the area of independent judgement of nurses. The main interest of another group of theorists was the answer to the question "How do nurses do what they do?". The answer to this question led to an interest in the interaction between nurses and patients; the theorists focused their attention on the process of care and the ongoing interaction between nurse and patient. Care was viewed as a humanistic act rather than a mechanistic one. These theorists, such as Peplau and Orlando, were among the first to view the patient as an equal partner in the nursing process. The focus of other theorists was on the outcome of nursing care or "Why do nurses do what they do?". Many of these theorists conceptualized the goal of nursing care as preservation of energy, harmony between the patient and the environment, and equilibrium. These models also provided nursing with a well-articulated view of human beings as nursing clients and of nursing as an external regulatory mechanism (Meleis, 1985).

As models were developed, debated, and discussed, a question arose: should nursing have only a single conceptual model or many? Riehl and Roy (1980), in their early writings, argued that one conceptual model would lend stability to the discipline. Others argued that one conceptual model would lead to premature closure on the options for the discipline (Stevens, 1981) and of the perceptions of the practitioner (Kristjanson, Tamblyn, and Kuypers, 1987). In addition, the use of several models would permit viewing nursing from several perspectives and increase our understanding of the scope and nature of the discipline (Feldman, 1980). Currently, there is consensus that several conceptual models are desirable. However, Fawcett (1989) warns that the validity of the position supporting multiple models has not yet been established.

Another issue surrounding conceptual models is determination of their credibility (Fawcett, 1989). Although the credibility of the conceptual model can not be determined directly, it can be determined indirectly by comparing the propositions and hypotheses derived from the model with empirical data, including nursing care outcomes and research findings. Another criterion for assessing credibility may be the determination of whether nursing models guide the development of nursing knowledge. Some nurse theorists assert that conceptual models provide a framework for the development of nursing knowledge. They argue that the model provides a focus by which decisions are made about phenomena of interest to the discipline and the precise nature of the problem to be studied (Fawcett, 1989) and provides a means for organizing and guiding research. Others have argued that models are inadequate for the theoretical and scientific development of the knowledge needed in nursing. They argue that models are "envisioned ideals", that is, they outline the oughts and shoulds of nursing and are not testable scientific theories, (Ellis, 1984), and "preparadigmatic", that is, they are at various levels of abstraction in their development, and the concepts and the statements which link them are differentially defined or not specified (Conway, 1985). This lack of specificity hinders attempts to arrive at a paradigm, thus enlarging the body of nursing science. Cowling (1987) counters these arguments by commenting that the distinction between nursing and scientific models as outlined by Ellis is not clear and that many of the models have been based on theorists' observations of realities of practice. Cowling (1987) also comments that Conway assumes that consensus on specifying conceptualizations is advantageous in advancing nursing science.

In a review of the use of nursing models in research, Silva (1987) and Allen and Hayes (1989) commented that their use has ranged from empirical validation of the models and with development of tools to measure concepts particular to the model, to inclusion by the researcher of a brief description of the relationship of the model to the study, however nebulous. These authors concluded that, although models have been used to guide research, there are several gaps and weaknesses in their usefulness for generating nursing knowledge, particularly the lack of testing of underlying assumptions of the model, proposed relationships between the concepts, and clarification of the concepts relevant to the model.

Silva (1987) also notes that there is little evidence that conceptual models of nursing, used as frameworks for research, have influenced nursing practice; and Castledine posed the question of why nurses should spend so much time "agonizing about theories which have yet to prove they have any value in the real world of looking after people" (1985, p. 22). However, Fawcett (1989) reports on several studies that provide evidence that planned, purposeful, nursing interventions, based on a conceptual model, were more effective than the absence of planned nursing interventions. All systematic inquiry requires a conceptual framework that serves as a guide to observations and a scheme for interpreting and organizing knowledge (Schlotfeldt, 1975). Although nursing models represent different views of nursing, they have helped identify the phenomena that are of interest to nursing, thereby providing direction for the generation of nursing knowledge (Fawcett, 1989; Fitzpatrick and Whall, 1989). With additional refinement, models can lead the profession to the exposition and discovery of the knowledge base for practice.

THEORY DEVELOPMENT IN NURSING

Theory development is the crucial element for the evolution of nursing into a professional discipline. The need for theory is no longer a matter of debate (Fawcett, 1984; Meleis, 1985); however, the content encompassing nursing science has not been agreed on. Confusion still exists about what phenomena should be included in a system of theoretical explanations in nursing science. As noted previously, theory development has progressed to acceptance of four domain concepts: person, environment, health, and nursing (Fawcett, 1984; Meleis, 1985); however, what constitutes nursing phenomena within these concepts is still unresolved. Boundaries of subject matter for scientific fields are revised through an evolutionary process (Kim, 1983). The grounds for defining boundaries of nursing may be considered superfluous or ambiguous. Nursing as a science must go through the process of claiming certain phenomena as subject matter, then abandoning and revising others as the definition of major scientific problems in nursing becomes clearer. What are questions relevant in nursing? What needs to be explained and why the explanations may be important for nursing are crucial issues (Kim, 1983). It may be, as Kim suggests, that we are at a stage where development of scientific knowledge has to go beyond "what nursing is all about" to what problems nursing knowledge can "take on" as its subject matter (1983, p. 77). Thus conceptual clarification is first-level scientific work that culminates in theories. A kaleidoscope must be developed that provides criteria or patterns for organizing knowledge that will ultimately influence the practice of nursing (Schlotfeldt, 1988). Nursing science entails assessment of theories brought to bear on problems that require nursing intervention. The problem-solving effectiveness of nursing theory should be assessed in terms of empirical problems solved, conceptual problems generated, and analogous problems unsolved.

What are the differences between "theories of nursing" and "theories for nursing" and their respective relevance, priority, and legitimacy in the science of nursing? "Theories for nursing" are developed through borrowing; nursing as an applied field must refine theories from other fields. In contrast, "theories of nursing" are those developed to explain and predict the phenomena of nursing. For these theories it is necessary to define and differentiate nursing phenomena from those of other fields. The use of adjunctive precepts, principles, and concepts is not inevitable but essential. As Levine (1988) states, "this is not borrowed knowledge, but knowledge required for appropriate nursing decisions." She also states that nursing cannot stand apart within a body of knowledge it shares with other health-care disciplines. Adjunctive concepts are antecedent to all nursing theory.

Analysis of theory in nursing is now dedicated to identifying the adjunctive sources and determining whether such use is warranted, thereby shifting the focus to the substantive content of the theory. The researcher finds hard data that support or refute the theorist's claims. The practitioner provides the ultimate test of relevance of the theorist's work. Tension exists within this helix. Practicing nurses question the relevance of much of nursing research to clinical work. Researchers are concerned about the diffusion of results into the practice of nursing. Theory drives research and practice. Findings should be used as concepts and principles, not as procedures or standardized rules. Theory guides clinical practice decisions.

The connection between theory and research is reasonably well understood, but that between theory and practice is not. It has been suggested that the latter are "fundamentally interdependent" (Chinn and Jacobs, 1983). Theory serves a variety of purposes that can be construed as attempts to describe, explain, predict, and control phenomena; thus the relationship of practice to research and knowledge development also becomes more apparent. Although practical applications of theory are rarely possible, theory can be of immeasurable assistance at a practical level. Enhanced thinking and understanding of situations and events in the clinical setting and the resulting acquisition of new approaches or orientations to problems through research are two of the ways in which the interrelationship of theory and practice benefits clinical nursing practice. Also, practice benefits theory through the generation of ideas developed in the context of practice. In a professional discipline such as nursing, the clinical setting provides a rich resource for the genesis of ideas as well as the observation and questioning of practices.

Nursing science is advancing from establishing frameworks to support research to focusing on the identification and study of phenomena that make up the body of knowledge required for practice. Meleis (1985) suggests the central focus of knowledge development will be on the substance and content of the nursing discipline. The development of knowledge reflects the interface between nursing science and research (Hinshaw, 1987, 1989).

PROCESS OF THEORY DEVELOPMENT IN NURSING

Nursing offers a plethora of research questions that arise from curiosity about phenomena in the field. Deciding on a mode of inquiry requires a full understanding of the nature of nursing phenomena. What is an appropriate framework for the science of nursing? There are numerous rival hypotheses on how a science develops. Theory guides a researcher about what to observe but does not provide direction about suitable methods for making such observations. Methods for observing phenomena may differ, depending on the nature of the phenomena, personal experience, and preference. What ends are served by a debate over the appropriate research strategy for developing nursing science? What paradigm can generate solutions to nursing problems? Freedom and flexibility are necessary to choose attributes of prevailing paradigms that best describe or explain nursing phenomena. An emergent challenge is to develop new methods of inquiry to study nursing phenomena more appropriately. The development and testing of a body of knowledge does not occur in a vacuum, but reflects a specific disciplinary perspective (Hinshaw, 1987, 1989). A pluralistic, eclectic approach is advocated by many theorists as opposed to an either-or approach, or one grand approach to capture the entirety of the domain of nursing (Fitzpatrick and Whall, 1989; Fawcett, 1984; Meleis, 1985). Evolution of theory is viewed as a process rather than a product. Dialectic reasoning assists in the synthesis of multiple modes of inquiry to derive nursing knowledge. A dialectic synthesis is viewed as representing the heart of knowledge development in nursing.

Value placed on basic and clinical studies are fundamental to the science of nursing. Nursing research will demonstrate increased use of explanatory designs and causal model testing to build on the growing descriptive body of nursing knowledge. Brown, Tanner, and Padrick (1984) noted a major limitation in nursing—failure to build a cumulative science. To amass knowledge, series of studies need to systematically address related questions in an area.

Induction and deduction are complementary and equally important processes for nursing science. Whether beginning with experience or theory, the circle must be completed. The deductive method of theory development evaluates theory by testing empirical adequacy, ascertaining whether predictions are borne out by relevant data. Such testing relies on null hypothesis tests of significance. Another type of inference involved in generation of theory is not inductive but retroductive (T. Maguire, personal communication, 1989). Certain observed phenomena come to the researcher's attention and are analyzed by detecting patterns. Once patterned, observations are explained by way of a retroductive theoretical reasoning process through the existence of an underlying causal mechanism. Theory appraisal is undertaken by comparing the hypothesized models, rather than by comparing them to other competitive theories, as in theory testing. This method begins with problems, not theories or observations. Stability of patterns gained through exploratory analysis is critically examined through the use of confirmatory data analysis. The theory evoked explains the reason for the pattern of the data. Retroductive methods are driven by "why" questions. Theories are created from and grounded in data (Glaser and Strauss, 1967); therefore, data are not used solely for testing existing theories. The data are theory driven, and competing theories could account equally well for the data. A number of explanatory theories are generated to explain the data, with the most plausible receiving additional development and appraisal. This method encourages and demands that a plurality of research procedures be used, and statistical inference will be used primarily to distinguish between systematic and haphazard trends in data.

Many patterns hold potential for providing scientific explanations in nursing. The shape and texture of nursing research has undergone dramatic change. Many problems in nursing cannot be solved by using quantitative strategies alone; focusing solely on quantity can lead to neglect of salient information. In addition, critical questions may be neglected if they do not fit into a numerical framework. Case study approaches, as well as qualitative strategies, have achieved respect in nursing research; it is recognized that the use of such strategies is essential in answering questions for which they are appropriate.

This does not mean there is not a role for statistical inference testing in nursing research. Statistical procedures cannot be avoided merely because they operate on data collected in the nursing situation characterized by small random samples. In addition, in nursing a unique manifestation of a construct is unlikely, and, therefore, a single measure will not capture all important aspects of the construct. Also, many measures currently in use have poor psychometric properties. Multiple measures of outcomes can be used to circumvent some of the problems of inappropriate measurement; triangulation is greatly valued in qualitative research (Denzin, 1987). A similar approach can be taken in quantitative research by using many dependent variables to describe a profile of outcomes. Multivariate strategies are increasingly viewed as helpful in nursing research. Statistical significance of a result should not be given without enough information to determine whether it is of substantive importance. Additional hypothesis testing should not treat each study as though it were the only one conducted on a question.

The development of nursing theory, therefore, requires a systematic process of inquiry. Components of that process include concept analysis, construction of theoretical relationships, testing of theoretical relationships, and practical validation of theory (Chinn and Jacobs, 1987). As a practice discipline, nursing requires that the theoretical relationship be tested and the theory be validated in the real world. The purpose of evaluating theory is to determine whether the theory can guide research or practice and to determine which type of research is required to modify the theory in order to meet the criteria of clarifying phenomena of interest to nursing. The level of knowledge about the phenomenon of interest directs the level of theory development and the type of questions asked in research. The approach used to develop theory will depend on the researcher's view of the world. The relationship among nursing theory, research, and practice is dialectic. The development of nursing theory arises from questions about the practice of nursing, is tested through research, and is used to enhance the practice of nursing.

CONCLUSION

The development of systematic knowledge should be a priority in planning the future of the discipline of nursing (Schlotfeldt, 1988). Critiques of knowledge development in nursing suggest that nurse scholars advance knowledge in a substantive area. In this chapter, the organization and development of nursing knowledge has been addressed. Different paradigms or models of nursing are seen as valuable. Maturation of a philosophy of nursing science as a base for knowledge development has been offered as a means to end the debate over which method is the right science. All modes of inquiry are necessary to form a knowledge base in nursing. The nature of human experience requires openness to numerous ways of knowing and scientific inquiry. As the world view of nursing is clarified, the essential questions in nursing will be asked, consistent with the practice of nursing.

REFERENCES

Allen, M.N., & Hayes, P. (1989). Models of nursing: Implications for research in nursing. *Recent Advances in Nursing, 24,* 77-92.

Brown, J.S., Tanner, C.A., & Padrick, K.P. (1984). Nursing's search for scientific knowledge. *Nursing Research, 33*(1), 26-33.

Carper, B.A. (1978). Fundamental patterns of knowing in nursing. *Advances in Nursing Science, 1*(1), 13-23.

Castledine, G. (1985). Where are the British models? *Nursing Times, 81*(43), 22.

Chinn, P.L., & Jacobs, M.K. (1987). *Theory and Nursing. A systematic approach* (2nd ed.). St. Louis: C.V. Mosby.

Chinn, P.L., & Jacobs, M.K. (1983). *Theory and nursing. A systematic approach.* St. Louis: C.V. Mosby.

Conway, M.E. (1985). Toward greater specificity in defining nursing's metaparadigm. *Advances in Nursing Science, 7*(4), 73-81.

Cowling, R.W. (1987). Metatheoretical issues. Development of new theory. *Journal of Gerontological Nursing, 13*(9), 10-13.

Denzin, N.K. (1987). *The research act* (2nd ed.). New York: McGraw-Hill.

Donaldson, S.K., & Crowley, D.M. (1978). The discipline of nursing. *Nursing Outlook, 26,* 113-120.

Ellis, R.E. (1984, October). *Theory development in nursing: The state of the art.* Paper presented at 50th Anniversary Celebration Hospital General Juif Sir Mortimer Davis, Montreal, Quebec.

Fawcett, J. (1989). *Analysis and evaluation of conceptual models of nursing* (2nd ed.). Philadelphia: F.A. Davis.

Feldman, H.R. (1980). Nursing research in the 1980's: Issues and implications. *Advances in Nursing Science, 3*(1), 85-92.

Fitzpatrick, J.J., & Whall, A.L. (1989). *Conceptual models of nursing. Analysis and application.* Norwalk, CT: Appleton & Lange.

Flexner, A. (1910). *Survey of medical education in the United States and Canada.* New York: Carnegie Corporation.

Glaser, B.G., & Strauss, A.L. (1967). *The discovery of grounded theory.* New York: Aldine Publishing Company.

Goode, W.J. (1969). The theoretical limits of professionalization. In A. E. Etzoni (ed.), *The semiprofessionals and their organizations: Teachers,* *nurses, social workers* (p. 280). New York: The Free Press.

Gortner, S.R. (1983). The history and philosophy of nursing science and research. *Advances in Nursing Science, 5*(2), 1-8.

Hinshaw, A.S. (1989). Response to "Structuring the nursing knowledge system: a typology of four domains." *Scholarly Inquiry for Nursing Practice, 1,* 111-114.

Hinshaw, A.S. (1989). Nursing Science: The challenge to develop knowledge. *Nursing Science Quarterly, 2,* 162-171.

Johnson, D.E. (1968). Theory in nursing: Borrowed and unique. *Nursing Research, 17,* 206-209.

Johnson, D.E. (1974). Development of theory: A requisite for nursing as a primary health profession, *Nursing Research, 23,* 372-377.

Kim, H.S. (1983). *The nature of theoretical thinking in nursing.* Norwalk, CT: Appleton-Century-Crofts.

Kristjanson, L.J., Tamblyn, R., & Kuypers, J.A. (1987). A model to guide development and application of multiple nursing theories. *Journal of Advanced Nursing, 12,* 523-529.

Lancaster, W., and Lancaster, J. (1981). Models and model building in nursing, *Advances in Nursing Science, 3*(3), 31-42.

Levine, M.E. (1988). Antecedents from adjunctive disciplines: Creation of nursing theory. *Nursing Science Quarterly, 1,* 16-21.

Meleis, A.L. (1985). *Theoretical nursing: Development and progress.* New York: J.B. Lippincott.

Nursing Development Conference Group: *Concept formalization in nursing. process and product.* Boston: Little, Brown & Co.

Reason, P., and Rowan, J. (1981). *Human inquiry. A sourcebook of new paradigm research.* New York: John Wiley & Sons.

Reilly, D.E. (1975). Why a conceptual framework? *Nursing Outlook, 23,* 566-569.

Riehl, J.P., & Roy, C. (1974). *Conceptual models for nursing practice.* New York: Appleton-Century-Crofts.

Riehl, J.P., & Roy, C. (1980). *Conceptual models for nursing practice* (2nd ed.). New York: Appleton-Century-Crofts.

Schlotfeldt, R.M. (1975). The need for a conceptual framework. In P.J. Verhonick (ed.),

Nursing Research I (pp. 3-24). Boston: Little, Brown & Co.

Schlotfeldt, R.M. (1988). Structuring nursing knowledge: A priority for creating nursing's future. *Nursing Science Quarterly, 1*, 35-38.

Schwab, J.L. (1962). The concept of the structure of a discipline. *Educational Record, 43*, 197-204.

Shaver, J. (1978). Research and the discipline of nursing. In M.C. Stainton, J.C. Kerr, & J. Moore (eds.), *Perspectives: Nursing education, practice and research* (pp. 104-123). Calgary, AB: Faculty of Nursing, University of Calgary.

Shermis, S. (1962). On becoming an intellectual discipline. *Phi Delta Kappan, 44*, 84-86.

Silva, M.C. (1987). Conceptual models of nursing. In J.J. Fitzpatrick & R.L. Taunton (eds.), *Annual review of nursing research* Vol 5. (pp. 229-246). New York: Springer Publishing Co.

Stevens, B.J. Nursing theories: One or many? In J.C. McCloskey & H.K. Grace, *Current issues in nursing* (pp. 35-43). Boston: Blackwell Scientific Publications.

Wald, F.S., & Leonard, R.C. (1964). Towards development of nursing practice theory. *Nursing Research, 13*, 309-313.

Wilensky, H.L. (1964). The professionalization of everyone. *American Journal of Sociology, 70*(2), 143-144.

CHAPTER NINE

Theory-Testing and Theory-Building: Research in Nursing

HEATHER F. CLARKE

During the past 20 years, theory building in nursing has focused on the development of theories of, for, and in nursing. Some nurse theorists such as Martha E. Rogers, Sister Callista Roy, and Imogene M. King, have been concerned with grand theories of nursing. Other nurses have developed theories and conceptual frameworks related to specific approaches for nursing care—Dorothea Orem's self-care and Madeleine Leininger's transcultural care. Still other theorists have given their attention to the generation and testing of constructs and concepts used in nursing, such as vulnerability, resilience, social support, and empty space. Regardless of the magnitude of the theory, nurse theorists seek to solve both undefined and acknowledged problems. Their ideas must be clearly explainable in the practice of nursing's therapeutic care. Theory-building and research aimed at generating and testing nursing theory must attempt to ground that theory in observations for the purpose of discovering nursing truths and ensuring that the theory has a reality base.

Both qualitative and quantitative research methodologies are required to ensure that data collection goes beyond the current emphasis on logical empiricism and deductive reasoning. If the gap between researchers and practitioners is to be reduced, inductive methods of theory generation and testing are essential.

In this chapter, the use of qualitative and quantitative methods will be discussed, concurrently or consecutively, for nursing research that aims to generate or test nursing theory. Although there has been an overwhelming tendency to give more credence to quantitative methods, equal status should be given to designs and results of qualitative methods where validity and reliability of the research are established.

Dr. Heather Clarke is Nursing Research Consultant for the Registered Nurses' Association of British Columbia.

PURPOSES AND OBJECTIVES
Purposes
The purposes of this chapter are to:

1. Demonstrate the need for nursing research that includes qualitative and quantitative methods for generation and testing of nursing theory;
2. Discuss requirements of the research process as it applies to the discipline of nursing; and
3. Present criteria for evaluating research reports.

OBJECTIVES
After studying the chapter, one should be able to:

1. Discuss at least two goals or purposes of nursing research for theory-building and theory-testing;
2. Compare the two major methods, qualitative and quantitative, used in nursing research;
3. Generate research questions or hypotheses and suggest appropriate methods for investigation; and
4. Critique a research report for methodological appropriateness, application of findings, and significance of recommendations.

NURSING PARADIGM
Definition of Nursing
From the time of Florence Nightingale, nurses have been charged with caring for the sick and the well, emphasizing restoration, promotion, and maintenance of health (Nightingale, 1969). Today, nurses are still defining the elements of nursing, determining the therapeutics of nursing care, and understanding the laws of health, behaviours of individuals and families, qualities of the changing environment, and transactions between individuals and their environments. The discipline of nursing is deeply involved in identifying its own unique knowledge base that includes four major concepts: individuals (as singular or group members of society); environment; health; and transactions between individuals, their environment(s), and health.

In Nightingale's *Notes on Nursing: What It Is and What It Is Not*, originally published in 1859, nursing was defined as having "charge of the personal health of somebody and what nursing has to do is to put the patient in the best condition for nature to act upon him" (1969, p. 133). A century later, Henderson defined nursing as:

> ... assisting the individual, sick or well, in the performance of those activities contributing to health or its recovery (or to a peaceful death) that he would perform unaided if he had the necessary strength, will or knowledge. And to do this in such a way as to help him gain independence as rapidly as possible (1961, p. 42).

Although these definitions illustrate the consistent orientation of nurses to the provision of care that promotes well-being in the people served, they do not reflect the influence of contemporary nursing theories and changing paradigms. For this chapter, the American Nurses Association's definition of nursing will be used, because it reflects the evolution of nursing, including theory application. "Nursing is the diagnosis and treatment of human responses to actual or potential health problems" (American Nurses Assocation, 1980, p. 9).

Nurses are concerned with two types of human response and behaviour:

1. Reactions of individuals and groups to *actual* health problems; and
2. Concerns of individuals and groups about *potential* health problems.

Health-restoring and health-supporting behaviours of both the well and the ill may vary with environmental influences and occur in single or multiple, episodic or continuous responses. Thus, nursing assessment, diagnosis, and therapeutic care are extremely complex activities, which must take into account both subjective and objective interpretations of health behaviours.

EVOLUTION OF A NURSING PARADIGM

Information, as a basis for determining nursing actions to be taken, comes from various sources: the individual, the environment, nursing theory, and nursing research. Nurses use theory in the form of concepts, constructs, and principles to improve their observations and to understand human responses and behaviour in wellness and illness. Research in theory-building and theory-testing must deal with the phenomena of human health behaviour and nursing therapeutics from both subjective and objective perspectives if there is to be advancement of the nursing paradigm.

Kuhn defines paradigms as "universally recognized scientific achievements that for a time provide(s) model problems and solutions to a community of practitioners" (1970, p. viii). Nursing has reached a state of maturity by developing a paradigm that includes theories and applications of nursing therapeutic care directed toward the health behaviours and responses of individuals and groups, in wellness and illness. However, research in both theory-building and theory-testing is continuously required to refine and expand the body of nursing knowledge and encourage its acceptance within the discipline of the nursing paradigm.

DEVELOPING NURSING KNOWLEDGE
Nursing Science and Theory

Several years ago, Donaldson and Crowley (1978) drew a distinction between the discipline of nursing and the profession of nursing. The latter refers to the activities of practitioners in the field; the former refers to the body of systematic knowledge. Nursing knowledge must be derived from a combination of humanitarian and scientific enquiries that deal with the meaning of the following phenomena and relationships among their variables: health, human behaviour, environment, and nurses' therapeutic care-giving (Fawcett, 1983). A nursing perspective focuses on the wholeness of human beings in interaction with their environments. Nursing needs scientific or empirical theories, as well as theories dealing with the art of nursing, theories concerned with personal knowledge of the therapeutic use of self, and ethical theories (Carper, 1978).

Benoliel suggests that " . . . the substance of the discipline of nursing needs to incorporate at least two broad components: professional foundations and nursing science" (1984, p. 2). The goal of knowledge development in professional foundations is to create prescriptive theories that direct the implementation of professional practice (e.g., code of ethics, practice principles) (Figure 9.1). The ultimate goal of knowledge and theory development in nursing science is " . . . the creation of descriptive and prescriptive theories that incorporate knowledge about the conditions necessary and sufficient for the promotion, maintenance and restoration of states of health in human beings" (Benoliel, 1984, p. 3).

RESEARCH AND THEORY

This chapter will deal with issues related to research and clarification and development of theories in *nursing science*. Like other practice professions, nursing uses knowledge and explanations invented by other disciplines, as well as

FIGURE 9.1 The discipline of nursing.

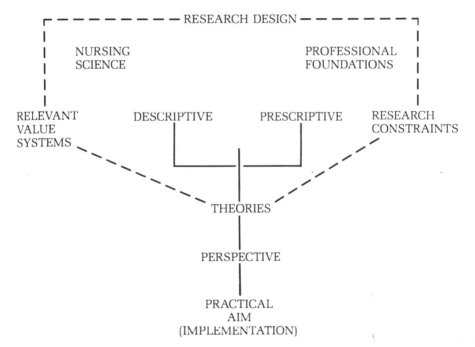

Modified from Donaldson, S.K., and Crowley, D.M. (1978) The discipline of nursing. *Nursing Outlook* 26(2), 113-120; Benoliel, J.Q. (1984) Advancing nursing science: Qualitative approaches. Communicating nursing research. Vol. 17: Advancing nursing science: Qualitative and quantitative approaches. Boulder: Western Interstate Commission for Higher Education.

those it develops itself. The goal of manipulating this information is different from other practice professions, and nursing must separate the knowledge that is important to the discipline from that which is not (Visintainer, 1986). The collection of knowledge specific to the nursing perspective and the subsequent discoveries resulting from that perspective must continue to provide the basis for the nursing discipline.

A nursing perspective of a situation considers meaning and function, individual differences, and the state of health or well-being in relation to the health concern. It defines the phenomena of any situation in more ways than just focus on disease, cure, emotional response, and reaction to stress. Nurses must use and develop knowledge from many sources, create new ways of investigating and testing concepts, constructs and theories, and explicate the results and applications to others within and beyond the nursing discipline. It is unlikely that one scientific theory or theoretic base will be adequate to describe all that is required in nursing science.

The work of nursing science is to conduct research and build theory that (1) is stimulated by questions derived from practice; (2) recognizes the need for new information; (3) integrates borrowed knowledge; (4) creates or builds on new perspectives; and (5) tests and validates proposed nursing theories.

Multiple and varied research efforts are required to accomplish these goals. The use of complementary qualitative and quantitative research methods creates a variety of options that need not compete with each other. We need only understand that they provide different information about the nature of the phenomena. The two major research methods, qualitative and quantitative, employ a variety of methods of generating and testing concepts, constructs, and theories. A major determinant of the method to be used is based on the type of research question posed. Quantitative research methods are designed specifically to answer deductive research questions, whereas qualitative methods are primarily used to address inductive research questions. Reductive research questions, using a combined inductive-deductive approach, require both quantitative and qualitative methods to be used concurrently or consecutively.

QUALITATIVE METHODS

Qualitative research is a systematic study of everyday experiences. It is concerned with understanding human beings and the nature of their transactions with each other and their environments. Nursing research includes the study of the interacting concepts: health, human behaviour, and the environment in the empirical social world (the natural, everyday world of human group life). The purpose is to discover meanings that might be hidden from public view. Human beings and their social worlds cannot be understood without considering that human beings create the worlds in which they live, and that the ongoing processes of social existence depend on shared meanings and negotiations (Benoliel, 1984). When nurses and their clients have different private perspectives for the same phenomenon, it is unlikely that nursing's goal of improving level of health and function will be attained.

Qualitative enquiry can be used to expand nursing knowledge about (1) health behaviour at many levels of existence (intrapersonal, interpersonal, social, cultural, transcultural, and transcendental); (2) decision making and adaptation to health and illness; (3) transactions between clients and nurses in relation to disability and change; and (4) interactions of people with their environment. In nursing, qualitative research provides a way to construct meaning that reflects nursing practice, as it aims to explain client situations from a perspective that is uniquely their own. Research methods include ethnography, phenomenology, and grounded theory approaches.

Nursing literature on qualitative research often carries a message that qualitative approaches to enquiry are primarily for the discovery of knowledge *to be tested* and are subsidiary to quantitative approaches in science. However, qualitative approaches in science are distinct modes of enquiry, oriented to variables of the phenomena of concern that require a different understanding than what is answered by a quantitative perspective (Benoliel, 1984).

Dickoff, James, and Wiedenbach (1968) identified four levels of nursing theory based on the relative maturity of the scientific base involved. Research approaches for testing, then, must match the level of the scientific base (Table 9.1). Qualitative methods are applicable when the researcher (1) has only a conceptual orientation as a guide, (2) is looking for descriptions of concepts and their relationships, (3) tests for correlational and predictive relationships among concepts and their variables, and (4) understands the situation from the client(s)' perspective(s) (levels I and II).

Although some quantitative methods may be helpful in defining concept relationships at level II, qualitative methodology must be applied as well.

TABLE 9.1 Levels of Nursing Theory and Potential Research Methods

Theory Level	Theory Characteristic	Purposes	Research Methodology
I. Naming	Conceptual orientation proposed	• Identify variables • Define concepts	Qualitative methods
II. Situation Depicting	Conceptual model available	• Define concept relationships • Answer question(s)	Qualitative and quantitative methods
III. Situation Relating	Theoretical framework developed	• Predict correlational and causal relationships • Test hypotheses	Qualitative and quantitative methods
IV. Situation Producing	Prescriptive-theory implementation	• Instruct on implementation of theory in nursing practice • Evaluate therapeutics	Qualitative and quantitative methods

QUANTITATIVE METHODS

Nurses also pose questions that require a more statistical, experimental approach based on reliable measurements. They may wish to test hypotheses, determine causal relationships, or evaluate therapeutic actions. For these purposes, a quantitative method is required.

Quantitative research methods are primarily applied to some aspect of theory-testing and further development, rather than initial theory development. They produce descriptive, correlational, or causal findings. Research designs for quantitative methods can be more rigorous in specifying assumptions and ruling out or specifying and measuring error sources than can qualitative methods.

A quantitative method can be defined as one which uses numbers, treated in a manner consistent with measurement principles, to represent the phenomena of interest (Atwood, 1984). Quantitative approaches use formal experimental studies, surveys, and nonexperimental causal modelling.

CONTROVERSY BETWEEN METHODS

Historically, there has been a clash between advocates of quantitative and qualitative methods for generation and verification of theory. Initially, qualitative data was used in a nonsystematic, nonrigorous way (Glaser and Strauss, 1967). However, later methodological advances demonstrated that accurate evidence could be produced, and qualitative research was employed to get surveys started. After this, quantitative research was to take over: discover facts and test current theory. Indeed, nursing can support the position taken by Glaser and Strauss that there is no fundamental clash between the purposes and the capacities of qualitative and quantitative methods or data.

> . . . We believe that each form of data is useful for both verification and generation of theory . . . In many instances, both forms of data are necessary . . . as supplements, as mutual verification, and . . . as different forms of data on the same subject, which when compared will generate theory (1967, pp. 17-18).

Today's researchers, including nurses, employing qualitative methods have developed methods and designs to the point where they offer assurance in their ability to assemble accurate evidence and to test hypotheses.

Chinn (1985) examined myths, persisting in the traditional male-defined scientific enterprise, that influence the methods used in nursing's search for new knowledge. Particularly significant are the myths related to "scientific supremacy," "empirical evidence," "objectivity," and "the perfect method." These myths can be "debunked" by (1) insisting on integration of all patterns of knowing (scientific, esthetic, ethical, and experimental) into the whole of knowing (Benoliel, 1984; Chinn, 1985); (2) recognizing the limitation of empirical evidence and integrating other methods of justification, criticism, and introspection into the knowledge base for understanding (Chinn, 1985); (3) acknowledging the nurse(s) responsible for the knowledge search, thus exposing underlying assumptions and views of their reality (Chinn, 1985); and (4) valuing alternative

TABLE 9.2 Data Collection Methods

Data Collection Method	Methodological Suitability	
	Qualitative	Quantitative
• Unstructured observation	X	
• Structured observation	X	X
• Open-ended interviews and questionnaires	X	
• Closed and mixed interviews and questionnaires		X
• Participant observation	X	
• Unwritten available data	X	
• Written available data	X	X
• Projective tests		X
• Other structured methods, e.g., physiological measurements		X

qualitative and quantitative methods in a fundamental way and not merely as stepping stones to the "perfect method" (Chinn, 1985; Benoliel, 1984; Atwood, 1984).

METHODOLOGIC ISSUES

Methods of data collection most suited to qualitative and quantitative methods are summarized in Table 9.2. Regardless of the methodologic perspective, selection of the methods must be congruent with the theoretical framework of research and bear directly on the question being asked or hypothesis being tested.

The study design depends on the level of nursing theory developed on the available knowledge base and/or conceptual framework. Research designs fall into one of two categories: descriptive or explanatory. Descriptive designs often use qualitative methods and result in descriptions, category definition and/or determination of basic statistical relationships. Explanatory designs attempt to establish causal relationships between variables. Qualitative methods can supplement the data generated in these designs, but primarily the quantitative data is generated through explanatory survey, as well as experimental and quasi-experimental designs (Brink and Wood, 1978; Campbell and Stanley, 1963).

In addition to qualitative/quantitative issues in research and the development of nursing knowledge and theory, consideration should be given to multiple triangulation, secondary analysis of data, and collaborative research.

Triangulation integrates both qualitative and quantitative methods and theoretical perspectives salient to the discipline of nursing (Mitchell, 1986). A triangulated study combines different theoretical perspectives, different data sources, different investigators, and different methods within a single study. It supports the study of the complex and dynamic phenomena of human behaviour.

Multiple triangulation, a complex form of triangulation, combines more than one type of triangulation into a study design (Denzin, 1970). This may be accomplished by including in the research design (Mitchell, 1986) two or more of the following:

1. Data sources that differ by person, place, or time
2. Two or more data collection methods that relate to qualitative and quantitative methods
3. Multiple questions to be answered or competing hypotheses to be tested
4. Involving multiple investigators

Collaborative research involves multiple investigators who study the same question, hypothesis, or theory in different populations; different aspects of the research problem in the same population; or a combination of the two. The use of multiple investigators helps to expand the generalizability of the results, to reduce the potential bias, impossible when only a single investigator is involved, and to improve the reliability of data collection and analysis (Denzin, 1970). The probability that a holistic approach to human behaviour will be taken is increased when researchers with differing expertise collaborate on the entire research process, from problem identification to report writing.

Secondary analysis of data collected for purposes other than the research problem currently being investigated can be valuable in research related to both the generation and testing of nursing theory. It provides another data source for triangulation. However, a number of factors must be considered when deciding whether to use data collected for other purposes: (1) whether the unit of analysis differs between original and proposed methods, (2) whether the lapse in time since the original collection of data makes the data obsolete or poses immense problems in interpretation, and (3) whether sufficient information is available on the methods of the primary study to make reliable interpretations of the data in secondary analysis.

CRITICALLY EVALUATING THE RESEARCH REPORTS

Nurses should be able to critically evaluate reports of theory generating and testing research to judge the applicability and significance of the results to their practice. The critique must be a critical, objective, and systematic analysis of the report based on specific criteria. The analysis includes examination of the researcher's interest, purposes, or goals of the study; the research problems or questions and significance of these; the theoretical or conceptual framework in relation to the questions, hypotheses, and purposes of the investigation; the methods, including design, sampling, instruments, data collection, and analysis; and results and discussion.

The following questions can be used as a basis for the critical evaluation:

1. PROBLEM
   a. Are the questions to be answered stated precisely and clearly?
   b. Is the significance of the problem discussed?

      c. Is the relevance of the problem convincing?
      d. Is the problem researchable?
      e. Are the variables and concepts identified and defined?
      f. Is the scope of the study identified?

2. THEORETICAL or CONCEPTUAL FRAMEWORK
      a. Are the researcher's assumptions stated? Are they valid and logical?
      b. Is the literature review comprehensive and pertinent to the research problem?
      c. Does the review include implications for the research problem under study?
      d. Are other competing or alternative theories, models or concepts presented?

3. METHODS
      a. Sample
        1. Is the subject population described?
        2. Is the sampling method described logical?
        3. Does it have the potential for generalizability?
        4. Are sources of bias identified?
        5. Are the principles of human subject protection followed?
      b. Data collection
        1. Are the measures and/or instruments sensitive and meaningful for the problem, the subjects?
        2. Is there evidence of instrument validity and reliability?
        3. Are major sources of bias recognized?
        4. Are procedures described?
      c. Data analysis
        1. Are the selected procedures appropriate, fully using the data?
        2. Is the level of significance discussed?
      d. Design
        1. Is the design appropriate to the research problem(s)?
        2. Is the description explicit enough to permit replication?
        3. Have data collection methods and instruments been pretested?

4. FINDINGS and DISCUSSION
      a. Are the limitations clearly specified?
      b. Are the results presented with clarity and precision and organized logically?
      c. Is there sufficient presented information to answer the research questions?
      d. Are the tabular and graphic presentations self-explanatory, supplementary to the text, easy to understand and complete?
      e. Are the conclusions warranted by the study results?
      f. Does the discussion compare the results to those of previous studies and present possible explanations for differences? Do the explanations indicate the extent to which objectives were achieved, questions answered or hypotheses supported?

g. Are the implications for theory, practice, education, or further research generative, innovative, and creative?

Despite lack of complete precision, systematic evaluation of research is a necessary process for any nurse. With thoughtful practice, one can soon identify major problems, shortcomings, omissions, strengths, and weaknesses of a study. The questions suggested above are by no means exhaustive, but they address important aspects of any study. It is up to individuals to draw their own conclusions and consider these in relation to knowledge development and use.

KNOWLEDGE AND RESEARCH UTILIZATION

Issues in knowledge and research utilization have been of concern to most disciplines (Loomis, 1985). Processes of understanding, accepting, reorienting, adopting, and applying the results of research and theory development to the world of practice are issues relevant to nurses. Throughout these processes, nurses must consider the validity, reliability, and generalizability of the knowledge base and research findings; relevance to clinical practice; context and readiness of situations in which adoption is to take place; interest, values, awareness, and perceptions of relevant policymakers and practitioners; communication network; and means of evaluating theory application (Glaser, Abelson, and Garrison, 1983; Loomis, 1985). Collaboration between researchers and practitioners in joint projects provides the greatest potential for maximum utilization of research findings and theory development in nursing.

REFERENCES

American Nurses Association. (1980). *Nursing: A social policy statement.* Kansas City, MO: Author.

Atwood, J.R. (1984). Advancing nursing science: Quantitative approaches. *Communicating nursing research. Vol. 17: Advancing nursing science: Qualitative and quantitative approaches.* Boulder: Western Interstate Commission for Higher Education.

Benoliel, J.Q. (1984). Advancing nursing science: Qualitative approaches. *Communicating nursing research. Vol. 17: Advancing nursing science: Qualitative and quantitative approaches.* Boulder: Western Interstate Commission for Higher Education.

Brink, P.J., and Wood, M.J. (1978). *Basic steps in planning nursing research.* Boston: Duxbury Press.

Campbell, D.T., and Stanley, J.C. (1963). *Experimental and quasi-experimental designs for research.* Boston: Houghton-Mifflin Co.

Carper, B.A. (1978). Fundamental patterns of knowing in nursing. *Advances in Nursing Science, 1*(1), 13-23.

Chinn, P.L. (1985). Debunking myths in nursing theory and research. *Image: The Journal of Nursing Scholarship, 17*(2), 45-49.

Denzin, N. (1970). Strategies of multiple triangulation. In N. Denzin (Ed.), *The research act* (pp. 297-313). New York: McGraw-Hill.

Dickoff, J., James, P., and Wiedenbach, E. (1968). Theory in a practice discipline. Parts I & II: Practice-oriented research. *Nursing Research, 17*(5 and 6), 415-435 and 545-554.

Donaldson, S.K., and Crowley, D.M. (1978). The discipline of nursing. *Nursing Outlook, 26*(2), 113-120.

Fawcett, J. (1983). Hallmarks of success in nursing theory development. In P.L. Chinn (Ed.), *Advances in nursing theory development* (pp. 3-17). Baltimore: Aspen Publications.

Glaser, B.G., and Strauss, A.L. (1967). *The discovery of grounded theory: Strategies for qualitative research.* Hawthorn, NY: Aldine Publishing.

Glaser, E.M., Abelson, H.H., and Garrison, K.H. (1983). *Putting knowledge to use.* San Francisco: Jossey-Bass.

Henderson, V. (1961). *Basic principles of nursing care*. London: International Council of Nurses.

Kuhn, T.S. (1970). *The structure of scientific revolutions*. Chicago: University of Chicago Press.

Loomis, M.E. (1985). Knowledge utilization and research utilization in nursing. *Image: The Journal of Nursing Scholarship, 17*(2), 35-39.

Mitchell, E.S. (1986). Multiple triangulation: A methodology for nursing science. *Advances in Nursing Science, 8*(3), 18-26.

Nightingale, F. (1969). *Notes on nursing: What it is, and what it is not*. New York: Dover Publications.

Visintainer, M.A. (1986). The nature of knowledge and theory in nursing. *Image: The Journal of Nursing Scholarship, 18*(2), 32-38.

CHAPTER TEN

Research-Mindedness in the Profession

JANNETTA MacPHAIL

T he term *research-mindedness* was first coined in relation to nursing research by Sir John Brotherston (1960). It is a useful term that conveys both awareness of and openness to nursing research.

In recent years, much has been written about the importance of increasing research in nursing practice since research is needed to advance knowledge and improve practice. Considerable attention has also been given to problems and inadequacies related to the dissemination and application of research findings in practice. Although the amount of research in nursing practice has increased in recent years, the process of research development in nursing has been slow. Even slower has been the incorporation of research findings into practice. Many factors contribute to this state of affairs, some of which can be identified as deterrents to the development of nursing. On the other hand, there are changes in nursing that facilitate research in practice and make it more relevant for all nurses.

RESEARCH-BASED NURSING PRACTICE

Research-based practice means nursing practice based on valid and reliable research findings obtained from scientific investigation of nursing practice problems. Much of nursing practice today is still based on opinion and experience, that is, on knowledge derived from trial and error or based on opinions and methods passed from generation to generation through books, articles, papers, conferences, workshops, and even educational programs in nursing. Nonetheless, an increasing number of nurses are recognizing the importance of research and are developing skills for critically evaluating research reports that are relevant to their practice. Johnson (1986, p. 1) states: "Research, as a basis for practice, is increasingly necessary as a professional nurse becomes less content with past reliance on instinct and tradition and wants hard data for planning nursing care."

Schlotfeldt (1971, p. 140) states: "Thus for nursing, as for any practice discipline, investigators must identify the central focus of practice and delineate the phenomena about which theories need to be developed." The central focus of

104

nursing practice is helping people, whether sick or well, to attain, maintain, or regain their optimal level of health and functioning. Nursing practice encompasses a variety of strategies or interventions, such as comfort measures, teaching, anticipatory guidance, support, and compensatory activities. Compensatory activities are actions taken by the nurse to compensate for what the patient cannot or will not do for himself or herself. They may include such activities as suctioning to maintain a clear airway, which is essential to respiration; assisting with ambulation to maintain circulation and joint and muscle function; and assisting with feeding to maintain nutritional status and elimination. All such strategies are designed to enhance the individual's health-seeking behaviours; to stimulate avoidance of disease and disability; to promote maximum use of the person's own resources in coping with disease or dysfunction; and to help persons cope with family responsibilities and crises. A holistic conception of human beings is appropriate for nurses because their interventions or strategies are designed to improve an individual's functioning as a total being (Scholtfeldt, 1971).

The nature of nursing practice makes it evident that nurses should study individual or group behaviour in relation to attaining, maintaining, or regaining health. The focus of research, to develop a scientific base for practice, involves the person's behaviour in relation to motivation to be healthy, as well as behaviour in coping with life crises. Life crises include such normal events as birth, developmental stages, and decline, as well as genetic failure, disease, and disability. Nursing research may also include behavioural responses to a wide variety of diagnostic and therapeutic interventions ordered by physicians. The feature that distinguishes nursing research from other research about human beings is the type of knowledge about persons that nurses need and use in practice. Consequently, research to advance knowledge and improve practice is concerned with people's behaviour in response to circumstances that require nursing action and their behaviour in response to that action (Schlotfeldt, 1971).

Schlotfeldt (1987, p. 66) states: "Nursing scholars should address pertinent questions that will guide observations and stimulate the generation of theoretical constructs about phenomena that are of particular concern to nurses and worthy of testing." She then poses six questions that pertain to identification and investigation of "innate human health-seeking mechanisms and innate and learned health-seeking behaviours [that] are of particular concern to nurses." Her questions concern naming, classifying, and characterizing mechanisms and behaviours and testing of nursing strategies to enhance them.

It is evident that scientific investigation of nursing practice has great potential for improving practice. Why then is there not more research, and why are the research findings that exist not applied to improve practice? Identifying some of the deterrents to doing research and having a research base for nursing practice will help anwser these questions.

DETERRENTS TO CONDUCTING RESEARCH

Before translating research into practice, research must be conducted. One of the major deterrents to research is the limited number of nurses prepared to conduct research. Although the number of nurses prepared at the doctoral and master's levels has increased considerably in the past decade in Canada and the United States, the proportion of nurses actually conducting research to strengthen the scientific base of practice is still limited. The number of nurses holding an earned doctorate in Canada increased from 81 in 1980 to 124 in 1982 and 193 in 1986 and the number of nurses involved in doctoral preparation increased from 72 in 1980 to 121 in 1982 and 224 in 1986 (Stinson, Larsen, and MacPhail, 1984; Stinson, MacPhail and Larsen, 1988). Thus, the number of nurses with an earned doctorate increased by 53% from 1980 to 1982 and by 56% from 1982 to 1986; the number of nurses engaged in doctoral study increased by 68% from 1980 to 1982 and by 85% from 1982 to 1986. The increases are expected to continue in both categories, particularly if those now in doctoral study complete degree requirements; however, the increments may become more gradual. In spite of the increased numbers, many nurses still study the nurse — that is, roles, relationships, and functions; education in nursing; or organization and management of nursing services. Although functional studies in nursing are important, they do not help strengthen the scientific base of nursing practice. Perhaps one of the reasons many nurses have studied functional aspects is that they were prepared, at the graduate level, in disciplines other than nursing and have studied phenomena with the orientation of disciplines such as education or administration. Nonetheless, nurse researchers have made remarkable progress in the past few years, since the introduction of the idea that nurses should systematically investigate their strategies or interventions, as do other professionals in practice fields. As discussed in Chapter 12, there has been an encouraging increase in clinical research reported at national conferences over the past seven years. This change is representative of ongoing trends in nursing research in Canada.

A second deterrent to increasing research in nursing practice is that many nurse researchers are not involved in, or knowledgeable about, nursing practice. Ellis states "One cannot formulate significant research questions in any field without knowledge of that field. No amount of knowledge of research methods can overcome lack of knowledge of nursing if one seeks to ask significant questions in the field of nursing" (1974, p. 32).

This does not imply that some nurse researchers have no knowledge of nursing practice, but that they have insufficient knowledge of current practice to ask meaningful research questions. Thus, we may see nurses prepared in other disciplines and out of touch with current practice studying phenomena from the perspective of those disciplines rather than from a nursing perspective. Insufficient knowledge of nursing may be displayed in the assumptions made, variables selected, instrumentation used, or any facet of the research process. Fortunately, ignorance or insufficient knowledge of nursing practice can be overcome, but only if recognized and acknowledged by the nurse investigator (Ellis, 1974).

A third deterrent to conducting research in practice is difficulty in asking the research question, which is the most complex and the most important task of any investigator. It is important to remember that research can solve problems, but not all problems are research questions. The question, "Why don't staff nurses use the medication cart as it was designed?" reflects a problem. It may imply the question of how to get them to do it. The problem may be a management or morale problem, but as stated, is not a research problem (Ellis, 1974).

There are two major types of questions that are not researchable. These are value or "should" questions and "yes" or "no" questions. Types of researchable questions as identified by Wilson (1985, p. 117) are:

1. Why are things this way? For example, why do cancer patients without hope participate in painful experiments?
2. What would happen if? For example, what would happen if sex education were taught in all schools?
3. Which approach would work better? For example, is group or individual counselling more effective with clients who abuse alcohol?
4. Who might benefit from this? For example, would hospitalized children have faster recovery if parents were permitted and taught to participate in their care?

Another categorization of types of research questions, as developed by Dickoff, James, and Wiedenbach (1968, p. 420) is:

1. Factor-isolating or "naming." For example, what are the stages of the grieving process?
2. Factor-relating or "what is happening here?" For example, what is the relationship of parents' own childhood experiences to engaging in subsequent child abuse or neglect?
3. Situation-relating or "what will happen if?" For example, will feedback training decrease suffering among chronic pain patients?
4. Situation-producing or "how can I make it happen?" For example, how can I intervene to prevent postoperative vomiting?

Bush (1985) believes that anything that can be described, quantified, or measured is potentially researchable. Brink and Wood (1983) define a researchable question as one that yields problem-solving information, produces new research, adds to theory, or improves practice. Lindeman and Schantz (1982) define it more narrowly as a question that can be answered by collecting observable data, includes reference to the relationship between two or more variables, and emanates from what is known about the phenomenon.

Defining researchable questions requires time and thought and a thorough search of literature to determine what is known about the phenomenon being considered. Only in this way can one decide if a question is worth investigating. Other factors that apply to the feasibility of studying the question are time, availability of subjects, cooperation of others, facilities and equipment, money, experience, and ethical considerations

A fourth impediment to the conduct of meaningful research is what Willems and Rausch (1969) identified as a lack of congruence between research purposes and research methods. Sometimes questions or problems are distorted to fit a method when the nature of the problem should determine the method. Although disjunction between purpose and method is not peculiar to nurses undertaking research, it may be a greater problem if the researchers are remote from practice and are trying to make research methods learned in another discipline fit questions.

Insufficient time has been identified by many authors as another impediment to conducting research. It is a concern of faculty members who devote much time to teaching, curriculum development, committee work, and professional activities. Time for research may be limited because of the orientation in nursing to "doing" and "being busy" and a tendency to want immediate results. A number of writers have indicated that practitioners may have difficulty understanding what investigators are doing with their time as they proceed through the research process. They have also indicated that nurses tend to want immediate results and fast action and have difficulty understanding that a hunch may not be borne out by research. On the other hand, educators may have difficulty using their time for research when they are accustomed to devoting it to teaching, curriculum study and revision, and committee work. This might also be related to lagging commitment, as termed by Werley (1972).

Another deterrent to research in practice may be lack of access to patients. Access may be limited by physicians who have certain prerogatives in relation to their patients, whether hospitalized, in clinics, or in offices. Access may also be limited by nurses who do not support or understand nursing research; nurses are in key positions to influence physicians, other nurses, and patients by educating them about the importance of research in nursing practice. This is not to suggest that patients' rights should not be protected, or that research proposals should not be subject to rigorous review for ethics and quality. Rather, it is to urge nurses to think about their influence on access to patients and promoting nursing research.

Insufficient funds to support research is an obstacle for all types of nursing research. It is a major problem in Canada because separate funding for nursing research has never been provided on the federal level. In the United States separate funding has helped investigators gain experience in research design and grant writing that is needed to be able to compete in the larger arena (Gortner, 1986). On the federal level the Canadian government provides research funds for the humanities and social sciences through the Social Sciences and Humanities Research Council (SSHRC), for the natural sciences and engineering through the Natural Sciences and Engineering Research Council (NSERC), and for medicine and other health related disciplines through the Medical Research Council (MRC). Although MRC funds are supposed to be available to health sciences other than medicine, the majority of the funds are awarded to medicine. Moreover, nursing has lobbied vigorously for representation on the MRC for a number of years, through individual nurse leaders and researchers and nursing organizations from the Canadian Nurses Association (CNA) and the Canadian Association of University Schools of Nursing (CAUSN). Because of discussions held in 1982, the MRC established a "Working Group on Nursing Research," composed of nursing leaders and researchers.

They proposed separate funding for nursing research that would include funds for doctoral study for nurses, but no action was taken by the MRC on these recommendations. In 1986 the MRC finally appointed a nurse to the Council, the Executive Director of the CNA, and appointed an ad hoc committee to recommend modifications in funding policy for nursing research. In 1987 nursing leaders and researchers in universities were encouraged by a new initiative announced by the MRC; separate funding would be available for programmatic research in nursing. Nursing faculties/schools in universities were invited to send a letter of intent to submit a full proposal for research funding organized around a central theme. Seventeen universities responded, from which the MRC selected six to submit a full grant proposal (Alberta, British Columbia, McGill, McMaster, Montreal, and Toronto). After much concentrated work and eager anticipation on the part of those writing the proposals, the outcome was very disappointing; no programmatic research grants were awarded. Three individual faculty members in different institutions were awarded funds to support research that was part of the programmatic research proposals. Moreover, when the term of the nurse on the MRC ended in 1989, she was replaced by a physiotherapist. CNA and CAUSN are continuing to lobby for nurse representation on the MRC; nursing is the largest health profession and desperately needs funds to support research and research development.

On the national level, nurses have access to small research grants through the Canadian Nurses Foundation (CNF); however, the grants are limited to $2500 or less. The CNF established the small research grants program in 1985 and has awarded a total of $42,423 to date. Some provincial nursing associations offer small research grants as well, but again, the amounts are limited. Nurses may apply for research funding through disease-oriented specialty organizations, such as heart, lung, diabetes and cancer, but again they are competing with medicine and other health disciplines.

There is another source of separate research funding for nursing: the Alberta Foundation for Nursing Research (AFNR) was established by ministerial order in 1982 as a response to lobbying by the Alberta Association of Registered Nurses (AARN) and leaders of the University of Alberta and the University of Calgary. A fund of $1,000,000 was allocated for use over a five-year period and a Board of Directors was appointed to establish research categories, guidelines and a review process and to award and administer the funds. Support services to administer the fund were provided by the Alberta Department of Advanced Education. At the end of the five-year period, negotiations and political pressure once again succeeded in obtaining $1,000,000 award for a five-year period (to 1993). The first awards were made in the 1983 to 1984 fiscal year, and a total of $1,200,210 had been awarded to Alberta nurses by the end of the 1988 to 1989 fiscal year. The amounts awarded per year and the number of awards made reflect remarkable progress, as evidenced by allocation of $19,015 to seven recipients in 1983 and 1984 and $280,404 for 33 awards in 1988 and 1989 (Alberta Foundation for Nursing Research [AFNR], 1989). Also encouraging is that a significant number of the studies funded by AFNR are being published and presented at national and international research conferences. With the establishment of the AFNR, Alberta became the first and only province or state worldwide to designate funds exclusively for nursing research. It is also the first research funding endeavour in Canada in which nurses have had a primary role in reviewing proposals and awarding funds.

DETERRENTS TO DISSEMINATING AND APPLYING RESEARCH FINDINGS

Another type of deterrent to research pertains to impediments to the dissemination and application of research findings. The majority of practising nurses cannot understand research reports or critically evaluate research results. This impediment is related to the fact that the majority of nurses are still prepared at less than a baccalaureate level and their programs did not include a research course or research-based teaching. In addition, nursing education has tended to nurture values other than those that foster inquiry, intellectualism, scientific investigation, and respect for "thinkers" as well as "doers."

Most nursing education takes place in institutions, such as hospital schools of nursing and community colleges, that do not expect faculty to be involved in research. Many of these institutions do not even require faculty to have a master's degree. They have been oriented to education as a value system that is reflected in expectations held for faculty and in the status system and rewards system, which are known to strongly influence faculty behaviour. Research must become an integral part of the faculty role; it is essential that faculty use research in teaching and help students evaluate research findings, applying those that are valid and reliable to practice. Since the majority of nurse educators have not been prepared for research and are not expected to conduct research and use it in teaching, it is not surprising that only a small proportion of nursing educators are using research in teaching.

Johnson identifies another barrier to research-based teaching in nursing-education programs: inadequacies in publishing policies and practice in nursing literature. She states:

> It is not universally accepted in nursing that authors of textbooks and articles for practitioners should rely heavily on scientific investigations to substantiate the knowledge transmitted and recommendations for activities. In some textbooks the documentation of the pronouncements is inadequate. One cannot determine if the information is the author's opinion, derived from theory, gained from experience, dictated by authority, or based on scientific investigation (1979, p. 128).

Johnson points out another problem, that should concern all nurses because of the possible consequences. She notes that several journals "published primarily for practitioners discourage authors from citing the sources of information they are conveying. In fact, some journals have editorial policies that prohibit citation of sources" (1979, p. 128). Such policies, developed by entrepreneurs who are taking advantage of nurses who are not aware of the importance of a scientific base for practice, do not help nursing in its effort to develop research or research-based teaching and practice.

A deterrent to both the development of research and the dissemination of research findings is inadequate preparation for research. This inadequacy may result in poor conceptualization of the problem, improper choice of research methods, inadequate attention to the validity and reliability of instruments, selection of an inadequate population from which to generalize findings, and other inadequacies in design. One of the consequences of poor research is results that are not worth disseminating. Fortunately, some reports are rejected by journals and by those who review abstracts for research conferences, although it may be difficult to assess the methods used from a brief abstract. In 1983, Downs noted that the quality of research submitted to the journal *Nursing Research* had improved over the previous four years, but the rejection rate still stood at 85%. She also noted that poor methods, which were once the greatest problem, are now secondary to poor logic in the for-mulation of research design. Another inadequacy she identified was a severe discrepancy between the concepts selected and their measurement; descriptive studies should be completed before proceeding with measurement (Downs, 1983).

Investigators have alleged that some journals give preference to quantitative research over qualitative research. Instead of dichotomizing the two research methods, investigators need to base selection of the method used on what is known about the phenomena being studied. Downs states that qualitative re-searchers criticize quantitative researchers for trying "to prove what is already known, has no meaning for nursing practice, and is generally of limited scope because the objective is to produce statistics"; meanwhile, quantitative research-ers allege that "qualitative research is unscientific and soft because it cannot be numerically categorized" (1983, p. 259). She asserts that the allegation that supporters of quantitative research are hindering the publication of qualitative studies is nonsense; she also identifies some of the inadequacies in reporting qualitative research that she perceives as problems, such as not explaining how conclusions are reached; why a sample was inadequate; or why the particular sample was appropriate. Some specification is necessary and must be supported by proper documentation (Downs, 1983). Qualitative research methods are ap-propriate for studying some of the phenomena in nursing because we know so little about them. Before quantifying a phenomenon, much has to be learned about it through descriptive and exploratory studies. Investigators using this method must apply proper rigour and interpret methods and findings clearly in relation to the conclusions that can be drawn.

Leaders' insufficient support for research, in nursing service and nursing education, may be another deterrent to conducting research and applying re-search findings. McClure (1981) has noted that support of research from the nurse executive requires a substantial knowledge of research methods and research literature, not only to provide a climate supportive of research but also to sponsor a study through various review committees and make the arrange-ments necessary for the investigation to proceed. She believes that the commit-ment of time and energy is essential to promoting and facilitating research and applying findings to practice.

STRATEGIES TO PROMOTE RESEARCH AND RESEARCH-BASED PRACTICE

The deterrents identified in relation to the development of research and the promotion of research-based practice in themselves suggest possible solutions; however, the solutions may be difficult to institute and will require strong commitment and determination on the part of nurses involved in research, education, and practice.

A basic requirement that is self-evident is to increase the proportion of nurses prepared at the baccalaureate level, which is the first level of nursing education in which students obtain an appreciation of the importance of research, an introduction to research methods, and beginning ability to critically evaluate research reports. Although there is increasing commitment to the goal of a baccalaureate degree requirement for entry to nursing practice by the year 2000, there is still resistance among some nurses and other groups. Careful attention should be given to this resistance while designing mechanisms and models for increasing the opportunities for persons entering nursing and registered nurses to earn a baccalaureate degree. In addition to increasing the proportion of baccalaureate prepared nurses, there is need to evaluate the nature of research preparation included in baccalaureate programs to ensure that it is not directed toward teaching people to do research, but rather increasing awareness of and openness to research and developing beginning ability to critique research and differentiate the findings that merit application.

A second strategy is to increase the proportion of nurses prepared at the master's and doctoral levels. To increase enrolments, more funding is needed for which all nurses should lobby. Funding for research training has been provided to other disciplines through NSERC, SSHRC, MRC and the National Health Research and Development Program (NHRDP), which is a program within the Health Promotion Directorate of Health and Welfare Canada. Over the past two decades, a number of nurses have been awarded fellowships from NHRDP for doctoral study in nursing in the United States and in other disciplines. In addition, a few nurses have been granted Health Research Scholar Awards, which provide funding to the university to support 75% of the recipient's time in research and other scholarly activities. For the nine recipients to date, this has resulted in a tremendous investment in furthering their research endeavours. Thus some nursing faculty have competed successfully for NHRDP funds to support research training and the actual conduct of research; however, the number has been small and the proportion almost infinitesimal when compared to funding for medicine and other disciplines.

In addition to increasing enrolments, attention must be given to the quality of graduate programs and the quality of research preparation within them. Nurses must be made aware of the importance of obtaining good research preparation in graduate study and not opt for the easiest and fastest route to a master's degree, which is the rationale given by some for selecting graduate programs. It is also important to ensure quality in nursing research and have faculty involved in their own research. Leaders in nursing education will need to develop a climate that supports and rewards research, obtaining resources to help faculty increase their research competence and grantsmanship skills, and holding faculty accountable for conducting research and disseminating findings. It is important to encourage nurses to pursue graduate study in nursing rather than in other disciplines so they will focus attention on studying nursing problems from a nursing perspective. Nurses should demand sound preparation in research and be helped to understand the importance of doing a thesis or independent investigation under expert guidance. Doctoral education in nursing must be developed in Canada, but only after the development of a sound research program by faculty, which implies the availability of faculty expertise in conducting research and guiding students in their research.

In recent years nursing literature has reflected increased efforts to promote, facilitate and implement collaborative strategies between nursing education and nursing practice in the interests of clinical nursing research.* While some strategies are facilitated by collaboration/unification models or by a system of joint appointments, others are much less formalized. All are based on basic principles of having a mutual sense of purpose; mutual commitment to common goals and ideals; maintaining open and frequent communication to engender trust and readiness for joint endeavours, at the operational level as well as at higher levels in the organizations; being flexible and patient; anticipating resistance, which is normal in any new endeavour, and being prepared to deal with it; and ensuring that both organizations benefit and gain recognition and visibility through research presentations, press releases and publication. Lancaster (1985) identified six Cs as a result of her experience in collaborative research: communication; credit; contribution; consensus; commitment and compatibility. Dennis, Howes and Zelauskas (1989) involved hospital nursing staff in the process of determining research priorities using the Delphi technique. They found that nurses at all levels were able to identify nursing practice issues needing further investigation. The investigators were reasonable in presuming that the issues would be stated as broad topics rather than as specific research questions, which even researchers often have difficulty formulating.

Janken, Dufault and Yeaw (1988) selected unit-based research roundtable discussions, undertaken jointly by faculty and nursing service, as an approach to increase awareness of the relevancy of research to practice and to disseminate research findings among staff nurses and nursing students. They report that the process required time, patience and persistence but resulted in more favourable attitudes toward research, application of research findings in practice, enhanced communications and development of a new respect between students and staff nurses.

Another strategy to promote and facilitate research in service settings is the appointment of a clinical nurse researcher, who plays an active role in identifying study topics and demonstrating involvement in and commitment to nursing

---

*Bergstrom et al, 1984; Engstrom, 1984; Lancaster, 1985; King et al, 1985; Frick, DelPo, and Robinson, 1988; Janken, Dufault, and Yeaw, 1988; Funk, Tornquist, and Champagne, 1989; Dennis, Howes, and Zelauskas, 1989.

research. The very presence of such a person increases the visibility of research and research activities. It is important to note that a clinical nurse researcher requires doctoral preparation with sound knowledge of research design and methods. The challenge is to create a research climate that encourages questioning and an awareness of the importance and potential of research. The clinical nurse researcher in an agency may have a problem of isolation. One solution to this problem is to involve the researcher in a joint appointment with the cost shared by the health-care agency and a university faculty of nursing. This is an approach that has been, and is being, applied effectively by several universities (Alberta, Calgary, Manitoba, McMaster, McGill, and Toronto) in collaboration with hospitals and other health-care agencies. A study conducted by the Western Interstate Commission for Higher Education in Nursing in the United States from 1973 to 1976 included 219 hospitals and 217 health-care agencies. Of the 219 hospitals, 8% had a full-time clinical nurse researcher and 31% had a part-time clinical nurse researcher. The percentage in community health agencies was 2% full-time and 22% part-time clinical nurse researchers (Krueger, 1978). A similar trend has occurred in Canada in the 1980s.

The role of the clinical nurse researcher, or faculty member in a dual appointment as part-time clinical nurse researcher, is to educate the staff about nursing research and increase awareness of research and its importance and potential for improving practice and to establish a proper research review process for screening nursing research proposals before they go to the agency review committee. The clinical nurse researcher helps nursing staff to interpret research findings, identify researchable problems, and assist in the conduct of research. Other important responsibilities are to serve as a role model by conducting research; to interpret research to other disciplines, notably medicine; and to serve as a reviewer of medical research proposals. It is important to ensure that the research review process is rigorous within the institution and to assist in the application of valid and reliable research findings in practice. The enactment of such a role requires a nurse who is skilled in communication, is sensitive to the reactions of others, applies theories of planned change, and is competent in research methods. It also requires strong administrative support.

Knafl, Bevis and Kirchhoff (1987) conducted a telephone survey of clinical nurse researchers in the United States to document the range of activities and responsibilities associated with the role and explore perceptions of how the role was developed and enacted. Despite considerable diversity in perceptions of enactment, most clinical nurse researchers reported devoting most of their time to research activities focused primarily on nursing practice studies and involving nursing staff in the identification of problems and conduct of research. Almost 50% of the research pertained to patient care and understanding patient behaviour and over 25% had been initiated by staff nurses. The clinical nurse researchers "view themselves and are viewed by their chief nurse executives as making a significant contribution to the hospital" (Knafl, Bevis and Kirchhoff, 1987, p. 252).

Providing research consultation is another strategy employed to promote and enhance development of nursing research. Consultation in research design is usually available in universities; however, such resources are not usually provided in health-care agencies except through joint appointments. Thurston, Tenove, Church, & Bach-Peterson, (1989) in their 1986 survey of nursing research being conducted in Canadian hospitals, found that 170 research projects were ongoing. The report does not specify what proportion of the projects were being conducted by graduate students in nursing or by nursing faculty; however, it is encouraging to find so much research activity. Research consultation has been provided to nurses in Saskatchewan through the Saskatchewan Nursing Research Unit (established in 1983 under the directorship of Norma Stewart, jointly sponsored by the College of Nursing at the University of Saskatchewan and the Saskatchewan Registered Nurses Association, and since September 1984, the Saskatchewan Union of Nurses). A similar model was established in Manitoba in 1985 with the appointment of Lesley Degner as Director of the Manitoba Nursing Research Unit (jointly funded by the School of Nursing of the University of Manitoba and the Manitoba Association of Registered Nurses). For the 1986 to 1987 fiscal year the AFNR provided research consultation to the nurses of Alberta through the secondment of Mary Renfrew Houston from the University of Lethbridge. This service was made possible by a one-time grant from the Alberta Department of Advanced Education. Extensive communication and publicity were used to advertise and interpret the research consultation services to nurses throughout the province. In the first six months, consultation was provided to over 100 nurses; 36% were from hospitals and nursing homes, 26% from colleges and universities, and 12% from professional associations and committees (AFNR, 1987). The response was gratifying and clearly reflected a great need for research consultation in Alberta.

Another strategy, proposed and supported by some nurse investigators, is to have researchers provide an interpretation of results in understandable form on a systematic basis. Kirchhoff raises the question: when staff nurses "need data base sources, should they struggle with the reported research journal or should they be satisfied with the short summaries provided by some of the clinically-oriented journals?" (1983, p. 246). Although the answer to this question may seem obvious, there is need to provide those informational sources through an intermediate step. One strategy, developed by Haller, Reynolds, and Horsley (1979) in Michigan was to provide research-based protocols for the nursing staff in several hospitals. This was a collaborative endeavour between education and service.

Another strategy was used by the American Association of Critical Care Nurses; reviews of studies in critical-care nursing with suggestions for practice were provided through their clinical journal, *Focus*. A similar approach was employed by the *Western Journal of Nursing Research* through their column "Using Research in Practice." However, it is essential to provide a scholarly critique of the original research and ensure that staff nurses realize that such protocols and suggestions cannot be applied without an interim step of interpretation by a competent investigator. Kirchhoff (1983) also suggests that research conferences might include a response to a research presentation entitled "Clinical Application," which is to be presented by a skilled researcher-clinician. Such an approach might encourage more practitioners to attend conferences.

Another strategy to facilitate the development of research is to organize research interest groups within the professional organization or within a health-care agency or group of agencies. It is important to have leaders with research expertise in such groups and to clearly define the purpose of the group. Is the purpose to learn to read and apply research findings, or to conduct research, or both? Should there be one general research group or should there be smaller groups focused around a particular clinical interest? Experience with such interest groups has demonstrated great potential if leadership is provided by nurses who are knowledgeable in research methods and able to utilize their knowledge in studying practice problems. Other approaches, in health-care agencies, are organizing research rounds, having research presentations at noon, and forming journal clubs in which discussion of research is led by a competent investigator. Another technique is to involve staff in data collection so they have a sense of what is involved in research and begin to learn that research results are not immediately forthcoming.

The opportunity to participate in the process of research review and ethical clearance is strategy which can be used under the direction and guidance of a competent researcher who works with staff to help them understand all the factors that must be considered. The problem is that one must assess the quality of a research proposal in order to give ethical clearance; if the study is not designed well it is not ethical to take the subjects' time. This means that the clinical nurse researcher or faculty member giving this leadership has to select a committee and educate the members in the review process. They must be introduced to nursing research and the requirements for reviewing and interpreting nursing research, which implies having at least a baccalaureate degree. Guidelines for such a re-search review process have been developed in some health-care agencies, such as the University of Alberta Hospitals, where a clinical nurse researcher provided leadership in the process. These guidelines are made available to others who are involved in promoting and facilitating research in other agencies.

Opportunities to share research findings can be provided through written media as well. Initially, this may be through the health care agency's monthly communique. Many have a communication mechanism of some type in nursing where a column can be devoted to research. This has been done in professional association newsletters but should be under the guidance of a capable researcher to ensure that quality is maintained and that the terminology is appropriate for research neophytes.

A final strategy to increase the dissemination of research findings is to increase opportunities to publish nursing research in Canada, possibly through a journal devoted to nursing research that will have an adequate readership to make it economically feasible. *Nursing Papers* has been devoted primarily to nursing research; however, until 1986, the title did not convey that it was a Canadian journal of nursing research. Even though the title now makes it clear that this is a research journal, other issues affect its viability. A change in name will not help in promoting research and applying research findings unless readership is increased. A major marketing effort is needed to increase reader-ship and convince nurses that the journal is a wise investment. If a subscription to the *Canadian Journal of Nursing Research* were incorporated into the regional annual fees for the Ontario and Quebec regions of CAUSN, as it is for the Atlantic and Western regions, readership would increase dramatically.

CONCLUSION

Increasing the quantity and quality of research endeavours in nursing and applying research results to practice will require strong commitment on the part of nursing educators and leaders in health-care agencies. Leadership is crucial to effecting changes in organizations or professions, but in this instance, there must also be competent nurse investigators to interpret knowledge of research and research findings in terms that can be understood by practising nurses. All must have the determination and commitment to pursue these goals and the ability to effect change in people and systems. Of utmost importance is that all nurses accept the challenge and take advantage of opportunities to commit themselves to increasing research endeavours, extending the scientific foundation for nursing practice, and ultimately improving practice through research.

REFERENCES

Alberta Foundation for Nursing Research. (1987, March 31). *Annual report.* Edmonton, Alberta: The Foundation.

Alberta Foundation for Nursing Research. (1989, March 31). *Annual report.* Edmonton, Alberta: The Foundation.

Bergstrom, N., Hansen, B.C., Grant, M., Hanson, R. Kulo, W., Padilla, G. and Wong, H.L. (1984) Collaborative nursing research: Anatomy of a successful collaboration. *Nursing Research,* 33(1), 20-25.

Brink, P.J., and Wood, M.J. (1983). *Basic steps in planning nursing research. from question to proposal* (2nd ed) Belmont, CA: Wadsworth Health Services.

Brotherston, J.A.F. (1960). Research-mindedness and the health professions. In *Learning to investigate nursing,* (p. 4). Geneva, Switzerland: International Council of Nurses and Florence Nightingale Fund.

Bush, C.T. (1985). *Nursing research.* Reston, VA: Reston Publishing.

Dennis, K.E., Howes, D.G. and Zelauskas, B. (1989). Identifying nursing research priorities: A first step in program development. *Applied Nursing Research,* 2(3), 108-113.

Dickoff, J., James, P., and Wiedenbach, E. (1968). Theory in a practice discipline: Part I. Practice oriented theory. *Nursing Research, 17*(5), 415-435.

Downs, F. (1983). One dark and stormy night [Editorial]. *Nursing Research,* 32(5), 259.

Downs, F. (1983). Oz revisited [Editorial]. *Nursing Research,* 32(1), 3.

Ellis, R. (1974). Asking the research question. In *Issues in research: Social, professional and methodological* (pp. 31-35). Kansas City, MO: American Nurses Association.

Engstrom, J. (1984). University, agency and collaborative models for nursing research: An overview. *Image: Journal of Nursing Scholarship,* 16(3), 76-80.

Frick, S.B., DelPo, E.G. and Robinson, T. (1988). The structure and process of a successful clinical research collaboration. *Nursing Connections,* 1(3), 69-75.

Funk, S.G., Tornquist, E.M., and Champagne, M.T. (1989). A model for improving the dissemination of nursing research, *Western Journal of Nursing Research,* 11(3), 361-367.

Gortner, S.R. (1986). Impact of the Division of Nursing on research development in the United States. In S.M. Stinson and J.C. Kerr (Eds.) *International Issues in Nursing Research* (pp. 113-130). London: Croon Helm.

Haller, K.B., Reynolds, M.A., and Horsley, J.A. (1979). Developing research-based innovation protocols: Process, criteria and issues. *Research in Nursing and Health* 2(2), 45-51.

Janken, J.K., Dufault, M.A., and Yeaw, E.M.S. Research round tables: Increasing student/staff awareness of the relevancy of research to practice. *Journal of Professional Nursing,* 4(3), 186-191.

Johnson, J.E. (1979). Translating research into practice. In *Power: Nursing's challenge for change* (pp. 125-133). Kansas City, MO: American Nurses Association.

King, J.M., White, M.A., Buckwalter, K.C., Whall, A., Leferman, R., Speer, J., Lasky, and R. McLane, A. (1985). A group dynamics view. *Western Journal of Nursing Research, 7*(1), 7-19.

Kirchhoff, K.T. (1983). Using research in practice: Should staff nurses be expected to use research? *Western Journal of Nursing Research, 5*(3), 245-247.

Knafl, K.A., Bevis, M.E. and Kirchhoff, K.T. (1987). Research activities of clinical nurse researchers. *Nursing Research, 36*(4), 249-252.

Krueger, J. (1978). Utilization of nursing research: The planning process. *Journal of Nursing Administration, 8*(1), 6-9.

Lancaster, J. (1985). The perils and joys of collaborative research. *Nursing Outlook, 33*(5), 231-238.

Lindeman, C.A., and Schantz, D. (1982). The research question. *Journal of Nursing Administration, 12*(1), 6-10.

McClure, M.L. (1981). Promoting practice-based research: A critical need. *Journal of Nursing Administration, 11*(11 & 12), 66-70.

Schlotfeldt, R.M., (1971). The significance of empirical research for nursing. *Nursing Research, 20*(2), 140-142.

Schlotfeldt, R.M. (1987). Defining nursing: A historic controversy. *Nursing Research, 36*(1), 64-67.

Stinson, S.M., Larsen, J., and MacPhail, J. (1984). *Canadian nursing doctoral statistics: 1982 update.* Ottawa: Canadian Nurses Association.

Stinson, S.M., MacPhail, J. and Larsen, J. (1988). *Canadian Nursing Doctoral Statistics: 1986 Update.* Ottawa: Canadian Nurses Association.

Thurston, N., Tenove, S., Church, J. and Bach-Paterson, K. (1989). Nursing research in Canadian Hospitals. *Canadian Journal of Nursing Administration, 2*(1), 8-10.

Werley, H. (1972). This I believe About clinical nursing research. *Nursing Outlook, 20*(11), 718-722.

Willems, E.P., and Rausch, H.L. (1969). *Naturalistic viewpoints in psychological research.* New York: Holt, Rinehart & Winston, Inc.

Wilson, H.S. (1985). *Research in nursing.* Don Mills, Ontario: Addison-Wesley Publishing Company.

CHAPTER ELEVEN

The Financing of Nursing Research in Canada

JANET ROSS KERR

G rowth of research activity in nursing has occurred gradually as a result of a slowly growing pool of nurses with research expertise. This development parallels the evolution of graduate education in nursing because teaching research methods and conducting research investigations to fulfil thesis requirements are important aspects of graduate education in nursing. Understandably, most research in any field takes place in university settings. Since graduate education in nursing was established little more than a quarter of a century ago, nursing research activities have increased in scope and number. Opportunities in master's degree programs in nursing are now available across the country, and, although admission is still very competitive, accessibility presents less of a problem than it once did. Doctoral programs in nursing are still on the horizon in Canada, but there are indications that the inception of the first program, with others to follow, will occur at the outset of the 1990s.

The establishment of the entire range of university programs in nursing, from baccalaureate through doctoral degree levels, is a process that is well underway, but by no means completed. Rationalizing the process rests on the view of the university as "a social institution, the specific mission of which is the transmission and the advancement of higher learning (Hurburtise and Rowat, 1970, p. 37)." The association between teaching and research has been described as a natural one, albeit complex: "Some kinds of research and some features of the research enterprise, are vital for good teaching: every university teacher should be involved in these kinds of features, and supported in them under the teaching budget (Bonneau and Corry, 1972, p. 23)."

At the conclusion of the stormy decade of the 1960s, Canadian universities began responding to the challenges and issues raised. One criticism of that period of rapid growth and student unrest was that too much time and energy were being expended on the research endeavour and too little on identifying and encouraging excellence in teaching. It is somewhat curious that universities came under fire for supposedly being preoccupied with research at precisely the same time as the nursing profession was engaged in the difficult struggle to establish its first graduate programs. During this process, the need for nursing's development of its research potential was underscored. Symons commented: "The slowness in developing graduate schools of nursing in Canada has, in turn, adversely affected the amount of research undertaken in this field. Little support has been available for publication, or for investigating problems in nursing and health care of particular interest to Canadians" (1975, p. 212).

In her exploration of the meaning of the concepts of professionalization and deprofessionalization, Stinson postulates that the development of the research function is a vital component of professionalization:

> Supplying professional services inheres in the principle that initiating research, training various kinds of research workers, and 'marketing' findings must not be left to the whims of chance or at the entire mercy of commercial interests. This means evolving not only intraprofessional mechanisms for the development and application of substantive knowledge but articulating these devices with those of other professions and those of the broader society (1969, p. 167).

Although the need and concomitant timeliness of research in nursing has been recognized both in and out of nursing, there have been problems in effecting change. It is likely that these problems will continue to be stumbling blocks for some time. The social reality of the last quarter of the twentieth century is that limits to growth of universities have appeared in the form of greatly decreased numbers of learners from the 18- to 22-year-old age group. This situation has occurred simultaneously with, at least in the early part of the period referred to, adverse and unstable world economic circumstances leading to shaky national economies and, subsequently, to financial stringency in all public institutions. However slow the basic development of research and graduate study in nursing, there is little doubt that the process will continue. Stinson asserts that successful delivery of nursing services to society will ultimately require "that three simultaneous processes be going on: (1) accumulation of the K-S (knowledge-skill) component, (2) transmission of it, and (3) extension of it, mainly through systematic research" (1969, pp. 156-157).

Concerted efforts to develop organizational support for nursing began in earnest in the early 1970s, when attention had been drawn to the crucial nature of that support: "A paradox of modern day research is that it is at once an intensely individual, personal endeavour, yet, if it is to be brought about, much less constitute benefits for society, it is immensely dependent upon organization — and highly complex organization at that" (Stinson, 1977, p. 10).

The first national conference on nursing research in Canada was held in Ottawa in 1971 under the auspices of the University of British Columbia, with federal assistance from the National Health Research and Development Program (NHRDP). As this was a "first" for the nursing profession in Canada, historical overviews were presented on the kinds of nursing research projects conducted over the years by governments, service agencies, professional associations, and universities (Griffin, 1971; Imai, 1971; Poole, 1971). These overviews document that most studies have been undertaken since 1965, and some were funded by a variety of sponsoring agencies. In relation to university based projects, Griffin commented,

> Funds for either faculty or graduate students' research have not been obtained for many projects. Of those reported, only 22 faculty and 23 students indicated some sponsorship. A few respondents indicated funds had not been obtained "yet" and doubtlessly the graduate students were indirectly funded for their research through funding during all or part of their graduate education programs (1971, p. 96).

FEDERAL SUPPORT FOR RESEARCH

The federal government first recognized a need for improved research and development because of the war effort, and the National Research Council (NRC) was formed in 1916. Its role was "undertaking, assisting and promoting scientific and industrial research in Canada" in certain specified areas (Secretary of State, 1975, p. 2). The Canada Council was established in 1957 to support research in the humanities and social sciences. The Medical Research Council (MRC) and the National Sciences and Engineering Research Council (NSERC) originally operated within the framework of the NRC of Canada, but the MRC became fully autonomous in 1969, as did the NSERC in 1978. The Social Sciences and Humanities Research Council (SSHRC), established in 1978, encompasses programs administered originally by the Canada Council. These three granting councils (MRC, NSERC, SSHRC) do not conduct intramural research programs of their own. Each is dedicated entirely to provision of grants and awards to support extramural research, conducted primarily in universities and their affiliated institutions. Each council is responsible for the areas of research indicated by its name. In addition, other agencies and departments of the federal government have always been involved in granting smaller amounts to support research. The NHRDP of Health and Welfare Canada is one such research-funding unit with particular relevance to nursing research support. (Peitchinis, 1971).

Three categories of federal research support provide funds: research grants, research fellowships, and auxiliary grants, the latter providing only indirect support for research. Funds may be awarded directly to faculty members and institutions "to assist them in the performance of projects initiated and controlled by the grant recipients" (Secretary of State, 1975, p. 35). Fellowships, are funds that are channelled directly to faculty members or graduate students for research training. Historically, NRC received the largest share of federal research funds; this is still evident in the amounts allocated to NSERC and MRC, which were originally encompassed within NRC. For the 1987 to 1988 fiscal year, research funding was provided through grants and fellowships; 52% to NSERC, 27% to MRC, 10% to SSHRC, and 11% to the Health Protection Program, which includes NHRDP (Statistics Canada, 1987). Since the early 1970s, there has been public conflict and debate over the levels of federal support available for research. From 1971 to 1974, federal research funding in Canada experienced a period of no growth, and in December 1975, the funds of the MRC were temporarily frozen. The result was that research teams across the country had to curtail or discontinue research activities. The "hard line" taken by the federal government toward medical research was vigorously denounced by the medical community:

> Those who downplay research show little inclination to give up its practical benefits. Only the cost is shunned, not the fruits. If Canadians want the high quality of health care they deserve, they must be prepared to pay for it. And a reasonable tab for medical research must remain prominently displayed on the invoice (Osmond, 1976, p. 10).

Since then, public debate has continued on the issue of federal research funding. Powerful lobbies for science and engineering research and for medical research appear to have reaped benefits. Undoubtedly, federal research-funding policy will continue to be the subject of considerable debate as the social merit of its decisions are weighed against the need for spending in other areas.

More recent developments, which may eventually have some impact on federal funding for health research, centre on provincial research-funding activities. In Ontario the proceeds of a lottery have been targeted for health research, and in Alberta in 1980, the provincial government created the Alberta Heritage Foundation for Medical Research (AHFMR), a research-granting agency, using $300 million from the Heritage Savings Trust Fund. The interest accrued on this principal is the source of medical research funding by the AHFMR.

SOURCES OF FUNDING FOR NURSING RESEARCH

The three primary areas for which external research support is sought are research projects, research training, and space and equipment for conducting nursing research. Discussion is limited to the first two sources because they precede and condition the eventual development of the third. However, it should be noted that the first Center for Nursing Research in Canada was established at McGill University in 1971 with federal support from Health and Welfare Canada. Until funding for nursing research became readily available as an integral part of the terms of reference of the NHRDP of Health and Welfare Canada, there were few sources of funds other than the limited funds of the Canadian Nurses Foundation (CNF) and those of private foundations and voluntary organizations. The 1971 documentation provided by Griffin reveals that research funding was not secured for many projects:

> It must be underlined that, to date, a substantial portion of Canadian nursing research has been done by graduate students at their own expense, and by nursing faculty and health agency members, often on their own time, and on a non-funded basis. As such, direct cost figures give us only a hint of the time, equipment, supplies and publication costs of all the nursing research being done (p. 22).

Slowly, almost imperceptibly, new sources of funding for nursing research have been opening up for nurses through the 1970s and 1980s. Some of these sources are provincial organizations, while others are national ones. Notable among the organizations which include nursing in their mandates are the British Columbia Health Care Research Foundation, the Canadian Cancer Society, the

Canadian Heart Foundation, the Hospital for Sick Children Foundation, the Kidney Foundation of Canada, the Manitoba Health Research Board, the Ontario Ministry of Health, the Quebec Ministry of Health and the Saskatchewan Health Research Board. One agency established by the Government of Alberta, the Alberta Foundation for Nursing Research (AFNR), is unique in that funding is exclusive to nursing research. Created in 1982 by ministerial order, the AFNR was designed to administer a grant of one million dollars for nursing research over a 5-year period. Funding categories included research projects, demonstration/evaluation projects, facilitation projects, research support for graduate students at the master's and doctoral levels, and conferences on nursing research. At the conclusion of the initial 5-year period of support, AFNR funding was extended at the same level on a yearly basis ($200,000).

FUNDING FOR RESEARCH PROJECTS IN NURSING AT THE FEDERAL LEVEL

A review of federal research grants for projects relating to health care between 1949 and 1963 revealed that no funding was awarded for research projects in university schools of nursing (Defence Research Board, 1963). Beginning in 1963, support became available for nursing research in progressively incremental amounts (see Table 11.1). Although these funds were reported as allocated for nursing research between 1964 and 1968, funding for only one investigation, conducted by a nurse co-principal investigator from a university school of nursing, could be identified from a review of lists of all health science projects funded in those years (Good, 1969). The nurse co-principal investigator was Helen M. Carpenter of the University of Toronto, whose cooperative project with an East York/ Leaside health unit investigator received a federal grant of $7100 (Defence Research Board, 1967, p. 18). A review of Table 11.1 ascertains that funding began to increase dramatically after 1968. During the 1975 to 1976

TABLE 11.1 Research Project Grants to Nurses From Federal Sources: 1964-1968 and 1972-1976

Year	Amount Awarded
1964-65	$ 11 300
1965-66	25 074
1966-67	27 414
1967-68	28 415
1972-73	48 840
1973-74	88 709
1974-75	318 002
1975-76	555 168

From Good, S. R. *Support of research in universities, 1964-68*, p. 12; *Directory of federally supported research in universities* (1972-73 to 1975-76). Ottawa: Canada Institute for Scientific and Technical Information, National Research Council.

fiscal year, $572,005 was awarded for nursing research projects in university schools of nursing, providing funding for 15 research projects under the direction of 10 nurse-principal investigators across the country. Not only was there a substantial increase in funding from 1964 to 1976, but the increase between the 1974 to 1975 fiscal year and the 1975 to 1976 fiscal year was a substantial 38% (Kerr, 1978).

RESEARCH PROJECT GRANTS TO NURSES FROM FEDERAL SOURCES: 1964 TO 1968 AND 1972 TO 1976

It became clear to nurses that even with the level of support provided by the NHRDP during the 1985 to 1986 fiscal year and funds awarded by other organizations, there was a critical need for funding from the federal government that was specifically designated for nursing. Of the three major granting councils, both the (MRC) and the (SSHRC) included nursing among the disciplines eligible for funding. Nevertheless, nursing researchers found it difficult to get either council to review proposals. Grant applications were often sent from one agency to another; many ended up being considered by NHRDP, a funding agency used extensively by medicine. Consequently, few nursing research project proposals were funded by either the MRC or the SSHRC. In response to Canadian Nurses Association (CNA) efforts to communicate nurses' concerns about this process and the resulting low level of federal funding for nursing research, the MRC established the Working Group on Nursing Research in 1982. Final recommendations in the Report of the Working Group in 1985 referred to the need to designate funds for nursing research within the MRC's structure and the need to assist in creating opportunities for the establishment of PhD in Nursing programs across the country. No federal action was taken on the recommendations until early 1988, when the MRC announced its decision to collaborate with NHRDP to make separate funding available for nursing research on a competitive basis. University nursing programs were invited to submit proposals, to be considered in the same manner as current development grants and program grants of MRC, for funding over approximately three years.

RESEARCH SUPPORTED BY UNIVERSITY SCHOOLS OF NURSING

Table 11.2 documents the results of an investigation of research support to university schools of nursing, including funds expended by schools for nursing research as reported by the individual universities (Kerr, 1978; 1986). The significance of the change in the extent of the research in university schools of nursing over time may be readily appreciated. From a very small endeavour in just a few schools, nursing research has become a more broadly based and better financed undertaking. Although the figures reported are aggregate sums that may include funds received from external granting agencies for program development, they give some indication of the "state of the art." It is interesting to

TABLE 11.2 Funds Expended for Nursing Research Reported by Canadian University Schools of Nursing, 1965-66 to 1985-86

	1985-86	1980-81	1975-76		1970-71		1965-66	
	Assisted Research: Nursing	Assisted Research: Nursing	Assisted Research: Nursing	Total University Research Funds (%)	Assisted Research: Nursing	Total University Research Funds (%)	Assisted Research: Nursing	Total University Research Funds (%)
University of British Columbia	81 290	13 074	104 333 385 296*	2.95	19 805 10 373*	0.27	1 519	0.03
University of Alberta	19 862	0	18 366	0.14	13 126	0.17	NA	NA
University of Calgary	20 280	0	NA	NA	NA	NA	NA	NA
University of Saskatchewan	35 712	7 135	NA	NA	NA	NA	NA	NA
University of Manitoba	6 140	0	88 728	0.10	0	0	NA	NA
University of Western Ontario	0	0	7 232	0.06	6 711	0.10	0	0
University of Toronto	32 643	89 070	171 574	0.58	84 723	0.44	12 091	0.14
McMaster University	78 887	101 517	145 825	1.12	80 613	1.13	NA	NA
Université de Montréal	18 669	0	61 363	0.32	0	0	NA	NA
McGill University	20 300	61 663	170 892	0.81	35 242	0.23	NA	NA
Queens University	10 644	0	NA	NA	NA	NA	NA	NA
Dalhousie University	0	0	0	0	92 606	2.69	37 063	NA

From Financial statements, accountants' records and records of the schools of nursing of the above universities; Reference List of Health Science Research in Canada, 1980-81 (source for 1980-81 information), and 1985-86 (source for 1985-86 information).

*"Special purpose" funds refer to program development funds.

NA, Not available.

note that all universities with graduate programs received funds for research in the 1980 to 1981 fiscal year, and one institution that had not yet initiated a program received external funds for nursing research.

From the rather bleak levels of research funding reported for the 1965 to 1966 fiscal year to the vastly increased amounts reported for the 1985 to 1986 fiscal year, it is evident that funding for nursing research in university schools of nursing has entered a new era. Undoubtedly, this change has been predicated on new expectations for faculty performance in research; without the development of research expertise among faculty it would not have been possible. Essential to the transition was the appointment of members of faculty qualified at the doctoral level who were prepared to undertake research. Despite the lack of availability of a doctoral program in nursing in Canada, nurses have found alternatives that enable them to develop research skills, such as entering doctoral programs in nursing in other countries, most notably the United States, and seeking admission to doctoral programs in other disciplines.

NURSING RESEARCH IN HEALTH-CARE AGENCIES

Nursing research has become an important sphere of activity in healthcare agencies, with greater recognition of the importance of nursing research to care and availability of research support, and the appointment of individuals to conduct and facilitate research. In many cases, collaboration between nursing researchers in health-care agencies and those in university schools of nursing has been mutually beneficial and joint appointments between these organizations have facilitated investigation of nursing research problems. Developing networks and collaborative work in nursing research undoubtedly result in important outcomes in terms of the nature of research questions asked and the quality of the research effort.

In a unique, state-of-the-art study of nursing research activities in Canadian teaching hospitals in 1985, 84 institutions were surveyed (Thurston, Tenove, and Church, 1987). The study documented completion of 170 investigations; 118 focused on nursing care, 44 focused on nursing care delivery, and 8 focused on other areas. Almost one third of the 59 projects identified were funded externally. and administrative commitment and support was the single most important factor in facilitating nursing research. The authors concluded: "Nursing research, although in an early state of development, had become a visible and credible activity in teaching hospitals (Thurston et al, 1987, p. i)." *The Reference List of Health Science Research in Canada* for 1985 to 1986 documents provision of $55,982 in research funds to nursing researchers in health-care agencies. (Canada Institute for Scientific and Technical Information, 1985-1986). Health-care agencies have a special interest in ascertaining the efficacy of methods of care as well as in exploring management questions that may lead to improved care. It is likely that there will be considerable expansion of nursing research in the future as health-care administrators observe the benefits of increased knowledge about nursing care and the most effective means of providing it in health-care environments.

REFERENCES

Bonneau, L.P. and Corry, J.A. (1972). *Quest for the optimum: Research policy in the universities of Canada*. Ottawa: Association of Universities and Colleges of Canada.

Canada Institute for Scientific and Technical Information. (1985-86). *Reference list of health science research in Canada*. Ottawa: The Institute.

Defence Research Board. (1963). *Medical research projects completed in Canada*. 1949-1963. Ottawa: The Board.

Defence Research Board. (1967). *Reference list of medical research projects in Canada*. Ottawa: The Board.

Good, S.R. (1969). *Submission to the study of support of research in universities for the Science Secretariat of the Privy Council*. Ottawa: Canadian Nurses Association and Canadian Nurses Foundation.

Griffin, A. (1971). Nursing research in Canadian universities. In *National Conference on Research in Nursing Practice*. Ottawa: School of Nursing, University of British Columbia.

Hurburtise, R. and Rowat, D.C. (1970). *The University, Society and Government: the report of the Commission on the Relations between Universities and Governments*. Ottawa: University of Ottawa Press.

Imai, R. (1971). Associations and research activities. In *National Conference on Research in Nursing Practice*. Ottawa: School of Nursing, University of British Columbia.

Kerr, J.C.R. (1978). Financing university nursing education in Canada: 1919-1976. PhD dissertation, Ann Arbor, MI: University of Michigan.

Kerr, J.C.R. (1986). Structure and funding of nursing research in Canada. In S.M. Stinson & J.C. Kerr (Eds.), *International issues in nursing research* (pp. 97-112). London: Croom Helm.

Medical Research Council. (1980). *Reference list of health science research in Canada*. Ottawa: The Council.

National Conference of Canadian Universities. (1944). *Proceedings*. Ottawa: The Conference.

Osmond, D.H. (1976). Sickness in Canada's health system. *The University of Toronto Graduate*, Spring, 10.

Peitchinis, S.H. *Financing post-secondary education in Canada*. Toronto. Council of Ministers of Education in Canada.

Poole, P.E. (1971). Research activities conducted or sponsored by government or service agencies. In *National Conference on Research in Nursing Practice*. Ottawa: School of Nursing, University of British Columbia.

Secretary of State. (1975). *Review of educational policies in Canada: Government of Canada report*. Toronto: Council of Ministers of Education in Canada.

Statistics Canada. (1987). *Federal science expenditures and personnel. 1987-88*. Ottawa: Statistics Canada.

Stinson, S.M. (1969). Deprofessionalization in nursing? Ed.D. dissertation. New York. Teachers' College, Columbia University.

Stinson, S.M. (1977). Central issues in Canadian nursing research. In B. LaSor and M.R. Elliot (Eds.), *Issues in Canadian nursing* (pp. 3-42). Scarborough: Prentice-Hall Canada Ltd.

Symons, T.H.B. (1975). *To know ourselves: The report of the Commission on Canadian Studies (Vol. I and II)*. Ottawa: Association of Universities and Colleges of Canada.

Thurston, N.E., Tenove, S., and Church, J. (1987). *Nursing research in Canadian teaching hospitals*, Calgary, Alberta: Department of Nursing, Foothills Provincial General Hospital and Faculty of Nursing, University of Calgary.

CHAPTER TWELVE

Scope of Research in Nursing Practice

JANNETTA MacPHAIL

T he scope of research in nursing practice is influenced by one's philosophy of nursing practice. For most nurses, nursing practice pertains to the direct care of individuals or groups, with a view to helping them attain, maintain, and regain their optimal level of health and functioning. For other nurses, practice includes educating nurses, conducting nursing research, and administering nursing services or nursing education. In general, nurse researchers classify nursing practice research as that involving studies of direct care.

DEVELOPMENT OF NURSING RESEARCH IN CANADA

The pattern of development of nursing research in Canada was similar to that of nursing education in universities; the initial focus was on functional nursing, that is, teaching and administration, as opposed to clinical nursing. This was also the trend in the development of nursing research in the United States (Gortner and Nahm, 1977; O'Connell and Duffey, 1978) and in the United Kingdom (Hockey, 1986). Cahoon (1986) points out that pressures to improve nursing education in Canada promoted a focus on nursing education studies until the mid-century and that clinical nursing studies were relatively infrequent until the late 1960s. Stinson (1986) notes that the focus shifted from nursing education to nursing service administration by the late 1960s and to research in nursing practice by the mid-1970s. Cahoon observed that "the majority of studies were conducted by university nursing faculty members and/or, as of the late 1960s, their graduate students" (1986, p. 164). This trend continued into the 1970s and 1980s, even though some large health-care agencies had established a position for a clinical nurse researcher. Thurston, Tenove and Church (1987) found, in a survey of Canadian teaching hospitals, that 150 nursing research projects were ongoing. The current trend emphasizes research in nursing practice designed to improve practice; there is less emphasis on research pertaining to nursing education and administration. This trend is probably due

128

to the increasing number of nurses prepared at the doctoral level in nursing and to the importance attached to nursing practice among the general population of nurses today.

CLASSIFICATION OF NURSING RESEARCH

A number of analyses have classified nursing research into categories (O'Connell and Duffey, 1978; Gortner, Bloch, and Phillips, 1976; Gortner and Nahm, 1977; Loomis, 1985; Hayter and Knafl, 1986). These analyses have been of nursing research in the United States, of nursing research published in nursing research journals in the United States, or, in the case of Loomis (1985), of dissertation titles and abstracts. No similar classification of nursing research has been conducted and reported by Canadians.

The major avenue for Canadian nurses to report their research findings and share ongoing research projects has been primarily through National Nursing Research Conferences, which were initiated in 1971 by the Canadian universities that offer graduate programs in nursing (Alberta, British Columbia, Calgary, Dalhousie, Manitoba, McGill, Montreal, Newfoundland, Saskatchewan, Toronto, and Western Ontario) and are held approximately every 18 months. The proceedings of the first ten conferences, held between 1971 and 1985, were published and served as an information source to analyze the scope of research in nursing practice and identify trends or themes that will be reported.

Another source of Canadian nursing research is the journal *Nursing Papers*, which was first published in 1968 by McGill University School of Nursing under the editorship of Dr. Moyra Allen, who is recognized for her vision and leadership in the development of nursing research in Canada. Although preference is given to articles based on research, *Nursing Papers* has not been devoted entirely to research. Beginning in 1986, the journal bore the added title of *The Canadian Journal of Nursing Research*. In recent years there has been some pressure to change the name to this title alone, but the change has not been made. Because the journal has not been devoted completely to research and because it is difficult to differentiate research articles from others, *Nursing Papers* was not used in analyzing nursing research in Canada for the purposes of this chapter.

Another source of Canadian nursing research is identified by Stinson (1986), who states that the *Index of Canadian Studies*, initiated in 1964 by the Canadian Nurses Association (CNA), is the most extensive cataloguing of Canadian nursing research; however, there is not yet a comprehensive repository of all Canadian nursing research.

ORGANIZATION AND FUNDING OF NATIONAL NURSING RESEARCH CONFERENCES

The First National Nursing Research Conference was held in 1971 in Ottawa; it was organized and sponsored by the University of British Columbia School of Nursing and supported by the Department of National Health and Welfare. Speakers were invited to address problems of research in professional practice.

Only one of the invited speakers was a nurse; not an unexpected situation at this early stage in the development of nursing research. The nurse speaker was Dr. Faye Abdellah, an eminent leader in the development of nursing research, who presented a historical perspective of nursing research in the United States. A symposium followed by discussion groups led by selected nurse leaders focused on current nursing research activities in Canada, as conducted or sponsored by government and service agencies, professional associations, and Canadian universities. In the Introduction the project director, Dr. Floris King, stated:

> Prior to 1960 there were few significant research studies in nursing practice reported in Canadian nursing literature. Research studies which appeared were primarily reports of surveys conducted to establish facts about activities in which nurses were engaged, income and employment conditions of nurses, supply and demand for nurses in particular geographic areas, and content of educational programmes. These were important starts in nursing research in Canada. (1971, p. 1).

At the end of the conference, the 380 participants presented resolutions that pertained to education of researchers, facilitation of nursing research in health care agencies, and the need to hold research conferences on a regular basis to present research findings and share research ideas.

Table 12.1 presents the years of the first 10 national nursing research conferences (1971 through 1985), the host universities, and sources of funding as reported in the proceedings of each conference.

The conferences were all organized by Canadian universities on a volunteer basis, and an offer to host the next conference was usually made at the end of each conference. The first five conferences were invitational, and all obtained external funding, initially from the Department of Health and Welfare and subsequently from the National Health Research and Development Program (NHRDP), which is part of the Department of Health and Welfare. The sixth conference was the first that was open to all persons; it was also the first to be supported solely by nurses through registration fees and contributions from the provincial nurses' associations of the two host provinces, Manitoba and Saskatchewan. Subsequent conferences have been supported by registration fees and a contribution from the provincial nurses' association of the host province or of the provinces involved in sponsorship and organization. In addition, continued federal funding through NHRDP or the Department of Health and Welfare has been apparent, although the amount has been reduced. The conferences held in 1983 and 1985 sought and received funding from the Secretary of State for simultaneous translation.

The 1985 National Nursing Research Conference in Toronto closed with a decision that no national nursing research conference would be planned for 1986 because the University of Alberta had announced in 1983 that the second International Nursing Research Conference would be hosted by the University of Alberta in May, 1986. Since plans had not been made for another national nursing research conference, the Executive Committee of the Canadian Association of University Schools of Nursing decided in the fall of 1986 to ask McMaster University to host a research conference in conjunction with the annual meeting of the Learned Societies in June 1987.

TABLE 12.1 Host Universities and Sources of Funding for National
Nursing Research Conferences

Year of Conference	Host Universities	Site	Sources of Funding
1971	British Columbia	Ottawa	Department of National Health and Welfare
1973	McGill & Montreal	Montreal	DHW
1974	McMaster, Toronto, & Western Ontario	Toronto	DHW
1975	Alberta, Calgary, Manitoba, & Saskatchewan	Edmonton	DHW
1977	Ottawa & Canadian Nurses Association	Ottawa	DHW
1978	Manitoba & Saskatchewan	Winnipeg	Registration fees and the two provincial nurses associations
1980	Dalhoise & four Atlantic Nurses' Associations	Halifax	Registration fees, four nurses' associations, and NHRDP
1982	British Columbia & Victoria	Victoria	Registration fees, RNABC, NHRDP, and BC Government
1983	McGill, Montreal, & Laval	Montreal	Registration fees, Quebec Nurses' Association, NHRDP, Secretary of State
1985	Toronto	Toronto	Registration fees, MRC, NHRDP, Secretary of State

After 1978, the published proceedings of the 10 National Nursing Research Conferences, were printed and provided to all participants. The cost was included in the registration fee initiated in 1978; however, as the cost of printing increased it became difficult to publish proceedings. Additional funding to continue this process was sought by the host universities.

DEMOGRAPHIC DATA AND FOCUS OF NATIONAL NURSING RESEARCH CONFERENCES

Demographic data for nine national nursing research conferences are presented in Table 12.2. These data indicate remarkable increases in the number of participants, the number of papers presented, and the number of investigators involved in the projects, particularly in later years. The first conference (1971) is not included in the analysis because it did not involve presentation of research papers. The number of participants was low in the early years, when attendance

TABLE 12.2 Demographic Data on National Nursing Research Conferences, 1973–1985

Data	1973	1974	1975	1977	1978	1980	1982	1983	1985
No. of participants	40	57	68	105	101	145	200+	354	300
No. of research papers presented	11	12	13	11	14	18	26	28	49
No. of authors — 1	11	6	12	10	6	10	15	14	26
— 2	—	3	1	1	8	4	7	6	10
— 3	—	3	—	—	—	2	2	7	5
— more	—	—	—	—	—	2	2	2	8
Discipline of — Nursing	11	17	15	13	20	27	40	51	83
Investigators — Other	—	4	—	—	—	8	4	10	15
Highest degree of researchers									
Nurses: Doctorate — Nursing	0	0	0	0	0	2	2	6	12
— Other	1	4	3	3	6	9	12	9	13
Master's — Nursing	7	10	6	6	9	11	19	21	39
— Other	3	2	2	3	3	2	6	5	10
Baccalaureate	0	0	1	0	1	2	1	1	8
No degree	0	1	1	0	1	0	0	1	1
Other									
disciplines: Doctorate — PhD	0	2	0	0	0	7	4	3	8
Doctorate — MD	0	2	0	0	0	0	0	1	5
Baccalaureate	0	0	0	0	0	1	0	0	2

was by invitation only. Although the number of participants did not increase in 1978, the first year that invitation was not required, a steady increase is evident in subsequent years. There has also been a significant increase in the number of abstracts submitted, from 38 in 1982, from which 26 papers were selected, to 110 in 1985, from which 49 papers were selected.

The number of papers presented increased in 1985 because this was the year that a standard procedure, a critique of each research paper given by a discussant, was eliminated. The increase in number of papers and abstracts reflects the augmentation in nurses' involvement in research over a period of 14 years and the standardization of presentation to research conferences in other disciplines. The trend has been to provide more opportunity for investigators to share their research findings and allow time for discussion by all attendees instead of limiting discussion of a paper to a planned discussant.

Two items of interest are the change in number of authors involved in preparing papers and the increase in the number of nurses involved as investigators as compared to the number of investigators from other disciplines. Also interesting is the change in the involvement of investigators from other disciplines versus nurses from 1980 to 1985. In 1980, 23% of the investigators were from other disciplines and two served as principal investigator. In 1982, only 9% were from other disciplines, and none served as principal investigator. In 1983 and 1985, the percentage of investigators from other disciplines was 16% and 15%, respectively, with none serving as principal investigator or co-principal investigator.

The change in the educational preparation of nurse investigators over the years is illustrated in Table 12.2. It is interesting to note that the number of nurses with doctoral preparation increased from 1 in 1973 to 25 in 1985. There were no nurse investigators with doctorates in nursing until 1980, when there were two; that number increased to 12 in a 5-year period. Through the years, the number of nurses who held a master's degree in nursing and were involved in research exceeded the number with preparation in a field other than nursing; of the 49 who held master's degrees in 1985, 39 had earned the degree in nursing. The nurses with baccalaureate degrees or diplomas were few, and their involvement in research was as assistants. The difference in the level of education between nurses and investigators from other disciplines demonstrates that in disciplines other than nursing, most of those involved in research are educated at the doctoral level.

ANALYSIS OF CONTENT OF THE NATIONAL NURSING RESEARCH CONFERENCES

Originally, the first two conferences did not have titles, and titles were adopted later to reflect a focus on nursing practice research and on particular concerns related to the preparation of investigators and problems to be addressed in developing nursing research. The 1974 conference was entitled "Decision-Making in Nursing Research"; however, the research presented was not all clinical in nature. The primary purpose of that conference, as stated by Cahoon, "was to enable Canadian nurse-researchers to share ideas about on-going research activities and to analyze determinants which influence decision-making in nursing research" (1974, p. 1). The title of the 1975 conference was "Development and Use of Indicators in Nursing Research," and its goal was to address physical, psychological, and social indicators. Hockey defined indicators as tools that attempt to extend knowledge and "help to focus disciplined attention to key issues and encourage logical thought progression" (1975, p. 8).

The 1977 conference, a workshop on research methods in nursing care, was designed to help nurse participants identify problems in methods of investigation and share solutions to these problems. The 1978 conference focused on issues, innovations, and problems related to methods of nursing-care research. The focus on research in nursing practice was continued in subsequent conferences, as indicated by their titles. They were designed to focus attention on use of the research process in nursing practice, with the goal of advancing nursing knowledge to improve nursing care.

Several reviews of nursing research have appeared in the literature, and each has developed a method of categorization suited to the particular purposes of that review. Hayter (1985) developed ten coding categories for review of research published in four research journals (*Nursing Research, Research in Nursing and Health, Advances in Nursing Science, Western Journal of Nursing Research*). The categories are as follows: nurses, nursing process, delivery systems, research activities, nursing education, theory and conceptual frameworks, historical studies and chronologies, patients/clients/consumers, basic research, and literature review. An attempt was made to use all of the categories but the last two to analyze the research reported in the proceedings of the 10 national nursing research conferences; however, after careful consideration, the categories used to organize the research papers presented at the 10th National Nursing Research Conference were deemed more appropriate for this review. The categories are as follows: practice differentiated into seven subcategories; health care delivery, including nursing administration; research methods/instruments; nurse and nurse role; clinical decisions/diagnosis; nursing education; philosophical/theoretical; and historical studies (Table 12.3).

The number of research studies pertaining to practice; increased dramatically from 5 in 1973 to 39 in 1985; however, the number should be compared to the total number of studies since practice represented almost half of the studies in 1973, 1974, and 1975. The proportion increased to 64% in 1977, decreased to 29% in 1978, and increased again, to 66% in 1980. The percentage of practice studies continued at a high level, with 68% in 1982, 64% in 1983, and 79.5% in 1985. Whether these percentages reflect the proportion of nursing research that focused on practice from 1973 to 1985 is not known. The figures indicate the high emphasis placed on nursing practice research by the organizers of the national nursing research conferences. This trend reflects nurses' efforts to establish a scientific base for practice and to extend and advance nursing knowledge.

Note the decreased interest in studies of the nurse, nursing roles, and nursing education, which dominated nursing research activities from the early part of the century into the 1950s. The analysis reflects limited interest or involvement in historical research and philosophical research, which should be a cause of concern to nurse researchers and leaders in Canadian nursing. This analysis of the content of research presentations at the 10 national nursing research conferences indi-

TABLE 12.3 Categories of Nursing Studies Reported at National Nursing Research Conferences, 1973 to 1985

Categories	1973	1974	1975	1977	1978	1980	1982	1983	1985
Practice	5	6	6	7	4	12	15	18	39
Aging	–	–	–	1	–	2	2	3	4
Chronicity & Meaning of Illness	2	–	1	–	–	–	1	1	5
Pain	–	–	–	1	–	1	–	2	6
Personal/Environment Interaction	1	5	4	2	2	5	5	3	4
Stress/Adaptation/ Social Support	–	–	–	1	–	–	–	3	8
Parenting	–	–	–	–	–	1	–	4	5
Parent & Child	2	1	1	2	2	3	7	2	7
Health Care Delivery (including Nursing Administration)	1	2	1	3	2	2	4	3	4
Research Methods/ Instruments	–	–	4	–	3	1	2	4	4
Nurse & Nurse Role	3	3	1	1	–	1	2	1	–
Clinical Decisions/ Diagnosis	–	–	1	–	–	–	1	1	–
Nursing Education	–	1	–	–	4	2	2	–	–
Philosophical/Theoretical	–	–	–	–	–	–	–	1	2
Historical	2	–	–	–	1	–	–	–	–
TOTAL	11	12	13	11	14	18	26	28	49

cates that, in Canada, there has been interest and emphasis on research in nursing practice and on problems pertaining to design and methods for the past 16 years. This trend, which has continued over the years, should be a source of pride for Canadian nurses. It reflects concern for the quality of nursing care since it is only through research that knowledge is advanced and care is improved.

ORGANIZATION OF ANNUAL NURSING RESEARCH CONFERENCES

The Canadian Association of University Schools of Nursing (CAUSN) began sponsoring an annual nursing research conference to be held in early June in connection with the annual meeting of the Learned Societies, because of their commitment to the development of nursing research in Canada. (CAUSN had sponsored annual conferences in conjunction with the Learned Societies before, but the papers presented were not necessarily research reports). The host university prepares for the review of abstracts by reviewers from other universities and assumes responsibility for organizing the conference and obtaining funds, in addition to registration fees, to cover expenses.

The first CAUSN-sponsored Annual Nursing Research Conference was hosted by McMaster University in 1987, the second by the University of Windsor

TABLE 12.4 Categories of nursing studies reported at annual nursing research conferences, 1987 to 1989

Categories	1987	1988	1989
Practice	22	45	70
Aging	3	8	6
Chronicity and meaning of illness	2	4	8
Pain	1	—	5
Personal/environmental interaction	1	8	11
Stress/adaptation/social support	3	9	13
Parenting	6	12	15
Parent and Child	3	1	8
Family	3	3	4
Health care delivery	5	2	12
(including nursing administration)			
Research methods/instruments	2	—	10
Nurse and nurse role	8	1	1
Clinical decisions/diagnosis	1	—	1
Nursing education	16	6	11
Philosophical/theoretical	1	—	—
Historical	1	1	1
Research networking	1	—	—
TOTAL	57	55	106

in 1988, and the third by Université Laval in 1989. "Innovation and Nursing Research" was the theme chosen for the fourth conference, hosted by the University of Victoria in 1990, at which 124 papers and 30 posters were presented (CAUSN Newsletter, 1990). There have been no reports of the annual conferences, but the programs given to participants in each of the conferences were used to analyze the nature of the research presented as a means of assessing the continued development of nursing research in Canada. Information about the number of participants was not available, nor was it possible to determine the educational credentials of the principal investigators or others involved in the research. This information could easily be made available by requesting that academic credentials be included on the abstracts submitted. Credentials *were* included in the abstracts of papers presented at the University of Windsor.

Table 12.4 identifies the categories of research studies presented at the three annual nursing research conferences for which programs were available; the categories are those used for analysis of the ten national nursing research conferences plus two others—Family and Research Networking. The topic for the 1987 conference, "Innovations in Nursing Education and Practice: The Role of Research" may have been the reason for the high percentage of nursing education studies reported at this conference (28% as compared to 11% in 1988 and 10% in 1989). There were also more studies pertaining to the nurse and nursing role in 1987 than in the other two years, 14% as compared to 2% and 1%. These two factors and the fact that 9% of the studies reported in 1987 were related to health care delivery questions resulted in nursing practice research representing only 39% of the studies in 1987, as compared to 82% in 1988 and 66% in 1989. The high proportion of practice studies in 1988 may have been influenced by that year's theme, "Women and Health." It is interesting and encouraging to note the increase in attention to instrument development and testing for validity and reliability since critiques of nursing research in recent years have identified inadequacy in these areas in many studies. This inadequacy has been evident at research conferences and in editorials in the major nursing research journals (see Chapter 10), especially in *Annual Reviews of Nursing Research*, volumes 1 through 8, edited by Werley, Fitzpatrick, and others. Such inadequacies merit serious consideration by researchers and reviewers of abstracts for research conferences, as does the need for adequate sampling from which to generalize findings and the need for more replication of nursing research studies. As discussed in Chapter 10, there is a tendency to generalize findings, even though researchers caution against it. Moreover, the consumers of research may not be aware of inadequacies in sampling procedures and the size of samples used.

Although for the most part it was not possible to examine the educational and research preparation of the researchers who shared their methods and findings at the three conferences, in instances where this information was provided, it caused some concern. For example, of the 33 principal investigators presenting papers at the 1988 conference, 24 were prepared at the master's level, 2 at the baccalaureate level, and only 7 at the doctoral level. This leads one to question whether the gradually increasing proportion of nurses in Canada with doctoral degrees, as reported by Stinson, MacPhail and Larsen (1988), are fulfilling their responsibility to conduct research and provide leadership to others in designing and conducting quality research. Perhaps the focus of this particular research conference influenced those who submitted abstracts; however, many persons are usually interested in studying women's health issues.

The number of abstracts submitted for the first three annual nursing research conferences, decreased from 109 in 1987 to 72 in 1988, then increased to 174 in 1989. In considering factors that may have caused these fluctuations, it may not be reasonable to expect a high level of participation every year; the time required to design and conduct research and the cost of travel across the country to present it are prohibitive. It may be important to plan each year's meeting location carefully, keeping these factors in mind. For example, the 1987 and 1988 conferences were both held in southwestern Ontario and 1989 conference was in Quebec; all of these locations are a long distance from the western provinces. Although the venue is not chosen by CAUSN but by the Learned Societies, it merits consideration.

The involvement of nursing service colleagues, particularly in 1987, is encouraging. Undoubtedly, this involvement was promoted and facilitated by the collaboration between nursing education and nursing practice at McMaster University-Chedoke McMaster Hospitals. Nurses in practice settings are studying important problems in health-care delivery as well as in nursing practice. Also interesting is the decreased attention to studies of the nurse and nursing roles and, to some extent, nursing education, which dominated nursing research in the first half of the century and even into the 1950s. The analysis reflects very limited interest and/or involvement in historical research and philosophical/ theoretical research; this should be a cause of concern to nurse researchers and leaders in Canadian nursing. Interest in historical research may be augmented through the organization of the Canadian Association for Nursing History, a group that has been meeting annually, in conjunction with other national nursing meetings, since 1987. Interest could also be stimulated through doctoral education in nursing, which has been identified as a priority in other chapters.

INFLUENCE OF A FOUNDATION ON RESEARCH IN NURSING PRACTICE

The Alberta Foundation for Nursing Research (AFNR), established by ministerial order in October 1982, began funding research in December 1983 after developing a process for receiving and reviewing grant applications and granting funds, giving visibility to the foundation's objectives and research funding opportunities, and developing a self-evaluation mechanism to enable the Board of Directors to assess performance on an annual basis. Grants were provided in accordance with the Board's assessment of areas of greatest importance in meeting AFNR's objectives, which included "research investigations which have relevance for nursing practice in any setting; educational training of researchers; and the communication of nursing research" (Alberta Foundation for Nursing Research [AFNR], 1984, p. 5). The six categories designated originally were:

1. A Research Project category for investigations which apply to the solution or management of problems pertaining to nursing practice;
2. A Demonstration/Evaluation Project category for projects which involve the implementation and evaluation of innovations in the organization or delivery of nursing care;
3. A Research Fellowship category which provides nurses with paid salary time solely for the purpose of conducting research investigations;
4. A Facilitation Grant category which provides funds to nurses who wish to develop innovative ideas into feasible research grant proposals;
5. A Student Research Allowance category which provides students with funds to help meet research related expenses; and,
6. A Conference and Workshop category for conferences or workshops designed to facilitate and/or communicate the development of nursing research.

The Board of Directors made changes in the categories and in the amounts awarded as new ideas evolved and experience indicated that some of the amounts designated were insufficient to achieve the research objectives.

Table 12.5 lists the grants awarded by the AFNR from the inception of the program in 1983 through March 31, 1989. Analysis of the report of awards made each year (AFNR, 1984, 1985, 1986, 1987, 1989) indicated that priority has been given to funding research in nursing practice, in keeping with the Board's original objectives. Priority has also been given to research training, through student research bursaries, research support services, and research trainee awards; and to the communication of nursing research, through support of research conferences.

TABLE 12.5 AFNR Grant Funds Awarded 1984 to March 31, 1989

Category of award	1983/84 ($)	1984/85 ($)	1985/86 ($)	1986/87 ($)	1987/88 ($)	1988/89 ($)	Total ($)
Research project	13,216	25,000	188,090	239,745	129,538	200,469	796,058
Demonstration project	1,379	0	0	0	0	22,519	23,898
Facilitation	1,420	9,296	17,075	17,450	29,130	9,333	83,704
Conference	0	25,000	5,860	10,000	28,180	0	69,040
Student bursaries	3,000	5,000	7,500	7,500	23,000	24,000	70,000
Research support service	0	0	61,314	0	0	24,083	85,397
Research trainee	0	0	25,000	47,113	0	0	72,113
Funds Awarded (TOTAL)	19,015	64,296	304,839	321,808	209,848	280,404	1,200,210

From Alberta Foundation for Nursing Research (1989). *Annual report.* Edmonton, Alberta: The Foundation.

The majority of the awards were for investigation of nursing practice problems, but a few grants supported development and testing of research instruments, studies of the nursing work environment, investigation of nursing administration problems with direct relevance to nursing practice, and studies pertaining to evaluation of nursing practice. All of the studies were pertinent to nursing practice and the climate in which practice and research take place.

Analysis of the content of research presentations at the national nursing research conferences and the annual nursing research conferences and research endeavours funded by the AFNR indicates that, in Canada, there has been continued interest in and emphasis on research in nursing practice and problems pertaining to design and methods for the past two decades. This trend reflects concern for quality of nursing care and for advancing knowledge to improve care. Canadian nurses recognize the need to increase and enhance nursing research and are giving priority to lobbying for funding, for research and doctoral education in nursing to attain their goals.

REFERENCES

Alberta Foundation for Nursing Research, (1984, March 31). *Annual report.* Edmonton, Alberta: The Foundation.

Alberta Foundation for Nursing Research. (1985, March 31). *Annual report.* Edmonton, Alberta: The Foundation.

Alberta Foundation for Nursing Research. (1986, March 31). *Annual report.* Edmonton, Alberta: The Foundation.

Alberta Foundation for Nursing Research. (1987, March 31). *Annual report.* Edmonton, Alberta: The Foundation.

Alberta Foundation for Nursing Research. (1989, March 31). *Annual report.* Edmonton, Alberta: The Foundation.

Allen, F.M., and Thibaudeau MF (Eds.). (1973). Proceedings of the Colloquium on Nursing Research, McGill University and Université de Montréal, March 28-30, 1973, Parts 1, 2, and 3.

Cahoon, M.C. (1974). Foreword. In Godden, J.O., and Cahoon, M. (Eds.). *Decision-making in nursing research.* Proceedings of the Third National Conference on Research in Nursing. Toronto: The University of Toronto.

Cahoon, M.C. (1986). Research developments in clinical settings: A Canadian perspective. In S.M. Stinson and J.C. Kerr (Eds.). *International issues in nursing research* (pp. 182-204). London and Sydney: Croom Helm.

Canadian Association of University Schools of Nursing. (1990 June). National Nursing Research Conference. *CAUSN Newsletter.*

Canadian Nurses Association. (1977). *Research methodology in nursing care.* Proceedings of the Workshop on Research Methodology in Nursing Care, November 9-11, 1977.

Crawford M., and Kyle, M. (Eds.). (1978). *Methodology in nursing care research: issues, innovations, problems.* Proceedings of the National Nursing Research Conference, University of Saskatchewan and University of Manitoba, December 13-15, 1978.

Godden, J.O., and Cahoon, M.C. (Eds.). (1974). *Decision-making in nursing research.* Proceedings of the Third National Conference on Research in Nursing, University of Toronto, May 21-23, 1974.

Gortner, S.R., Bloch, D., and Phillips, T.P. (1976). Contributions of nursing research to patient care. *Journal of Nursing Administration 6(3).* 23-28.

Gortner, S.R., and Nahm, H. (1977). An overview of nursing research in the United States. *Nursing Research 26(1).* 10-33.

Hayter, J. (1985). Institutional sources of articles published in thirteen nursing journals 1978 to 1982 (Research). *Nursing Research 33(6).* 357-362.

Hayter, M.J., and Knafl, K.A. (1986). Generating nursing knowledge: Whose work? In J.C. McCloskey and H.K. Grace (Eds.). *Current issues in nursing* (2nd ed.) (pp. 149-160). Boston: Blackwell Scientific Publications.

Hockey, L. (1975). Indicators in Nursing Research with Emphasis on Social Indicators. In Zilm, J., Steed, M., and Overton, P. (Eds.) *Development and use of indicators in nursing research.* Edmonton: University of Alberta School of Nursing.

Hockey, L. (1986). Nursing research in the United Kingdom: The state of the art. In S.M. Stinson and J.C. Kerr (Eds). *International issues in nursing research* (pp. 216-235). London & Sydney: Croom Helm.

King, F. (Ed.). (1971). *National Conference on Research in Nursing Practice.* Proceedings of First National Nursing Research Conference, University of British Columbia, February 16-18, 1971.

King, K., Prodrick, E., and Bauer, B. (Eds.). (1985). *Nursing research: Science for quality care.* Proceedings of the 10th National Nursing Research Conference, University of Toronto, April 9-11, 1985.

Kravitz, M., and Laurin, J. (Eds.). *Nursing research:*

A base for practice. Proceedings of the 9th National Nursing Research Conference, McGill University and Université de Montréal, October 12-14, 1983.

Loomis, M.E. (1985). Emerging content in nursing: An analysis of dissertation abstracts and titles: 1976 to 1982. *Nursing Research 34(2).* 113-119.

McKay, R.C. and Zilm, G. (Eds.). (1980). *Research for practice.* Proceedings of the National Nursing Research Conference, Dalhousie University, October 22-24, 1980.

McMaster University School of Nursing and Canadian Association of University Schools of Nursing/The Learned Societies. National Nursing Research Conference. *Innovations in nursing education and practice: The role of research,* Hamilton, Ontario, June 6-7, 1987.

O'Connell, K.A. and Duffey, M. (1978). Research in nursing practice: Its present scope. In N.L. Chaska (Ed.), *The nursing profession: Views through the mist.* (161-174). New York: McGraw-Hill Book Co.

Stinson, S.M. (1986). Nursing research in Canada. In S.M. Stinson and J.C. Kerr (Eds). *International issues in nursing research.* (236-258). London & Sydney: Croom Helm.

Stinson, S.M., MacPhail, J. and Larsen, J. (1988). *Canadian Nursing Doctoral statistics: 1986 Update.* Ottawa: Canadian Nurses Association.

Thurston N., Tenove S., and Church, J. (1987). *Nursing research in Canadian teaching hospitals.* Calgary: Foothills Provincial General Hospital and University of Calgary Faculty of Nursing.

University of Windsor School of Nursing, Canadian Association of University Schools of Nursing, The Learned Societies Conference. *Women and Health.* Windsor, Ontario, June 10-11, 1988.

Université Laval, Ecole des Sciences Infirmières and Association Canadienne des Ecoles Universitaires de Nursing. Congrès des Sociétés Savantes 1989. *Colloque Annuel de recherche en sciences infirmières,* Québec, Québec, 8-9 juin, 1989.

Zilm G.N., Stinson, S.M., Steed, M.E., and Overton, P. (Eds.). *Development and use of indicators in nursing research.* Proceedings of the 1975 National Nursing Research Conference, Universities of Alberta, Calgary, Manitoba and Saskatchewan, November 3-5, 1975.

Zilm, G., Hilton, A., and Richmond, M. (Eds.). (1982). *Nursing research: A base for practice, service and education.* Proceedings of the National Nursing Research Conference, University of British Columbia, April 28-30, 1982.

PART III

Nursing Care Delivery

CHAPTER THIRTEEN

Quality Assessment in Nursing in Health-Care Agencies

JANET ROSS KERR

Increasing diversification and sophistication in the health-care field have been accompanied by steady increases in national expenditures for health care. Concomitantly, changing social values about health characterize the general population. Better informed health consumers are demanding increased accountability in health care. Investigative and consciousness-raising activities of consumer rights groups have resulted in a high media profile; health lobbyists have argued for environmental protection, health promotion, and provision of health-care services that are available, effective, and appropriate. As a result, North American attitudes toward health care and health care professionals have undergone a significant transition. Health care is considered a right rather than a privilege, and health care professionals are expected not just to provide care, but to provide quality care.

The relationship between accessible, cost-effective, high quality patient care and institutional excellence has been explored in several studies on magnet hospitals (Kramer and Schmalenberg, 1988; McClure et al, 1982). In identifying hospital organizations that had developed a reputation for vitality and innovation, other factors of considerable interest to the nursing department emerged. These included low turnover, less frequent need for orientation of new staff, high commitment and identification with institutional values on the part of staff, less use of inexperienced staff or agency personnel, and cooperative working relationships among staff members (Kramer and Schmalenberg, 1988). The highly desirable nature of these variables and the fact that they are associated with excellence in care underscores the importance and relevance of efforts to ensure quality patient care.

Historically, quality assurance in health care was defined as the self-regulating activities of the various professions. The prevailing view that only relevant health-care professionals could describe the nature of competent practice meant that physicians, nurses, and other professionals were not challenged in the way that they dealt with matters of professional misconduct. Today, the situation is very different. While professional groups granted the privilege of autonomously conducting regulatory functions still have those privileges, there is more public scrutiny of the process. In many provinces, lay members of professional governing boards and their disciplinary committees are appointed by the Lieutenant-Governor-in-Council to represent the interests of the public in professional deliberations. Professional groups are constantly pressured by the media for full and open disclosure of the results of disciplinary operations. Thus, the professional conduct of physicians, nurses, and other health care professionals may easily become a subject for public discussion and debate, something that was unheard of in the past.

External pressure for quality assurance programs in nursing has come directly from accreditation standards and requirements. The Canadian Council on Hospital Accreditation (CCHA) has standards requiring the presence of an ongoing quality assurance program for accreditation of a health-care agency. This requirement alone has undoubtedly provided the major incentive for the increased development of quality assurance programs in hospitals across the country.

RATIONALE FOR QUALITY MONITORING

The assessment of quality of nursing care is believed to be an important and essential strategy for monitoring and stimulating excellence in nursing practice, administration, education, and research. Credit for the first documented study in health care and nursing, based on the use of standards, is attributed to Florence Nightingale, who in 1858 investigated the quality of care rendered to military personnel (Nightingale, 1858). In the United States, the idea of developing standards for health care was formalized in 1918. The American standards were subsequently adopted in Canadian hospitals. In 1952, the Joint Committee on Accreditation of Hospitals was formed, and, until 1958, this organization also assumed responsibility for accrediting Canadian hospitals. In 1958, The CCHA was formed for accrediting health-care agencies in Canada.

In the 1970s a surge of activity in quality assurance produced improved CCHA standards for accreditation; for the first time, standards were developed for long-term care and mental health agencies. Provincial professional associations in nursing also instituted quality assurance activities; guidelines for implementing quality assurance programs and nursing practice standards were developed by many of these organizations. Nursing consultants with quality assurance expertise have been retained by the professional associations to provide assistance to nursing service departments in provincial health care agencies in developing programs or ongoing activities in quality assurance.

The idea that quality of patient care cannot be taken for granted is fundamental to establishing standards and programs. Since consumers clearly expect health care to be efficient, effective, and equitable, nursing, as the largest department in the hospital, can expect close scrutiny of its service. Nursing care is provided by individual practitioners who bear individual, professional responsibility for the care provided. Accountability at the individual level is important to the client as well as to the profession.

Since health-care agencies are ultimately responsible, legally and ethically, for the actions of employees, considerable effort has been made to develop formal programs for assessing, monitoring, and improving care. This effort has been headed by nurses, since nursing expertise is critical to developing and implementing successful quality assurance programs (Sliefert, 1985). Nursing expertise has also been important in developing standards at the level of the Board of Directors of the CCHA, where the Canadian Nurses Association (CNA) is represented through two seats on the governing board.

Clearly, the quest for quality assurance in nursing has been driven by a number of forces. As important as quality assurance in any one discipline is, the objective from the consumer standpoint is quality assurance in all phases of health care. The primary focus to date has been on developing quality monitoring programs in nursing, undoubtedly because nursing is the largest, most visible, and most critically important service in health-care agencies. Interdisciplinary quality assurance programs, somewhat rare in the past, should be encouraged to demonstrate system-wide responsibility and accountability. Such encouragement has been provided through standards for accreditation approved by the CCHA; since 1986 a hospital-wide quality assurance program that covers all hospital services has been required for 3-year accreditation, the maximum available under the program.

ORGANIZING FOR QUALITY ASSURANCE

The common denominator of quality assurance programs is standards. Donabedian (1980) proposed three levels for assessing quality: structure, process, and outcome. Structural standards focus on the human and material resources available and their organization in a health care setting. Examples include the philosophy of the institution, resources and supplies, staffing patterns, and characteristics of the environment of care. Process standards focus on the role of the nurse and on nursing activities performed in the interest of meeting patient care goals. Examples of process standards are the nursing process, communication between nurses and clients, and nursing activities. Outcome standards are mainly client oriented, and describe the anticipated results of the care process. Outcomes generally refer to the results of health care. It is difficult to attribute outcomes to any one health care profession because a team effort is necessary to achieve results.

The majority of the effort in quality assurance programs is directed at the process level of care because the activities of a health-care profession can be assessed and measured directly at this level. The assessment may be concurrent or retrospective. If concurrent, nursing care is reviewed or measured at the time the care is delivered; if retrospective, the review takes place at some time after the provision of care. The advantages of the concurrent method include the potential for collecting more and better information and availability of direct information from clients. Because the information is gathered sooner, changes can be made more quickly. Disadvantages may include increased cost implications and possible disruptions to the activities of the nursing unit. Retrospective reviews may be attractive because cost implications tend to be lower and there is less disruption to the nursing unit because the client's record is usually the focus of this review. However, with this type of review it is not usually possible to collect information directly from the client, and nurses responsible for the data on the chart may not be available to elaborate on it or to answer questions that arise. Because there is evidence that both concurrent and retrospective reviews provide valuable and unique information about the process of care, many agencies are using both types in their quality assurance programs.

The development of standards for measuring care raises a number of questions. For example, who should determine the standards for agencies? Historically, beginning with Florence Nightingale's work, nurses have assumed responsibility for development of standards. Professional nursing associations across the country have developed nursing practice standards and guidelines for quality assurance programs to help health-care agencies develop their own programs. Within the accrediting body, nurses have also been influential in developing approved standards for accreditation of the nursing department. Within agencies, nurses and have assumed responsibility for designing and implementing programs.

In many agencies, staff nurses have been asked to assist with the implementation process as data collectors. Those responsible for the programs feel that this is important, as it allows evaluees to become a part of the monitoring process; it is generally believed that involvement enhances commitment to the program. It also allows nurses to become involved in a peer review process for evaluating nursing care. Researchers have noted that there may be disadvantages in random involvement of untrained and inexperienced observers in the data collection process, indicating that quality of the information collected may be less than adequate in terms of reliability and validity. There are techniques to combine appropriate methods and involve staff nurses in the process; however, those responsible for program management must be informed and understand measurement and statistical issues.

The components of quality assurance programs appear to be the same in all professions. They include standards that describe quality, systems of data collection around the achievement of standards, and methods of bringing performance in line with standards. There are difficulties in separating contributions to client care by members of the health-care team. For nursing in particular, the development of outcome measures has been fraught with problems. Isolating the contribution of nursing to client health status is difficult and challenging, particularly since outcome measures appropriate for one patient are not necessarily appropriate for another. Also, the idiosyncratic nature of outcome criteria makes it difficult to find enough clients with similar characteristics to identify common criteria.

INSTRUMENTS FOR MEASURING THE QUALITY OF NURSING CARE

The literature on quality assurance is plentiful and increasing rapidly; most publications can be described as descriptive, covering areas such as nature of quality; components of a quality assurance model/framework; categorizations of quality; rationale for developing quality assurance techniques and programs; and establishing, maintaining, and improving quality assurance programs. The sector of the literature that deals with research on quality assessment is limited, focusing primarily on instrument development. Although there has been a great deal of research in the area of instrument development, there has been little attention to the type of testing that should be an integral part of the process. Most instruments in current use demonstrate little more than face validity, raising questions about the value of results in quality assurance programs that use inadequately tested instruments. It also poses problems for the interpretation of research utilizing instruments purporting to measure the quality of nursing care.

Ventura's work in testing instruments that are designed to measure quality in instruments commonly used in tertiary care institutions has produced some interesting results. Studies were conducted at the Veterans Administration Medical Center in Buffalo, New York to investigate the relationship between QualPacs and the Phaneuf nursing audit. A Pearson product moment correlation of 0.01 was obtained for total scale scores using 97 patients (Ventura et al, 1980). Another study, correlating scales of QualPacs and the Rush-Medicus instrument, indicated that some subscales were related, whereas others bore little relationship to each other. This led to the conclusion that different dimensions of quality were addressed in each instrument and further exploration of the nature of the concept of quality was necessary (Ventura et al, 1982). Results support those of an earlier investigation by Trussel and Strand (1978), which identified differences between concurrent and retrospective reviews of the same patients.

Examination of interrater reliability of these same instruments identified difficulties with the QualPacs and the Rush-Medicus instruments. Minimal standards for evaluating results were not met by the QualPacs instrument; the Rush-Medicus instrument only met them in some instances of testing in situations where the test conditions were carefully controlled. Ventura et al (1980) recommended that interrater reliability be calculated on a regular basis, using the intraclass correlation coefficient (ICC) before and after data collection. Also, Ventura et al. indicated that a minimum standard for measuring results would be an ICC of at least 0.75 (1980).

A study conducted at the University of Alberta in Edmonton, Alberta, assessed the reliability and validity of the Rush-Medicus process audit, an in-house tool for measuring quality developed by one hospital — the Process Chart Audit; and the MAPS Outcome Audit, an instrument developed by the Alberta Hospital Association (Alberta Hospital Association, 1983). ICCs in two data collection periods were calculated for each instrument. On the Rush-Medicus instrument, ICCs were 0.76 in the first period and 0.93 in the second; on the Process Chart Audit, ICCs were 0.77 and 0.75; and on the MAPS Outcome Audit, ICCs were 0.94 and 0.89. No significant differences were noted between the ratings of the two observers; ICCs that were greater than the recommended standard of 0.75 were obtained for all three instruments in both testing periods based on total scale scores. A discrepancy was noted in the ICC obtained for the Medicus instrument in both testing periods that could not be explained. In terms of subscale results, improvement from the first data set to the second was noted. For the Medicus process audit, all subscales of the second data set were above the 0.75 ICC standard. Results of the MAPS Outcome Audit, in terms of the ICC values for subscales, also met the 0.75 standard and were the most impressive, suggesting a high level of reliability. ICC values for the subscales of the Process Chart Audit varied widely in both data collection periods, a finding that might be expected considering the lack of testing of this instrument. These investigators concluded that the recommended 0.75 ICC level for interrater reliability may be too low and should be closer to 0.85 (Giovannetti et al, 1986).

The validity testing portion of the study assessed the relationship between the instruments being tested using Pearson correlations. The coefficient for Rush-Medicus and MAPS was 0.27; for Rush-Medicus and the Process Chart Audit, 0.23; for MAPS and the Chart Audit, 0.29. It is obvious that correlations were very low; in fact, none explained more than 9% of the variance. Based on Ventura's earlier findings these results were not unexpected. The conclusions of these researchers were consistent with Ventura's; the three instruments measure different dimensions of quality (Giovannetti et al, 1986).

Many health-care agencies place considerable emphasis on selecting and implementing a workable and well-recognized quality assurance program for quality monitoring and control in the nursing department. The methods used to accomplish the agency's goals vary. There are concurrent and retrospective process audits and outcome audits; a number of these methods include review of the chart, questionnaires to be completed by nurse or client, interviews of clients or nurses, or direct observation of the process of nursing care. It is important to select methods that yield information that will help the agency meet its goals. A number of firms that have high international standings in quality assurance use vigorous marketing strategies, offering to provide a quality assurance program for the institution. Their assistance comes at a considerable cost and agencies must understand both the positive features and limitations of the purchased service. The recent availability of research findings on most of the programs currently in use should be used in making decisions about purchase of a quality assurance program, even if it is necessary to employ consultants to assist with the process.

PROBLEMS IN QUALITY ASSESSMENT

Reference has been made to problems with quality assurance programs and monitoring. A major difficulty facing executive officers of agencies, in times of limited financial resources, is financing the quality assurance programs. The number of people required for successful operation of quality monitoring programs has increased, and so have the costs associated with programs that are implemented by firms that specialize in this area. Funds expended on quality assurance are likely to be considerable; therefore it is imperative that the programs used in agencies be effective and appropriate and that the budget allocated to this sector of activity be justified.

A second area of concern is whether those responsible for designing and implementing programs are knowledgeable in research and quality assessment. Knowledge about the research literature is important, as is ability to assess the strengths and weaknesses of various approaches to quality to maximize the former and minimize the latter in programs selected for implementation. Many nurses who have been responsible for inservice education are now responsible for managing quality assurance activities in health care agencies. This is an expedient way for agencies to implement quality monitoring, but it is important to assess whether those responsible have the time, interest, background, and expertise to function effectively in this sphere.

The limited reliability and validity testing of instruments used for quality monitoring continues to be a major concern for the nursing department in health-care agencies. If instruments do not measure dimensions of quality consistently, from one session to another and from one rater to another, the information collected is of little value to those who wish to judge performance within the institution from the results obtained. Also, if there is little correlation between instruments that are to measure the same dimensions of quality, major conceptual problems about what is being measured must be addressed before decisions can be made on findings. Considerable research on the psychometric attributes of quality monitoring instruments is needed to address these questions.

Ventura et al (1980) and Giovannetti et al (1986) have noted that measurement must be made carefully so the quality monitoring process yields reliable findings. Controlled conditions are necessary, and raters must be carefully trained and monitored. Although agencies like to involve as many staff nurses as possible in the process of data collection, the principles of control must be strictly followed if the process is to yield meaningful information. This may mean that certain nurses are seconded to the program for a period of time, given preparation in methods of assessment, and then included in practice sessions until interrater reliability reaches an acceptable level. Ventura et al. (1980) and Goodwin and Prescott (1981) have argued that use of the intraclass correlation statistic as a method of assessing interrater reliability is superior to the time-honoured percentage of agreement technique. This method is superior because it accounts for error in level and ranking disagreements. Interrater reliability testing should be continuous to ensure that results are meaningful, since even minor changes in circumstances surrounding the testing can cause changes in results. Thus, interrater reliability cannot be assumed.

FUTURE DIRECTIONS IN QUALITY ASSESSMENT

Considering the relatively recent interest in and knowledge of this area, the increasing technology and sophistication that characterize quality monitoring programs is impressive. Nurses have learned a great deal about the level of excellence of client care and have displayed interest and enthusiasm for approaches that will improve the outcomes of care. Nursing researchers are evaluating the process of measuring quality; and the questions that have been raised, as well as the interest in this area, will stimulate further research into methods, procedures, and dimensions of quality. It is essential that nurses continue to direct quality monitoring of nursing care. Collaboration with health care agencies is important because the majority of nursing services are provided under the auspices of such agencies. Future efforts to improve public accountability by refining and modifying quality assessment procedures and practices are important to development in this area. Health care agencies and the nursing profession will continue to work together in this shared responsibility to the public.

REFERENCES

Alberta Hospital Association. (1983). *Management analysis and planning systems.* Edmonton, Alberta: Unpublished materials.

Donabedian, A. (1980). The definition of quality and approaches to its assessment. In *Explorations in quality assessment and monitoring* (Vol 1). Ann Arbor, MI: Health Administration Press.

Giovannetti, P., Kerr, J.C., Bay, K., and Buchan, J. (1986). *Measuring quality of nursing care: Analysis of reliability and validity of selected instruments—final report.* Edmonton, Alberta: Faculty of Nursing, University of Alberta.

Goodwin, L.D. and Prescott, P.A. (1981). Issues and approaches to estimating interrater reliability in nursing research. *Research in Nursing and Health, 4*(3). 323-327.

Kramer, M., and Schmalenberg, C. (1988). Magnet Hospitals: Part I—Institutions of excellence. *Journal of Nursing Administration, 18*(1). 13-24

McClure, M., Poulin, M., Sovie, M., and Wandelt, M. (1982). *Magnet hospitals: Attraction and retention of professional nurses.* Kansas City, MO: American Nurses Association.

Nightingale, F. (1858). *Notes on matters affecting the health, efficiency and hospital administration of the British Army.* London: Harrison and Sons.

Sliefert, M. (1985). Quality control: Professional or institutional responsibility? In J. McCloskey and H. Grace. (Eds.). *Current issues in nursing* (443-456). Boston: Blackwell Scientific Publications.

Trussel, P.M. and Strand, N. (1978). A comparison of concurrent and retrospective audits of the same patients. *Journal of Nursing Administration, 8*(5). 33-38

Ventura, M., Hageman, P.T., Slakter, M.J., and Fox, R.N. (1980). Interrater reliabilities for two measures of nursing care quality. *Research in Nursing and Health, 3*(1). 25-32.

Ventura, M., Hageman, P.T., Slakter, M.J., and Fox, R.N. (1982). Correlations of two quality of nursing care measures. *Research in Nursing and Health, 5.* 37-43.

CHAPTER FOURTEEN

The Canadian Nurse Shortage: Real or Imagined?

ELEANOR ROSS

N ursing is invaluable to the health of Canadians. The importance of recruiting and retaining nurses cannot be overemphasized. Canadians recognize that "nursing manpower shortages . . . have serious, negative repercussions on the availability of, access to and scope of health services — precisely those attributes of the Canadian Health system on which we pride ourselves." (Canadian Hospital Association [CHA], 1988). One of the most challenging tasks for nursing, hospital administrators, governments, and society is to ensure that enough nurses are available to provide care now and in the future. Many studies in Canada (Alberta Association of Registered Nurses, 1988; Hospital Council of Metro Toronto, 1988; Meltz and Marzetti, 1988; Ontario Nurses Association, 1988; Ordre des Infirmières et Infirmiers du Québec, 1989; Newfoundland Ministry of Health, 1988) and in the United States (American Organization of Nurse Executives, 1988; Secretary's Commission on Nursing, 1988) have indicated that "the remedies for the difficulties of recruitment of nurses and for the problems in salaries and working conditions depend on the recognition of the nursing profession, on the autonomy of nursing practice, on their educational requirements and on their enormous and distinctive contribution to the health system." (Ordre des Infirmières et Infirmiers du Québec, 1989).

This chapter describes trends in employment of nurses, supply of nurses, supply imbalances, challenges facing the profession, and recommendations for change. The discussion is based on available data, with the recognition that certain data have limitations due to a variance in definitions over time and among sources of data collection.

TRENDS IN EMPLOYMENT OF NURSES

Registered Nurses (RNs) now form the largest occupation group in Canada. The RN workforce has increased rapidly: The number of RNs increased by 33%

Eleanor Ross is Clinical Nurse Specialist at Sunnybrook Health Science Centre in Toronto. She is also a doctoral candidate at the University of Toronto.

1961 to 1971 and by 68% from 1971 to 1981 (see Table 14.1). A review of Registered Nurses Management Data 1988 indicates that there were 249,673 RNs in Canada in 1988; an estimated 227,213 were employed in nursing (Statistics Canada, 1990).

Nurses and others believe that a large number of RNs are either inactive or working at jobs outside health care; however, studies in Canada (Meltz and Marzetti, 1988) and the United States (Aiken and Mullinix, 1987) have demonstrated that the profession of nursing has one of the highest rates of participation and retention in predominantly female occupations. Eighty percent or more are actively employed either full- or part-time. Since the profession of nursing is predominantly female and women continue to be primarily responsible for child rearing and other household duties, an employment rate of 80% may be as high as can be anticipated. Thus it is doubtful that unemployed nurses are a potential resource for hospital employment if shortages exist.

Table 14.1 presents census data for 1971, 1981, and 1986 for occupations in nursing. While the number of RNs increased rapidly, the number of Registered Nurse Assistants (RNAs), aides and orderlies increased slowly and actually decreased in the 1980s. Change in number of nursing supervisors exhibited a similar pattern. The percentage of increase for therapists and those employed in unclassified nursing and therapy occupations was higher than that of RNs.

The rapid increase in the number of RNs was due to at least four factors. The first factor was the increase in nurse employment in and outside hospitals. Although some observers suggested that there was a shortage of hospital RNs,

TABLE 14.1 Nurses and Other Selected Occupations in the Labour Force

	Number			Percentage Change		
	1971	1981	1986	1971 to 1981 (%)	1981 to 1986 (%)	1971 to 1986 (%)
CANADA						
Nurses, registered, graduate, and nurses-in-training	104,635	175,825	221,980	68.0	26.3	112.1
Supervisors, nursing	14,550	21,270	19,700	46.2	−7.4	35.4
Nursing assistants	27,285	44,900	35,470	64.6	−21.0	30.0
Nursing aides and orderlies	70,940	85,670	81,465	20.8	−4.9	14.8
Physical, occupational, and other therapists	6,250	13,680	18,680	118.9	36.5	198.9
Nursing and therapy occupations not otherwise classified	9,480	14,180	27,415	49.6	93.3	189.2

From Meltz, Noah and Marzetti, Jill. (1988). *The shortage of Registered Nurses: An analysis in a labour market context.* Toronto. Registered Nurses Association of Ontario.

possibly due to the increased demand for nursing in home and ambulatory care, studies indicated that, although the number of RNs employed in the community had increased, the number employed in hospitals had also increased.

Table 14.2 presents data about where nurses work; the categories are standard Statistics Canada classifications. Despite small decreases in the proportion of RNs working in hospitals over the 15 years presented, 73% of RNs were still working in hospitals in 1986. Although the proportion for related health care institutions (nursing homes and homes for the aged) was small, the number of RNs working in this category has increased from 10,585 in 1981 to 26,790 in 1986. The number of RNs in the diagnostic and therapeutic services group (visiting home nurses) has almost tripled from 1981 to 1986. In summary, two thirds of the increase in the number of nurses employed was in hospitals and one third outside, particularly in related health care institutions, such as nursing homes, and in diagnostic and therapeutic services, such as visiting home nurses.

The second factor in the increase in the number of employed RNs was the trend of reduction in bed to RN ratio or more RNs per bed (Meltz and Marzetti, 1988). In 1977, the ratio in Ontario was 1.88; by 1985, the ratio had dropped to 1.45. This trend may have been due to the increased acuity and complexity of patient care, which required more RNs around the clock, and the shorter average length of stay. However, there is a paucity of research to support this explanation.

The third factor, which can be seen in Table 14.1, was the reduced number of assistants, aides, and orderlies. In 1971, the number of RNs (104,635) was slightly smaller than the total number of supervisors, assistants, aides, and orderlies (112,775). By 1986, however, the number of RNs (221,980) was almost double that of the other three groups (136,635). In Ontario the shift was even more dramatic: 42,740 RNs compared with 39,780 supervisors, assistants, aides and orderlies in 1971; 84,415 RNs compared with 33,145 in the other three groups in 1986. The number of RNs was two-and-one-half times the total number of the other three groups in Ontario (Meltz and Marzetti, 1988). RNs increased from 21.3% to 32.7% of the total employees in hospitals, whereas assistants, aides, and orderlies decreased from 20.3% to 11.87% (Meltz and Marzetti, 1988). Although this trend has been explained by the fact that hospitalized patients were sicker and required more care than in years past, in reality, RNs are paid a low relative wage and are very adaptable. As Aiken and Mullinex (1987) stated:

> Registered Nurses, as versatile employees, can provide all the services which hospitals sometimes employ nurses' aides and licensed practical nurses, and they can also often perform a wide range of other functions, including those assigned at other times to secretarial and clerical personnel, laboratory technicians, pharmacists, physical therapists, and social workers. Nurses substitute for physicians under some circumstances, and commonly assume hospital management roles after regular work hours. Thus, when nurses' relative wages are low as compared with other workers', it is advantageous for hospitals to employ them in greater numbers and in lieu of other kinds of workers. Even if nurses' wages are 20 to 30 percent higher than those of licensed practical nurses or secretaries, it may still be more economical to hire nurses, because they require little supervision and can assume responsibility for a wide range of duties. The increased demand for nurses created by low relative wages can lead to shortages . . .

TABLE 14.2 Where Nurses Work in Canada

	Number			Percentage Change		
	1971	1981	1986	1971 (%)	1981 (%)	1986 (%)
Community, business and personal service industries						
Health and welfare services						
Hospitals	75,405	133,295	162,515	79.5	75.9	73.2
Related health-care institutions	1,880	10,585	26,790	2.0	6.0	12.1
Welfare organizations	2,410	6,815		2.5	3.9	
Offices of physicians and surgeons	3,565	5,280	6,480	3.8	3.0	2.9
Diagnostic and therapeutic services (not elsewhere specified)	*	2,625	7,105	—	1.5	3.2
All other health and welfare	3,600*	5,090	4,075	3.8	2.9	1.8
TOTAL	86,860	163,690	206,975	91.6	93.2	93.2
Education and related services	1,390	1,900	1,895	1.5	1.1	0.9
All other community and business service	1,120	2,730	3,290	1.2	1.6	1.5
TOTAL	89,370	168,320	212,160	94.3	95.9	95.6
Manufacturing	980	1,335	1,390	1.0	0.8	0.8
Construction	40	80	15	0.0	0.0	0.0
Transportation, communication, and other utilities	90	175	295	0.1	0.1	0.1
Trade	245	425	440	0.3	0.2	0.2
Finance, insurance, and real estate	155	300	320	0.2	0.2	0.2
Public administration and defence	3,820	4,770	6,360	4.0	2.7	2.9
Agriculture, forestry, fishing, trapping, and mining	95	160	225	0.1	0.1	0.1
All industries (TOTAL)	94,795†	175,575‡	221,980§	100.0	100.0	100.0

From Meltz, Noah and Marzetti, Jill. (1988). *The shortage of Registered Nurses: An analysis in a labour market context.* Toronto. Registered Nurses Association of Ontario.
*1971 data include "Diagnostic and therapeutic service" in "All other health and welfare."
†Excludes 9,835 nurses in training (because the data does not provide anything to compare them with in future years).
‡Figure differs from the total of above because of rounding.
§Includes 775 industry unspecified.

TABLE 14.3   Percentage of Canadian Nurses Working Part-Time*

	Females (%)			Males (%)		
	1970	1980	1985	1970	1980	1985
Nurses, registered, graduate, and nurses in training	27.6	38.9	43.4	10.6	15.8	18.2
Supervisors, nursing	13.2	23.2	26.2	3.2	8.5	7.3
Nursing assistants	17.4	38.0	45.9	6.0	18.2	20.2
Nursing aids and orderlies	23.6	39.0	45.4	8.8	21.1	31.2

From Census of Canada.
*Based on persons who worked mostly part-time during each year, by self-declaration or basic data-gathering instrument.

The fourth factor was the increase in the proportion of RNs working part-time. The increase from 27% in 1970 to 43% in 1985, in the number of RNs working mostly part-time is illustrated in Table 14.3. Almost half of the RNs in Canada were working part-time in 1985. Undoubtedly, a change in the number of hours worked by almost 100,000 nurses could substantially affect the number of full-time equivalent nurses.

TRENDS IN SUPPLY

The sources of RNs in Canada are recent graduates from hospital programs, community colleges, and university programs; immigrants from other countries who have had nursing education; and former RNs returning to the workforce. Since there are few studies of the career patterns of Canadian RNs, it is difficult to estimate the number that returned to nursing (Baumgart, 1988).

In 1986, 87.5% of the employed RNs had graduated from Canadian schools of nursing; 9.1% had graduated from schools in other countries. Whereas nursing school programs in Canada have continued to achieve maximum enrolment, enrolment in nursing programs in the United States has dropped by 20% since 1983 (Aiken and Mullinix, 1987). However, observers in Canada indicate that a decrease in the number of applicants for nursing programs is occurring, a trend similar to that in the United States. Moreover, in the United States, the shrinking applicant pools have forced nursing programs to lower admission standards (Rosenfeld, 1987). High school students interested in nursing scored lower than the national average on university entrance exams.

Interest in nursing as a career may be declining for a number of reasons, including increased career opportunities for women, lack of long-term career opportunity in salary structures for nurses, and lack of economic return for degrees in nursing. Also, the number of students is decreasing due to a declining number of 18-year-olds, and fewer young adults are entering the workforce.

SUPPLY-DEMAND IMBALANCES

Imbalances in a labour market can occur through unfilled vacancies or un-employment and underemployment (Meltz and Marzetti, 1988). Vacancies indicate an inability to recruit people for or retain them in a particular position. The vacancy rate is calculated by dividing the number of positions vacant for some period of time (e.g., 42 days) by the average number of positions and multiplying by 100 to obtain a percentage.

Although increasing vacancy rates have been reported in some areas across Canada, the rates vary tremendously. For example, in October 1989, Ontario vacancy rates varied depending on the area of specialty and the type and location of the hospital. Whereas the provincial RN vacancy rate in Ontario was 4.1%, the vacancy rate in Metro Toronto was 9.1%, and the average provincial vacancy rate excluding Metro Toronto was 1.7% (Ontario Ministry of Health, 1990). Critical and long term care nursing had the highest vacancy rates at 6.3% and 6.1%, respectively. Meltz and Marzetti (1988) found that critical and long term care consistently had high vacancy rates, and vacancy rates for chronic care, psychiatric, and active teaching hospitals were also well above the provincial average.

A low unemployment rate can indicate a shortage; a high rate can indicate a potential source of supply of RNs. The data available on unemployment of nurses in Canada show consistently low rates, and rates that are 50% or less of the overall unemployment rates across Canada. The data also suggest that unemployed nurses do not form a large untapped pool of workers.

CHALLENGES FACING THE PROFESSION

Our health care system depends overwhelmingly on the work of women. Four out of five workers in health related occupations are women; four out of ten workers overall are women (Ryten, 1988). Because of the large number of women in health care, part-time work is more prevalent in health care than in the general economy (33% vs. 21%); part time work is also more prevalent among women health providers than among women in the rest of the economy (39% vs. 33%) (Ryten, 1988). In 1985, only 57% of employed women graduate nurses worked full-time; 43% worked part-time (see Table 14.3).

Work patterns vary between men and women and between different health care occupations. For example, 88% of male pharmacists and 70% of female pharmacists worked full-time, but 82% of female physicians worked full-time, and 57% of registered nurses worked full-time (Ryten, 1988). Ryten (1988) questioned whether the "proportion of women working full-time is almost an indicator of the social and economic status of its practitioners" (p. 7).

During the past 25 years, women have entered traditionally male occupations such as medicine and engineering; however, men have not entered traditionally female occupations, such as nursing, at the same rate. In the past 10 years, more women than men have graduated from universities. Women have made great strides in pursuing higher education, but their participation has benefited fields of study that are not predominantly female (Ryten, 1988). Fagin and Maraldo (1988) state "The nursing shortage will worsen, because little girls do not want to grow up to be nurses anymore. Nursing is considered women's work, and despite the strides made by the women's movement, women's work is as undervalued as ever."

A key characteristic of the Canadian labour market in the 1980s and the 1990s is the continually increasing demand for well-educated and skilled workers. "This trend reflects both changes in the occupational 'mix' of employment toward managerial and professional jobs, which require higher levels of education and skills, as well as increases in the skill content and educational requirements of most occupations" (Feature, 1988). This trend in the labour market is also evident in the health care industry, in hospitals, and in the nursing profession. Nevertheless, the health care system and hospitals have been slow to recognize and support the RNs' need for additional skills and knowledge. Campbell (1987) described nursing's challenge in today's cost-containment environment:

> Nurses provide today, as they always have, an essential element of health care. Organizational support for their work, however, remains as low as it has been in past decades. Sophisticated new management methods systematically devalue nurses' knowledge and displace their professional judgment in the process of organizing funding restraint in health care institutions. Being required to absorb a disproportionately heavy burden of cost containment must be seen as a gender-specific form of oppression of nurses. The contemporary approach to cost containment looks uncomfortably like the solution to hospital funding problems of an earlier era when nursing students provided unpaid labour.

A review of the Canadian labour market in general and the female workforce in health care specifically identifies two trends: Women are pursuing higher education but are ascribing to different work patterns than men after entering the workforce. The profession of nursing has been in the forefront of these trends.

A review of data suggests that nurses have not been leaving the profession as is often suggested, but are actually working and attempting to make changes in the system so that nurses can provide the kind of patient care for which they were educated. The profession of nursing has become more vocal; illegal strikes have even occurred in the 1980s. The anger and unrest among nurses may provide the positive stimulus needed to effect some of the systemic changes that would empower nurses.

Every study in Canada (Alberta Association of Registered Nurses, 1988; Meltz and Marzetti, 1988; Ontario Ministry of Health, 1988; Ontario Nurses Association, 1988; Order des Infirmières et Infirmiers du Québec, 1989; Newfoundland Ministry of Health, 1988; Registered Nurses Association of Ontario, 1988) and in the United States (American Organization of Nurse Executives, 1988; Government of the United States, 1988; Wandelt, 1986) has recommended structural changes that would address unsatisfactory conditions of nursing work.

RECOMMENDATIONS FOR CHANGE

The review of trends in employment of nurses, supply of nurses, and supply imbalances indicates that Canada does not have a "shortage" of RNs. However, there are specialties, hospitals and other nursing areas in Canada that do have high vacancy rates at this time. Almost 50% of RNs in Canada work part-time, since the vacancies exist in spite of an increasing number of RNs, increasing the number of nurses is not a solution. The present "nursing shortage" phenomenon is complex and requires a comprehensive and collaborative approach to address the various issues. Government officials, hospital administrators, and nurses all have roles to play.

Since health care is a provincial matter in Canada, the provincial governments, in planning for health care, should have a coordinated health human resource strategy to address the imbalances in supply and demand for RNs. The World Health Organization and others (Bankowski and Fulop, 1987; Edmonstone, 1988; Hall, 1988; Hsu and Lovelace, 1986; Terris, 1988) have highlighted the health human resource issues and have provided guidelines for human resource planning, but Canada and the provincial governments have continued to focus on single-profession and limited human resource planning. The need for a coordinated health human resource plan based on the health needs of Canadian citizens cannot be overemphasized.

Governments have a responsibility to review and update legislation that would enact structural changes that give nurses the authority to participate in decision making. This legislation is needed to ensure that nurses' participation in decision making is not simply by virtue of invitation, as it is at present in most provinces.

Administrators of health-care delivery organizations should preserve the RN's time for direct care of patients and families. Staffing affects quality and cost of patient care (Flood and Diers, 1988). Organizations should design and implement innovative, cost-effective staffing methods that include job restructuring, use of support personnel, flexible scheduling plans, and labour-saving technology (Aiken and Mullinex, 1987; Glandon, Colbert, and Thomasma, 1989; Donnelly, Yarbrough and Jaffe, 1989). Also, administrators should consider nursing as a revenue centre rather than a cost centre and thus begin to value and recognize nursing's contribution to the organization (Johnson, 1989).

Management should introduce incentives to encourage experienced nurses to remain in clinical care. Wage structures and benefit packages that recognize experience and advanced education are urgently needed. As Benner and Wrubel (1989) stated:

> Like other professional groups made up predominantly of women, nurses have been viewed as short-term workers rather than career workers .... Nursing administrators have not uniformly treated the nurse as a knowledge worker. To cope with high turnover rates, they often set up extensive rules, guidelines, and protocols inappropriate to the level of discretionary decision making required of the professional nurse .... Empowering the practicing nurse is the best remedial action for the organization.

Depressed wages for RNs will increase their demand for nurses because low wages allow nurses to be substituted for other personnel; as a result, vacancies for nurses will occur. Nursing recruitment will be adversely affected by the absence of a salary range that rewards skill and experience (Aiken and Mullinix, 1987).

Nurses also have a part to play in addressing some of the issues. Each nurse must value and recognize the importance of nursing care and be able to articulate that value. Nurses should realize the strength of nursing; it includes many different groups, organizations, and specialties. External groups have suggested that a major problem in nursing is a lack of unity or unified voice. However, this may be a "blame the victim" phenomenon similar to those seen in other women's issues. Such comments by government and administrators maintain the status quo; they need not do anything about the nursing problems since they are "nursing's problem." Therefore systemic and legislative changes, which would deal with worklife issues are not addressed. Nurses should take pride in their differences and recognize that other nurses perceive the "shortage" issue to be a result of worklife and workplace problems common to nurses everywhere.

Nursing must also become more politically aware. Legislation and policies that direct who and how decisions are made need to be fully appreciated by all nurses. Hayes and Fritsch (1988) state:

> Nurses are part of a large, potentially powerful group, yet they often complain that they feel powerless to effect changes either in health care or in their daily practice. They are uncomfortable with the notion of power, especially political power and despite their political potential, traditionally have remained inactive. Some of this discomfort arises from nurses' socialization as women, with their inability to control their personal and professional life space, as well as from their socialization into the nursing profession itself with its affective ideals of uniformity and docility.

CONCLUSION

Data indicate that Canada does not have a shortage of RNs at present; however, there are a number of problems related to working conditions, especially in hospitals, where the majority of nurses work. The problems include inadequate financial reward; limited autonomy in clinical situations; and inability to participate in management decisions about resource allocation and, therefore, support services and staffing. Collaboration between government, administrators, and nurses is required to deal adequately and comprehensively with the various quality of worklife issues facing nursing in Canada today.

REFERENCES

Aiken, L., and Mullinix C. (1987). Special report: The nurse shortage—myth or reality? *New England Journal of Medicine. 317*(10), 641-646.

Alberta Association of Registered Nurses. (1988). *Brief on concerns of Registered Nurses employed in* *Alberta hospitals and nursing homes to the Premier's Commission on Future Health Care for Albertans.* Edmonton, Alberta: The Association.

American Organization of Nurse Executives. (1988). *Proceedings of the invitational conference on the nursing shortage: Issues and strategies.* Chicago: American Hospital Association, October 7, 1988.

Bankowski, Z. and Fulop, T. (Eds). (1987). Health manpower out of balance: Conflicts and prospects. *Highlights of the XXth CIOMS Conference.* Acapulco, Mexico, September 7-12, 1986, Geneva: Council for International Organizations of Medical Sciences.

Baumgart, A.J. (1988). The nursing workforce in Canada. In *Canadian nursing faces the future: Development and change.* Toronto: CV Mosby Co.

Benner, P., and Wrubel, J. (1989). *The primacy of caring.* Menlo Park, CA: Addison-Wesley.

Campbell, M. (1987). Productivity in Canadian nursing: Administering cuts. In Coburn, D'Arcy, Torrance, and New (Eds.). *Health and Canadian society: Sociological perspectives.* Markham: Fitzhenry & Whiteside.

Canadian Hospital Association. (1988). *Issues concerning the Canadian health care system and its funding.* Submission to the Standing Committee on National Health and Welfare. Ottawa: The Association.

Donnelly, L.J., Yarbrough, D., and Jaffe, H. (1989). Organizational management systems decrease nursing costs. *Nursing Management. 20*(7), 20-21.

Edmonstone, J. (1988). Managing the manpower resource: The nature of the problem. *Hospital and Health Services Review.* February, 13-15.

Fagin, C.M. and Maraldo, P.J. (1988). Feminism and the nursing shortage: Do women have a choice? *Nursing and Health Care.* September, 365-367.

Feature article. (1988). The changing nature of the Canadian labour market: The increased importance of education and training. *Quarterly Labour Market and Productivity Review.* Winter, 17-23.

Flood, S.D., and Diers, D. (1988). Nurse staffing, patient outcomes and cost. *Nursing Management. 19*(5), 34-43.

Government of the United States. *Secretary's Commission on Nursing: Final report. 1*(12).

Hall, T. (1988). Guidelines for health workforce planners. *World Health Forum. 9*, 409-413.

Hayes, E. and Fritsch, R. (1988). An untapped resource: The political potential of nurses. *Nursing Administration Quarterly. 13*(1), 33-39.

Hospital Council of Metro Toronto. (1988). *Report of the HCMT Nursing Manpower Task Force.* Toronto: The Council.

Hsu, D. and Lovelace, J.C. (1986). Health human resources in Canada. *Educ Med Salud. 20*(3), 351-362.

Johnson, M. (1989). Perspectives on costing nursing. *Nursing Administration Quarterly. 14*(1), 65-71.

Meltz, N., and Marzetti, J. (1988). *The shortage of Registered Nurses: An analysis in a labour market context.* Toronto: Registered Nurses Association of Ontario.

Newfoundland Ministry of Health. (1988). *Report of the advisory committee on nursing workforce.* St. John's, Newfoundland: The Ministry.

Ontario Ministry of Health. (1988). *Report on nursing manpower.* Toronto: Advisory Committee on Nursing Manpower.

Ontario Ministry of Health. (1990). *Report of the hospital nurse staffing survey: October, 1989.* Toronto: Health Manpower Planning Section/Policy Development and Co-ordination Division.

Ontario Nurses Association. (1988). *The nursing shortage in Ontario.* Toronto: The Goldfarb Corporation.

Ordre des Infirmières et Infirmiers du Québec. (1989). *Hypertension: An urgent need for action.* Montreal: The Ordre.

Registered Nurses Association of Ontario. (1988). *Sorry no care available due to nursing shortage: A prescription for reforming human resource planning in health care.* Toronto: The Association.

Rosenfeld, P. (1988b). *Nursing student census with policy implications.* New York: National League for Nursing.

Ryten, E. (1988). *Women as deliverers of health care.* Unpublished speech presented at the Canadian Association of University Schools of Nursing Annual Conference, University of Windsor, Windsor, Ontario: June, 1988.

Statistics Canada. (1990). *Registered Nurses management date, 1988.* Health Ottawa: Health Manpower Statistics Section, Health Division.

Terris, M. (1988). Editorial. Meeting the needs for health workers: Proportions, prerogatives, and priorities. *Journal of Public Health Policy. 9*(3), 309-318.

Wandelt, M. et al. (1986). Why nurses leave nursing and what can be done about it. *American Journal of Nursing. 81*(1), 72-77.

CHAPTER FIFTEEN

Political Awareness in Nursing

JANET ROSS KERR

T he health-care system in Canada is in a period of turmoil and change. More sophisticated methods of care and treatment, high technology solutions to previously unsolvable problems, and increased specialization in the health professions have led to a need to prioritize health care needs and identify the nature and types of health-care services that are and can be made available. The fact that physicians have continued as sole gatekeepers to the health care system has led to continuing problems for those who wish to access the system and to higher costs than would be incurred if nonphysician health-care professionals were used more effectively in the system. Nurses in particular have historically been underused; a number of Canadian studies have demonstrated the effectiveness of services provided by nurses (Chambers et al, 1977; Hoey, McCallum, and LePage, 1982; Ramsay, McKenzie, and Fish, 1982).

The health-care system is "big business" in Canada, with over 7% of the gross national product expended for health. Health expenditures are almost entirely in the public sector due to the institution of national health insurance operated by provincial governments under public auspices. Any public sector activity that involves substantial expenditure of tax dollars engenders considerable debate and competition among providers of the service. This is obvious in the health-care arena, where the various health-care professions are competing to increase their "shares of the pie". Physicians have been extraordinarily successful in increasing income earned for services provided. Physicians' incomes have increased considerably over the past half century; the substantial increase attests to the success physicians have had in the political arena. Nurses have been demonstrating increasing ability to argue for proportionately increased compensation for their services, and significant gains have been made in the past 15 years.

The fact that nursing is and has been a sex-segregated profession since its inception in Canada must be considered a factor; historically, members of the profession have had to struggle to gain appropriate recognition, respect, and

161

remuneration for their services. Increased awareness of the need for respect for women's rights has occurred gradually over the past century; important gains have been made in the last three decades. The parallel rise of the women's movement and unionism in nursing, which began in the 1960s, has been a significant development; members of the profession are challenging the status quo assiduously and assertively, striving for higher salaries and better working conditions. Nurses have gradually gained understanding of the processes and skills involved in influencing others, becoming more powerful and exercising more control over the factors that influence their working lives.

Although nurses are commonly thought of as political novices, Krampitz has noted that "the actions of nurses as political activists are well recorded in the profession's proud history" (1985, p. 10). In the early history of Canadian nursing, Jeanne Mance could be considered a political activist *par excellence;* she raised and sustained support for her hospital in New France. Florence Nightingale's accomplishments are legendary and "as a reformer and political activist she helped establish a new attitude toward the contributions of nurses in a military environment and the education of women" (Dock [cited in Krampitz, 1985, p. 10]). Florence Nightingale's skill as a researcher was impressive, and her interpretation of the statistics she collected led to important and lasting changes in the organization of the health services of the British Army (Nightingale, 1858). She demonstrated the positive effect of good nursing on the health of soldiers; the principles apply to health care in general. There were important offshoots from her work, for the British populace and indeed for people in other nations, as the Nightingale model of nursing was carried far afield.

Nurses in Canada argued strongly for legislation encompassing registration for nurses between 1900 and 1922. This campaign was successful and every province had such legislation by the end of 1922. More recent political activity by nurses was also successful; the lobbying carried out by the Canadian Nurses Association (CNA) for the Canada Health Act of 1984 resulted in an amendment to the Act, after it was tabled in Parliament, that permitted federal funding for "health practitioners." This legislation also made it possible for a provincial health plan to fund services of nurses or other health professionals on a direct reimbursement basis, as the services of physicians and dental surgeons have been financed since the Medical Care Act of 1968 was passed.

THE IMPORTANCE OF DEVELOPING POLITICAL AWARENESS

The term "politics" is used in many different ways. For some it may stimulate images of smoke-filled rooms, devious dealings, or power in the hands of the few. For others, the images have a different and more generic meaning. Maraldo noted, "politics is ubiquitous, occurring wherever two or more people are gathered" (1985, p. 81). Among the earliest philosophers who attempted to understand the relationship between politics and people were Aristotle and Plato. Plato discusses the development of political leaders in some depth in *The Republic,* describing the qualities of leadership. Maraldo observes that "Aristotle's and Plato's views of politics as intrinsic to human behaviour have not been heeded over the years" (1985, p. 82); neither the ways that political leaders worked nor the factors that shape political behaviour have been studied to any extent.

Politics can be viewed as the art of influencing another person. In practical terms, political activity means influencing for the purpose of allocating scarce resources wisely. In the health-care arena, there is new realization of the limits to growth; this effectively means limits placed on care and treatment. Expensive high-technology health care for all is not affordable in the Western World. Developed countries are learning what developing countries have known all along—that decisions must be made about health-care priorities and that not everyone can be the recipient of expensive care and treatment. Certain individuals will be responsible for deciding how to allocate the available resources, and others will have a political responsibility to provide the reasons for allocating resources in one way or another. As Maraldo noted, "the truth of the matter, however, is that everyone who functions in society must be, to some extent, a political animal. There is no escaping politics in any arena" (1985, p. 81).

Many nurses recognize the importance of developing political skills, realizing that these skills are as important on the nursing unit as they are in other spheres of social activity where decisions must be made. As Mason and McCarthy have stated, "the ultimate reason for enhancing the nurse's political power, be it in the workplace, community, government, or professional organization, is to improve the health care that patients receive" (1985, p. 38). There tends to be more awareness of the importance of political factors in development of policy than in working or other everyday situations. Where service is the primary activity, the politics of patient care may be less visible, but they are important and essential to good care.

Nurses as a group have sometimes expressed a sense of powerlessness. Many nurses believe that nursing is low in the health care hierarchy in terms of power and influence. They adopt an indifferent approach believing that expressing their views will not be useful because they will not be heard. A nurse who adopts such an approach will not be able to argue for the needs of patients. These negative attitudes are based on false assumptions about society; fortunately, more nurses are taking an active interest in political activity and in learning how to influence others. Although professional groups have always recognized the value of lobbying for their objectives and using political skills to advantage, they are now attempting to educate members about developing political skills to enhance success in achieving objectives.

Nurses may have to work harder to establish a power base than other professional groups. There is strength in numbers, and that is an important factor where nursing is concerned since nurses are the largest group of health care professionals. However, nurses also have the lowest level of academic preparation among the health care professions. Less than 15% of practising nurses in Canada hold a baccalaureate degree; in other health professions the baccalaureate degree is usually a minimum requirement for entry to practice. In addition, nurses have struggled with an image of subservience, partially because nursing has been sex stereotyped; currently, over 98% of the profession is female. The medical profession has historically been male dominated, but this is rapidly changing. In some medical schools over 50% of the students are women; however, the sex-stereotype in nursing is deeper, and men are not yet entering the nursing profession in increased proportions, certainly not at the rate women are entering traditionally male-dominated professions. Nevertheless, many changes are occurring because of the women's movement, increased recognition of human rights, and increased recognition of nursing's contribution to health care. These factors bode well for nursing in the future, as arguments for restructuring and policy change within the health-care system are likely to engender considerable interest and support.

CREATING POLITICAL AWARENESS: UNDERSTANDING THE FUNDAMENTALS OF POLITICAL ACTION

Understanding the formal and informal systems in the workplace is a basic necessity for effective political action. By learning how to work within these systems, nurses can greatly enhance the achievement of goals. Although it is essential to understand both, comprehending the informal structures and processes of an organization is a more difficult and less defined task than understanding formal ones. It is also important to develop good communication skills, working with other individuals in the organization to understand their roles and functions and the problems they face. Those wielding a substantial amount of power within the organization should be identified as key individuals, and the development of working relationships with these individuals is essential. Informal groups within the organization may also be important; although they may be organized around activities unrelated to the organization, they may represent networks for exchange of information. Social contacts may also be helpful in developing useful channels for political activity.

Talbott and Nichols have referred to some principles for political action:

- Look at the big picture
- Do your homework
- Nothing ventured, nothing gained
- Get a toe in the door
- Quid pro quo
- Walk a mile in another's moccasins
- Strike while the iron is hot
- Read between the lines
- Half a loaf is better than none
- Rome was not built in a day (1985, p. 157)

There is no substitute for understanding how an organization works or for thinking carefully about the nature and scope of problems and how they might be solved. Nurses must be risk takers; no gains will be made if no action is taken. Timing is essential to achieving a goal. It is necessary to understand all sides of the question to develop a more effective strategy, and negotiation and compromise may be required in the final solution. A high degree of communication skill is required.

INTERPERSONAL COMMUNICATION

The most important factor in the political arena is effective interpersonal communication. Because politics involves influencing others, effective relationships are essential. It is impossible to influence others if interpersonal activity is not positive and dynamic. Vance has stated that "the exercise of influence involves three components, on the 'three C's' of political influence: communication, collectivity, and collegiality" (1985, p. 166). In this hierarchy, communication is the fundamental skill, as all of the other techniques build upon it. By communicating effectively with others, goals may be enhanced and attained. Joining with others in pursuit of common goals is a very effective technique and is also recognized as an effective political strategy. It is important to work cooperatively and willingly with others in pursuing collective goals. Approaching others with respect and understanding increases the possibility that political activity will be enhanced and more effective.

Although communication is important on every level, its fundamental tenets remain the same. Attention has recently focused on networking, or joining together with others to achieve common goals. This can be accomplished in many ways. Networking is an important political strategy and it may be personally rewarding. Nursing curricula usually contain courses designed to enhance interpersonal effectiveness. Since nurses are in close contact with patients preparation in the area of interpersonal communication is essential to good patient care. This is a subject that is emphasized in baccalaureate degree programs.

DEVELOPING A BASE OF SUPPORT

Consolidating and developing a base of support often takes considerable skill and time. Credibility must be established, and the desire to work in the best interests of the organization and its goals must be demonstrated. In professional associations, this means working with the public interest in mind. It is important to demonstrate that clear and careful thought preceded the development of a campaign for support on a particular issue, as this may be a powerful factor in convincing potential supporters that the issue is worth supporting. As noted previously, there is power in numbers and nursing has a great advantage in this respect. The campaign is more likely to be successful if many people are committed to working toward the goal. Nurses have not always recognized the strength in their numbers; they have only mobilized group support on the most crucial of issues. Many nursing organizations now recognize this potent force and are using its power to advantage.

THE PURSUIT OF GOALS

Effective political strategy is a labour intensive process that requires clear thinking and ability to recognize factors, processes, and actors of importance. Identifying an issue or problem is important. Its relative importance must be measured against that of other issues or problems that arise. Action cannot be taken in all matters, so it is important to *choose one's issues*. There is always some cost in pursuing a problem to its conclusion in the political sphere, and the possible negative consequences must be weighed against the positive benefits that may result. Bowman has referred to this process as "risk analysis. The risks and payoff of challenging an issue must be measured in the goal-setting process. What will be lost if the issue is not pursued? What will be gained if it is? How certain are those losses or gains? What are the short term and long term effects of either choice?" (1985, p. 202)

Analysis of the issue is essential to determine if pursuing the issue is reasonable. Once a decision has been made to pursue a particular goal, additional analysis would determine what other resources might be helpful.

The CNA has historically taken courses of action designed to result in maximum benefit to the health of consumers. Recently, the CNA addressed the Standing Committee on Social Affairs, Science and Technology of the Senate of Canada, urging them to "refocus the system to a better balance of illness care, rehabilitation, prevention and promotion" and discussing "effective utilization of all our resources" (CNA Connection, 1990, pp. 8, 10). The action the CNA took relative to offensive advertising before the opening of Expo '86 in Vancouver is an example of an organization identifying a specific issue, then moving quickly toward effecting some change. A federal government advertisement encouraging attendance portrayed a group of nurses in chorus-girl-type roles expressing the merits of attending the Exposition. The CNA, on receiving complaints from nurses as the first ads were aired, moved swiftly through the Executive to protest the negative portrayal of nursing. The protest was made at the federal Cabinet level, the matter was dealt with quickly, and the controversial ads were swiftly withdrawn.

Since every issue is different, a plan of action must be outlined for the benefit of all those involved in the campaign. It is important to determine how the issue will be dealt with, both formally and informally. It is possible that many avenues will need to be taken to argue for or against the issue of concern; these need to be outlined at the outset and revised as necessary. One person alone may be able to make the case for change, or it may be necessary for an entire organization to be involved. This was the case in 1982 and 1983, when the Alberta Association of Registered Nurses lobbied for the passage of a new Registered Nurses Act incorporating mandatory registration. The entire membership was asked to send letters of support to members of the Legislative Assembly and the Cabinet. Ultimately, the fact that so many of the members got involved influenced the legislators to decide to move forward with the Act. Bowman (1985) refers to professional strategies, public strategies, and procedural strategies as categories that can be considered when plans are being developed to pursue an issue. A contemporary issue, of interest across the country, is legalization of nurse midwifery in Canada. The Ontario government has made a commitment to legalizing midwifery and has received a report from the task force it established to study the issues involved and to identify how legalization can be accomplished. Currently, other provinces are studying the issues. Clearly, this is an area where nurses must identify the issues and analyze the situation very carefully. It is essential that the legal and professional framework for the practice of nurse midwifery be outlined very carefully to ensure that the public interest is protected.

BENEFITS OF ENHANCED POLITICAL AWARENESS

Much can be gained by developing a cadre of politically skilled professional nurses. There are important public implications for such activity, both at the individual and collective levels. The priorities of patient care are subject to politics at all levels. Nurses spend more time with patients than any other group of health care professionals and are in an excellent position to understand, appreciate, and argue for consideration of their needs and concerns. Nurses must also continue to work for optimum conditions in the workplace, for the quality of nursing care will be enhanced through the pursuit of such a goal. In collective bargaining, political skills are essential tools that will make the process a smoother and more satisfying one for all concerned. Collaboration between nurses and other health-care professionals can do much to enhance effectiveness of nurses. Most important of all, understanding the political process and recognizing political strategy is an important first step in developing the ability to influence others. Zander has summed this up: "Application of the tools of organizational analysis, . . . together with change strategies, including heightened political sensitivity, will enable nurses to create magnetic environments" (1985, p. 239).

REFERENCES

Bowman, R.A. (1985). Recognizing, developing, and pursuing an issue. In D.J. Mason and S.W. Talbott (Eds.). *Political action handbook for nurses* (196-204). Menlo Park, CA: Addison-Wesley.

CNA Connection (1990). *The Canadian Nurse.* 86(4), 8-10.

Chambers, L.W., Bruce-Lockhart, P., Balck, D.P., Sampson, E., and Burke, M. (1977). A controlled trial of the impact of the family practice nurse on volume, quality, and cost of rural health service. *Medical Care.* 15(12), 971-981.

Hoey, J.R., McCallum, H.P., and Lepage, E.M. (1982). Expanding the nurse's role to improve preventive service in an outpatient clinic. *Canadian Medical Association Journal.* 127(1), 27-28.

Krampitz, S.D. (1985). Historical overview of nursing and politics. In D.J. Mason and S.W. Talbott (Eds.). *Political action handbook for nurses* (10-22). Menlo Park, CA: Addison-Wesley.

Maraldo, P. (1985). Politics is people. In D.J. Mason and S.W. Talbott (Eds.). *Political action handbook for nurses* (81-87). Menlo Park, CA: Addison-Wesley.

Mason, D.J., and McCarthy, A.M. (1985). Politics of patient care. In D.J. Mason and S.W. Talbott (Eds.). *Political action handbook for nurses* (38-52). Menlo Park, CA: Addison-Wesley.

Nightingale, F. (1858). *Notes on matters affecting the health, efficiency and hospital administration of the British Army.* London: Harrison & Sons.

Ramsay, J.A., McKenzie, J.K., and Fish, D.G. (1982). Physicians and nurse practitioners: Do they provide equivalent health care? *American Journal of Public Health.* 72(1), 55-57.

Talbott, S.W. and Nichols, B. (1985). Political analysis: structures and processes. In D.J. Mason & S.W. Talbott (Eds.). *Political action handbook for nurses* (143-164). Menlo Park, CA: Addison-Wesley.

Vance, C.N. (1985). Political influence: building effective interpersonal skills. In D.J. Mason & S.W. Talbott (Eds.). *Political action handbook for nurses* (165-180). Menlo Park, CA: Addison-Wesley.

Zander, K. (1985) Analyzing your workplace. In D.J. Mason and S.W. Talbott (Eds.). *Political action handbook for nurses* (227-239). Menlo Park, CA: Addison-Wesley.

CHAPTER SIXTEEN

The Organization and Financing of Health Care: Issues for Nursing

JANET ROSS KERR

Although nursing is an essential health-care service and represents one of the largest professional components of the health-care budget, health-care financing is an area that is generally not well understood by nurses, undoubtedly because the health-care system is based on national health insurance and the majority of nurses are employees of health-care agencies. The study of health care financing, including nursing, is generally left to the health-care economists and health administrators; few curricula in schools of nursing have attempted to address the subject. It is important for nurses to understand how the system operates, because health-care financing can affect the nature of nursing services and the form in which they can be offered. Comprehending the complex system of arrangements for federal-provincial cost-sharing and knowing how nursing is affected is necessary if nurses are to exercise their professional responsibility to interact with and influence government, the public, and other health professions in changing and restructuring the system.

THE HEALTH-CARE SYSTEM: A COMPARATIVE VIEW

Health-care financing in Canada shifted from the private to the public sector in 1957. Since the 1867 passage of the British North America Act at the time of Confederation, responsibility for health has rested with the provinces. The Constitution Act of 1982 confirmed the historical division of power between the federal government and the provinces. Canada's arrangement is different from those of other nations that have centralized health-care systems where power in this area is vested in the federal government; the United Kingdom (UK), France, and Sweden are examples of countries where responsibility for health care is federal. Wallace observed that:

... the fathers of Confederation clearly thought they were assigning the provinces the less important and inexpensive functions of government, among which education, hospitals, charities and municipal institutions were then reasonably numbered. They could scarcely have foreseen the way in which time would reverse their expectations, so that the costliness of the responsibilities laid upon the provinces subsequently increased to the point where it was financially impossible to defray them. Within thirty years after Confederation social and economic conditions had so altered that public opinion was demanding government action on matters held in 1867 to be primarily personal and of no concern to the state. (1980, p. 27).

The constitutional division of authority and responsibility for health care also provides a partial explanation for the length of time it took to implement a national health insurance program. Because jurisdictional responsibility for health lies within the provinces, achievement of uniform changes to benefit the entire country is a difficult task. Over the years, federal interest in this sector of provincial responsibility has been high because of the value placed on health and its importance in the life of society. The greater taxing power of the federal government in a publicly funded system has led the provinces to look to the government for help in financing the operation of the system.

The United States has not yet implemented a national health insurance program. Although the division of powers in relation to health are similar in that country, members of one party are not required to vote as one unit. This means that lobbying by interested individuals and groups must be directed toward individual members of the House of Representatives and the Senate and those who hold the reins of party power. The achievement of unanimity on a matter of national importance, such as a national plan of health insurance, is clearly difficult. These considerations, along with a value system centred on individual responsibility and free enterprise, explain why a form of Medicare in the United States has only been achieved for those over 65.

In contrast, the United Kingdom introduced its National Health Service in 1948, providing a model for Commonwealth countries in particular, for health-care financing. There are differences, however, in the national health plan adopted by the United Kingdom and that introduced in Canada; Canada did not restructure the existing health care system, it provided a framework for financing the system. A two-tiered system of health-care financing has emerged in the United Kingdom, the inefficiencies and shortcomings of the public system giving rise to a private one for those of means, complete with third-party insurance.

THE DEVELOPMENT OF A NATIONAL SYSTEM OF MEDICARE: A HISTORICAL PERSPECTIVE

Although universal health insurance was first suggested in 1919, it took a long time to implement the system. Taylor has commented that:

... our heritage of the Elizabethan Poor Law had placed responsibility for the sick poor on local government, but many cities, towns and especially rural municipalities in Canada quickly reached the point of near or actual bankruptcy from the combination of declining revenues and expanding relief payments for food, clothing and shelter. Medical care, except in the direst emergency conditions, was a luxury that only few individuals or municipalities could afford. (1987, p. 4)

The continuing financial problems facing hospitals during the early decades of this century have been reported and analyzed. The struggle was greater in the voluntary hospital, but even among municipally owned institutions, the reluctance to provide adequate funds made financing a continuing nightmare for trustees and administrators (Agnew, 1974, p. 149). During the Depression years, a difficult situation deteriorated further, until many hospitals had large deficits. In the 1930s, only 40% to 50% of the patient days in public hospitals had been paid in full by 55% to 60% of the patients. Eight percent of patients paid for part of their hospital stay, and one third of those remaining were unable to pay their bill (Agnew, 1974, p. 151). In addition, "a fairly sharp division was usually drawn between paying and non-paying patients" (Agnew, 1974, p. 153), and extra payment for private accommodation was used to help offset deficits.

Physicians and professional nurses also experienced difficulties during this period. Since the proportion of patients unable to pay medical bills had escalated, many physicians had a difficult time financially. In Saskatchewan in "December, 1932, the provincial government through its Relief Commission made a grant of $75.00 a month to doctors in 56 rural municipalities in Relief Area 'A' and $50.00 a month in 103 rural municipalities in Relief Area 'B' " (Canadian Medical Assoc J, 1953, p. 671). Nurses also felt the pinch, and graduate nurses' positions in private duty nursing evaporated with the stock market crash. In Calgary,

> General Hospital graduates, unable to get positions as special nurses, were glad to be taken on the hospital staff at a monthly salary of thirty dollars in addition to room and board. Many supervisory nurses, already on staff, had to take substantial salary reductions as the city slashed and re-slashed its hospital budget in a desperate attempt to make ends meet with the reduced taxes it was able to collect (Agnew, 1974, p. 150).

Beginning in the 1920s, a number of small prepayment plans for hospital care were developed to provide for hospital services. Care was prepaid for all who were covered by the plan. There were many factors that encouraged thinking about using a system of insurance on a wider scale, to create a health-care system that would eliminate hardships for persons who became ill, allow hospitals to operate on other than a hand-to-mouth basis, and ensure that health-care professionals received remuneration for services provided. The Depression years, followed by World War II, were difficult for Canadians; in 1937, Canada ranked seventeenth in infant mortality among developed nations (Advisory Committee on Health Insurance, 1943, [as cited in Taylor, 1987, p. 5]). The views of politicians are also an important factor, particularly those of the party leader. Taylor commented on this reference to the views of Prime Minister MacKenzie King:

> In the initiation of any government proposal, the personal objectives and commitment of the party leader who occupies the position of premier or prime minister at a particular juncture in history is frequently the most crucial factor in the decision to act

or not to act . . . . But that his views were a powerful force in incorporating health insurance and other social security measures in the post-war reconstruction proposals is clear (1980, pp. 9-10).

EARLY HEALTH INSURANCE PLANS

Commercial insurance companies began developing plans in the 1930s, and publicly sponsored arrangements for prepaid care were initiated by municipalities, hospitals, and regional groups soon after. The first known voluntary plan for prepayment of hospital care in Canada was the Edmonton Group Hospitalization Plan, introduced by the four major general hospitals in that city in 1934. Initial efforts to establish a Blue Cross Plan in the province had met resistance from some institutions, so the four hospitals started their own small plan. This plan was extended to the rest of Alberta, as a Blue Cross Plan under the sponsorship of the provincial hospital association, in 1948. Hospitalization benefits were provided, when needed, as prepaid fees for those who enroled (Agnew, 1974). The first province-wide Blue Cross Plan in Canada, initiated in 1937, was created by an act of the Manitoba legislature and administered by the Manitoba Hospital Service Association. Similar plans were implemented in other provinces: Ontario (1941); Quebec (1942); and Nova Scotia, New Brunswick, Prince Edward Island, and British Columbia (1943) (Agnew, 1974). Many of the plans eventually added medical and surgical services to the plans they offered. Because different authorities were responsible for developing and maintaining plans offered in different provinces, there was considerable variation in benefits from plan to plan. The basis of most of the plans was payment of premiums by enrolees. A substantial segment of the Canadian population was not covered by any form of prepaid insurance due to ineligibility for plans limited to specific groups of people, or inability to pay the required premium.

THE ROAD TO NATIONAL HEALTH INSURANCE

Federal involvement in financing health care had been discussed since the Honourable W.L. MacKenzie King developed a proposal for health insurance in the platform of the Liberal Party in the election of 1919. In 1929, the standing committee on industrial and international relations of the House of Commons recommended that "with regard to sickness insurance, the Department of Pensions and National Health be requested to initiate a comprehensive survey of the field of public health, with special reference to a national health programme" (Agnew, 1974, p. 165). The report was approved in 1933, and in 1935 the Employment and Social Insurance Act provided for collecting information and advising groups in provinces planning a health insurance program. Because the Act was declared unconstitutional in the courts, it was not until 1942 that a federal committee on health insurance was established to study the issues. At that time, the Canadian Medical Association (CMA) endorsed the principles of health insurance, and although it preferred fee for service as the method of payment for medical services, it indicated that a capitation, or salary method of remunerating physicians, might also be needed.

A Federal-Provincial Conference, convened in 1945, "proposed universal health insurance with federal-provincial cost sharing" and "produced a model draft health-care bill for the provinces" (Vayda, Evans & Mindell, 1979, p. 218). Due to concern that such legislation would interfere with provincial autonomy and that Canada's health-care facilities and personnel were inadequate to carry the load that health insurance would bring, the legislation failed. The province of Saskatchewan, under the leadership of Premier TC Douglas, instituted a hospital insurance plan financed entirely by the province in 1947. Payment of premiums was basic to this plan and that every Saskatchewan resident was required to register for it. The plan was subsidized from general revenues, and in 1948 the provincial sales tax was increased to help finance it. In 1949, a similar program was established in British Columbia.

FEDERAL LEGISLATION FOR HEALTH-CARE FINANCING

The federal government's first foray into health-care financing occurred in 1948 through the National Health Grants Program. Assistance was provided for hospital construction, public and mental health programs, and professional training to "gear up" for hospital insurance. At a federal-provincial conference held in 1955, an agreement was reached about the details of a national hospital insurance plan; the details were translated into legislation in the form of the Hospital Insurance and Diagnostic Services Act of 1957. Provinces were given the option to join, with the federal government paying "an amount equal to 25% of its own per capita cost (less authorized charges) plus 25% of the national per capita cost multiplied by the number of insured persons" (Brown, 1980, p. 523). Programs were required to provide universal coverage, portability of coverage from province to province, comprehensive coverage for all in-hospital care in general and certain other designated care, and public, nonprofit administration of plans was mandatory (LeClair, 1975). Administration of the plans was to be carried out by the individual provinces. All provinces had accepted the terms of the Act by 1961 (Vayda, Evans, and Mindell, 1979).

The next struggle was to include medical care in the insurance plan. The Royal Commission on Health Services of 1964 emphasized the importance of including medical care in the national health insurance program. Again, it took many years to reach agreement on the nature and form of the legislation, and the federal program was preceded by a program developed by the province of Saskatchewan (1962). Physicians opposed the plan, and the 1962 Saskatchewan physicians' strike will be long remembered. In 1968, the federal Medical Care Act was established to provide reimbursement to provincial health insurance plans for physicians' services. This was provided under the same cost-sharing conditions as assistance for hospital services. Again there was opposition from physicians, who feared interference in the physician/patient relationship and the possibility that the fee-for-service system of remuneration for physicians would be abandoned as the plan was implemented. New

Brunswick joined in 1971 and the provisions of the Act then applied to all provinces.

In the 1970s, the federal government became concerned about escalation in health-care costs. With the unlimited 50%-50% cost-sharing arrangement, there was no ceiling on the federal share of health-care cost reimbursement. As the federal deficit increased, the government passed the Fiscal Arrangements and Established Programs Financing Act of 1977. The provisions of this Act, which applied to hospital care, medical care, and postsecondary education, provided for block funding, reducing the federal contribution to health care to 25%, with additional federal contributions based on increases in the Gross National Product. Federal income taxes were decreased to allow the provinces to increase their taxes to offset the federal reductions. For the first time, funding was provided for extended and home care. In 1982 the federal government changed the method of calculating contributions through amendments to the health-care financing legislation of 1977. This meant that provinces received considerably less federal assistance than before. The federal government responded to provincial objections to decreased funding by reiterating that decreases in federal income taxes had left room for increases in provincial income taxes.

The federal government was disturbed by the increasing incidence of extra billing and user fees in the provinces and by the premiums charged in some provinces. Brown (1980) commented that, after the passage of the 1977 act, "user charges have increased both in prevalence and in amount. Extra-billing by physicians over medicare payments increased markedly during 1978 and 1979" (Brown, 1980, p. 522). Provinces had considerably more flexibility under the new rules for federal financing of health care; they could reduce their contributions to health care; to compensate, user charges for various health-care services could be instituted. If provinces decreased funding of medical services relative to the fee schedule, the practice of extra billing was stimulated. According to Brown :

> Allowing doctors to extra bill not only thwarts the social objective of free care, but also promotes a system under which total costs (public costs plus private costs) will be higher than they would be either under completely socialized medicine or under an unregulated market. Hospital user charges, on the other hand, suggest fewer problems because their development would not suggest a corresponding loss in government control over prices (1980, p. 531).

THE CANADA HEALTH ACT OF 1984

Another confrontation between the federal government and the provinces occurred over the way health-care dollars would be expended. The federal government took the position that extra billing and user fees were eroding Medicare and further that if those practices were allowed to continue and increase, a two-tiered system of health care would develop, one for the rich and another for the poor. There was a great deal of variation among the provinces in the extent to which user charges and extra billing were practiced. Quebec had the most restrictive rules on extra billing: physicians who extra billed were required to opt out of the plan and bill patients directly; and their patients could not seek reimbursement from the plan. A number of provinces, including New Brunswick, Nova Scotia, Prince Edward Island, Saskatchewan, and Alberta, allowed physicians to extra bill and remain in the plan. At the time the legislation was introduced, two provinces, British Columbia and Newfoundland, had user charges for daily stays in acute care beds, but Alberta had an admission charge. Chronic care patients were assessed a daily charge in some provinces: British Columbia, Alberta, Manitoba, Ontario, Quebec, and New Brunswick. Only British Columbia, Alberta, and Ontario charged premiums (Health and Welfare Canada, 1983).

The Canadian Nurses Association (CNA) was strong in its representation to the federal government on its position on provisions in the proposed legislation. This position was very clear: Health care should be provided regardless of ability to pay; extra billing by physicians and user charges by health-care agencies should be disallowed; health professionals should be remunerated on a salary-based system; and insured services should be extended to include community, home care, and long-term care services provided by qualified health-care professionals. The CNA also supported the idea of financial incentives for provinces that developed lower cost health programs and services by using the skills of health-care professionals more effectively:

> We need to develop alternatives to our high cost, high tech health care service and begin to better utilize other lower cost, highly qualified health care providers and services. The Canadian Nurses Association advocates the further development of multidisciplinary community health centres and home care services, with nurses and other health care providers serving as a first contact with the system for assessment, referral and care (Canadian Nurses Association, 1983b, p. 4).

The representation was vigorous and prolonged. Members of the CNA Board lobbied members of Parliament on several occasions in 1983 and 1984; reports and analyses of individual meetings were published in bulletins and distributed to the membership. The CNA Executive and Staff held meetings with key members of the federal government and members of the civil service with responsibility for developing legislation. In a letter to members of the CNA Board, President Helen Glass urged:

> It's our responsibility to make nursing's voice heard—and soon. Even if you have already contacted your minister of health, we strongly urge you to keep up your lobbying efforts. Health department officials, leaders of opposition parties, opposition health critics and members of standing committees on health will be key targets (1983, p. 1).

The Honourable Monique Bégin, Minister of National Health and Welfare, faced the difficult task of drafting the legislation and shepherding it through committees of the Cabinet and House of Commons before it could be introduced as a bill to be debated and acted on in the House of Commons. In her opening statement to the Conference of Federal and Provincial Ministers of Health in Ottawa in 1982, Bégin said:

The health care system for which we are responsible is one of Canada's greatest social policy achievements. For Canadians it is the single most popular government program. To outside observers it is a source of great envy . . . However, our commitment to health care insurance in Canada is no easy task. Our governments are faced with major problems of financing in tough economic times . . . It is clear that Canadians today are particularly concerned about the future of their health care system (pp. 1-4).

The pressure to implement more directly and carefully the five basic principles identified, but loosely applied, in initial health insurance legislation was intense:

The militancy of our associations of health care professionals has never been higher. Recurrent confrontations with doctors, nurses and hospital workers have troubled our system. Concern about the phenomena of opting out and extra-billing, about user fees and about the level of services provided in our hospitals is high. Most Canadians still have adequate access to health care, but many of them fear for the future of the health care system. I feel certain that most of us here today share these concerns. It is clearly up to us to act and act quickly (Bégin, 1982, p. 4).

The new legislation was passed in early April of 1984, amid intense publicity. Bégin became a high-profile figure, and the media focused on confrontations with health ministers in a number of provinces where elected officials considered the Canada Health Act an intrusion into the constitutional rights of the provinces to make laws on health care. The CNA lobbied hard and was rewarded for its efforts with legislation that effectively ended the practices of extra billing and user fees and with the introduction of a statement that provided federal funding for services provided by "health practitioners." The door was thus open for the inclusion in provincial health plans of specialized nursing services that were eligible for reimbursement for the first time. The wording of the legislation could also apply to services provided by other health-care professionals. Clearly, this was the first step in achieving the stated CNA goals: better utilization of nurses and more cost-effective health care. The CMA lobbied equally hard against the legislation, but due to the popularity of national health insurance, the unpopularity of extra billing and user fees, and strong political support for the legislation, it was unable to prevent the passage of the Canada Health Act.

PRIVATIZATION OF HEALTH CARE

The shortage of resources and general retrenchment in the health-care system has led to discussions of privatization of health care. Although the percentage of the gross domestic product that Canadians spend on health care is substantially lower than that of the United States, where public health-care financing arrangements exist only for the old, allowing the private sector to operate hospitals at a profit, assuming that they could do it at lower cost, continues to be a subject of debate. At least two provinces are conducting experiments; governments have provided funding to private organizations to run hospitals at Port Hawksbury in Ontario and at Athabasca and Olds in Alberta. These ventures violate, at least in spirit, one of the five basic principles on which health legislation in Canada was founded (i.e., public administration); however, there are many supporters of privatization. It is likely that considerable opposition would surface if anything more than token experiments in privatization were undertaken. Despite its problems, most Canadians value their health-care system, and most would not want the system of public financing to be significantly altered.

PHILOSOPHICAL BASIS OF HEALTH-CARE FINANCING LEGISLATION

The combined effect of the provisions of the 1948 federal legislation supporting hospital construction and the 1957 hospital insurance legislation set in motion a system in which "hospital-based patterns of practice were solidified" (Vayda, Evans, and Mindell, 1979). The number of hospital beds increased at twice the rate of population increase between 1961 and 1971, and occupancy rates were around 80% (Vayda, Evans, and Mindell, 1979). Since outpatient care was not eligible for federal cost sharing, there was an incentive for choosing more costly hospital care over outpatient or home care. Community health services were also excluded from federal financing, and provinces were required to finance the operation of such services without assistance.

Another point that pertains to nursing and the services offered by other health-care professionals is that medical care insurance legislation provided federal cost sharing only for physicians' services. This was intended to constrain the development of the health-care system by providing a financial incentive for the proliferation of physicians' services. Since these were the most costly services of all of the health professions, this decision had serious financial repercussions for the health-care system.

> One of the factors associated with the volume of health care services is the number of physicians. More surgeons are correlated with higher discretionary surgical rates and more physicians with an increased volume of medical services, just as more hospital beds are associated with greater bed use (Vayda, Evans, and Mindell, 1979, p. 220).

Projections of the number of physicians needed to care for the Canadian population were grossly overestimated in the 1960s. The Royal Commission on Health Services Report of 1964 assumed there would be a shortage, based on its projections of 1961 patterns of health services utilization, and failed to account for "changes in technology and productivity" (Vayda et al, 1979, p. 219). The ratio of physicians to population rose dramatically, from 1:850 in 1961 to 1:600 by 1973 (Health Manpower Directorate, 1974). The financial repercussions for a physician-driven system in which the skills of other health professionals are not effectively employed are obvious. As Vayda, Evans, and Mindell have pointed out, "There are dangers inherent in health care decisions that are predicated solely on financial considerations; yet now governments not only know what the total health care bill is, they also have to pay that bill and deal with the issues (1979, p. 230)."

RESTRUCTURING THE HEALTH-CARE SYSTEM

There is ample evidence that "although universal hospital insurance in Canada provided payment to hospitals, it did not mandate an organizational framework to deal with problems of efficiency or duplication of services" (Vayda, Evans, and Mindell, 1979, p. 219). When insurance for medical services was imposed on the existing structure of services, the environment for care was clearly the hospital. When new funding arrangements were implemented in the legislation of 1977, the federal government attempted to stop open-ended health-care financing by placing limits on the total amount of federal spending. Thus, it sought to constrain its own financial commitment in a more predictable way, one that would encourage the provinces to manage their programs more efficiently (by removing any illusion that they are spending 50 cent dollars). The cost has been a loss in control over health insurance programs. In retrospect, it appears that the federal government was somewhat naïve in believing that the nature of Medicare and hospital insurance would make them immune to provincial government encroachment (Brown, 1980, p. 525). It is not difficult to understand why restructuring and reorganizing the health-care system were not included in federal legislative proposals for funding provincial health-care services. The need for change had been recognized for some time; the Royal Commission on Health Services had recommended reorganization of health services in its 1964 report. Political considerations, the fierce determination of the provinces to retain their constitutional prerogatives for health care, and the opposition of powerful lobbyists were all factors that deterred needed change in the system. In the process of enacting new health-care financing legislation, such as the Canada Health Act of 1984, the federal government encountered difficulty implementing even a few changes; they were opposed by physicians and provinces. The need for a new approach to health care remains and is more urgent than ever, but the agenda for legislative change is a political minefield. The federal government that next addresses the need for action in health care will require a firm commitment to change and the courage of its convictions in the presence of strong political opposition.

Canada cannot afford to continue to support a system in which the physician is the "gatekeeper" to virtually all health-care services. Research indicates that using the services of nurses and other health professionals is a sensible and cost-effective approach to the provision of health-care services. A study of nurses providing primary care in rural Newfoundland demonstrated that acute-care hospital services decreased by 5%, while in the control area there was a 39% increase in a physician-based acute care-centred system. The cost of providing services to the population in the experimental group was substantially lower (24%) than in the control group (Chambers et al, 1977, p. 971). An investigation in Manitoba demonstrated that physicians were less successful than nurse practitioners in helping comparable groups of patients to control blood pressure and lose weight (Ramsay, McKenzie, and Fish, 1982). In a controlled trial, nurses were more successful in vaccinating elderly patients for influenza than were physicians, nurses immunizing 35% of clients as opposed to 2% by physicians (Hoey, McCallum, & LePage, 1982, p. 27). Canada is one of few countries in the world where nurse midwives are not legally permitted to practise. Several provinces are currently studying this matter; it is likely that provincial health-care legislation will be amended in the future to permit the practice of mid-wifery by nurses.

Because physicians are likely to oppose efforts to include services provided by nurses among those eligible for direct reimbursement in provincial health-care plans, it will not be easy to change existing provisions. Nevertheless, nurses provide a viable and cost-effective alternative in delivering certain kinds of health-care services, particularly those involving health promotion, health main-tenance, and counselling activities in relation to health. Health-care legislation has imposed financial constraints on nursing roles and functions since nursing's inception in Canada. This has meant that change that might have occurred naturally in a free and open health-care environment has not occurred. To date, powerful physician-dominated lobby groups have successfully prevented major departures from access to physician health care. Nurses are learning to develop effective lobby groups of their own to help politicians understand the contribu-tion nurses can make to the health-care system. Governments will be forced to consider alternatives, despite the pressure to resist change, as the limits of the public purse and the demand for improved health are recognized.

REFERENCES

Agnew, G.H. (1974). *Canadian hospitals, 1920 to 1970: A dramatic half century.* Toronto: University of Toronto Press.

Bégin, M. (1982, May 26). Opening statement to Conference of Federal and Provincial Ministers of Health. Ottawa.

Brown, M.C. (1980). The implications of estab-lished program finance for national health in-surance. *Canadian Public Policy. 3,* 521-532.

Canadian Medical Assoc J (1953). *28,* 671.

Canadian Nurses Association. (1983a). The Can-ada Health Act: Where we stand. *Canada Health Act Bulletin IV.* Ottawa: The Association.

Canadian Nurses Association. (1983b). The Can-ada Health Act: Where we stand. *Canada Health Act Bulletin.* Ottawa: The Association.

Chambers, L.W. et al. (1977). A controlled trial of the impact of the family practice nurse on vol-ume, quality, and cost of rural health services. *Medical Care. 15*(12), 971-981.

Glass, H.P. (1983). Letter to Dr. Janet Kerr. *Pro-vincial health insurance plans: extra-billing/user charges by hospitals.* Ottawa: Health and Wel-fare Canada.

Health Manpower Directorate. (1974). *Canada health manpower inventory.* Ottawa: National Health and Welfare.

Hoey, J.R., McCallum, H.P., and Lepage, E.M. (1982). Expanding the nurse's role to improve preventive service in an outpatient clinic. *Ca-nad Med Assoc J 127.* (1), 27-28.

LeClair, M. (1975). The Canadian health care sys-tem. In S. Andrepoulos (Ed.). *National health insurance: Can we learn from Canada?* New York: John Wiley & Sons.

Ramsay, J.A., McKenzie, J.K., and Fish, D.G. (1982). Physicians and nurse practitioners: do they provide equivalent health care? *American Journal of Public Health. 72*(1), 55-57.

Taylor, M.G. (1987). Health insurance and Cana-dian public policy: The seven decisions that created the Canadian health insurance system and their outcomes. Montreal: McGill-Queen's University Press.

Vayda, E., Evans, R., and Mindell, W.R. (1979). Universal health insurance in Canada: History, problems, trends. *Journal of Community Health* 4(3), 217-231.

Wallace, E. (1980). The origin of the social wel-fare state in Canada, 1867-1900. In C.A. Meil-icke and J.L. Storch (Ed.). *Perspectives on Cana-dian health and social services policy: History and emerging trends.* Ann Arbor: Health Administra-tion Press.

CHAPTER SEVENTEEN

Organizing for Nursing Care: Primary Nursing, Traditional Approaches, or Both?

JANNETTA MacPHAIL

I dentifying the ideal system for organizing staff to provide nursing care has been a goal of nursing service administrators for at least four decades. Because many factors influence assignment patterns and are influenced by them, identifying the ideal system offers a challenge to administrators and their staffs. The administrator is concerned not only about quality and costs of care, but also about the satisfaction of nursing staff and the patients in their care. A historical review of the major organizational modes used since the early part of the century will provide a perspective of this continual challenge to administrators and nursing staffs.

TYPES OF ORGANIZATIONAL MODES

Four major types of organizational modes can be identified from the literature and from accounts of nurses who have practised since the 1920s: functional assignment, case assignment, team nursing, and primary nursing. In the functional assignment mode, care is assigned by task or function; the primary considerations are efficiency and cost control. This mode was based on the work of Frederick W. Taylor, the "father of scientific management," whose work dates back to the 1880s. Taylor's management concepts were first published in 1912. Drucker (1974, p. 24) states, "Taylor was the first man in the known history of mankind who did not take work for granted, but looked at it and studied it." Unfortunately, his focus was on the individual task, not the end product, which he always took for granted (Drucker, 1974). The premises of his theory of management were that managers "are capable of thinking and planning" and that "the worker is viewed as needing close supervision and constant direction"

179

(Beswetherick, 1979, p. 18). The functional system is task-oriented and highly structured, with the charge nurse reigning supreme and operating according to rules, regulations, and procedures. Tasks are assigned according to ability and status of the various members of the nursing staff. Until World War II, and in some cases after that time, the staff consisted primarily of nursing students and assignments were made according to their level of progression in the hospital diploma programs. Decisions were made by the charge nurse, to whom all reported and by whom all were evaluated. The charge nurse was the main communicator; thus the charge nurse, usually a registered nurse on days and a senior nursing student on nights, was in a position of power and control. This arrangement could be beneficial or detrimental to patients and staff, depending on the charge nurse's knowledge base, decision-making ability, and leadership style. The advantages of this system were efficiency and cost. For example, if the ratio of staff to patients was low, it conserved both costs and energy. This system is still used, particularly when staff is limited. Three disadvantages of functional assignment are fragmented care, with the patients attended by many persons who have responsibility for only one or two aspects of care; limited responsibility on the part of the nursing staff; and limited opportunity to learn about decision making.

The case assignment method developed as a result of recognizing the limitations of the functional method and the need to provide continuity of care, a concern that was intensified by the change from 12- to 8-hour duty, which occurred in the 1940s and 1950s. Case assignment was recognized by nurse educators as a way to teach total patient care, which became increasingly important after the middle of the century. It was also the method of assignment used by private-duty nurses, who were prevalent in the first half of the century, practising in the home and hospital. In the case assignment system, the nursing student or staff nurse was assigned a certain number of patients for their total hospital stay; a new patient was assigned when one was discharged. Assignment was based on the severity of illness of patients and the abilities of the staff. Although it was still task-oriented to a great extent, the staff member provided total care. The charge nurse remained the central control figure and the main communicator in this system; she made all assignments and all staff reported to her. The advantages of this system are greater continuity of care and a more consistent view of the patient as a whole. The disadvantages are that control is still centralized and opportunities to learn decision making and responsibility are still limited, but greater than under the functional system. Another disadvantage of the system is that experienced staff with well-rounded abilities are needed to make this system work, and in many situations staff are not well qualified. Changes began to occur in the way nurses viewed nursing. They began to identify nursing problems and realize that nursing was not merely a collection of tasks to be performed.

The third method of organizing nursing staff is team nursing. This mode was influenced by the shortage of nurses that occurred during World War II, when many nurses enlisted and the number of nursing students left to staff hospitals was not sufficient. As a result, assistants to nurses, usually nursing aides and nursing assistants or practical nurses, were recruited. The focus of this mode is the work group or team, which includes professional nurses and nonprofessional staff. The team is headed by a team leader, to whom members of the team report; the team leader reports to the head nurse. The team leader is responsible for care of all patients assigned to the team and for supervision of team members. The number of teams on a nursing unit depends on the size of the unit and the number of staff available. An advantage of this mode, as noted by proponents of team nursing (Lambertsen, 1953; Brooks, 1961; Williams, 1964; Kron, 1966; Douglass & Bevis, 1970) is that it improves patient care by using the diverse skills of team members to their full potential under the guidance of registered nurses. Other advantages are the ability to function with more nonprofessionals on the unit; increase in opportunities for learning clinical decision making, particularly by the team leader; opportunities for the team leader to learn leadership and group skills; availability of a nurse's judgement to a larger number of patients; decreased number of staff needed to care for a patient; increased opportunity to share responsibility; and better use of individual abilities. Disadvantages of the team system are fragmentation of care; a tendency not to assume responsibility and place blame on others; possible resistance by nonprofessionals to direction by the team leader, which affects new graduates particularly; an insufficient number of team leaders who have the skills needed to direct staff; time devoted to supervising others instead of assessing care; and a tendency for staff dissatisfaction.

To address the disadvantages of team nursing and increase nurse and patient satisfaction, a fourth system of organization was created in the 1970s—primary nursing. Hegyvary (1982, p. 3) perceives primary nursing as "both a philosophy of care and an organizational design . . . not simply a way of assigning nurses to patients, but rather a view of nursing as professional, patient-centred practice." Although there are many definitions of primary nursing in the literature and in practice, it means essentially:

> . . . the nursing care of a specific patient is under the continuous guidance of one nurse from admission through discharge. One nurse on each shift provides total care for the same group of patients day after day. Round-the-clock care is coordinated for each patient by the nurse designated as the primary nurse for that patient (Hegyvary, 1982, p. 3).

Four essential elements of the primary nursing model, identified by Hegyvary (1982), are accountability to the patient, family, professional colleagues, and the institution; autonomy, in that the nurse decides and acts on decisions about nursing care; coordination of care, which promotes consistency and harmony; and comprehensive care, or total patient care.

Several authors indicate that in this mode of organization the registered nurse's activities are changed from manager of care and organizer of personnel to care manager/care implementer (Ciske, 1974; Manthey, 1973; Manthey and Kramer, 1970; Manthey et al, 1971; Marram, 1976; Williams, 1975). Munson and Clinton (1979) also note that in this system, nurse's aide activities focus on equipment and supplies, not on direct contact with patients as in team nursing.

Many advantages of primary nursing are explicated in the literature. They include continuity of care, increased accountability, total patient care, highly individualized care, opportunity to implement the total process of nursing care and evaluate outcomes, increased autonomy and authority, and comprehensive and better coordinated care. Some have also claimed that there is improved quality of care (Felton, 1975; Leonard, 1975; Marram, 1976); faster recuperation for certain patients, with a corresponding decrease in length of stay and in cost per patient day (Brown, 1976; Henderson, 1964; Jones, 1975); increased patient satisfaction (Isler, 1976; Nenner, Curtis, and Eckhoff, 1977); increased nurse satisfaction, with a corresponding reduction in turnover rates and absenteeism (Ciske, 1974; Isler, 1976; Knecht, Schlegel, and Marram, 1973); and reduction in errors of commission and omission (Cicatiello, Zimmer, and Christman, 1977) and improved relationships between nurses and physicians (Cicatiello, Zimmer, and Christman, 1977). Although not identified as disadvantages, some of the problems in implementing primary nursing are the difficulty encountered by some hospitals in maintaining a well-qualified staff because of turnover or poor staffing and the changes required in hospital philosophy, structure, and process to accommodate the increased independence and autonomy of the primary nurses that is essential to the system.

Munson and Clinton (1979) note that it is impossible to generalize the findings of various reports on primary nursing because of conflict among them, even though the findings may have been valid and relevant for the particular setting in which the research or activities occurred. In addition, finding a clear and definitive model of one of the modes in operation consistently is unlikely in most settings. Rather, there may be many combinations of the four modes, which makes comparison difficult and generalization of findings unreliable.

COMPARISON OF ORGANIZATIONAL MODES

The four major organizational modes can be compared from many perspectives, although Munson and Clinton (1979) could not define them clearly enough to make rigorous comparisons. Key factors identified by Giovanetti (1986) are major focus, accountability, lines of authority, communication patterns, basis of personnel assignment, and patient-care planning.

The major focus in functional assignment is on tasks, in case assignment on patients and tasks, in team nursing on patients and managing team members, and in primary nursing on patients.

Accountability is to the charge nurse in functional assignment and case assignment, to the team leader in team nursing, and to the patient in primary nursing. Lines of authority are as follows: The charge nurse is in complete control in functional and case assignment; the team leader reports to the charge nurse in team nursing; and the primary nurse is in charge in primary nursing. Communication is channelled through the charge nurse in functional and case assignment and through the team leader to the charge nurse in team nursing; in primary nursing all communication is directed to the primary nurse. Personnel assignment in both functional and case methods is based on task and level of preparation of the worker. In team nursing, personnel are assigned according to the severity of illness of patients and the level of preparation of team members. In primary nursing, personnel are assigned according to patient needs. Involvement in patient-care planning and opportunity for making clinical decisions is centred in the charge nurse in functional and case assignment, in the team leader in team nursing, and in the primary nurse in primary nursing.

ASSESSMENT OF PRIMARY NURSING

Primary nursing, introduced in the early 1970s, has become very popular; it has been advocated as the solution to many problems in organizing nursing staff to give quality care and increasing job satisfaction for nurses and patient satisfaction with care (Corpuz, 1977; Dawson and Wilson, 1983). A great many articles, reports, and books have been devoted to primary nursing, particularly in the nursing literature. Young, Giovannetti, Lewison, and Thoms (1981) identified over 150 articles and reports on primary nursing, nearly 80% of which were not research based and overwhelmingly supported the concept. Giovannetti (1986) stated that "the remaining research literature, consisting of evaluative studies and explorative non-comparative studies, also concluded with strong support for primary nursing, but in-depth analysis revealed serious methodological flaws leading the reviewers to question the largely positive results (1986, p. 127)."

Giovannetti (1986) conducted a comprehensive survey of published and unpublished works pertaining to primary nursing between 1970 and 1984 to identify studies that met these criteria: "(1) be an evaluative study citing primary nursing as an independent variable; (2) be systematic; (3) include information on the methods and procedures for data collection; (4) present findings; and (5) be written and translated into English." Only 29 studies met these criteria. Several hundred articles, reports, and comparative studies were excluded. A major problem indentified was the lack of an operational definition of primary nursing or of any other organizational mode studied. Although many investigators recognized this as a limitation and few stated that their findings could be generalized, Giovannetti identified this lack as a major problem. Moreover, although investigators did not suggest that their results could be generalized, many nurses in practice and administrators tend to do so.

Giovannetti completed an insightful critique of these 29 studies and identified basic problems with the research. She states:

> Although many methodological issues could be identified in research on primary nursing, instrumentation and research design are of particular importance. With few exceptions, the instruments used to measure the criterion variables lacked adequate reliability and validity assessment In many instances, no reference was made to the psychometric attributes of the measurements. In the instances where standardized measures were used, many investigators appeared to assume that previously established reliability and validity estimates were transferable. The inadequacies associated with instrumentation, coupled with the problems related to the operationalization of the independent variable, are not inconsequential. If it is not known what is going to

be measured, and it is not known whether the instruments really measure what is to be measured, intelligible interpretations of the research effort cannot be made (1986, pp. 130-131).

Several other investigators have noted similar inadequacies with the research of primary nursing. Steckel (1980, p. 77) states, "There are insufficient data to demonstrate that primary nursing improves the quality of care, increases nurse or patient satisfaction, or is cost-effective." Prescott and Sorenson (1978) identified flaws in research design or outcome measures used in evaluations of primary nursing. Betz (1981) criticizes the wide variations in time periods used to compute turnover rates and failure to fully discuss the sample and methods used in reporting studies. Betz (1981, p. 151) also states: "The claims in other reports are made so easily and with such cavalier disregard for the methods by which their data are measured, obtained, and computed that one does not know how seriously to read, let alone generalize, the findings."

Despite the lack of research evidence available to determine whether implementation of primary nursing will achieve all that it is purported to accomplish, the use of primary nursing has become widespread. There are few negative reports in the literature, and those that are negative are not research based (Hylands and Sarnavka, 1984; Chavigny and Lewis, 1984). Because research evidence could not be found in the literature to support a change from team nursing to primary nursing in a Veteran's Administration (VA) Hospital, Chavigny and Lewis (1984) conducted an epidemiologic cohort design study to determine if there were differences between the two organizational modes in patient health status, quality of care, costs, and job satisfaction. The only significant difference noted was in direct care time: Team nursing resulted in more contact with patients than did primary nursing, which supports the findings of Giovannetti (1981) and Shukla (1982a). The survey of nurses' job satisfaction indicated that the nursing staff perceived primary nursing as difficult and stressful; 73% of the registered nurses in the VA Hospital thought this method should not be used. Their decision to reject primary nursing was based on opinion, not on comparative data.

In an effort to find a sound scientific base for choosing primary nursing over team nursing, Shukla (1982a, 1982b, 1983) has begun extensive research to evaluate the cost benefits of the two modes. He controlled for the quality and quantity of registered nurses in the models compared, which had not been done in other studies. Shukla (1982b) concluded that individual factors, such as nurse competency, affect quality to a greater extent than the structural differences between team nursing and primary nursing. He states: "While the structure for primary nursing is generally found to be a better system for organizing care, its effectiveness is obviously not uniform for all types of nurses, patients, hospitals, and even nursing units within a single hospital" (Shukla, 1982b, p. 12). He identified two critical factors that should influence the choice of organizational mode: the efficiency of nursing support systems and the patients' degree of independence. The support systems include transportation systems, distribution systems, communication systems, and the unit management system. The more efficient these systems, the less time nurses have to spend on indirect care activities and the more time they can devote to direct patient care. This has been the basis for development and improvement of support systems in hospitals over the past four decades. In spite of the improvement, one of the chief complaints of nurses today, as indicated by surveys and study commissions in both Canada and the United States, is their frustration from having insufficient time to devote to direct care because of the time required for indirect care, due to inefficiencies or inadequacies in the nursing support systems. Efficient support systems for nurses, such as the Friesen Concept, were designed 20 years ago. Some aspects of the concept existed 40 years ago when the designer, Gordon Friesen, was a visionary and creative hospital administrator. Why then, do efficient support systems still not exist in all hospitals today? Cost is often cited as the reason. Would the cost not be offset by the reduction in costs of rapid nurse turnover, inefficiencies, dissatisfaction, and nurses leaving nursing?

Another factor to consider in selecting an organizational mode is nurses' satisfaction with the various delivery models. Betz and O'Connell (1987) conducted two studies to compare job satisfaction of nurses on primary nursing units and nurses on team nursing units. Like other investigators, they found no significant difference in satisfaction from the quantitative data collected (Alexander et al, 1981). Some researchers have speculated abstractly about their results, whereas others have searched further. Betz and O'Connell (1987) collected qualitative data as well and found that nurses practising in the primary nursing mode were enthusiastic about their increased autonomy, increased involvement in and responsibility for direct patient care, better nurse/patient ratios, and increased knowledge about their patients with which to make clinical decisions; dissatisfaction arose from insufficient help with low-level tasks and too much paperwork. The investigators suggest that the move to primary nursing contributes to two types of role strain: role overload and role ambiguity. Role overload is the result of increased responsibility and inadequate support systems for managing the increased responsibilities. Role ambiguity is a part of any role change, but it may be increased in cases where preparation for the change was insufficient, as has been reported by registered nurse students who had been involved in changes from team nursing to primary nursing in their work settings. Other research indicates that increased autonomy may not lead to increased satisfaction unless autonomy leads to control over pace and conditions of work (Karasek, 1976). The primary nurses who are responsible for low-level tasks that should be performed by efficient support systems do not have this control.

Nursing costs have been increasingly important to hospitals since the advent of diagnostic-related group (DRG)-based payment systems in the early 1980s, and are even more critical with the shortage of nurses. Studies of the costs of primary nursing have indicated inconsistencies; some results show primary nursing to be less costly than team nursing (Marram, 1976); some show it to be more costly (Shukla, 1982a); and some show no significant difference in costs (Chavigny and Lewis, 1984). Wolf, Lesic, and Leak (1986) compared direct nursing care costs within specific DRGs between a primary nursing unit and a team nursing unit in a 474-bed acute care community hospital. They endeavoured to control for patient acuity but found the acuity level 28% higher on the primary nursing unit. This may have been due to a factor that was previously unknown to the investigators; physicians were asking the Admitting Department to admit their more acute patients to the primary nursing unit because of the reputation it had earned for providing quality care. The findings showed that "the primary nursing unit's average daily cost per patient per DRG was $1.30 less than on the team unit" (Wolf, Lesic, and Leak, 1986, p. 11). Researchers speculate that the primary nursing structure may allow nurses to care for patients more efficiently, but they emphasize the need for additional study of the cost of primary nursing within the prospective payment system.

Glandon, Colbert, and Thomasma (1989) completed an extensive analysis of the cost of nursing in 392 nursing units in 62 US hospitals that are part of the Medicus Systems Corporation. They compared nursing costs among four organizational modes: primary nursing, team nursing, modular nursing, and total patient care. Modular nursing is defined as "a geographic assignment of patients that encourages continuity of care by organizing a group of staff to work with a group of patients. The fixed geographic areas typically represent 10-12 patients per module" (Hegyvary, 1977, p. 189). It is a pragmatic mixture of team and primary nursing. Total patient care is "a case method for organizing nursing care where nurses are responsible for total care of a patient but only for the hours that specific nurse is present" (Hegyvary, 1977). The findings of the Glandon et al. analysis revealed that small, primary nursing units using a high mix of registered nurses are the most costly per patient day, even after controlling for the patients' average nursing care needs. The investigators note that the nursing care delivery model used, size of nursing unit, and extent to which registered nurses are used all have significant effects on nursing costs. Moreover, they note that the delivery model and use of registered nurses are closely interrelated; they plan to use regression analysis to separate possible confounding influences. Glandon et al. emphasize that their analysis did not account for differences in quality of care and that decisions cannot be made solely on the basis of cost; the quality of care must also be considered. They conclude that "in the current health care environment, there does not appear to be one best method to deliver care in a cost effective manner" and that "more research is needed on the relationship of nursing care delivery to the quality of care and nurse satisfaction" (Glandon, Colbert, and Thomasma, 1989, p. 33).

THE FUTURE IN ORGANIZATIONAL MODES

Identifying the best methods of organizing nursing staff to provide quality nursing care remains a challenge to all nurses. Because nurses are dissatisfied with existing systems, they seek other approaches and are strongly influenced by the proponents of new methods presented in the literature and at conferences. They are asked to demonstrate cost-benefit ratios before implementing a new approach, although this is not usually required of other health professionals with new ideas. In many settings, primary nursing, or the application of some attributes of primary nursing, seems to be achieving the desired outcomes in nurse satisfaction and patient satisfaction. Although it is not unusual that they wish to share their ideas with others, it is important that scientifically sound research be completed to evaluate the outcomes of different approaches before they are used so that false claims are not made. It is important that the research be designed with expert consultation to ensure its quality and ability to be replicated. Replication of research is needed to provide nursing with a sound base for proceeding in new directions.

Giovannetti (1986) suggests that, if primary nursing is partially a philosophy of care, (as many have suggested [Hegyvary, 1982; Marram, Schlegel & Bevis, 1974]), we should proceed with philosophic rather than with scientific enquiry. Attempts at measuring the effects of primary nursing using scientific means alone are premature; without philosophic enquiry the measurements will continue to be ineffective. Philosophic questions are not answerable through the scientific method. Whatever the source of these problems, they must be addressed; to ignore them is to assure that research in nursing does not provide a sound basis for making decisions about improving nursing care (Giovanetti, 1986).

The major factors that influence assignment patterns are patient characteristics, nursing resources, and organizational support. The method of combining these factors will influence the degree of continuity and integration and the type of coordination that can be achieved. The challenge for the future is to consider all factors and support sound scientific and philosophical enquiry that will help identify the best methods for organizing nursing care. There may not be a "best" mode, due to the variability of patient characteristics and nursing resources that exist in the various health-care settings that constitute Canada's health-care system. The goal in all settings is to promote, facilitate, and support professional nursing practice.

REFERENCES

Alexander, C.S., Weisman, C.S., and Chase, G.A. (1981). Evaluating primary nursing in hospitals: examination of effects on nursing staff. *Medical Care* 19(1). 80-89.

Beswetherick, M. (1979). A review of past and current systems of nursing care delivery. *The Canadian Nurse* 75(5). 18-22.

Betz, M. (1981). Some hidden costs of primary nursing. *Nursing and Health Care* 2(3). 150-154.

Betz, M., Dickerson, T., and Wyatt, D. (1980). Cost and quality: primary and team nursing compared. *Nursing and Health Care* 1(3). 150-157.

Betz, M. and O'Connell, L. (1987). Primary nursing: panacea or problem? *Nursing and Health Care* 8(8). 457-460.

Brooks, E.A. (1961). Team nursing: 1961. *AJN* 61(4). 87-91.

Brown, B. (1976). The autonomous nurse and primary nursing. *Nurs Admin Q* 1(3). 31-36.

Carlsen, R.H. and Malley, J.D. (1981). Job satisfaction of staff registered nurses in primary and team nursing delivery systems. *Research in Nursing and Health* 4(2). 251-260.

Chavigny, K. and Lewis, A. (1984). Team or primary nursing care? *Nursing Outlook* 32(6). 322-327.

Cicatiello, J., Zimmer, M.J., and Christman, L. (1977). NAQ forum: Primary nursing—why not? *Nurs Admin Q* 1(2). 82-83.

Ciske, K.L. (1974). Primary nursing: an organization that promoted professional practice. *J Nurs Admin* 4(1). 28-31.

Corpuz, T. (1977). Primary nursing meets needs, expectations of patient and staff. *Hospitals* 51(6). 95-96.

Dawson, P. and Wilson, N.M. (1983). What nurses say about primary nursing. *The Canadian Nurse* 79(6). 37-41.

Douglass, L.M. and Bevis, E.D. (1970). Team leadership in action: principles and application to staff nursing situations. St. Louis: The C.V. Mosby Co.

Drucker, P.F. (1974). Management: Tasks, responsibilities, practices. New York: Harper & Row.

Felton, G. (1975). Increasing the quality of nursing care by introducing the concept of primary nursing: A model project. *Nursing Research* 24(1). 27-32.

Giovannetti, P. (1981). A comparative study of team and primary nursing care. Unpublished doctoral dissertation. Baltimore; Johns Hopkins University.

Giovannetti, P. (1986). Evaluation of primary nursing. In H. Werley, J. Fitzpatrick, and R.L. Taunton (Ed.). *Annual review of nursing research*, vol. 4. New York: Springer.

Glandon, G.L., Colbert, K.W., and Thomasma, M. (1989). Nursing delivery models and RN mix: Cost implications. *Nursing Management* 20(5). 30-33.

Hegyvary, S.T. (1977). Foundations of primary nursing. *Nurs Clin North Am* 12(6). 187-196.

Hegyvary, S.T. (1982). The change to primary nursing: a cross-cultural view of professional nursing practice. St. Louis: The CV Mosby Co.

Henderson, C. (1982). Can nursing care hasten recovery? *AJN* 64(6). 80-83.

Hylands, J. and Sarnavka, A. (1984). Primary nursing or total patient care? *Dimensions* 61(9). 36-38.

Isler, C. (1976). Rx for a sick hospital: Primary nursing care. *RN* 39(2). 60-65.

Jones, K. (1975). Study documents effect of primary nursing on renal transplant patients. *Hospitals* 49(24). 85-89.

Karasek, R. (1976). Impact of work environment on life outside the job. Unpublished doctoral dissertation. Boston: Massachusetts Institute of Technology.

Knecht, A.A., Schlegel, M.W., and Marram, G.D. (1973). *Innovation on four tower west (3 parts)*. *AJN* 73(5). 808-816.

Kron, T. (1966). *Nursing team leadership*. ed 2. Philadelphia: WB Saunders.

Lambertsen, E.C. (1953). *Nursing team organization and functioning*. New York: Bureau of Publications, Teachers College, Columbia University.

Leonard, M. (1975). Health issues and primary nursing in nephrology care. *Nurs Clin North Am* 10(3). 413-420.

Manthey, C., et al. (1971). Primary nursing: A return to the concept of "my nurse" and "my patient." *Nursing Forum* 9(1). 65-83.

Manthey, M., and Kramer, M. (1970). A dialogue on primary nursing. *Nursing Forum* 9(4). 356-379.

Manthey, M. (1973). Primary nursing is alive and well in the hospital. *AJN* 73(1). 83-87.

Marram, G.D. (1976). The comparative costs of operating a team and primary nursing unit. *J Nurs Admin* 3(4). 21-24.

Marram, G.D., Schlegel, M.W., and Bevis, E.O. (1974). *Primary nursing: A model for individualized care*. St. Louis: The CV Mosby Co.

Munson, F.C. and Clinton, J. (1979). Defining nursing assignment patterns. *Nursing Research* 28(4). 243-249.

Nenner, V.C., Curtis, E.M., and Eckhoff, C.M. (1977). Primary nursing. *Supervisor Nurse* 8(5). 14-16.

Prescott, P. and Sorenson, J. Cost effectiveness analysis: An approach to evaluating nursing programs. *Nurs Admin Q* 3(3). 17-39, 1978.

Roberts, L.E. (1980). Primary nursing. *The Canadian Nurse* 76(12). 20-28.

Shukla, R.K. (1982a). Nursing care structures and productivity. *Hospital and Health Services Administration* 27(16). 45-58.

Shukla, R.K. (1982b). Primary or team nursing? Two conditions determine the choice. *J Nurs Admin* 12(11). 12-15.

Shukla, R.K. (1983). All-RN model of nursing care delivery: A cost-benefit evaluation. *Inquiry* 20. 173-184.

Steckel, S. (1980). Introduction to the study of primary nursing. *Nursing Dimensions* 7(4). 74-77.

Taylor, F.W. (1912). *The principles of scientific management*. New York: Harper & Row.

Williams, L.B. (1975). Evaluation of nursing care: A primary nursing project. 1. Report of the controlled study. *Supervisor Nurse* 6(1). 32, 35-36, 38-39.

Williams, M.A. (1964). The myths and assumptions about team nursing. *Nursing Forum* 3(4). 61-73.

Wolf, G.A., Lesic, L.K., and Leak, A.G. (1986). Primary nursing: the impact on nursing costs within DRGs. *J Nurs Admin* 16(3). 9-11.

Young, G.P., et al. (1981). Factors affecting nurse staffing in acute care hospitals: A review and critique of the literature (DHEW Publication No. HRP 0501801). Hyattsville, Md: Department of Health, Education and Welfare.

CHAPTER EIGHTEEN

The Practising Nurse and the Law

JANET ROSS KERR

L egal challenges to nursing activities were once rare and posed little concern in the nursing profession. There were also very few legal disputes involving medical practice in Canada. This situation is changing: The consumer movement, extension of the nurse's scope of practice, substantial improvements in salaries and working conditions for nurses, and a greater propensity for the public to seek damages for professional negligence are all reasons for nurses to be aware of their responsibilities and the law to avoid civil suits and criminal prosecutions.

This chapter provides an overview of the law and the principal areas of nurses' involvement in the legal system. This information is not intended as a comprehensive treatment of the subject, but rather as a cursory review to emphasize areas of concern, stimulate thinking about issues, and encourage additional research. The potential benefit of understanding rights and responsibilities under the law, particularly as they apply to the health-care field, is easily identified by considering the close and continuing contact between patients and nurses in health care environments.

AN OVERVIEW OF THE LAW

Canadian law was derived from Roman civil law and English common law. Roman law can be traced to the Twelve Tables of Rome (450 BC), codification by Justinian in 533 and development of the French Code Napoleon in 1804 (Merryman, 1969). English common law has a more recent history, beginning with the Norman conquest of 1066 (Plucknett, 1956). In Canada, English common law forms the basis of the legal system in all provinces except Quebec, where Roman civil law is the dominant influence. As Dais has noted,"The two traditions have much in common in terms of the legal rules they apply. Their essential difference has to do with culturally conditioned attitudes about the relation of law to society, the limits on government in using law, and the techniques and intellectual skills for making, interpreting, applying and teaching law (1973, p. 4)."

Although the law refers to a clearly defined system of rules for the conduct of human activities and of sanctions for violations of these, in practical terms, law is viewed in a wider sense and is

> . . . seen as a set of institutions, roles and procedures for ordering human behaviour in accordance with social values and political policies . . . It punishes deviance from basic social values (criminal law). It remedies harms intentionally, negligently or accidentally inflicted (tort law). It allocates scarce resources for satisfying human needs (property law). It facilitates productive enterprises (contract law), (Dais, 1973, p. 4).

In our society, the institutions that serve the law are the legislatures of the provinces and the Parliament of Canada by making laws, the police by enforcing laws, the courts by judging disputes, and the prisons by applying punishments.

Case law and enacted law are the two primary types of law. In the Roman tradition, enacted law assumes greater importance because less freedom for judicial interpretation is allowed; under English common law, case law is dominant. The judicial process begins when there is disagreement about whether a matter meets the terms of the law. The courts are often thought of as the principal component of the judicial system; however, other important components include the legal profession and the adversary system. It should be noted that jury trials are rare in civil cases in Canada because of the expense involved; jury trials are primarily conducted in criminal cases.

It is helpful to know the distinctions between the various types of law. Civil law, also known as private law, comprises contract law, tort law, and property law, while public law is concerned with constitutional law, administrative law, and criminal law. International law may be considered private law when it involves concerns between individuals and public law when the dispute is between governments (Dais, 1973).

RESPONSIBILITIES OF NURSES UNDER THE LAW

In a professional field such as nursing, legal obligations to the public are particularly important. Nurses are entrusted with the lives and health of other people in the course of their duties. The law has become increasingly complex, and it is important for all citizens to be aware of the laws that govern everyday life. On a daily basis, nurses are at great risk of violating the legal rights of others. The public expects nurses to practise competently and to do no harm to those who entrust nurses with their care. The concept of the provision of a reasonable standard of nursing care has been upheld by the courts in case law. Thus it is essential that nurses be knowledgeable and competent in the practice of their profession as well as being aware of and respecting the legal rights of their clients.

RIGHTS OF THE HEALTH-CARE CONSUMER

As Storch (1982) has pointed out, rights are the product of social history and are based in law and ethics. As a self-governing profession, nursing has a statutory responsibility to protect the public interest in the provision of nursing care. Reference to a code of ethics or ethical principles is embodied in provincial statutes regulating nursing. A code of ethics, one of the hallmarks of a profession, represents an attempt to document appropriate conduct.

It was not until after World War II that codes of ethics were developed and accepted by nursing organizations. Unacceptable experimentation on and treatment of human beings during the war led to the Declaration of Universal Human Rights in 1948, and the health-care professions focused attention on the necessity of protecting individuals from unscrupulous, unethical, and incompetent practitioners. The Code of Ethics developed by the International Council of Nurses in 1953 was used as the standard for measuring nurses' conduct for many years. The Canadian Nurses Association's (CNA) first code of ethics, developed in 1980, was replaced by a new version in 1985. Today, most provincial nursing associations use the CNA code as the standard.

As important as codes of ethics may be, they are not a panacea for all the ethical concerns and dilemmas that arise in nursing practice. The difficulties have been noted by Storch (1982): "Health-care codes . . . may not include all issues of concern to the patient . . . codes are limited because moral dilemmas in health care and nursing do not generally occur as a series of problems and questions to be solved with a series of guidelines. Rather, moral dilemmas are situations of complexity and conflict." Codes of ethics may be used by the profession to promote function in an ethical manner, but nurses must also have good intent, understand the facts of a situation that has ethical dimensions, exhibit clear thinking in weighing a situation, and be able to use basic ethical principles or theory in decision making (Storch, 1982).

Consumer rights in health care, as proclaimed by the Consumers' Association of Canada, include

> . . . the right to be informed, the right to be respected as the individual with the major responsibility for his own health care, the right to participate in decision-making affecting his health, and the right to equal access to health care regardless of the individual's economic status, sex, age, creed, ethnic origin and location (Storch, 1982, p. 186)

The right of individuals to be informed about their health care is protected legally in tort law, which requires informed consent, and ethically in the principles of autonomy, veracity, and beneficence. The client's right to read and examine health-care records about personal health is an issue that arises in discussing this right. The right to be respected as an individual is a more elusive concern, raising ethical questions of autonomy, nonmaleficence, and beneficence. From a legal standpoint, the patient's right to confidentiality and to refuse treatment is associated with the right to be respected and the right to privacy. The right to participate in decision making about health care is primarily ethical in nature; the principles of autonomy and responsibility are at issue. The right to equal access to health care finds its origin in the principle of justice (Storch, 1982).

CONSENT TO NURSING CARE

A fundamental human right, historically respected in law, is the right to be free from interference. The tort of battery involves intentional touching of another person; there need not be any injury for the charge to be upheld by the courts. Because nursing practice involves a great deal of touching clients, it is important that client consent be obtained for any nursing procedures that involve touching. In most cases, clients will not initiate legal proceedings unless serious harm has resulted from the touching, but nurses must be aware of the importance of client consent. Nurses are taught the importance of explaining to a patient, before beginning a nursing procedure, what is involved and why it is necessary. The importance of communicating effectively and ascertaining client consent to nursing care cannot be overstated.

Nurses often encounter problems in obtaining informed consent. The consent is legally valid only if a number of conditions are met, including the requirement that the client be properly informed about the procedure and clearly understand its nature and risks. Age, health, and mental status of clients and circumstances surrounding the situation often make it difficult for nurse to obtain informed consent. Nurses usually rely on the client's verbal expression of consent to nursing care activities. In the past, the majority of these activities have been considered low risk; however, with the steady expansion of the scope of nursing practice and the increase in independent nursing functions, many current nursing-care procedures are considered high risk. Consent to care may be expressed, implied, or inferred. Philpott asserted that health-care workers who rely on implied consent in the absence of emergency or for high-risk procedures are exposing patients to unauthorized invasion and themselves to possible liability (1985, p. 55).

Philpott identified six elements that must be present in legal consent:

1. The consent must be genuine and voluntary.
2. The procedure must not be an illegal procedure.
3. The consent must authorize the particular performer of the treatment or care.
4. The consenter must have legal capacity to consent.
5. The consenter must have the necessary mental competency to consent.
6. The consenter must be informed (1985, p. 57).

TELEPHONE ORDERS

A related concern is the problem inherent in nurses' acceptance of telephone orders from physicians for patient treatment. Many health-care agencies accept telephone orders only in emergency situations. If telephone orders are considered acceptable by an agency, the nurse may be liable in the event of later disagreement about the orders. If telephone orders are deemed acceptable by the agency, provision should be made for validation of the order, such as taping the conversation or having a second person confirm the orders with the physician.

The complexity of health care and the potential for problems with modern drugs and treatments increase legal risks for nurses. If there is disagreement between physician and nurse on what transpired, external validation of the orders would strengthen the nurse's legal position. The decreased potential for error benefits the client as well.

NEGLIGENCE

Complaints of negligence are the basis of most lawsuits against health-care professionals. Negligence is commonly defined as that which a reasonable and prudent nurse would do or not do in particular health care circumstances. Philpott has noted that certain conditions must be present for a defendant to be liable in actions involving negligence and for damages to be awarded by the court:

1. The presence of a duty of care by the defendant to the plaintiff.
2. The defendant's conduct must constitute a breach of that duty of care, i.e., must have failed to comply with the required standard of care.
3. The plaintiff must have suffered a material injury.
4. The negligent conduct must have been the proximate cause of the injury.
5. There must not have been contributory negligence on the part of the plaintiff and he must not have voluntarily assumed the risk (1985, p. 25).

The standard of care the reasonable and prudent nurse would use in a particular situation is established by the courts in a number of ways: articles and books by nursing authors that document the acceptability of certain practices, nursing practice standards developed by national and provincial professional nursing associations, curriculum content in schools of nursing, and testimony by expert witnesses who are nurses. The individual nurse's practice, educational background, and experience will be scrutinized by the court. The professional activities of a nurse whose practice is being questioned may also be considered relevant. In one important case, a nurse was found negligent after the court learned that the nurse, who had worked in a physician's office in Alberta for 22 years, had failed to take any continuing education courses since the year after she had graduated, 40 years before (*Dowey v. Rothwell*, 1974).

Krever (1973) states that the term *malpractice* is commonly used as a synonym for negligence. He points out that, although malpractice is a popular term that has even found its way into writings of the Supreme Court of Canada, it is a term "which tends to cause confusion, because of its very imprecision" (1973, p. 109). As Krever notes, not only does the term malpractice refer to negligent practice by someone authorized to practice a profession, it also includes the practice of a profession by an unauthorized person. The latter situation would fall under the category of battery.

Although health-care professionals, including nurses, tend to view actions involving negligence as negative to reputation and integrity, Krever (1973) points out that "moral blamelessness is not involved" (1973, p. 109). The purpose of the law pertaining to torts is to compensate the party who is injured through the actions of another. The issue here is not punishment; it is compensating the plaintiff for injury by moving responsibility for loss from the plaintiff to the defendant.

Noting that any citizen can be sued for negligence, Krever (1973) states that a higher standard of care is expected of the professional. The question of foreseeability of outcome of nursing-care activity or lack of activity is important in cases involving negligence. Kever states: "A person must take reasonable care to avoid acts or omissions which he can reasonably foresee would be likely to injure other persons so closely and directly affected by his act that he ought reasonably to have them in contemplation as being so affected when he is directing his mind to the acts or omission in question (1973, p. 110)."

Commenting on a determination of negligence when burns resulted from a diathermy treatment that was improperly performed, Krever (1973) points out that "it was clearly foreseeable that burns would result from a failure to use that degree of care which objectively could be expected from a reasonable person with the nurses' training" (1973, p. 112). The client had placed his trust in the nurse and had a right to expect the best possible care based on a reasonable standard of skill and knowledge.

NURSES' NOTES

Nurses' records of the care and progress of patients in their care are important documents. In 1970 nurses' notes were declared admissible as evidence by the Supreme Court of Canada:

> Hospital records, including nurses notes made contemporaneously by someone having a personal knowledge of the matters then being recorded and under a duty to make the entry or record should be received in evidence as *prima facie* proof of the facts stated therein. This should, in no way preclude a party wishing to challenge the accuracy of the records or entries from doing so.

Before this decision, nurses' notes were considered hearsay evidence and were not admissable in court. As Grady has observed, the legal system has gained a great deal from this decision, for: (*Ares v. Venner*, 1970, p. 608)

> . . . if the nurse is (1) dead; or (2) for any sufficient reason unavailable to give evidence . . . or (3) unable to testify with regard to the accuracy of the facts stated in nurses' notes (for example, because of the many patients attended and the time lapse since the notes were taken), these notes may be introduced as evidence and proof of the facts stated therein. Such facts could be used to support a case, either for or against a nurse, doctor, or hospital (1973, p. 128).

There are differences, however, among provinces as to whether various kinds of nursing records that form a part of the hospital record are admissible as evidence in court. Philpott (1985) notes that the Canada Evidence Act and the majority of provincial laws concerning evidence accept those parts of the record that are considered business records; however, there are variations in nursing records from agency to agency, and whether any or all of a record is consistent with the definition of business records is decided by the province involved.

The importance of "the virtues of accuracy, legibility, brevity practised faithfully by the nurse" in recording descriptions of care or patient progress is emphasized by Ross (1973, p. 102), who also refers to descriptions of unusual occurrences involving patients. These "unusual occurrence" or "incident" records are most often written by nurses, who may or may not have been present when the events took place. The desired characteristics of nursing notes, as previously mentioned, could include the need for contemporaneous recording by the nurse who had firsthand knowledge of what was described in the record and who was responsible for the record. The importance of a "cool, dispassionate, and thoughtful" approach to preparing a "factual, concise and totally objective" record of the event is reinforced by the fact that the record could be introduced as legal evidence to support or defend a damage claim (Ross, 1973, pp. 102-103).

In many cases, problems with nursing notes introduced as evidence in court have engendered criticism in court records of the proceedings. Frequent criticisms include the failure to record events contemporaneously, gaps in recording, and recording of care by someone other than the nurse who provided the care. In general, it is difficult to verify that any care not recorded was actually provided. Cases often come to trial long after the events in question occurred; in these circumstances it is difficult for principals to remember details of what happened; thus, clear, accurate, and complete recording of events is essential.

There have also been cases of falsification and destruction of nursing records by nurses. These occurrences are sad commentaries on the trust and confidence placed in nurses by a public that expects honesty and integrity in all aspects of care. Nurses may be considered negligent in these cases simply because the court must assume that important facts were hidden, and the person or persons responsible for the falsification or destruction of records was acting in self-interest. It is evident that dishonesty in matters pertaining to care will usually be discerned in court proceedings and will not reflect positively on the character, conduct, or professionalism of the nurse(s).

The advent of computerization in hospitals is changing the way hospital records are developed and maintained. Programs written to support computerized nursing records are designed to facilitate nurses' recording of notes. Typewritten entries eliminate legibility problems, but the issues associated with the nature and quality of the recording remain. Computer programs can also be designed to note the correct time on all entries and to eliminate interlineations. Although signatures are not possible, a unique identifying code can be assigned to each user to attribute entries to the correct individuals. It is possible that hospital records will no longer be kept on paper or microfilm, but rather in computer files, which can be stored and retrieved easily.

CONFIDENTIALITY

Statutes of the provinces that include laws that address the patient's right to confidentiality in health records are usually included in hospital acts, although acts that regulate nursing also contain provisions that reiterate the nurse's professional responsibility to maintain client confidentiality. To fail in this responsibility is to be subject to allegations of professional misconduct. Other areas of law where client confidentiality is protected include contractual and common law. Four provinces protect the right of privacy by statutory means: Quebec, British Columbia, Manitoba, and Saskatchewan. In other provinces, there is no recourse to invasion of privacy. It has been noted that "where statutory rights to privacy are recognized, the patient's right to consent and withdraw consent to privacy is valued and enforceable" (Philpott, 1985, p. 134). However, such is not the case in other provinces, where the only references to privacy are in hospital acts, which do not provide the same protection.

Exceptions to the responsibility for maintaining confidentiality include (1) client consent for disclosure of personal information to persons other than those named in the hospital act of the province, (2) statutory provisions for reporting certain diseases and child abuse to appropriate health and social services personnel, and (3) court orders, which are often used to obtain health records for the use of plaintiffs or defendants in trials.

In the past, the client's right to view personal records has been a controversial issue. Historically, lawyers acting for clients in suits against a hospital or its employees have had to gain access to the records by court order. Health-care agencies have traditionally been reluctant to release client records. However, there has been recognition that clients have the right to see their records, and the development of new legislation dealing with confidentiality should allow clients easier access to their own records.

UNDERSTANDING LEGAL ASPECTS OF NURSING

It is evident that the professional nurse must have some knowledge of the law, legal processes, the judicial system, and client rights. The increasing complexity of professional practice has been associated with increased risks in nursing procedures, and higher risk procedures increase the potential for legal action. There have been many changes in the nurse's role over time, and the pace of development has accelerated in recent years. The effort to establish the baccalaureate standard for entry to practice in the profession is likely to result in even more change in the direction of augmented responsibility and increased risks for the nurse.

The assumption is that the knowledgeable nurse will have a good understanding of the legal aspects of the relationship with the client, but few schools of nursing devote courses or units within courses to legal issues in nursing practice. Likewise, there are few continuing education programs that offer topics on legal issues for staff nurses who wish to enhance their understanding of the law as it relates to professional practice. Indeed, the inservice education departments of acute-care agencies deal with this subject only rarely in the programs they offer, perhaps because those who are responsible for teaching and programming have not had formal instruction in the legal aspects of nursing and may not consider this area an essential component in the curriculum or inservice education programs. They may also be unaware of the increasing legal risks for nurses in practice. However, as the twenty-first century approaches, new educational standards will be needed for the professional environment. The nurse of the future will need extensive knowledge and skills for competent and ethically based practice. Nursing practice will require a fundamental understanding of the law and the legal aspects of nursing.

REFERENCES

Ares v Venner (1970). S.C.R., 14, D.L.R. (3d) 4 (S.C.C.), p. 608.

Dais, E.E. (1973). Canadian law: an overview. In S.R. Good and J.C. Kerr (Eds.). *Contemporary issues in Canadian law for nurses* (3-14). Toronto: Holt, Rinehart & Winston.

Dowey, v Rothwell (1974). 5 W.W.R. 311.

Grady, P.E. (1973). The law and nurses' notes. In S.R. Good and J.C. Kerr (Eds.), *Contemporary issues in Canadian law for nurses* (127-129). Toronto: Holt, Rinehart & Winston.

Krever, H. (1973). Liability for negligence. In S.R. Good and J.C. Kerr (Eds.), *Contemporary issues in Canadian law for nurses* (pp. 107-116). Toronto: Holt, Rinehart & Winston.

Merryman, J.H. (1969). *The civil law tradition.* Palo Alto, Calif: Stanford University Press.

Philpott, M. (1985). *Legal liability and the nursing process.* Toronto: W.B. Saunders.

Plucknett, T.F.T. (1956). *A concise history of the common law.* Boston: Little, Brown & Co.

Ross, M.W. (1973). The nurse as an employee. In S.R. Good and J.C. Kerr (Eds.), *Contemporary issues in Canadian law for nurses* (95-106). Toronto: Holt, Rinehart & Winston.

Storch, J. (1982). *Patients' rights: Ethical and legal issues in health care and nursing.* Toronto: McGraw-Hill Ryerson Ltd.

CHAPTER NINETEEN

Ethical Issues and Dilemmas in Nursing Practice

JANNETTA MacPHAIL

C losely related to the issues pertaining to legal aspects of nursing practice are issues and dilemmas concerning professional ethics. Health professionals have always been faced with ethical dilemmas and have had to make ethical decisions; however, the dilemmas are more complex today. Factors contributing to this complexity are the rapidly expanding body of medical knowledge and the development of new technologies to save or prolong human life. At the same time, changes in societal values have increased recognition of individual rights and freedoms and responsibility for protecting those rights.

Another influential factor is the availability of education, resulting in a better-informed public who are more questioning and expect to be more involved in decisions about their own lives and health. Because of the eradication of many diseases, control over other diseases, and improved living standards, people are also living longer, which creates new ethical questions in terms of making decisions about prolonging life. The finite amount of resources available is another factor that raises questions about priorities in the health-care system; when there are insufficient resources to meet all needs, complex decisions must be made about who will receive care and how funds will be spent.

Because of these interacting factors, health professionals face many dilemmas. Who decides what is right for the individual or family involved? Is there always a right answer? Curtin (1982, p. 1) defines ethics as "a discipline in which we attempt to identify, organize, analyze, and justify human acts by applying certain principles to determine the right thing to do in a given situation." Thus, ethics is concerned with judgement of actions, not judgement of human beings.

CODES OF ETHICS

A code of ethics is one of the characteristics of a profession. It is defined by the profession through the professional association and serves to inform members of that profession and society about the profession's expectations in ethical matters. For many years, physicians have taken the Hippocratic Oath, which was derived from the time of Hippocrates, on graduating from medical school. Although it provides some ethical direction, it also commits the physician to saving and prolonging life at any cost, which is one of the factors leading to difficulties between physicians and nurses today. For example, there is often a difference of opinion between these two professions about prolonging life. This difference has led to stressful interprofessional relationships in terms of who should make the decision. Many physicians believe it is their responsibility, whereas many nurses believe the individual or family should be involved in making a decision that affects their lives.

Although some nurses have taken the Florence Nightingale pledge (which did not originate with Florence Nightingale but with Harper Hospital School of Nursing in Detroit), this pledge does not provide ethical direction for the issues and dilemmas encountered in practice. In 1955, the Canadian Nurses Association (CNA) adopted the code of ethics developed in 1953 by the International Council of Nurses (ICN) and replaced in 1973 by *The ICN Code For Nurses — Ethical Concepts Applied to Nursing,* which guided members in ethical decision making until the 1970s. At its 1978 annual meeting, the CNA made the development of a new national code a priority. A new code was approved in 1980, but revisions were deemed necessary soon after. An ad hoc committee appointed to make the revisions sought input from nurses across Canada and, after lengthy deliberations, published *Code of Ethics for Nursing* in 1985 (Canadian Nurses Association [CNA], 1985). A tentative code of ethics for nurses in the United States, adopted by the American Nurses Association (ANA) in 1926, was revised a number of times over the years. The ANA code of ethics for professional nurses, adopted in 1950, was revised in 1960 to become the *Code for Professional Nurses.* With additional revision in 1976, the ANA adopted the *Code for Nurses with Interpretive Statements* (American Nurses Association, 1976; Flanagan, 1976). Earlier codes of ethics, prescriptive in nature, were essentially rules to govern the personal and professional conduct of members of a profession; recent codes are more similar to guidelines for practice that provide a framework for nurses to make ethical decisions and fulfil their responsibilities to the public and the profession. Although codes of ethics may or may not be part of statutory regulations, in most provinces there is statutory requirement within the Act governing the nursing profession, which mandates that nurses uphold ethical standards as defined by the nursing profession. This means that not only are individual nurses expected to uphold the precepts contained in codes of ethics, but also hold colleagues accountable for adhering to them.

Because of the complexity of the ethical dilemmas nurses confront today, they need more than a code of ethics. Storch (1982) believes that at least four conditions are necessary for ethical decision making: (1) desire and commitment to do what is right and good; (2) knowledge of relevant facts of the particular situation; (3) clarity of thought, rather than emotionalism, in dealing with the facts; and (4) some understanding of basic principles or concepts of ethics. In recent years, nurses and other health-care professionals have recognized the importance of examining and clarifying values that may influence their actions and of becoming more sensitive to the values of their patients or clients. Rather than prescribing a set of values for nurses and nursing students as in the past, values clarification strategies are being used increasingly in both nursing education programs and continuing education programs for practising nurses.

PRINCIPLES AND CONCEPTS OF ETHICS

A prerequisite to applying ethics in nursing is having a theoretical base in ethics, just as basic knowledge in the biologic and behaviourial sciences is requisite to the application of principles and concepts from those sciences to nursing. Without a theoretical base, discussion of ethical issues may be merely sharing of opinions. Although it is not feasible to provide a theoretical base for ethical decision making in this context, basic concepts of ethics can be identified. They include: (1) personhood, of which self-awareness is a basic quality (Storch, 1982); (2) autonomy, which implies not only freedom to decide and to act, but also to acknowledge and respect the dignity and autonomy of others (Francoeur, 1983); (3) veracity, which includes obligation to tell the truth and to use good judgement in determining what the patient wants to know or can withstand; (4) paternalism, which refers to restricting the liberty of an individual without his or her consent with the justification of trying to do good, such as not telling a person about his or her diagnosis and condition because of a poor prognosis; (5) confidentiality, which must be maintained but balanced against the rights of others, including society (Francoeur, 1983); (6) beneficence, or doing what is best for an individual while balancing the risks and benefits in a given situation; (7) nonmaleficence, or not inflicting intentional harm or risk of harm and preventing evil or harm whenever possible; and (8) justice, which pertains to ensuring that individuals get what they deserve according to individual need, worth, and merit and to enforcing the concept of distributive justice, which "has to do with the distribution of good and evil, of burdens and benefits in any society when resources are limited" (Davis and Aroskar, 1983, p. 45). The question of justice is an ethical dilemma frequently described in the literature today with the shortage of nurses and nurses having to make difficult decisions about apportioning care when all needs cannot be met. A thorough knowledge of basic ethical concepts is necessary for nurses to be able to address the increasingly complex issues encountered daily in practice settings. Although there is a tendency to consider only the dilemmas faced in acute care settings, the issues are different but equally complex for practitioners in long-term care and home and community settings due to increased longevity, early discharge from hospitals, and the use of technologies in the home that were previously limited to acute care settings. Robillard et al (1989, p. 9) point out that there has been little research on the ethical issues in primary care, although most health care is provided in primary care settings. Their study revealed that the issues are most frequently pragmatic, not dramatic, and are concerned with "patient self-determination, adequacy of care and professional responsibility, and distribution of resources" (Robillard et al, 1989, p. 9). Thus nurses practising in all types of health-care settings need a knowledge base in ethical concepts and principles, as well as support and expert resources to assist them in ensuring that basic human rights are recognized and respected.

BASIC HUMAN RIGHTS ABOUT HEALTH AND HEALTH CARE

Basic human rights in health care, which are increasingly recognized today, are the right to be informed, the right to be respected, and the right to self-determination. Each has great implications for ethical decision making and the responsibility of health professionals to protect these rights. These rights also cause debate over some ethical issues and are the bases for confrontation between nurses and physicians. For example, there may be differences of opinion between nurses and physicians about the meaning of being informed and whose responsibility it is to inform the individual or family. A confrontation may occur when information is withheld by a physician who believes this is in the best interest of the patient when the nurse believes that the patient should be informed and is asked directly for such information. The right to be informed has increased the need for obtaining informed consent before medical interventions are instituted and before patients or clients are asked to participate in research. Until the 1970s, there was no expectation or requirement for obtaining informed consent for participation in research, and people were sometimes exploited. For example, in an experiment at the Allen Memorial Institute in Montreal in the late 1940s, patients were given mind-altering drugs, such as lysergic acid diethylamide (LSD), which had far-reaching effects, and recompense was sought in the mid-1980s.

The right to be respected has great implications in approaches to patients and is interrelated with the right to be informed. Providing an interpretation of care and explaining medical conditions are two methods of showing respect for an individual. Respect also has implications for confidentiality, which has been a problem in terms of information shared among health professionals. Although nurses and physicians may respect confidentiality to the point of not sharing information with persons outside the health professions, there has been a tendency to share information openly in discussion where it can be overheard. Confidentiality also requires that written records be carefully protected, which has great implications for the protection of rights with the development of computers.

The right to self-determination implies that individuals or families have the right to make decisions about matters that affect their health and their lives. Ensuring that this right is protected is complex; for example, it involves deciding if an individual is capable of making decisions and if not, who should be involved in the decision making. Making decisions about matters that affect a patient's health and life involves giving people the opportunity to decide not to have treatment recommended by a physician. This is a difficult situation for health professionals because they are faced with an individual refusing treatment that they believe is best for the individual. There may be circumstances in which not consenting to treatment is logical in terms of an individual's prognosis and desire not to undergo adverse side effects known to result from some treatments, such as cancer therapy when the disease has progressed beyond redemption. On the other hand, some individuals choose to have treatment almost to the end, even if there is no hope of cure or remission.

Self-determination is not limited to life and death matters, but also involves making decisions about life-style. For example, individuals make decisions to continue with life-styles and behaviour patterns that are known to be detrimental to their health and well-being, such as smoking, overeating, excessive drinking, refusing to wear seat belts, and engaging in sexual relations with people likely to be carriers of the acquired immunodeficiency virus. Although efforts to educate the public about the hazards of such habits are more successful, many persons still choose to do things that are harmful to their health.

THE RIGHT TO MAKE CHOICES IN RELATION TO DEATH

Dying and death give rise to many ethical issues and dilemmas. Davis and Aroskar (1983) identify three issues: (1) possible interventions by health professionals, such as resuscitation and passive euthanasia; (2) possible interventions by the family or significant others, such as helping a terminally ill person to hasten death and end suffering; and (3) possible interventions by the afflicted person, such as suicide, use of a living will, and claiming "a right to die."

> The ethical, legal, medical, social, cultural, psychologic, and economic factors to be considered in types of intervention will vary with the individual and family involved. Decisions about types of intervention are extremely complex for everyone involved because of the numbers and kinds of factors intersecting in each individual situation. There are significant implications from the decisions made in individual situations for individuals and the community in terms of the moral principles of respect for the person, doing no harm, and justice. (Davis and Aroskar, 1983, pp. 136-137).

The word *euthanasia* derives from Greek meaning good or pleasant death. Is death ever preferable to life? That question is difficult to answer; it must consider the specific situation and distinguish this from the interests and values of the care provider and the institution. Some believe that euthanasia should be considered only for those who can ask to die, which would eliminate newborns, infants, and individuals who are kept alive by machines and are unable to speak for themselves. Others believe that in certain circumstances some severely deformed newborns should be allowed to die by withdrawing or withholding treatment, and that the decision should be made by the parents and their professional advisors, who are usually physicians (Duff and Campbell, 1973; McCormick, 1974; Shaw, 1973).

Passive euthanasia, or "letting someone die," may be done by not initiating treatment or by stopping treatment, with or without the consent of the individual. These measures, although used in some hospitals, are still morally controversial. Active euthanasia is providing an individual with the means to end life or directly bringing about the individual's death with or without consent (Brody, 1976). How does the concept of protecting human rights fit into euthanasia? Does a person ever have the right to die? Can one refuse life-saving treatment? Is lack of clear-cut policies and guidelines to help health professionals in addressing such complex questions a reflection of there being no right or wrong answer? Some believe that death should never be hastened; others believe that a person whose death is imminent should be allowed to die to relieve pain and suffering, and that the right to refuse treatment should be respected. Some fear that if euthanasia as a kindly act—beneficent euthanasia—can be morally justified, euthanasia for other purposes may also be justified and practised (Dyck, 1975).

Little is written about the ethical dilemmas faced by nurses in "no code" orders. If there are no written orders for "no code" and a patient develops cardiac arrest, is the nurse expected to "code" the patient? Some hospitals are making an effort to develop guidelines for resuscitation. These have been encouraged by a joint effort of the Canadian Medical Association (CMA), the CNA, Canadian Hospital Association (CHA), and the Canadian Bar Association (CBA), which resulted in a joint statement on terminal illness published in 1984 in *The Canadian Nurse* (1984). There is opportunity for nursing input in developing guidelines, but it is the physician's responsibility to write the order for not resuscitating and to convey the order to nursing staff. Davis and Aroskar (1983, p. 149) point out that "nurses are in a key position to notify the physician if the patient's condition changes, which change would indicate that the orders may need reassessment." This reinforces the need for careful nursing assessment and clear communication with physicians and the need for flexibility and wise judgement in applying orders based on changes in the patient's condition.

THE RIGHT TO LIVE AS PERSONS AND RESPONSIBILITIES FOR CHANGING BEHAVIOUR

Many complex ethical questions derive from efforts to effect a change in deviant behaviour. Bandman and Bandman state:

> Once a set of persons occupies a place within the circle of life, the problem of the right to live as persons arises. The limits to this right are found in the right a person has to be free to live well, without unjustified interferences of his or her freedom. Conversely, being free—and one can only be free if unmolested and free from unjustified harm, injury or threat of violence—is the presence of rules and norms for changing undesirable behavior. To induce changed behavior, reward and punishment are commonly used (1978, p. 4).

Although few people would argue about the need to control violence against others, what constitutes deviant behaviour? What establishes norms of standard behaviour? What authorizes persons to try to change behaviour that does not meet these norms and under what conditions? Specific groups in society, such as prisoners, children, older persons, and the mentally ill, are particularly vulnerable to having their rights disregarded when professionals use behaviour modification methods.

Peplau identified a major problem in defining mental illness with the contradictory views of professionals. She believes that "the difficulties of the 'mentally ill' are conceptualized in different ways by health professionals, and each viewpoint gives rise to a different form of treatment" (1978, p. 208). She also notes that problems with self-identity, relationships, and function within social systems do not fit easily into the cause-effect, disease-oriented medical model. How do we ensure protection of the human rights of the "mentally ill" who have long been considered incompetent and unable to judge the necessity of treatment? They are not given the opportunity to refuse treatment. Moreover, many of the therapies used for these patients have been designed to change behaviour in the direction of obedience, compliance, and conformity. Coercion has been used to force patients to accept treatment. Whittington (1975) believes it would be best to admit we often do not know what is best for an individual or group and give them more choices.

Another concern about allowing the mentally ill to refuse treatment is that, if untreated, their conditions will become chronic and they will become an economic burden on society. Peplau (1978) believes that releasing these patients into the community, which has been done in Canada and the United States for more than a decade, is not as much a matter of their being a danger to society as their being a burden on others. In addition, they are in danger of being exploited by others ready to take advantage of the already disadvantaged. It is probably more appropriate to give them the opportunity to choose from available treatments or grant them the right to refuse treatment after participating in "sessions designed to investigate conceptions of treatment offered and reasons for refusing" (Peplau, 1978, p. 212).

ETHICAL DILEMMAS RELATED TO CHILDBEARING

One of the major ethical issues pertaining to childbearing is abortion. The issue is "the status of the fetus as a member of the human species when the existence of the fetus poses a threat to the physical, psychological or social well-being of a pregnant woman and/or other family members" (Curtin, 1982, p. 240). Antiabortionists claim that the personhood of the fetus is being denied, whereas proabortionists maintain that the woman's right to self-determination cannot be denied. They emphasize the burden imposed on society by an unwanted pregnancy and the possible outcomes for the welfare of the child in the future. Between the two extremes are those who favour abortions depending on circumstances surrounding the pregnancy, such as rape and incest.

The question of abortion presents problems for the individual nurse who is expected to participate in abortions within a health-care agency. It is important that the nurse know the agency's policies about such participation before accepting a position. Health-care agencies must have clearly defined policies that can be communicated to potential employees and referred to when situations arise that present an ethical dilemma to staff members. The nurse is responsible, legally and morally, for ensuring that patients' needs are met and that patients are not neglected because of differing values (Curtin, 1982). The Supreme Court of Canada's decision, made in 1988, endorses women's rights to self-determination in relation to abortion.

Other ethical issues pertaining to childbearing are genetic engineering and surrogate motherhood (Campbell, 1984). Bill C43, passed in 1990 by the House of Commons, will permit abortion only if a continued pregnancy would jeopardize the woman's physical or mental health, as diagnosed by one physician only. Physicians are adamantly opposed to this change because of the possibility of criminal charges against them, and because they will be required to provide pre-abortion and post-abortion counselling. As with all ethical dilemmas, there are no easy answers, and health professionals must be guided by their own values and their legal and ethical responsibilities in deciding on a course of action for care of these patients.

ALLOCATION OF HEALTH-CARE RESOURCES

Ethical issues pertaining to allocation of health-care resources may be encountered at several levels. At the government level, public policies are established that determine what type of health care can be provided. Nurses and other health professionals have a responsibility to exercise their prerogatives and communicate with legislators to influence these policies. For example, as a result of a government's decision not to require seat belt use by law, a considerable portion of the health-care dollar is spent on persons involved in automobile accidents.

Policies that influence the use of health-care resources are also established at the institutional level. Too often, nurses have little influence on such policies and they need to take action to affect decision making and priority setting. Decisions to develop programs are often made without adequate consideration of the implications for nursing practice; new medical programs, such as heart transplants and hip replacements, have enormous impact on the need for nursing care and could affect nurses' ability to respond to the demands placed on them. At the unit level, nurses have to delineate problems that result from new programs and provide data that will facilitate a reasoned decision, although values and emotions often enter into these decisions. Fortunately, nurses have become more vocal in expressing their concerns and in providing facts that can influence decision making, rather than merely responding to the decisions made by physicians and hospital administrators.

Is it ethically and morally right to support activities that may jeopardize the patient or result in unequal or unfair distribution of resources among different programs within a health-care institution? Who decides the priorities in allocating resources, and what facts are considered? With the increasing proportion of older persons in Canada and other developed countries, the question of age may influence decisions. For example, a 99-year-old man had surgery for removal of an esophageal pouch that was making adequate nutrition impossible. He had been advised 17 years earlier not to have surgery because of his age, but the predictors of his life expectancy were inaccurate. Although he survived the surgery, it might have been easier at age 82. Many disadvantaged groups such as the physically handicapped, the retarded, the poor, and ethnic minorities, are also exploited by such decisions and their rights are neglected.

Other factors that influence allocation of resources in health-care legislation include consumer unrest and the patients' rights movement. Davis and Aroskar (1983, p. 206) believe that "health care policy cannot be the monopoly of providers any more than scientists should have the only say on biomedical research." Reasons for such a position are possible conflicts of interest; that large amounts of taxes are used to provide health care; that nonmedical dimensions of health problems may be critical aspects; and that "individual liberty and autonomy extend not only into the political arena but also into health care" (Davis and Aroskar, 1983, p. 206). Although nurses, individually and collectively, have become more involved in influencing public policy through lobbying and working effectively with consumers and providers of care, their involvement needs to be increased. In addition to responding to particular issues, the professional organizations can work to influence public policy about allocation of health-care resources.

STRATEGIES FOR ADDRESSING ETHICAL DILEMMAS IN PRACTICE

The number and variety of ethical dilemmas that nurses encounter in practice have increased because of advancements in scientific knowledge and development of technologies. Nurses and physicians often become embroiled in ethical dilemmas in which opinions differ, leading to decreased communication and failure to work together in the interests of patients. These results can be detrimental to patient care and to the mental health and well-being of nursing staff, particularly in intensive care units, where nurses and physicians may disagree on life and death decisions, on approaches to care, and on setting priorities.

Some health-care agencies address these dilemmas through an ethics committee, which is called on an *ad hoc* basis to address dilemmas presented by nurses or physicians. In some large teaching hospitals an ethicist is employed to provide expert assistance and guidance. At Montreal General Hospital, Dr. David Roy, an internationally recognized physician-ethicist, has been helping nursing and medical staff address complex issues for several years.

A strategy of a preventive nature is to improve the teaching of ethics in nursing education by ensuring that ethics is an official part of nursing curricula on the undergraduate and graduate levels and is taught by experts, not left to "chance" to be integrated into all teaching. Thompson and Thompson (1989) are advocates of this approach. They identify the goals of teaching ethics to professional students and professionals as: "to stimulate the moral imagination; recognize ethical issues; elicit a sense of moral obligation; develop analytical skills; and tolerate and reduce disagreements and ambiguity" (1989, p. 86). They recommend using case studies, as do many textbooks on ethics; however, there must be expert guidance in the process of analyzing the ethical issues and dilemmas presented.

Since many practising nurses who face ethical dilemmas every day have not had the benefit of this education, discussion of ethics should be included in inservice education and continuing education. After nurses have learned the theoretical foundation of ethics, ongoing Bioethics Rounds can be organized for nurses and physicians. Bioethics Rounds are not intended to address ethical issues encountered in the care of a specific patient, but to provide opportunities for open discussion of ethical issues when the professionals involved can consider various viewpoints and are not facing a specific ethical issue requiring an immediate decision. This approach is being developed through a Joint-Faculties Bioethics Project undertaken in 1987 by the University of Alberta, the University of Alberta Hospitals, and the Cross Cancer Institute. The project, a result of a collaborative effort to address ethical dilemmas, has equal representation from medicine, nursing, and philosophy through directors who plan and conduct Bioethics Rounds and are responsible for joint teaching in ethics for nursing and medical students. Such a collaborative approach facilitates addressing issues involving both professions so they are deliberated together, and collaborative decisions are reached that are in the best interests of the patients and the health-care providers. This approach is based on the belief that collaboration in the delivery of health care is required to address complex ethical dilemmas; there are no right or wrong answers, but decisions must be made that will meet the needs of the consumers of health care.

CONCLUSION

This chapter has highlighted a few ethical issues and dilemmas; many more are addressed in books and journals for health professionals. The amount of literature on ethics has increased at a phenomenal rate in the past two decades, helping health professionals determine what action to take ethically in situations encountered in practice. Although there are no easy answers to ethical questions, health professionals must have resources available, in the literature and through ethicists, and they must use these resources in dealing with complex issues and dilemmas.

REFERENCES

American Nurses Association (1976). *Code for nurses with interpretive statements.* Kansas City, MO: American Nurses Association.

Bandman, E.L. and Bandman, B. (1978). *Bioethics and human rights.* Boston: Little, Brown & Company.

Brody, H. (1976). *Ethical decisions in medicine.* Boston: Little, Brown & Company.

Campbell, D. (1984). Surrogate mothers—controversy continues. *Nursing Mirror, 158*(5), 5.

Canadian Nurses Association. (1985). *Code of ethics for nursing.* Ottawa: Author.

Canadian Nurses Association, Canadian Medical Association, and Canadian Hospital Association. (1984). Joint statement on terminal illness: A protocol for health professionals regarding resuscitative intervention for the terminally ill. *The Canadian Nurse, 80*(4), 24.

Curtin, L.L. (1982). Case study v: Abortion, privacy and conscience. In L. Curtin & M.J. Flaherty, *Nursing ethics: Theories and pragmatics,*

(pp. 239-254). Bowie, MD: Robert J. Brady Company.

Curtin, L.L. (1985). Developing a professional ethic. *AARN Newsletter, 41*(10), 1, 3-6.

Davis, A.J. and Aroskar, M.A. (1983). *Ethical dilemmas and nursing practice,* (2nd ed). Norwalk, CT: Appleton-Century-Crofts.

Duff, R.S. and Campbell, A.G.M. (1973). Moral and ethical dilemmas in the special-care nursery. *New England Journal of Medicine, 289,* 890-894.

Dyck, A.J. (1975). Beneficent euthanasia and benemortasia: Alternative view of mercy. In M. Kohl (Ed.), *Beneficent euthanasia,* (pp. 120-126). Buffalo, NY: Prometheus.

Flanagan, L. (1976). *One strong voice: The story of the American Nurses Association.* Kansas City, MO: American Nurses Association.

Francoeur, R.T. (1983). *Biomedical ethics: a guide to decision making.* Toronto: John Wiley & Sons.

International Council of Nurses. (1973). *ICN Code for nurses—ethical concepts applied to nursing.* Geneva: International Council of Nurses.

McCormick, R.A. (1974). To save or let live: The dilemma of modern medicine. *Journal of the American Medical Association, 229,* 172-176.

Peplau, H.E. (1978). The right to change behaviour: Rights of the mentally ill. In E.L. Bandman & B. Bandman, *Bioethics and human rights,* (pp. 207-212). Boston: Little, Brown & Company.

Robillard, H.M., High, D.M., Sebastian, J.G., Pisaneschi, J.I., Perritt, L.J. and Mahler, D.M. (1989). Ethical issues in primary care: A survey of practitioners' perceptions, *Journal of Community Health, 14*(1), 9-17.

Shaw, A. (1973). Dilemmas of "informed consent" in children. *New England Journal of Medicine, 289,* 885-890.

Storch, J.L. (1982). *Patients' rights: Ethical and legal issues in health care and nursing.* Toronto: McGraw-Hill Ryerson.

Thompson, J.E. and Thompson, H.O. (1989). Teaching ethics to nursing students. *Nursing Outlook, 37*(2), 84-88.

Whittington, H.G. (1975). A case for private enterprise in mental health. *Administration in Mental Health, 25*(1), 23-27.

CHAPTER TWENTY

Emergence of Nursing Unions as a Social Force in Canada

JANET ROSS KERR

A prediction made 25 years ago about the direction and management of determining nurses' salaries would make interesting reading today. Whether the rise of powerful and independent nursing unions was foreseen is not known, but it is probable that this development would have seemed unlikely. One wonders how the health-care system and the public in general would have reacted if nurses had used the ultimate union weapon, the strike, a quarter of a century ago (Muyskens, 1982). Since striking employees in the public sector are viewed negatively by a certain proportion of the public even today, the image of nurses on picket lines would probably have seemed far-fetched, if not impossible (Rotkovich, 1980).

The approach of the twenty-first century has brought with it many changes that once seemed improbable. Nurses in Canada today are at the helms of organizations that promote their social and economic welfare by influencing and participating in the collective bargaining process. When collective bargaining activity in nursing began, nurses made an effort to become knowledgeable about labour relations, anticipating control of salaries and wages through mastery of the process. Have they been successful? Although there is considerable variation among provinces in approach and achievement, the initial developmental stage seems to be over. Consolidation and continued skill development will likely be stressed as nursing unions focus on applying their new expertise to the world of labour and management (Ponak, 1981).

THE RISE OF NURSING UNIONS

In Canada, as well as in other countries, professional nursing associations have played key roles in development of nursing unions. However, since 1973, events in Canada can be differentiated from those in other countries by the decision made in a Saskatchewan case that was appealed to the Supreme Court of Canada. The issue was a dispute between the Service Employees International Union and the Saskatchewan Registered Nurses Association (SRNA) over the SRNA's application for certification as a bargaining agent. The union charged that the SRNA should not be permitted to act as a trade union because its Board of Directors included nurse managers.The decision, which ruled in favour of the union, radically altered labour relations in nursing in Canada in little more than a decade. Because the SRNA elected nurse managers to its governing body, it was presumed to have an inherent bias or conflict of interest, which precluded participation in collective bargaining, and the way was paved for establishing of new organizations across the country. The new unions took over the collective bargaining functions that had been performed exclusively by the professional associations.

Both the Canadian Nurses Association (CNA) and the American Nurses Association (ANA) approved the principle of collective bargaining for nurses in the 1940s, and both affirmed that the bargaining agent at provincial or state level should be the professional association. Each was also on record as supporting a no-strike policy. This stand became controversial two decades later and was repealed by both organizations in the 1960s. The passage of the Labour Relations Act at the national level in 1944, which gave federal employees collective bargaining rights, was probably instrumental in the 1944 CNA decision to support collective bargaining among its member associations.

Rowsell (1982) notes that nurses were concerned about possible management domination from the boards of directors of provincial associations after the 1944 decision. Since there was no formal collective bargaining at that time, the provincial associations struggled with the issues inherent in being at the forefront of the process. Shortly after that, having studied the issues, member organizations informed the CNA that it was not legally possible for them to act as bargaining agents. The first breakthrough in provincial labour legislation appeared in 1946, when the Registered Nurses Association of British Columbia (RNABC) became the first provincial association to apply successfully for certification as a bargaining agent under a labour relations act, beginning a movement that would eventually involve all provinces.

Although they were not permitted to be formally involved in collective bargaining, the other associations became involved in promoting the social and economic welfare of their memberships in a less formal and proactive manner. It became customary in most provinces to publish annual personnel policies that included recommendations about salaries and working conditions. The associations discussed the recommendations with employers or hospital associations. Although the recommendations in the document resulted from agreement of the parties, they were not binding and often not implemented, which led to progressive disillusionment with the process and its results. The recognition of failure to make any progress using the personnel policy approach led to the associations' search for a more effective method of involvement influencing salary and wage decisions.

During the expansionist decade of the 1960s, the majority of the provincial associations began to be assertive in applying for the right to bargain collectively for the large groups of nurses employed in provincial health-care agencies. A number of factors were important in setting the stage for this new phase of development in nursing organizations. With the economy finally booming after gradual recovery through the postwar period, workers were making gains in financial status because the country could finally afford it. There were new opportunities for students as an egalitarian mood swept the postsecondary education system, and ability and willingness to work diligently became the new entrance standards. Financial and social status were no longer required as competitive scholarships became available to the most academically qualified students. The Royal Commission on the Status of Women drew attention to the need for equal opportunity for women in society and for removing inequities in a system that inadequately remunerated women. The new optimism in society brought what had seemed impossible in the past into the realm of the possible.

Because provincial nursing associations in all provinces except British Columbia could not be certified under provincial labour laws in the early 1960s, the associations established an important role for themselves by teaching staff nurses in hospitals and community health agencies about collective bargaining and helping them organize staff nurses' associations at the agency level. These organizations became the bargaining units that were eventually certified under the various labour acts. The exception to this process was Prince Edward Island; collective bargaining rights were written into the Prince Edward Island Nurses' Act (PEI Nurses' Act).

The provincial associations laid the ground work for involvement in the collective bargaining process. By the time the Supreme Court decision was made that led to the separation of professional associations and unions, nurses had gained some experience and expertise in collective bargaining, and the transition from a single organization to two was facilitated. There were difficulties in moving from one structure to another in some provinces, but by 1981, the process was complete and the dual structure was in place in all provinces; the last to complete the process was Prince Edward Island.

There were many advantages to the new organizational structure. Professional associations became more credible. Because they were not responsible for collective bargaining, they were no longer protecting their economic interests in public statements on health-care issues, particularly those that involved financing health care. Annual membership fees to the professional association no longer supported collective bargaining. Since collective bargaining is a labour-intensive process that involves extensive time commitments from a bargaining team and involvement of labour relations consultants, lawyers, and others, it is an expensive process. Management involvement in professional associations and the fact that fees from members supported collective bargaining had always been sensitive issues. Complaints about the associations' strong thrust in the bargaining arena came from those not affected by the bargaining process. The creation of two organizations from one addressed these complaints. Also, the removal of responsibility for collective bargaining enabled the professional association to focus on serving the public interest through self-regulatory functions; improving standards of nursing education and practice, promoting nursing research, and interacting with government and other health-care professions as the official voice of the profession (Beletz, 1980; Eldridge et al, 1982; Hopping, 1976; Jacox, 1980).

Many were disappointed when the alternatives narrowed as a result of the Supreme Court decision, and the inevitability of separation of professional associations and unions across the country became clear. It was difficult for nurses to think about separating and maintaining distinct and autonomous organizations (Cleland, 1978). It was also difficult for many nurses to understand that the professional association now stood truly apart from the bargaining function and could no longer intervene at difficult times to support a union stance in the face of a strike action.

This did not keep some provinces from developing excellent working relationships between the professional association and the union (Conroy and Hibberd, 1983). In Ontario there was a good working relationship between the organizations until 1988. In 1961 self-regulatory functions were transferred to the College of Nurses; the Registered Nurses Association of Ontario (RNAO) performed all other professional functions, including bargaining. After the Ontario Nurses Association (ONA), the major nursing union, was created in 1975, there were three organizations, and each was concerned with a different area of professional activity. When the RNAO began losing members at a rapid pace in the late 1970s and early 1980s, it established an agreement with the ONA. The terms of the agreement, which became effective in 1983, enabled the union to purchase a block membership in the RNAO. The agreement also provided for a reduced RNAO membership fee for union members, with no reduction in services. Although there was some concern that the terms of the agreement might compromise the RNAO's autonomy and freedom to address health-care issues, this was an excellent example of cooperation and collaboration between the two organizations. A change in union leadership in 1987 destroyed the collaborative relationship and block membership was terminated.

THE ORGANIZATIONS: ESTABLISHMENT AND CONSOLIDATION

The development of separate and unique organizations for collective bargaining occurred within a relatively short time after the Supreme Court decision in 1973. Only eight years elapsed between the inception of the first such organization, the Saskatchewan Union of Nurses, and the conclusion of the process with the establishment of the last, the PEI Nurses Union, in 1981.

BRITISH COLUMBIA

As previously noted, the organization that first acquired formal authority, in that it was legally recognized as the official bargaining agent for nurses in the province, was the RNABC. In the early years it operated on the basis of personnel policies approved each year at the annual meeting; the bargaining that took place between the RNABC and the hospital boards was based on these approved recommendations. This process was similar to that used in other provinces; the difference was the legal recognition of the RNABC's role of bargaining agent. In British Columbia and other provinces, dissatisfaction arose with the personnel policies route by 1959; many disputes went to conciliation and strike votes were taken in a number of health-care agencies. It was evident that a different approach was needed.

The new approach was collective bargaining as it is used today: The agencies and the nurses each have a primary bargaining agent who bargains on behalf of all that wish to be a part of the process. This proved to be a reasonably successful approach over the next decade and a half; the bargaining structure within the association remained stable until 1974, when the RNABC disassociated the collective bargaining program from other association activity. This initial response to the Supreme Court decision may have been an attempt to determine if anything other than total separation was possible and obviate the need for developing a totally separate organization for collective bargaining.

In 1974, the British Columbia government approved legislation that gave government employees the right to bargain collectively and the right to strike. However, a decade later, new legislation revoked the right to strike for those designated as essential employees, which included nurses. Although there was been much protest, the government stood firm in its decision. An illegal nurses' strike in May and June 1989 provided an interesting example of the lack of solidarity between the union and its leadership because the membership repudiated a memorandum of agreement approved by union leaders. An agreement was reached eventually, but the startling image of members who were angry with their union leaders endures.

ALBERTA

Nurses in Alberta became concerned about their social and economic status in the early 1960s, and organizational meetings were held to decide what should be done. The Alberta Association of Registered Nurses (AARN) led this movement and worked to help nurses in hospitals develop staff nurses' associations for bargaining. Amendments made to the Registered Nurses Act in 1965 allowed the AARN to act as bargaining agent for the nurses. The AARN, like the RNABC, made bylaw changes in 1974 to create a unit for collective bargaining that would function separately from the rest of the Association. However, nurses in Alberta made the decision that a separate and autonomous structure for collective bargaining was really what they wanted, and, in 1977, the United Nurses of Alberta was selected to act in this capacity. Shortly thereafter, the first nurses strike occurred. Seven hospitals and 2000 nurses participated. Government intervened and ordered the nurses back to work, appointing a tribunal to rule on the items in dispute. Subsequently, two nurses' strikes occurred in Alberta, one in 1980 and another in 1982. In 1983, the Alberta government enacted legislation that made it illegal for hospital nurses to strike; however, in January 1988, Alberta nurses defied the Labour Act and went out on an 18-day illegal strike.

SASKATCHEWAN

In Saskatchewan, the SRNA became involved in collective bargaining before 1973, primarily in response to a demand from members employed in nongovernmental positions. Government-employed nurses who were represented by unions achieved significant improvement in salaries throughout the 1960s, whereas SRNA members who had had no bargaining agent before 1968 did not. By 1972, collective agreements between the SRNA and the Saskatchewan Hospital Association encompassed about half of Saskatchewan hospitals (Botterill-Conroy, 1980).

As previously noted, the amendment to the Trade Union Act that resulted from the question of the legality of the SRNA's role as bargaining agent for the nurses was ratified by the Supreme Court's 1973 decision. The Saskatchewan Union of Nurses, created after the decision was made, has continued its efforts to improve the social and economic welfare of nurses.

MANITOBA

Although nurses in Manitoba asked the Manitoba Association of Registered Nurses (MARN) to represent them in collective bargaining as early as 1953, the MARN did not become formally involved in this activity until 1969. Because the MARN had not begun to participate actively in bargaining, the Winnipeg Civic Registered Nurses' Association was organized in 1965 to serve as an alternative to the provincial employee union, the Federation of Civil Employees. Even after 1969, when the MARN became involved in bargaining, some ambivalence about that involvement continued within the Association, because the Labour Relations Act clearly specified that unions must operate separately from management. As a result, the MARN followed the precedents set in Alberta and British Columbia where the collective bargaining sector of the organization was segregated to function at arm's length from the rest of the Association. As in the other provinces, this was a short-term solution to the problem. In 1975, the Manitoba Organization of Nurses Association (MONA) was established; since that time it has addressed the social and economic welfare issues of its staff nurse members (Botterill-Conroy, 1980).

ONTARIO

As previously discussed, events took a different course in Ontario, beginning with the creation in 1961 of a quasigovernmental body, the College of Nurses. Collective bargaining rights were not secured easily in Ontario, and nurses tried unsuccessfully from 1958 until 1965 to gain legal recognition of bargaining for nurses. Even so, after 1965, bargaining had to be done individually, agency by agency. Not until 1973 did the Ontario Hospital Association approve centralized bargaining, on monetary issues only, for nurses (Botterill-Conroy, 1980). Although the RNAO had assumed the bargaining function for many years, a decision to form a nurses union was made at an annual RNAO meeting, and the ONA was established. The ONA separated from the RNAO in 1975, following the trend that by now was well established in the rest of the country, but bargaining at the provincial level was not begun until 1979. Legislation passed in 1965 had prevented nurses from striking since that time.

QUEBEC

In Quebec, nurses were given legislative approval for collective bargaining in 1946 under the Quebec Nurses Act. However, the Association of Nurses of the Province of Quebec did not develop a bargaining program. The reasons for this are unclear; however, after the enactment of the omnibus legislation, which applied to a number of professional groups, and the Professional Code in Chapter 43, which applied to nursing, registration in the province became mandatory. The Order of Nurses of the Province of Quebec (ONQ) was disqualified as bargaining agent; not because of management domination but because the right of free association guaranteed by the Quebec Labour Code was precluded by the mandatory membership provisions of the Act; therefore, nurses sought other representation in the socio-economic domain. Several unions were formed—l'Alliance des Infirmières et Infirmiers du Québec, la Fédération des Syndicats Professionels d'Infirmières du Québec (FSPIIQ), and in 1967, the United Nurses of Montreal (UNM). L'Alliance and FSPIIQ bargained separately for staff nurses and management nurses whereas the UNM represented all nurses, including management nurses. This changed in 1970 when the UNM split into separate staff and management organizations—United Nurses' Inc. (UNInc.) and United Management Nurses' Inc (UMNInc.)

In 1972, many public services were affected by a strike of the Quebec Federation of Labour that involved nurses who were members of l'Alliance. These nurses were ordered to return to work when the Quebec National Assembly passed legislation to end the interruption in public services. In 1975, UNInc. joined the Corps des Organismes Professionels de la Santé (COPS) for the purpose of bargaining. Representing the vast majority of unionized nurses in Quebec, the organization also included the FSPIIQ and many other groups in the health professions among its members. (Botterill-Conroy, 1980). a number of strikes have occurred in Quebec since the one in 1972; however, because of the number of organizations that serve as bargaining agents in Quebec, the strikes have usually involved only certain sectors of the nurse population and other health workers.

Three nursing unions merged in December 1988 to form the Federation of Nurses of Quebec, resulting in greater union strength in bargaining for salary increases for nurses in Quebec, traditionally among the lowest paid nurses in Canada. The illegal walkout of members of the new organization and the subsequent standoff between the nurses and the Premier and his government in the midst of an election campaign unified nurses and gained them considerable public support for their cause. Their gains in this confrontation were impressive, and their public image improved.

NEW BRUNSWICK

In the 1960s, nurses in New Brunswick became concerned about their socioeconomic status and disenchanted with the procedure for determining salaries. Originally, the New Brunswick Association of Registered Nurses

(NBARN) provided recommendations on salaries and working conditions to the government on an annual basis. The first step in the process that would accord nurses more power was the NBARN's Social and Economic Welfare Committee's acquisition of standing committee status in 1967. After acquiring this status, the committee began helping nurses in health-care agencies to organize staff associations throughout the province. In 1968, the NBARN Provincial Collective Bargaining Council was established as a separate entity from the NBARN.

The first serious collective bargaining in New Brunswick began in 1969, when employers agreed to negotiate with the NBARN Provincial Collective Bargaining Council. When a stalemate occurred in the negotiations, the majority of New Brunswick nurses resigned. These resignations were withdrawn when the employer group agreed to go back to the bargaining table to negotiate in a fair and equitable manner. An agreement was signed by both parties soon after. In the same year, provisions of the Public Service Labour Relations Act gave nurses in the public sector the right to bargain collectively. The right was extended to the private sector two years later, through the Industrial Relations Act. The NBARN Provincial Collective Bargaining Council disassociated itself from the NBARN by becoming the New Brunswick Nurses' Provincial Collective Bargaining Council, although it had been a distinct and separate organization from its inception. Due to the legislative division between public and private sector bargaining provisions, another organization was formed: the New Brunswick Civil Service Nurses' Provincial Collective Bargaining Council. The two organizations merged in 1978 and became the New Brunswick Nurses Union (Botterill-Conroy, 1980).

NOVA SCOTIA

In 1966, the Registered Nurses Association of Nova Scotia (RNANS) organized a Committee on Social and Economic Welfare as a tangible means of increasing their influence on salaries and working conditions. In 1968, members decided that the RNANS should act as a bargaining agent for nurses employed in agencies, but professional nursing legislation made no provision for collective bargaining. The RNANS helped nurses in health-care agencies to seek certification as bargaining agents through the Trade Union Act. The first certifications were granted in 1969, and nurses began to consider the possibility of bargaining collectively. The staff associations first worked as a committee under the RNANS, but in keeping with the national trend, organized the Staff Nurses' Association of Nova Scotia. This organization was the forerunner of the Nova Scotia Nurses Union, organized three years later in 1976.

In 1971, a brief strike at Amherst Hospital, resulted in an agreement. Longer strikes took place at two institutions in 1972, and in 1975, nurses in 15 institutions withdrew their services because of a bargaining impasse. At that time, bargaining was still primarily at the local level, but nurses realized that greater gains could be made by working together. The first joint bargaining session took place in 1978; by 1979 most agencies were involved in the process (Botterill-Conroy, 1980).

PRINCE EDWARD ISLAND

As previously noted, collective bargaining rights for nurses were included in the PEI Nurses' Act when it was amended in 1972. The reason for that amendment was that nurses were specifically excluded from the PEI Labour Act. This legislation made the Provincial Collective Bargaining Committee, an arm of the Association of Nurses of Prince Edward Island (ANPEI), legally responsible for collective bargaining for nurses in the province. Although the Act was amended in 1972, the first collective agreement was not produced until 1974 because the government and the ANPEI did not agree on the regulations to implement the Act. A "showdown" between the nurses and the government was resolved when the government agreed to a compromise after most of the nurses threatened to resign. For a time it seemed that Prince Edward Island might be the only province that would not establish a separate organization for collective bargaining, but in 1982, the PEI Nurses' Act was amended to remove responsibility for collective bargaining from the ANPEI and the Labour Act was amended to ensure that nurses would not be excluded from its provisions.

NEWFOUNDLAND

The Association of Registered Nurses of Newfoundland (ARNN) prepared recommendations for salaries for nurses on an annual basis and submitted them as part of a brief to the Cabinet until 1970, when the process was discontinued because no action was being taken. The nurses then voted to establish the ARNN as their bargaining agent to engage in collective bargaining with government, for nurses in civil service, and the Newfoundland Hospital Association, for those employed by nongovernmental agencies. The process occurred on a voluntary basis at the outset, and the first collective agreement was concluded in 1970. The passage of the Public Service Act in 1972 provided legal recognition of collective bargaining rights for nurses and other health workers. This legislation reflected the spirit and intent of the 1973 Supreme Court decision; therefore, the ARNN was precluded from involvement in collective bargaining. The Newfoundland Nurses' Union was established in 1974 to take responsibility for the socioeconomic welfare of nurses.

UNION OR MANAGEMENT: WHERE TO DRAW THE LINE

It is difficult to describe the bargaining unit because of uncertainty about the appropriate classification of some supervisory positions. The dilemma is most prevalent at the level of first-line managers, and there are differences of opinion among the provinces as to whether certain employees can be included in the bargaining unit. In some areas, the "hiring and firing" standard has been used; managers who perform these functions are disqualified. In some instances management has redefined functions to ensure that first-line managers are not included in the bargaining unit. This redefinition has often occurred in provinces where the union has the right to strike; management may perceive the need for expert assistance on the front lines in the event of strike.

Many nurses do not wish to be removed from the bargaining unit because they will no longer have the security of a contract. There is little protection for management nurses in comparison to that provided by the collective agreement. Only the province of Quebec has a union for nurse managers that actively represents them. Nurses who hold administrative positions are thus at the mercy of their employers as far as salaries and benefits are concerned. Perhaps more important, they are also vulnerable in terms of job tenure. Employers are aware of the potential power of the nursing department, the largest sector of activity in any hospital. In some instances, administrators have been so threatened by strong nursing leaders that they have dismissed them and replaced them with an individual, or a new arrangement, that appeared to be less threatening.

PROFESSIONAL RESPONSIBILITY CLAUSES

In recent years, one of the trends in negotiations across the country has been to focus on the climate of the setting in which nurses are expected to function. The advent of professional responsibility clauses as part of collective agreements is tangible evidence of this trend, which may be the beginning of a new phase in collective bargaining. Emphasis may be shifting away from the concern with salaries and wages. Nurses are concerned about the quality and safety of the care they can provide in certain settings. Structuring the collective agreement to allow nurses to negotiate with the employer about certain resources that may be necessary to provide safe care is attractive to many unions. Examples of diffi-culty in providing adequate care, as documented in waivers, or disclaimer of responsibility forms, and diaries, have been used to provide data to support concerns discussed at meetings with management on professional responsibility committees.

IMPACT OF LOSS OF THE RIGHT TO STRIKE

The denial of the right of a particular professional group to strike is unusual and represents legislative interference with freedom to engage in the usual processes associated with collective bargaining (Anderson and Anderson, 1982). Ontario nurses lost the right to strike when the Hospital Disputes Arbitration Act of 1965 was passed (Botterill-Conroy, 1980). The right to strike was denied to nurses employed in hospitals in Alberta in 1983, after a period of acrimonious labour relations among Alberta nurses, the provincial government, and the Alberta Hospital Association. Three nurses' strikes between 1977 and 1982 moti-vated the Alberta government to enact legislation that denied hospital nurses (and some other workers) the right to strike because their services were essen-tial. This legislation imposed severe penalties on those who defied the law. It is possible that events in Alberta convinced the government of British Columbia that legislation to prevent nurses' strikes was necessary. A question that is often asked is whether the presence or absence of freedom to strike compromises a union's position at the bargaining table (Amundsen, 1975). In Ontario, nurses have not had the right to strike for two decades, but salary levels appear to be comparable with those in other provinces; until Alberta nurses asserted themselves in the wake of a booming economy in the late 1970s and early 1980s, Ontario nurses had the highest salaries in Canada.

PUBLIC IMPACT OF COLLECTIVE BARGAINING IN NURSING

It is difficult to determine the effect of the collective bargaining movement in nursing on public perceptions of nurses (McClelland, 1983). Stereotypic images of nurses as passive and unassertive have been undermined, particularly in provinces where nursing unions have been militant, and relations with employer groups and governments have been acrimonious (Baumgard, 1983; Kalisch and Kalisch, 1983; Kluge, 1982). Public response to nurses' strikes has varied. In Alberta in 1977, public sympathy was against the nurses; however, in 1979, there was a virtual outpouring of sympathy for the bargaining position of the nurses, and the public as well as members of other unions joined the picket lines, resulting in a large salary settlement. When Alberta's nurses went on strike again in 1982, there was little public support. In 1988, the Alberta public was reasonably supportive of the nurses during their illegal strike. Except for the fines levied against the union, few repercussions against nurses resulted from this illegal walkout.

There have been some notable and successful efforts by provincial governments in Alberta and British Columbia to restrict the activities and processes that unions can use to exert pressure on their employers in the collective bargaining process. The fact that public protest did not persuade either government to reconsider its decision about passing the legislation and in fact exerted pressure to stimulate the development of the legislation suggests a lack of public support for the unions and their activities. The fact that both provinces were entering periods of recession when this legislation was enacted indicates that the factors and pressures that influenced its development were economic.

Nurses represent the largest group of health professionals in the labour force, and even small increases in nurses' salaries will have a great impact on the total budget of a health-care agency; thus, employers may keep nurses' salaries at minimum level to effect cost savings and balance budgets. Although collective bargaining rights for nurses did not appear to change the goals of employer negotiating groups, it gave the process of negotiation a higher profile and gave nurses more power (Luttman, 1982; Zimmerman, 1985). Having fought hard for and achieved the right to bargain collectively with their employers, it is unlikely that nurses will ever again be remunerated so inadequately for their services (Stern, 1982; Numerof and Abrams, 1984). Financing of the healthcare system has acquired new dimensions since nurses' salaries showed higher proportionate increases to other comparably prepared professionals, and governments at federal and provincial levels have been hard pressed to resolve the inevitable economic problems of publicly funded health-care systems.

REFERENCES

Amundsen, N. (1975). Alternatives to strike in collective bargaining. *J Nurs Admin* 5(1). 11-12.

Anderson, J., and Anderson, M. (Eds.). (1982). Union-management relations in Canada. Don Mills, Ontario: Addison-Wesley.

Baumgart, A. (1983). The conflicting demands of professionalism and unionism. *AARN Newsletter* 39(6). 2-7.

Beletz, E. (1980). Organized nurses view their collective bargaining agent. *Supervisor Nurse* 9. 319-346.

Botterill-Conroy, M.D. (1980). Labour Relations, collective bargaining and nursing. Unpublished manuscript. Edmonton: Division of Health Services Administration and Community Medicine, The University of Alberta.

Cleland, V.S. Shared governance in a professional model of collective bargaining. *J Nurs Admin* 8(5). 39-43.

Conroy, M.D. and Hibberd, J. (1983). Areas for cooperation and conflict between nursing associations and negotiating bodies. In S. Quinn (Ed.). Cooperation and conflict: caring for the carers. Geneva: International Council of Nurses.

Eldridge, I. and Levi, M. (1982). Collective bargaining as a power resolution for professional goals. *Nurs Admin Q* 6(2). 29-40.

Hopping, B. (1976). Professionalism and unionism: conflicting ideologies. *Nursing Forum* 15(4). 372-383.

Jacox, A. (1980). Collective action; the basis for professionalism. *Supervisor Nurse* 9(9). 22-24.

Kalisch, B., Kalisch, P., and Young, R. (1983). Television news coverage of nurses' strikes: a resource management perspective. *Nursing Research* 33(3). 175-180.

Kluge, E.W. (1982). The profession of nursing and the right to strike. *Westminster Institute Review Fall* 3-6.

Luttman, P.A. (1982). Collective bargaining and professionalism: incompatible ideologies. *Nurs Admin Q* 6(2). 21-28.

McClelland, J. (1983). Professionalism and collective bargaining: a new reality for nurses and managers. *J Nurs Admin* 13(11). 36-38.

Muyskens, J.L. (1982). Nurses' collective responsibility and the strike weapon. *J Med Philos* 7. 101-112.

Numerof, R.E. and Abrams, M.N. (1984). Collective bargaining among nurses: Current issues and future prospects. *Health Care Management Review* 9(2). 61-67.

Ponak, A.M. (1981). Unionized professionals and scope of bargaining: A study of nurses. *Industrial and Labor Relations Review* 34(3). 396-407.

Rotkovich, R. (1980). Do labor union actions decrease professionalism? *Supervisor Nurse* 9(9). 16-18.

Rowsell, G. (1982). Bargaining: a means of conflict resolution. *International Nursing Review* 29(5). 141-145.

Stern, E.M. (1982). Bargaining: A means of conflict resolution. *Nurs Admin Q* 6(2). 9-21.

Zimmerman, A. (1985). Collective bargaining in the hospital: The nurse's right, the professional association's responsibility. In J. McCloskey and H. Grace (Eds.). *Current issues in nursing.* Boston: Blackwell Scientific Publications.

CHAPTER TWENTY ONE

Unionism and Professionalism: Conflicting or Compatible Processes?

JANET ROSS KERR

T he establishment of independent nursing unions, leading to at least two powerful organizations representing nurses in each province, has brought to the fore issues of relationships between professional organizations and unions. Historically, the collective bargaining function in each of Canada's 10 provinces was assigned to a branch of the professional association, and it gradually became an important part of the association mandate. The situation changed markedly after the 1973 Supreme Court decision, *Service Employees International Union v. Saskatchewan Registered Nurses Association* (SRNA). The Court agreed with the union's contention that the SRNA could not legally represent staff nurses in Saskatchewan because of management domination. This decision led to separation of professional associations and unions across the country (Rowsell, 1982).

Because the core memberships and professional and socioeconomic welfare interests of both organizations are the same, their relationships are strong. In most provinces, the professional nursing association is the largest professional organization and, although in most cases nursing unions are smaller than the professional organizations, their memberships are substantial. Since the public finances health-care services, and thus the major portion of salary budget for nursing, activities of nursing unions engender considerable public interest and media comment.

CHARACTERISTICS OF PROFESSIONAL ASSOCIATIONS AND UNIONS

Professional associations and unions have many common characteristics, including promoting welfare of members and improving their working conditions. Since professional associations include many who are not members of

221

nursing unions and whose economic interests are not served directly by unions, they continue to play an important role in advising and assisting; most nurses in management are included in this group. Professional associations are also interested in ensuring that salaries and benefits for staff nurses are maintained at sufficiently high levels to maintain the status of the profession and to encourage prospective candidates to enter nursing. All professions have an interest in seeing that members are appropriately remunerated, since the value that society places on services is reflected, at least in part, by the level of remuneration.

Professional associations and unions in nursing also share a concern for professional ethics, although it is the provincial association that is responsible for ensuring that the code of ethics is enforced. Professional maturity has been observed during the past decade in the attention given to developing and approving a code of ethics at the national level. Before the Canadian Nurses Association (CNA) Code of Ethics was approved and published in 1985, most provincial professional associations accepted the standard established by the International Council of Nurses (ICN) Code.

Although they have common interests, professional organizations and unions are different in many ways. The service ideal that is deeply embedded in the professional consciousness is reflected in legislation that regulates discipline of their members. This is true in every province except Ontario, where the College of Nurses of Ontario, a separate, quasi-autonomous body partially funded by government, is responsible for regulatory functions. Thus the focus of professional associations on the health and safety of recipients of nursing services is in the public interest. Standards of practice that support the public right to safe and competent care are of paramount importance. Unions are not legally bound to protecting the public interest; they focus almost exclusively on the socioeconomic needs of members.

Unions are concerned with the development of legally binding agreements that regulate staff nurses' salaries, working conditions, and other negotiable benefits. Professional associations, although concerned that salaries remain at appropriate levels and that good working conditions be maintained, are not responsible for developing these agreements and, therefore, are not active in this area. In fact, professional associations must avoid involvement in the collective bargaining process because any interference may be viewed negatively by sectors of the membership and result in controversy and conflict. In times of labour unrest, many professional associations have been pressured by both union members and management nurses to take a position on issues on the negotiating table. These situations are difficult for professional associations, and any action must be based on maintaining appropriate standards of nursing care and serving the public interest.

The mandate of professional associations is also aimed at improving and maintaining standards of nursing education. In most provinces, the professional association is legally authorized to monitor standards in programs of basic nursing education. However, in Alberta, this responsibility is delegated to the Universities Coordinating Council through the provisions of the Nursing Profession Act. In Ontario, the responsibility belongs to the Ministry of Colleges and Universities of the Government of Ontario under the Health Disciplines Act. In Quebec, where nursing programs are governed by the Ministry of Higher Education and Science, a mechanism for approval of diploma nursing programs has been developed with the advice of the Ordre des Infirmières et Infirmiers du Québec (OIIQ), and university nursing programs are subject to the approval process of all educational programs in their respective universities. Since the mid-1950s, there has been a drive to establish master's programs in nursing and to ensure their availability in various regions of the country. More recently, professional associations have focused their efforts on promoting doctoral education in nursing in Canada. It is possible that the first such program in Canada will be established during the next decade along with a number of other programs. Efforts to ensure opportunities for graduate study have coincided with a movement toward baccalaureate education in nursing as a requirement for entry to practice. The CNA and all member associations except one now support the requirement of baccalaureate status for entry to practice by the year 2000. Although there has been union support for educational standards and improvements in programs, unions tend to be less concerned with education and educational standards, even for advancement in the profession. The principle of seniority is normally the basis for unions' approaches to advancement and other workforce decisions. Competence, skill, and educational background are not usually the primary considerations when unions choose staff members for positions; opportunity is based on seniority in the health-care agency.

Finally, professional associations tend to value autonomy and independent action on the basis of individual evaluation and judgement. An individual approach to solving problems is contradictory to the approach taken by unions to achieve goals in collective bargaining. Individual needs are supplanted by those of the majority when pressing for contract demands, and the egalitarian view prevails: What is good for the average member is good for all members. Professional associations attempt to respond to the needs of various sectors of the membership and take public stands that will enhance standards of care and address needs of different categories of members. Unions must negotiate agreements that incorporate all the items agreed to by unions and management; therefore, the needs of the "average" member prevail.

FACTORS INFLUENCING COOPERATION AND CONFLICT

There is considerable controversy about whether it is possible for professional associations and unions to coexist in areas in which their objectives are sufficiently dissimilar to engender conflict. Conroy and Hibberd have postulated two propositions to address the question: "where collective bargaining is controlled by nurses and where professional values predominate, the greater the likelihood of cooperation between the professional body and the negotiating body" and "where collective bargaining is controlled by nurses and where union values predominate, the greater the likelihood of conflict between the professional body and the negotiating body" (1983, p. 84).

The underlying principle is that predominantly professional values are believed to encourage good relationships and cooperation, whereas the reverse may lead to conflict between the organizations.

In Quebec, where there are many large nurses' unions, the OIIQ took an unusual step in 1982; they issued a public statement that the professional association would not endorse the use of strike tactics if patient care was jeopardized:

> Governed by its mandate to ensure the protection of the public, the Bureau of the Ordre declares it is against withdrawal of services in the health field. This is the position it has taken following its study, having considered the different components of the context of the organization of health services, those of labour relations and the harm suffered by the population (Order of Nurses of the Province of Quebec, 1982, p. 14).

At the same time, the OIIQ suggested to the Commission Permanente du Travail et de la Main-d'Oeuvre de l'Assemblée Nationale du Québec that a new approach to collective bargaining was needed, recommending compulsory arbitration that would require participation by professionals and consumers. Very few professional associations in nursing or in other professions have taken a similar stand, undoubtedly because of the likelihood of a negative interpretation by a large section of the membership. The ability of the OIIQ to take this stand is impressive; it may be partially due to the fact that union membership in Quebec is scattered across several organizations. Another factor is the strength of Quebec legislation for nursing to incorporate mandatory registration and empowering the OIIQ to vigorously monitor standards of nursing practice in the province.

Unions, a new genre of nursing organization since 1973, have introduced a range of new interorganizational and intraorganizational challenges. The development of leadership and of organizational culture and norms takes time, as both are evolutionary processes. Nurses have had to learn about the collective bargaining process and how to use collective power to advantage. Professional nursing associations, dating formally from 1910 and informally for many years before that, have had a much longer history than nursing unions. The maturity that characterizes the relationship between professional associations and unions is extremely important, as it will define the nature of the interactions between them. The initial growth period of unions has been characterized by positive and negative relationships between these organizations. The fact that unions were organizational newcomers and professional associations may not have expected such independent and determined challenges from them may have caused some tension.

The potential or actual use of the strike as a weapon may also be a source of conflict between professional organizations and unions. Historically, nurses have been ambivalent about the use of strike; the no-strike policy of the CNA was not eliminated until 1982, after collective bargaining became a serious concern and was legally recognized. Although it may have been difficult for many of them, nurses were prepared to go on strike if labour negotiations did not produce the necessary outcomes. Kluge has examined the arguments about whether it is ethical for the nurse to withdraw services: "it is by no means a foregone conclusion that depriving individuals within society, no matter how strategically placed they may be, of their fundamental rights as persons will advance the public good" (1982, p. 6). However, Kluge (1982) did conclude that such a right exists "because of the nature of contracts and the fact that the nurse herself is an autonomous moral agent with the usual corresponding rights; qualified because she is a member of a monopolistic service group" (1982, p. 6). Nevertheless, the right is deemed to be "severely limited" (1982) by the public welfare concern.

Initially, nurses had the right to strike in all provinces except Prince Edward Island. However, as some of the provincial governments realized the tremendous impact of nurses' strikes, they attempted to eliminate the strike option. The right to strike was eliminated in Ontario in 1973 and in Alberta in 1983. In New Brunswick and Newfoundland the right to strike still exists, but there is legislation that requires designated employees to remain on the job to maintain essential services in the event of a strike. In British Columbia it is now illegal for nurses and other public sector workers to strike, and Newfoundland is currently reviewing its legislation with a view to eliminating public sector employees' right to strike. In Quebec the right to strike still exists, but legislation passed in 1981 and modified in 1986 requires nurses to maintain 90% staffing in health-care agencies; therefore, the impact of strike action is considerably limited. In Manitoba, the right to strike still exists, but there is an agreement between labour and management to maintain essential services in the event of a strike (K. Connors, personal communication, June 22, 1987). Although elimination of the right to strike is believed to hamper bargaining power, nurses' salaries in Ontario have been among the highest in the country during the decade and a half since the right to strike was denied. The legislation that the Alberta government introduced to deny essential workers, including nurses, the right to strike involved imposing severe penalties for violations, indicating that there was concern and within government ranks that nurses might engage in illegal walkouts. The 19-day illegal strike of Alberta nurses in 1988 substantiated this concern, and it resulted in heavy fines for the union and the appointment of a government commission to study the issues. In Quebec, an illegal walkout of nurses in 1989 resulted in a confrontation between the striking nurses, the Premier, and other government officials. The nurses emerged from the bitter confrontation relatively unscathed and their salary demands were met. Although striking nurses were subject to lose their seniority in health-care agencies, most agencies failed to implement this punitive measure.

RELATIONSHIPS BETWEEN PROFESSIONAL ASSOCIATIONS AND UNIONS

The history of collective bargaining in Canada indicates that the development of nursing unions was influenced by professional associations. In some cases, there have been "growing pains" as fledgling unions separated from the professional associations. A few of the provincial nurses unions have joined the trade union movement and severed their connections with the more profession-ally directed organizations, perhaps reflecting a process of maturation as the new organization searches its own identity. This association with the trade union movement, however, could adversely affect some members and the pro-fessional association. Because trade unions were originally founded by factory workers and employees in the unskilled labour category, the processes, lan-guage, and strategies used are not those of professionals. The image of nurses adopting the language and actions of general trade unionists may be abhorrent to many professional nurses, the professional nursing association, and other professional associations.

Although trade union alliances for nursing unions may result in fewer benefi-cial outcomes due to lack of member support for a less professional image, solidar-ity between groups in the trade union movement could benefit the union mem-bership as a whole. The sharing of resources, strategies, financial assistance, and moral support may benefit a nursing union. The professional association cannot provide support during periods of labour unrest because of its statutory mandate to serve the public interest before the professional interest. Nevertheless, the price of closer ties may require members to march with locals of other unions on strike. Media coverage that might ensue may not be pleasing to all members of the professional organization and may engender a less professional public image.

The development of a professional model of collective bargaining has been proposed by Cleland (1978). In essence, this model would promote stronger professional ties for the nursing unions. Although the Cleland model was devel-oped for the United States, where state nurses associations are often involved in bargaining, it includes some important perspectives on professional unionism that apply to the Canadian situation. New developments in unionism have resulted in the formation of more professional unions from highly educated professional groups, such as professors. Although most physicians are self-employed, the advent of medicare since 1957 has meant that payment for services comes primarily from the public purse; economic decline, the accumu-lation of large federal deficits, and the need to control public sector spending have led to controls on reimbursement of medical services under provincial health-care plans. Physicians' strikes have been infrequent, the two most notable being Saskatchewan in 1962 and Ontario in 1986. The increasing size of the professional sector of the union movement allows for the development of alli-ances, whereas nursing unions previously had little alternative but to form alliances with the trade union sector.

The American Nurses Association's Commission on Nursing Services devel-oped a statement designed to encourage good relationships between profes-sional and negotiating bodies entitled the "Characteristics of a Professional Climate of Administration and Practice in a Nursing Department" (1979). The characteristics include a system of shared governance; planning for quality of nursing staff as well as optimal staffing levels to meet patient needs; encourag-ing continuing education for staff; recognizing educational background, profes-sional experience, and level of clinical competence; appointing administrators with educational and experiential background appropriate for their positions; emphasizing nursing research in the practice setting; and establishing a joint practice committee to promote collegial relations between nurses and physicians (American Nurses Association, 1979).

Professional associations and nursing unions in most jurisdictions in Canada will probably establish relationships that allow each to perform its functions to the best advantage. Intolerance of the unique mandate of the negotiating body and the professional body may have clouded perceptions of the appropriateness of the other's actions in the past. With time may come understanding and acceptance of the role and functions of each type of organization. Many agencies, alliances, and relationships may be needed to help the profession accomplish its goals in the diverse areas noted. Communicating with the large membership complement of the profession to increase understanding on the part of its members presents challenges, which are difficult but not insurmountable. No doubt, compromise will characterize relationships between groups and affect the development of positive relationships. As Zimmerman has noted, "The history of organized nursing has been the history of a profession seeking to assert itself, to define and control its own body of knowledge and practice, to win recognition, respect and just reward for its contributions" (1983, p. 603).

REFERENCES

American Nurses Association. (1979). *Characteristics of a professional climate of administration and practice in a nursing department.* Kansas City, MO: The Association.

Cleland, V.S. (1978). Shared governance in a professional model of collective bargaining. *Journal of Nursing Administration, 8*(6), 39-43.

Conroy, M.D. and Hibberd, J.M. (1983). Areas for cooperation and conflict between nursing associations and negotiating bodies. In Quinn, S. (Ed.), *Cooperation and conflict: caring for the carers.* Geneva: International Council of Nurses.

Kluge, E.W. (1982). The profession of nursing and the right to strike. *Westminster Institute Review,* pp. 3-6.

Order of Nurses of the Province of Quebec. (1982). *Labour relations and withdrawal of services within the health sector.* Brief presented at the meeting of the Comitée Permanante du Travail et de la Main-d'Oeuvre de l'Assemblée Nationale du Québec. Quebec: The Association.

Rowsell, G. (1982). Changing trends in labour relations: effects on collective bargaining for nurses. *International Nursing Review, 29*(5), 141-145.

Zimmerman, A. (1983). Collective bargaining in the hospital: The nurse's right, the professional association's responsibility. In McCloskey, J. and Grace, H. (Eds.), *Current issues in nursing.* Boston: Blackwell Scientific Publications.

BIBLIOGRAPHY

Amundsen, N. (1975). Alternatives to strike in collective bargaining. *Journal of Nursing Administration, 5*(1), 11-12.

Anderson, J. and Anderson, M. (Eds.). *Union—management relations in Canada.* Don Mills, Ontario: Addison-Wesley.

Baumgart, A. (1983). The conflicting demands of professionalism and unionism. *AARN Newsletter, 39*(6), 2-7.

Beletz, E. (1980). Organized nurses view their collective bargaining agent. *Supervisor Nurse, 11*(9), 39-41.

Botterill-Conroy, M.D. (1980). *Labour relations, collective bargaining and nursing.* Unpublished manuscript, Division of Health Services Administration and Community Medicine. Edmonton, Alberta: University of Alberta.

Canadian Nurses Association. (1989). *Code of ethics.* Ottawa: The Association.

Eldridge, I. and Levi, M. (1982). Collective bargaining as a power resolution for professional goals. *Nursing Administration Quarterly, 6*(2), 29-40.

Hopping, B. (1976). Professionalism and unionism: Conflicting ideologies. *Nursing Forum, 15*(4), 372-383.

Jacox, A. (1980). Collective Action: The basis for professionalism. *Supervisor Nurse, 11*(9), 22-24.

Kalisch, B. Kalisch, P. and Young, R. (1983). Television news coverage of nurses' strikes: A resource management perspective. *Nursing Research, 33*(3), 175-180.

Luttman, P.A. (1982). Collective bargaining and professionalism: Incompatible ideologies. *Nursing Administration Quarterly, 6*(2), 21-28.

McClelland, J. (1983). Professionalism and collective bargaining: A new reality for nurses and managers, *Journal of Nursing Administrators, 13*(11), 36-38.

Muyskens, J.L. (1982). Nurses' collective responsibility and the strike weapon. *Journal of Medical Philosophy, 7*(1), 101-112.

Numerof, R.E. and Abrams, M.N. (1984). Collective bargaining among nurses: Current issues and future prospects, *Health Care Management Review, 9*(2), 61-67.

Ponak, A.M. (1981). Unionized professionals and scope of bargaining: A study of nurses, *Industrial and Labor Relations Review, 34*(3), 396-407.

Rotkovich, R. (1980). Do labor union actions decrease professionalism? *Supervisor Nurse, 11*(9), 16-18.

Stern, E.M. (1982). Bargaining: a means of conflict resolution. *Nursing Administration Quarterly, 6*(2), 9-21.

PART IV

Educating Nurses for the Future

CHAPTER TWENTY TWO

The Orgins of Nursing Education in Canada: An Overview of the Emergence and Growth of Diploma Programs: 1874 to 1974

JANET ROSS KERR

H igher education in formal settings outside the home was not available to women at the beginning of the nineteenth century. Just before the turn of the century, during which a crusade to allow women to gain entry into institutions of higher education began; Mary Wollstonecraft presented an articulate case for the schooling of women (1786, 1792). However, it was not until the middle of the century that the struggle to open the universities and professions to women began to gain momentum. Teaching was among the first professions to accept women, and in the western United States, seminaries and normal schools for women were founded:

> . . . where from the 1830s onward women teachers were churned out by the thousands for the numerous but very elementary schools of the expanding American republic. When universities opened in the new mid-western and western states in the 1860s and 70s, for example in Michigan, Wisconsin, Iowa and Utah, the need for fees fully as much as frontier egalitarianism dictated that these state-funded land-grant institutions would be coeducational from the outset (Jackel, 1985).

The more tradition-bound eastern states did not move as quickly. As a substitute for the full admission of women to existing institutions, such as Harvard and Yale, a number of universities, such as Radcliffe, Smith, Vassar, Bryn Mawr and Wellesley, were formed expressly for women. In Great Britain, the outcome of the debate about the education of women was affected by the fact that women greatly outnumbered men: at mid-century by 650,000 and in 1900 by 1½ million. Jackel notes:

> "Distressed gentlewomen," as impoverished middle-class women were called, was no mere phrase, therefore; the privations of these women when male breadwinners died or lost their incomes were very real, and they were not only material, but psychological and emotional as well. Consequently the plight of the single educated woman without means became one of the most widely debated social issues of nineteenth-century Britain (1982, pp. xiv-xvii).

The situation was particularly acute for middle-class women because social norms dictated that an unmarried woman should depend on her male relatives for financial and social support; however, the surplus of women supported the argument to allow women to become educated and use their skills in gainful employment so that they would not be dependent on male family members. Many women became active in the movement for higher education for women, including Florence Nightingale, who eloquently put the question as follows: "Why have women passion, intellect and moral activity — these three — and a place in society where no one of the three can be exercised?" (1929, p. 396).

EARLY PREPARATION FOR NURSING PRACTICE

Although nurses had some preparation for practice in the early days of the profession, it was largely informal. Observation, passing of knowledge from one person to another, and on-the-job training were the principal forms of educational preparation for nurses in the seventeenth, eighteenth, and nineteenth centuries. The three Augustinian nuns who share the distinction of being the first trained nurses practising in Canada from their arrival in 1639 received their preparation within their order, which had dedicated itself to the care of the sick. Jeanne Mance, the first lay nurse with preparation, designed her own course of study, travelling to several centres in France to learn methods used in care before emigrating to Canada to take up her vocation. For several centuries, women who joined religious orders were taught the skills of nursing by experienced members of the sisterhood.

THE NIGHTINGALE MODEL

The setting in which education for the practice of nursing was born and nurtured was the hospital. The founding of the first school of nursing, by Florence Nightingale in 1860 in conjunction with St. Thomas' Hospital in London, was evidently a development that was needed in Western society, for the idea swept the world and many hospital training schools were established throughout Europe and America. The term "historical accident," coined by Esther Lucile Brown, referred to the failure to apply the fundamental philosophy of the Nightingale model in the majority of the new schools (Brown, 1948, p. 164). In many of the new schools, the concept of autonomy was lost in the financial administration of the enterprise. Such schools became completely dependent on the financial stability of the hospital with which they were associated, and their policies were dictated by a board of trustees. The educational orientation was forgotten as the new schools-cum-service ministered to the needs of the sick. As a result, little attention was given to opportunities for instruction in the classroom or during clinical experience, and educational preparation was considered secondary to the needs of the hospital nursing service.

Certain principles of the first Nightingale school were present in new schools: Women who were as well prepared in nursing as possible were placed in charge of the schools, courses were spread over a period of two or three years, and incidental instruction was accompanied by extended periods of practice. It was an apprenticeship system that lacked a master craftsman. In North America, students who did not have responsibilities for patient care on the nursing units attended one or two hours of lectures that were given each week by a physician or the superintendent of nurses. Those who could attend related the information to those who could not.

One of the first schools in North America to advocate the principles of Florence Nightingale was the Bellevue Training School for Nurses; it was established in New York in 1873 by Sister Helen Bowden, an Anglican sister who had been educated at University College Hospital in England. Many Canadian women went to the United States to study during this period, and some, including Isabel Hampton Robb, Mary Adelaide Nutting, and Isabel Maitland Stewart, later became leaders in American nursing. Close contact was maintained between nurses in Canada and the United States through professional nursing organizations.

THE FIRST CANADIAN NURSING SCHOOLS

The first hospital diploma school in Canada, the St. Catharine's Training School, was initiated on June 10, 1874 by Dr. Theophilus Mack, an Irish-born physician who was convinced that "the prejudice held by many sick people against going into public hospitals could best be overcome by building up a profession of trained lay nurses" (Gibbon and Mathewson, 1947, p. 144). Healey (1990, pp. 31-32) notes that the date of the inception of the school "so closely parallels the start of Bellevue that in later years there will be those who seek to prove it was the first on the Continent to incorporate Nightingale's ideas" (1990). She also indicates that "Dr. Mack is credited with having the idea [for the establishment of the school] as early as 1864" (1990, p. 43). Constraints were again imposed, as "nursing was considered an undesirable vocation for a refined lady, the only acceptable profession being teaching" (Healey, 1990, p. 44).

Admission standards were "plain English education, good character, and Christian motives" (St. Catharines Annual Report [cited in Healey, 1989]). The philosophy of the school is reflected in a statement concerning instruction (Healey, 1989):

> Every possible opportunity is seized to impart instruction of a practical nature in the art of nursing, while teachings will be given in Chemistry, Sanitary Science, Popular Physiology and Anatomy, hygiene and all such branches of the healing art as

a nurse ought to be familiar with. . . . The vocation of nursing goes hand in hand with that of physician and surgeon, and are absolutely indispensable one to the other. Incompetency on the part of a nurse renders nugatory the best effects of the doctor in the critical moments and has frequently resulted in loss of life. All the most brilliant achievements of modern surgery are dependent to a great extent upon careful and intelligent nursing . . . The skilled nurse, by minutely watching the temperature, conditions of skin, pulse, respirations, the various functions of all the organs and reporting faithfully to the attending physician, must increase the chances of recovery twofold" (Healey, 1990, pp. 45-46).

The School for Nurses associated with the Toronto General Hospital was established in 1881; 17 students enrolled, but 8 resigned or were dismissed (Gibbon and Mathewson, 1947). When Miss Mary Agnes Snively was appointed Superintendent of the School in 1884, there were no systems for work or study, no written orders, no history records, and no systems for obtaining ward supplies. The living conditions were distressing. The School was gradually reorganized and the modern plan developed (Gibbon and Mathewson, 1947). In 1894, 53 candidates for the program were selected from 647 applications. Also in 1894 21 graduands and 4 graduate nurses held staff positions. The programs's size made it the largest nursing education program in Canada (Gibbon and Mathewson 1947). Miss Snively worked hard to improve the educational component of the program as it developed. In 1896 a three-year course was introduced that included "84 hours of practical nursing and 119 hours of instruction by the medical staff" (Gibbon and Mathewson, 1947, p. 154).

Miss Snively's involvement with the International Council of Nurses (ICN) began in 1899 the year the council was founded. She became the first honourary treasurer of the organization, and her efforts in establishing the Canadian National Association of Trained Nurses (later the Canadian Nurses Association [CNA])and in serving as its first president are an indication of the stature she achieved (Canadian Nurses Association [CNA], 1968). Written records of CNA meetings indicate that Miss Snively supported changes designed to improve nursing education programs. Commenting on the recently introduced plan to devote the first part of the training period to a preliminary course at a meeting, she stated:

> They are also taught anatomy, physiology and simple lessons in nursing and practical demonstrations during the three-months period. We have a room fitted up with bedding and linen and all the necessaries, there the nurses are taught to do practically all the work that will be required of them after they enter the school as nurses. At the end of three months, probationers pass an examination in all they have been taught theoretically, and also in practical work (Gibbon and Mathewson, 1947, p. 155).

At the Montreal General Hospital, which was founded in 1822, early interest in establishing a school of nursing led to the Committee of Management's correspondence in 1874 to secure assistance in developing "a system of trained hospital nurses such as approved of in England" (MacDermot, 1940, p. 17). Communication may have been initiated by Miss Maria Machin, a native of Quebec who was engaged in nursing in London at the Nightingale Home (Baly,

1986, p. 143). Baly notes that: "It is unlikely that Miss Nightingale would have selected Miss Machin, for her loss as Home Sister to the Nightingale Home would be irreparable for she had not long been installed and was regarded as the one person who could keep the peace with Mrs. Wardroper." (Baly, 1986, p. 144).

Correspondence that ensued with Florence Nightingale and her brother-in-law Henry Bonham Carter, the President of the Fund, dealt primarily with plans for the new hospital building that had been promised by the Committee of Management. Miss Machin set out for Montreal with four Nightingale nurses, but the mission failed. The difficulties that arose during Miss Machin's tenure at the hospital included a high staff turnover rate, and "there is reason to believe there was 'a lack of adaptability on the part of Miss Machin whose uncompromising purpose was to apply Nightingale principles of nursing care at whatever cost and without much thought for diplomacy'" (Redpath [cited in Baly, 1986, p. 146]). The problems she encountered and her failure to accomplish her initial objective, establishing a training school for nurses, led to her perception of failure in her mission and she returned to England in 1878. Baly notes that the Council of the Nightingale Fund did not make much of their efforts in Montreal or elsewhere because Cook (Nightingale's biographer) had only given Montreal a passing reference, and Carter clearly thought that the entire issue should be forgotten (Baly, 1986). Recently Baly has taken issue with "nursing historians" who "have claimed that Nightingale missioners took reformed nursing to both Canada and Australia and have made much out of little evidence" (Baly, 1986).

The School for Nurses at the Montreal General Hospital was finally initiated in 1890, under the direction of Miss Nora Livingston, the daughter of English parents who was born in Sault Ste. Marie, Michigan, raised in Como, Quebec, and educated at the New York Hospital's Training School for Nurses. When she arrived, "Conditions at the General were deplorable . . . and within a year of her entrance she had so revolutionized the organization of the hospital as to make it almost unrecognizable compared with conditions of the previous year" (*Famous nurses in history*, undated).

The popularity of the School increased rapidly. Miss Livingston reported 169 applications in the first year, 80 of which were accepted on approbation. Of the 80 that were accepted, 42 of them proved satisfactory, 4 resigned, and 2 were dismissed (Gibbon and Mathewson, 1947). Recollections (Desjardins) of Miss Livingston's abilities are positive:

> . . . what an extraordinary amount of tact and gumption this remarkable woman possessed. Not only had she to change the incredible conditions of nursing but above all she had to change the attitudes of the administrators, men animated by good intentions but more accustomed to conducting the affairs of business than those of a hospital (1971, p. 103).

The nursing education program gradually took shape; one of the early graduates recalls: "Thinking of those days so long ago, I think I hear Miss Livingston say—'Nurse—the patient—always the patient first!' I think that spirit still lives within these old walls" (Gibbon and Mathewson, 1947, p. 149).

The move to establish hospital schools of nursing swept the country. The Winnipeg General Hospital initiated the first Training School for Nurses in the West in 1887, which served all of the West in its early years. Gibbon and Mathewson note that 134 graduates of that school served as matrons and nursing sisters in World War I (1947). In the maritime provinces, the Saint John General Hospital in Fredericton and the Victoria Public Hospital, in Saint John, opened Training Schools for Nurses in 1887 and the Victoria General in Halifax and the Prince Edward Island Hospital in Charlottetown followed in 1890. In Vancouver, the General Hospital began an educational program in 1891 and in Alberta, a school was initiated at Medicine Hat in 1894. By 1930, there were approximately 330 schools of nursing in Canada (Canadian Nurses Association, 1968).

RECOGNIZING THE NEED FOR IMPROVEMENT IN STANDARDS

Because hospitals were staffed primarily by students in the late nineteenth and early twentieth centuries, there were few opportunities for securing a staff position after graduation. Graduates who practised their profession usually did so as private duty nurses in the homes of the sick. Therefore, one of nurses' first struggles after the hospital-based system of nursing education was established involved replacing students with graduate nurses as the primary providers of nursing care. Mabel Holt writes of an "experiment" in a Montreal hospital in which a nursing unit was totally staffed with graduate nurses and justified the endeavour as follows:

> There are, however, other and even more important benefits, affecting the nursing profession as a whole, which have come about as a direct result of this new policy. Instead of adding to the output of graduate nurses during these difficult years by increasing the enrolment of our school of nursing, we have created employment for those who otherwise would have been obliged to enter an overcrowded and highly competitive field. I also consider it to be a great factor in the education of the public concerning its responsibility to nurses and nursing that a Board of Directors should be willing to try out the difficult experiment of staffing a complete unit with graduate nurses (1936, p. 10).

In view of the firm establishment and acceptance of the hospital-based educational system, the difficulty that the university-based system encountered in establishing its credibility in the eyes of patients, the public, and even nurses is easily understood. Bonin (1976) commented: "So deeply time-honoured became this system of nursing education that it became difficult to imagine nursing, like other professions, as belonging to a university setting for the education of its practitioners" (1976, pp. xii-xiii).

Increased awareness of deficiencies resulted in a number of surveys of nursing education in Canada and the United States. In 1923 the Goldmark Report, commissioned by the Rockefeller Foundation to investigate conditions in schools of nursing in the United States, described appalling conditions in nursing schools. The report advocated more attention for the educational preparation of nurses, more stringent admission requirements for nursing schools, and provision of federal grants to assist schools in raising their educational standards. In *Nurses, Patients and Pocketbooks* (Burgess, 1928) and *Nursing Schools Today and Tomorrow* (Committee on the Grading of Nursing Schools, 1934), reports of a joint committee of several professional nursing associations and professional organizations of related health fields on the grading of schools of nursing restated the shortcomings of the system. It was concluded that:

> 1. No hospital should be expected to bear the cost of nursing education out of funds collected for the care of the sick. The education of nurses is as much a public responsibility as the education of physicians, public school teachers, librarians, ministers, lawyers, and other students planning to engage in professional public service, and the cost of such education should come, not out of the hospital budget, but from private or public funds.
> 2. The fact that a hospital is faced with serious financial difficulties should have no bearing upon whether or not it will conduct a school of nursing. The need of a hospital for cheap labour should not be considered a legitimate argument for maintaining such a school (Burgess, 1928, p. 447).

Regarding the institutions that conduct schools of nursing: "The Grading Committee reports showed clearly that the system of hospital-owned and-operated schools of nursing was still practically universal. The proportion of university schools was so small in 1932 that they scarcely figured numerically, however important their influence might be individually" (Stewart, 1947, p. 213).

The significance of the 1910 Flexner Report on medical education and its impact on nursing education have been noted by Allemang (1974). Funded by the Carnegie Foundation, the Flexner Report was commissioned because of concern for the quality of medical practice and medical education and the concomitant inability of the American Medical Association and the Council on Medical Education to achieve reforms. As a result of the Flexner Report, the character of medical education changed quickly; the proprietary schools that operated for profit were closed, and standards in medical education began to rise as the universities assumed major responsibility for the support and direction of the enterprise. According to Allemang: "The Flexner report on medical education provided a model for the new approach to nursing reforms" (1974, p. 115-116). Thus the call for improved standards of nursing education became more intense as the twentieth century began.

In Canada, unrest similar to that in the United States surfaced a few years later over conditions in schools and hospitals. In 1927, a joint committee of the Canadian Medical Association (CMA) and the CNA was organized to study the problems. The Committee appointed Dr. George Weir, of the Department of Education at the University of British Columbia, to conduct a survey to address these matters. The study documented the problems and drew attention to the changes needed to improve standards of education and service. The fact that small hospitals had established schools of nursing led to a presumption that the size of a hospital was important because there could be a lack of variety in clinical experience in small institutions. The survey indicated that this presumption was educationally unsound, but it also indicated that schools associated with hospitals with fewer that 75 beds were more concerned with the financial needs of the hospital than with the educational needs of nursing students in operating programs (CNA, 1968; Gibbon and Mathewson, 1947; Weir, 1932). This suspicion about the general motives of hospitals in offering educational programs led to the recommendation that authority and responsibility for schools of nursing be vested within the general provincial system of education: "The development of training schools for nurses primarily as educational institutions functioning as an integral part of the general educational system of the province and financed on the same principle as are normal schools, should be made an immediate objective" (Weir, 1932, p. 116).

This recommendation was repeated many times in the years before the basic diploma nursing education program began to move within the purview of the general postsecondary system of education. After the Weir Report was tabled, nurses turned their attention to developing strategies to improve the quality of education in schools of nursing.

> Moved by the recommendations in the Weir Report indicating the need for immediate correction of defects in administrative and teaching policies of hospital schools of nursing, in 1932, the Canadian Nurses' Association . . . organized a National Curriculum Committee with the responsibility of constructing a curriculum guide (Letourneau, 1975, p. 6).

The curriculum guide, published in 1936, was intended to serve as an interim measure that would help schools of nursing during their transfer to provincial educational systems (CNA, 1936).

The Demonstration School

The minimal progress through the next decade led the CNA to secure Red Cross funding for a demonstration school that would ascertain the feasibility of preparing a nurse in less than three years. The school, known as the Demonstration School, was established in 1948 in conjunction with the Metropolitan Hospital in Windsor, Ontario. Red Cross funding enabled the Demonstration School to be financially independent from the hospital. The experiment continued until 1952, when the Demonstration School reverted to its former status of financial dependence on the hospital. An extensive evaluation, conducted by a joint committee of the CNA and the Canadian Education Association (CEA) that was chaired by A. R. Lord, indicated that the venture was a success; it was possible to prepare a nurse for practice in two years:

> The conclusion is inescapable. When the school has complete control of students, nurses can be trained at least as satisfactorily in two years as in three, and under better conditions, but the training must be paid for in money instead of in services. Few students can afford substantial fees nor can the hospital pass on such additional costs to the "paying patient". Some new source of revenue is the only solution (Lord, 1952, p. 54).

The Centralized Teaching Program

In Saskatchewan there was increasing consternation about the lack of foundational courses in basic sciences for nursing students in diploma programs and the general shortage of suitably qualified faculty. The Saskatchewan Registered Nurses Association (SRNA) sought and secured financial support from the W.K. Kellogg Foundation to centralize teaching of basic sciences for all schools of nursing in the Saskatoon and Regina areas. The program provided for:

> . . . a duly authorized sixteen weeks' program of instruction in the basic sciences for nursing students. It is an integral part of the curriculum plan of the hospital school of nursing provided apart from the hospital school at a designated centre permitting centralization of effort and resources not immediately available in the local setting of the participating schools (Schmitt, 1957, p. 6).

Although considerable effort was directed to organizing this effort and it was declared a success, it was not considered a panacea for the ills of basic nursing education. Although many areas of the country decided not to offer basic science instruction on regional basis, this endeavour provided a solution to some problems and issues in basic diploma nursing education.

Accreditation

The CNA next directed attention to the quality of instruction in schools of nursing. A pilot project under the direction of Executive Director Helen Mussallem was designed to determine whether schools were ready for a national voluntary accreditation program. The findings were somewhat disappointing; only 16% of schools met the criteria for accreditation. It was also determined that little progress had been made in improving the quality of schools since Dr. Weir had made his Report public some 30 years before. Dr. Mussallem thus recommended that the CNA not embark on an accreditation program, but rather a school improvement program that would lead to accreditation in the future (Mussallem, 1960). The CNA implemented Dr. Mussallem's recommendation, and accreditation was not seriously discussed again until the late 1970s. At that time, because of the costs associated with accreditation, it was not considered for diploma schools in the absence of an organization willing to provide the necessary funds.

The Royal Commission on Health Services

A trend gradually became evident in the majority of the two-year schools that were established. In the brief presented to the Royal Commission on Health Services, the CNA favoured "introducing diploma schools of nursing into the post-high school system of the country" (Mussallem, 1964, p. 137). The Royal Commission on Health Services, or the Hall Commission, surveyed the entire range of health services (including nursing) that were provided and reported in 1964. Nursing education programs that took fewer than three years and functioned independently from the hospital were recommended:

> The Commission believes this to be the right approach. The educational system for nursing should be organized and financed like other forms of professional education. An additional reason for the change in nursing education is not only that we shall obtain equally, if not better, qualified personnel in shorter time, but that a substantial part of hospitalized patient-care will no longer depend, as it does now, upon apprentices (Government of Canada, 1964, pp. 64-69).

A certain momentum, created by the increased pace of change after the release of the Hall Commission Report, may have led to the CNA's plan for the development of nursing education programs within the general educational system. Mussallem declares that:

> Whether nursing education should be placed within the general educational system can no longer be considered a point of debate. It is possible and it can be done . . . The Canadian Nurses' Association, in cooperation with its provincial counterparts, should take steps to implement the plan present in the study . . . leading to the inclusion of all nursing education within the general educational system of each province (1964, pp. 183-185) .

THE MOVEMENT TO ESTABLISH TWO-YEAR SCHOOLS
Saskatchewan

Saskatchewan was the first province to consider implementing two-year diploma nursing schools. The Regina Grey Nuns Hospital School of Nursing requested and received permission from the SRNA to develop a two-year diploma program in nursing on an experimental basis. This led to the establishment of two year diploma programs in the two major cities of the province in 1967. Letourneau cites the difficulties that occurred because "Saskatchewan had forged ahead in legislating change without having an educational system fully established to absorb programs" (1975, p. 25). To avoid the development of isolated institutions that would be for nursing only, the SRNA insisted "that diploma nursing for nurses be established in post-secondary institutions for higher education" (Saskatchewan Registered Nurses' Association [SRNA], 1966, p. 1). In Saskatchewan "the trend was not for hospital schools of nursing to transmute to an educational institution, but rather to gradually phase out by ceasing to admit students" (Letourneau, 1975, p. 27). The two new two-year programs in Saskatchewan were developed at the Kelsey Institute in Saskatoon and at Wascana Institute in Regina.

Quebec

In Quebec, the Royal Commission of Inquiry on Education, also known as the Parent Commission, reported its findings in 1966, recommending not starting one or two two-year schools suggested by the Association of Nurses of the Province of Quebec (ANPQ), but a total transfer of programs to the general system of education. The contention of this report was that the entire education system was examined by the Commission, and the nursing recommendations were totally consistent with findings in other fields. Campbell has commented about the impact of the Parent Commission's report: "It would be difficult to name any royal commission in the history of Canadian education whose judgements more profoundly altered the structure and process of the entire educational system of a province and with greater speed" (1971, p. 54).

In 1967, three programs were selected for transfer to the Colleges d'Enseignement General et Professionnel (CEGEP) to serve as a pilot projects; 17 were selected in 1968, and others after that: "In 1972, the last Schools of Nursing attached to hospitals closed, ending three-quarters of a century of history. Now a network of 40 nursing options exist throughout 'la belle province'" (Association of Nurses of the Province of Quebec, 1972, p. 1) with the two English-language CEGEPs that have diploma programs, the number of programs was 42. Also, "A distinctively unique characteristic of education offered in a CEGEP is that it is tuition free for all full-time students" (Letourneau, 1975, p. 77). Thus, as nursing schools became part of the community college system in Quebec, nursing students began receiving the same educational benefits as students studying in other professions and vocations.

Ontario

Elsewhere in Canada, models for two-year programs emerged as independent, freestanding institutions. The Nightingale School of Nursing in Toronto, established in 1960, was financed by the Ontario Hospital Services Commission. Situated in close proximity to New Mount Sinai Hospital where clinical experience was obtained, the school was administered by an independent board of directors. The Quo Vadis School of Nursing was established in 1964 under the auspices of the Catholic Hospital Conference of Ontario. Again, financial support was provided by the Ontario Hospital Services Commission and the school was administered by an independent board of directors. This school had a mandate to structure its educational program to attract mature students (McLean, 1964).

The School of Nursing established at Ryerson Polytechnical Institute in Toronto in 1964 had the distinction of being the first nursing diploma program in Canada to be initiated in an educational institution (Letourneau, 1975). The efforts of the Registered Nurses Association of Ontario (RNAO) were influential in instigating this effort; Ryerson's administration and board reviewed the RNAO's proposal carefully, decided to establish the school, and accepted the first class in 1964. Similar programs were developed in colleges across the country. Although Ryerson's program was initially structured as a three-year program, it was later converted to a two-year program. Dr. Moyra Allen of McGill University and Professor Mary Reidy of the University of Montreal evaluated the Ryerson program after five years and confirmed the soundness of the program. The findings "point to the potential value of preparing a nurse in a college-level institution within the general system of education" (Allen and Reidy, 1971, p. 262).

In 1967, 20 Colleges of Applied Arts and Technology (CAAT) were created in the province by order of the Ontario government. In 1969, Humber College was the first of these institutions to develop a nursing program. Ontario moved ahead on another front before it began to develop schools of nursing within the CAAT system on a large scale; freestanding schools of nursing called regional schools were developed apart from the general education system. There were no regional schools in 1965, but "by the end of 1967 there were eight, and ten more ... expected within the next five years" (Murray, 1970, p. 132). The government also decided, in spite of the reservations expressed by the College of Nurses of Ontario, to move to "two plus one" programs, initially in a "ten-year plan leading to a gradual shortening and regionalization of schools of nursing" (Letourneau, 1975, p. 144). This change occurred rapidly, but it was a passing phenomenon; the move to establish two year schools under the aegis of the CAATs was overwhelming, and "in 1972, policies with regard to free room and board were altered; the year of internship was discontinued, and nursing students were required to pay tuition fees" (Letourneau, 1975, p. 145). Thus by 1973 56 schools had been absorbed by 23 CAATs.

British Columbia

In British Columbia, the first diploma nursing program to be established within the general educational system was a jointly planned venture of the British Columbia Institute of Technology (BCIT) and the Registered Nurses Association of British Columbia (RNABC) in 1967. The RNABC's position was well known:

> Nursing can no longer be taught by apprenticeship methods; yet the students are part of the hosptial service personnel . . . We believe that the method of financing nursing education partly through hospital operating costs and partly through service rendered by students is no longer an adequate or desirable one (1967, p. 20).

Funding for this program was obtained through an agreement between the federal and provincial governments for vocational-technical education. During the development of the program the RNABC successfully lobbied for changes in existing legislation to allow for development of new and innovative models of diploma nursing programs. Thus, community colleges throughout the province were able to develop nursing programs, and in 1965 Vancouver City College in Langara and Selkirk College in Castlegar initiated programs. By 1974, four programs had been developed, and several others were in the planning stages; although four hospital diploma programs still remained in operation.

Alberta

In Alberta, the transfer of diploma programs to the community colleges also was incomplete by 1974. Mount Royal College in Calgary was the first college in the province to develop a diploma nursing program in 1967. Others included Red Deer College and College St. Jean (merged with Grant MacEwan Community College in 1972) in 1968, Lethbridge Community College in 1969, Medicine Hat College in 1970, and Grant MacEwan Community College in 1972. Although seven hospitals had phased out their schools, six were still in operation in the province in 1974 (Letourneau, 1975). A report prepared by Dr. G. R. Fast in 1971 recommended the transfer of remaining diploma programs to the Alberta college system; however, the recommendation was not well received by all stakeholder groups, reportedly because of a lack of consultation and discussion preceding the release of the report.

Manitoba

The transfer of diploma nursing programs to the colleges in Manitoba was also incomplete by 1974, with five hospital-based programs continuing to operate.

The first and only college diploma program was established at Red River Community College in 1970, the result of "action on the part of the Departments of Health and Education and the adjoining cooperative efforts of the MARN" (Letourneau, 1975, p. 253). The Manitoba Association of Registered Nurses (MARN) was influential in establishing the program because it supported the inclusion of diploma nursing programs in the general system of education and shortening their duration to two years (Manitoba Association of Registered Nurses [MARN], 1968).

The Atlantic Provinces

By the end of 1974 there had been some activity in the Atlantic provinces in relation to the movement that was sweeping other parts of the country, but activity was limited. A study conducted by Katherine MacLaggan of nursing education in New Brunswick resulted in a recommendation that the general educational system be vested with responsibility for diploma nursing education (MacLaggan, 1965). According to Letourneau: "conflicting forces have rendered impossible the actual transfer of hospital programs to the system of education" (1975, p. 275) In 1971, the Abbis Report recommended that four independent schools be established similar to a pilot program at the Saint John School of Nursing, which had been converted to a two-year program, but financed through health dollars from the Department of Health (Study Committee on Nursing Education, 1971). Because the document contained controversial recommendations about registration and standards in addition to recommendations about diploma nursing education that were not entirely satisfactory, the New Brunswick Association of Registered Nurses indicated that it was "gravely alarmed at the import of these recommendations and quite surprised that they appear in the Report . . . earnestly recommend that they be rejected" (NBARN, 1971, p. 23)

Because there was no authority for establishing community colleges in New Brunswick until 1974, transfer of diploma nursing programs to the system of general education across the province was not possible. Thus four independent schools and one hospital school were established in Bathurst, Edmunston, Moncton, and Saint John (Letourneau, 1975). These programs were autonomous in all respects except finance. However, as Letourneau (1975) observed: "Trends point to an eventual orderly transfer of independent programs to the provincial system of education, but first the community college system must develop sufficiently to absorb these programs" (1975, p. 290).

The Registered Nurses Association of Nova Scotia (RNANS) had a leading role in pressing for changes in the system of nursing education in that province. The RNANS' appointment of a curriculum council to determine each school's plan for change may have hastened and facilitated self-study by the schools so that: "Seven hospital schools of nursing were authorized, in the period extending from 1969 to 1970, to begin a two-year program or to effect a change in this direction" (Letourneau, 1975, p. 293). As with nurses across the country, in 1969 nurses in Nova Scotia had to stop an attempt to remove the regulatory powers vested in their association. Nova Scotia also faced the problem of having a community college system that needed to "develop sufficiently to absorb these programs" (Letourneau, 1975, p. 290).

The Association of Nurses of Prince Edward Island (ANPEI) requested that the three existing hospital schools of nursing in its province be phased out and replaced by one program to make the best use of staff and facilities and to provide the best possible education for students (Letourneau, 1975). The organization also sponsored a study to assess the climate and readiness for change in the diploma nursing education system; this study indicated that it was not the right time right for major change (Rowe, 1967). In 1968, the ANPEI again pressed for change in the system, and this time the government responded by providing authority for developing one independent "two plus one" program for the province, replacing the three hospital schools (Letourneau, 1975). Efforts in 1974 to link the school with a community college, Holland College (1975) were unsuccessful.

Letourneau stated: "The transfer of hospital schools of nursing to the system of education is, as in other Atlantic provinces, non-existent in Newfoundland" (1975, p. 308). Four hospital schools of nursing continued to exist there, although the Association of Registered Nurses of Newfoundland (ARNN) tried to encourage change. Arpin, a consultant hired by the ARNN to help formulate goals, recommended that "the three schools of nursing in St. John's develop their curriculum plans so that the theory and experience essential for meeting the school objectives is included in the first two years of the program" (Arpin, 1972, p. 1). By 1973, the three schools in St. John's had established "two plus one" programs and the Corner Brook program had reduced its length to two years.

CONCLUSION

In 1974, 100 hundred years after the inception of the Mack Training School for Nurses in St. Catharines, the system of diploma nursing education had undergone a transformation. In 1874, despite the wide recognition of Florence Nightingale's work around the world and despite the historic work of the nursing sisterhoods in Canada dating from the seventeenth century, it was still not socially acceptable for a woman to do nursing in a hospital or leave home to enter a school to acquire knowledge and skills for that work. In 1974, 109 basic diploma schools of nursing (Letourneau, 1975) operated across the country, and widespread debate continued about the quality of instruction and the expectations for nursing students in comparison to those for other students in the system of postsecondary education. Issues change over time; the comparison of diploma nursing education to that provided at the university level as the most appropriate level for beginning practice is a current issue of concern in the profession that is discussed in more detail in Chapters 23 and 24. Nevertheless, one can see both a progression and transition of nurses' ideas about their educational system. It is evident that there is a fundamental concern for standards of education and practice in view of the responsibility for safe patient care. With the development of the discipline and the expansion of the knowledge base, the appropriateness of the environment in which learning takes place is at issue. The fact that nursing is one of the last sex-segregated professions has led to attention to the potential for differential treatment, with improvement in the status of women as they gradually gained fundamental rights and privileges previously accorded only to men. Although it is difficult to say what the next 100 years will mean to nursing and nursing education, it is likely that nurses will continue to work to improve standards of education and practice.

REFERENCES

Allemang, M.M. (1974). *Nursing education in the United States and Canada, 1873-1950: Leading figures, forces, views on education.* Ph.D. dissertation, Seattle: University of Washington.

Allen, Moyra and Reidy, Mary. (1971). *Learning to nurse: The first five years of the Ryerson nursing program.* Ontario: Registered Nurses Association of Ontario.

Arpin, Kathleen. (1972). *Report of visit to the Association of Registered Nurses of Newfoundland.* St. John's: AARN.

Association of Nurses of the Province of Quebec. *CEGEP nursing education after five years.* Montreal: Author.

Baly, Monica. (1986). *Florence Nightingale and the nursing legacy.* London: Croom Helm.

Bonin, M.A. (1976). *Trends in integrated basic degree nursing programs in Canada: 1942-1972.* Ph.D. dissertation. Ottawa: University of Ottawa.

Brown, E.L. (1948). *Nursing for the future.* New York: Russell Sage Foundation.

Burgess, M.A. (1928). *Nurses, patients and pocketbooks.* New York: Committee on the Grading of Nursing Schools.

Campbell, Gordon. (1971). *Community colleges in Canada.* Toronto: McGraw-Hill.

Canadian Nurses Association. (1936). *A proposed curriculum for schools of nursing in Canada.* Montreal: Author.

Canadian Nurses Association. (1968). *The leaf and the lamp.* Ottawa: Author.

Committee on the Grading of Nursing Schools. (1934). *Nursing schools today and tomorrow.* New York: Author.

Desjardins, Edouard. (1971). *Heritage: History of the nursing profession in the province of Quebec.* Quebec: Association of Nurses of the Province of Quebec.

Famous nurses in history. undated. "Gertrude Elizabeth Livingston." Guelph: The Sterling Rubber Company Ltd.

Gibbon, J.M. and Mathewson, M.S. (1947). *Three centuries of Canadian nursing.* Toronto: Macmillan.

Government of Canada. (1964). *Royal Commission on health services,* vol. I. (Emmett M. Hall, Chairman). Ottawa: Queen's Printer.

Healey, Phyllis. (1990). *The Mack training school for nurses.* Unpublished Ph.D. dissertation. Austin, TX: University of Texas.

Holt, M. (1936). Staffing with graduate nurses. *The Canadian nurse, 32*(1), 5-10.

Jackel, Susan. (1985). "Women in Canadian universities: A historical overview". Keynote address to the Conference and Annual Meeting, Western Region, Canadian Association of University Schools of Nursing, University of Alberta, Edmonton, Alberta.

Jackel, Susan (Ed.). (1982). *A flannel shirt & liberty.* Vancouver: University of British Columbia Press.

Letourneau, Marguerite. (1975). *Trends in basic diploma nursing programs within the provincial systems of education in Canada 1964-1974.* Ph.D. dissertation. Ottawa: University of Ottawa.

Lord, A.R. (1952). *Report of the evaluation of the Metropolitan School of Nursing, Windsor, Ontario.* Ottawa: Canadian Nurses Association.

MacDermot, H.E. (1940). *History of the School of Nursing of the Montreal General Hospital.* Montreal: The Alumnae Association.

MacLaggan, Katherine. (1965). *Portrait of nursing: A plan for the education of nurses in the province of New Brunswick.* Fredericton: New Brunswick Association of Registered Nurses.

Manitoba Association of Registered Nurses. (1968). *A position paper on nursing in Manitoba.* Winnipeg: Author.

McLean, Catherine D. (1964). *A report on the establishment of the Quo Vadis School of Nursing and the selection of the first class of students.* Toronto: Quo Vadis School of Nursing.

Murray, V.V. (1970). *Nursing in Ontario: A study for the committee on the healing arts.* Toronto: Queen's Printer.

Mussallem, Helen K. (1964). *A path to quality: A plan for the development of nursing education programs within the general educational system of Canada.* Ottawa: Canadian Nurses Association.

Mussallem, Helen K. (1960). *Spotlight on nursing education: The report of the pilot project of the evaluation of schools of nursing in Canada.* Ottawa: Canadian Nurses Association.

New Brunswick Association of Registered Nurses. (1971). *Position paper.* Fredericton: Author.

Nightingale, Florence. (1929). *Cassandra: An essay.* Old Westbury, NY: Feminist Press.

Registered Nurses' Association of British Columbia. (1967). *A proposed plan for the orderly development of nursing education in British Columbia: Part One—Basic nursing education.* Vancouver: RNABC.

Rowe, H.R. (1967). *A study of transition in nursing education in Prince Edward Island.* Charlottetown: ANPEI.

Saskatchewan Registered Nurses' Association. (1966). *Brief presented to the joint committee on higher education.* Regina: Author.

Schmitt, Louise M. (1957). *Basic nursing education study: Report of the status of basic nursing education programs in Saskatchewan.* Regina: Saskatchewan Registered Nurses Association.

Stewart, I.M. (1947). *The education of nurses.* New York: Macmillan.

Study Committee on Nursing Education. (1971). *A study committee on nursing education.* New Brunswick: Department of Health.

The first annual report of the St. Catharines training school and nurses' home in connection with the general and marine hospital. (1875). As cited in Healey, Phyllis. (1989). "The Mack training school for nurses." Unpublished manuscript.

Weir, G.M. (1932). *Survey of nursing education in Canada.* Toronto: University of Toronto Press.

Wollstonecraft, Mary. (1787). *Thoughts on the education of daughters.* Clifton, NJ: A.M. Kelley.

Wollstonecraft, Mary. (1792). *A vindication of the rights of woman.* London: J. Johnson.

CHAPTER TWENTY THREE

A Historical Approach to the Evolution of University Nursing Education in Canada (1919 to 1974)

JANET ROSS KERR

T he history of nursing education in Canada parallels that of the country, as it is intimately related to social and economic developments. The health-care system has tended to expand and move ahead in times of prosperity. This has included building more hospitals and health-care facilities, all of which require nursing staff. As the recruitment of nurses has direct implications for nursing education, developments in schools of nursing have been conditioned by society. Standards of education in schools of nursing have been an important concern of the profession over the years and, therefore, have been subjected to considerable scrutiny and discussion. This chapter focuses on some of the major forces that have shaped the nature and form of the current system of nursing education at the university level in Canada. The focus is on undergraduate nursing education; graduate education is dealt with in some detail in Chapter 31.

EMERGENCE OF UNIVERSITY SCHOOLS OF NURSING

University education for nurses was the subject of an address by Dr. Malcolm T. MacEachern to the British Columbia Hospitals Association in July 1919, after the May 26 Board of Governors' decision to approve the Senate's recommendation that a department of nursing be established at the University of British Columbia (Street, 1973). The founding of this department, a precedent in the history of Canadian nursing, occurred four years later, largely through the efforts of Dr. MacEachern, the progressive medical superintendent of the

Vancouver General Hospital. Universities were founded in the West as early as the second decade of the twentieth century, when agricultural and technical education were receiving attention from the federal government. The utilitarian philosophic orientation of the new Western universities rationalizes the location of the first school of nursing in the West—in British Columbia.

When the decision was made to establish the University of British Columbia's Department of Nursing, the source of funding for the school was reviewed.

> The Board was advised that the Department would not involve any additional expense to the University. The minutes of this meeting do not add a fact of which the Board was aware: that the Vancouver General Hospital would pay the full salary of its director of nursing, who would also take charge of the University's Department of Nursing (Street, 1973, pp. 118-119).

In subsequent communication to the Senate to inform members of the disposition of the recommendation, it was "emphasized that the action was taken on the understanding that the establishment of this Department would not involve any additional expense to the University" (Street, 1973, pp. 118-119). Under the terms of such a favourable arrangement, where the operating costs of the new department were to be borne by the hospital, the university was undoubtedly more easily persuaded by the persistent Dr. MacEachern that the entry of nursing to the academic world of the University was both possible and desirable.

The appointment of Miss Ethel Johns as Director of the new Department was fortuitous; she was energetic, articulate, and of independent spirit. These qualities would be an asset, because in the beginning, the way would not be easy for the first university school of nursing in the country. Street alludes to the "precarious early years" (1973, p. 115) of the new program. In an address to a joint session of the British Columbia Hospitals Association and the Canadian Public Health Association in Vancouver in June 1920, Miss Johns had an opportunity to appeal for positive attitudes, which had prevailed among physicians, toward the new development in nursing education:

> To those who are in opposition or are in doubt, one last word, if there are any of such here: Will you not listen to the appeal of those upon whose shoulders you yourselves lay such heavy burdens? You see so many faults, so many blunders in our nursing service. So do we; they are not hidden from us. You cannot imagine why things should not run more smoothly, but we can; we know it is because of insufficient teaching and supervision. You do not realize how complex your own profession has become. How can we expect you to realize how difficult it is for us, with few of your educational advantages, to keep up with the advance shown in medicine? (Street, 1973, p. 132).

The degree program thus established was based on the prevailing American model and "became the Canadian prototype of the pattern which came to be known as the non-integrated degree nursing course, of the 2+2+1 or 1+3+1 course, in which the university assumed no responsibility for the two or three years of nursing preparation in a hospital school of nursing" (Bonin, 1976, p. 7).

The new program began to establish itself. After the program was approved for its fifth year there was a request from the Library Committee:

... for a grant of two hundred fifty dollars with which to purchase books for the Department of Nursing. But the Board had a long memory. After some discussion, it was decided to direct the attention of the Library Committee to the undertaking of the Hospital authorities that the University would not be asked to assume any financial responsibility in respect to the Department of Nursing. It was decided that a sum not to exceed one hundred dollars should be granted for books (Street, 1973, p. 127).

THE IMPACT OF RED CROSS FUNDING

After World War I, the Canadian Red Cross Society participated in the formation of the League of Red Cross Societies and the planning of an international program for peacetime activity in public health: "It was decided that there should be a great worldwide public health organization to help bring up the standards of physical and mental fitness of the world ... the promotion of health, the prevention of disease and the mitigation of suffering throughout the world" (Gibbon and Mathewson, 1947, p. 342).

In Canada, the Red Cross Society first directed its efforts to providing funds for the provision of facilities for postgraduate instruction in public health nursing "by subsidizing special courses for three years at the Universities of Toronto, McGill, British Columbia, Alberta, and Dalhousie" (Gibbon and Mathewson, 1947, p. 342). The financial incentive provided by these grants contributed to the creation of departments for the study of nursing at four of the institutions and encouraged the extension of what had been initiated the previous year at the University of British Columbia:

> In April 1920 the University of British Columbia accepted a proposal from the Provincial branch of the Canadian Red Cross Society to the effect that a Red Cross Chair of Public Health be established. For a period of three years from date of acceptance by the University, the Red Cross Society would pay five thousand dollars toward the salary of the professor. The expectation was that "the cause of Public Health, which everywhere is being regarded as of great importance, will be materially advanced throughout British Columbia." The Senate approved the proposal (Street, 1973, p. 128).

The Red Cross funds must have seemed like a windfall to the young institution, which had been founded during wartime and had received little tangible support from the Liberal government that was in power in the Province at the time.

In addition to providing funds to the institutions to stimulate the creation of new programs in public health nursing, the Canadian Red Cross Society provided financial aid to students who wanted to attend programs initiated under their sponsorship (King, 1970, p. 70). These actions were met with enthusiasm, and continued increases in enrolment ensured the survival of most of the universities after the three-year period of institutional grants had ended. Not surprisingly, these certificate courses became the first in a series of such courses that were offered by the universities and also led to the development of degree programs in most of the institutions.

However, these developments in 1920 were preceded by years of effort on the part of nurses to secure advanced preparation. King notes that:

> The first documentation concerning efforts to establish a university nursing program in Canada appeared in 1905 when a memorandum was submitted by the Graduate Nurses' Association of Ontario to the University of Toronto requesting the university "to offer a course of training and education of nurses" (King, 1970, p. 70).

In 1918 Dr. Helen MacMurchy, a physician and the first editor of *The Canadian Nurse*, wrote to the presidents of the universities to urge them to encourage establishment of nursing programs at their institutions (MacMurchy, 1918). Although the influence of such communication remains a matter of speculation, it is reasonable to assume that it at least made administrators of higher education more aware of the needs and issues in nursing education. As one author concluded: "One of the most significant developments during the period from 1910 to 1930 was the growth of positive attitudes toward university education for nurses" (Allemang, 1974, p. 137).

The one exception to the lasting success of the stimulus provided by the Red Cross for establishment of university nursing education was the public health nursing certificate program begun at Dalhousie University, which was also the first of its kind to be initiated (Tunis, 1966). The program at Dalhousie was short-lived and, for financial and perhaps other reasons, did not survive after 1922. It is noteworthy here that, although Dalhousie's program was the first to be initiated through Red Cross funds, the nature of the support differed; it consisted of direct funding of students rather than institutional grants. Thus the assistance provided to Dalhousie was far less substantial than that given to other universities during those same years.

CRISIS AT McGILL

The year 1929 spelled the end of a decade in which university nursing education in Canada improved by leaps and bounds. According to Allemang (1974), the stock market crash in the fall of 1929 "and the economic depression that followed brought unemployment and hardship to nurses" (1974, p. 172). Nurses had experienced difficulties in securing employment before 1929, and because of the worldwide economic depression, the situation rapidly worsened. Patients could no longer afford to employ private-duty nurses, and private duty had been the most promising area of employment for graduate nurses (Gunn, 1933, p. 141).

For universities in general, the Depression meant a period of significant adjustment, which included reduced revenues, staff layoffs, and difficult working conditions. However, despite this adverse environment, enrolments continued to show generally slow but steady growth throughout the decade; perhaps because no employment was available for people who had completed their high school educations, many chose to remain in school. The impact of the Depression on an institution in Canada was determined to a large extent by the amount of external support it received from government and private sources.

The Depression was hard on McGill University. McGill received only token funding from its provincial government from the earliest times. As a private institution, its mandate was to raise funds from private sources to operate its programs or reduce the size of its enterprise. This mandate made financing difficult enough during prosperous times; during the lean years of the Depression, it became an onerous task. The School for Graduate Nurses at McGill was subjected to the impact of the financial crunch for more than a decade.

Although Helen Reid had originally envisioned a two-year degree course at McGill, advice from Isabel M. Stewart in 1920 suggested that "to attempt at present in any way to arrange for two-year courses would be a real injury to the undertaking" (Tunis, 1966, p. 22). The final announcement of the course reflected the intent to begin a degree program "in the near future" (Tunis, 1966, p. 22). The issue was raised again after the death of Flora Madeline Shaw in 1927, and the matter was referred to committee (Tunis, 1966, p. 22). After the appointment of Bertha Harmer, a distinguished Canadian-born nurse educator, author, and administrator from Yale, as Director of the School in 1928, the Committee recommended "that a six-year undergraduate course leading to a degree be established at the School for Graduate Nurses" (Tunis, 1966, p. 42). It is reported that the attitude of the Principal and Vice-Chancellor was encouraging, as exemplified in his promise to Miss Reid: "When we establish the degree course we can promise that Miss Harmer's rank will be that of professor" (Tunis, 1966, p. 42).

Because there was reason for optimism, work went forward under Miss Harmer's direction to develop a framework for the curriculum that would facilitate the transition to the degree program when it was established. Students could select from five new areas of focus, each of which could lead to a university diploma rather than a certificate after two years of study. To implement the new programs, four new faculty members were appointed for the 1929 to 1930 academic year. Despite the optimism, however, the financial uncertainty under which the school operated after the termination of Red Cross funding in 1923 was a threat to its viability. To the new Director this uncertainty must have been a continuing source of anxiety, which can be detected in her query to the Acting Principal:

> I have just returned to the office after a repeated attack of illness and had hoped to find a favourable decision of the Finance Committee awaiting me. At the risk of seeming to trouble you unduly I am writing to ask the decision of the Finance Committee in regard to our budget. I should not trouble you if it were not that so many important matters are depending on it (Harmer, 6 May 1929).

The undercurrent of suspicion toward the place of nursing in the university environment surfaced again: "There are so many professors in the University who most cordially disapprove of schools of this kind. Their antagonism becomes more marked because of the necessity of reducing their salaries" (Currie, 27 June 1932).

A crisis was imminent and the facts were given to Miss Harmer by Sir Arthur Currie, the Acting Principal:

> I quite agree with you that the School has had an increasing attendance, that it has done excellent work, and that the influence of its graduates on nursing and nursing

education and administration has been most valuable. But there is the eternal question of finance. How are we to get the money to continue this School? (Currie, 27 June 1932).

In the face of the university's economic difficulties because of the Depression, the school would not be permitted to continue to drain McGill's financial resources. It was given only one alternative to closure; it would have the opportunity to raise an endowment of $40,000 to provide for the annual operating expenses of $8000, "which would keep it going for the next five years, in the hope that by that time financial conditions would be such that the expense of the School could be more readily provided for" (Currie, 27 June 1932).

The Alumnae Association and the Advisory Committee convened in joint session to consider the crisis that had beset the School and offered support for a national fund-raising effort (Tunis, 1966). An appeal was sent to the presidents of all provincial nursing associations to assist with the campaign. In Miss Harmer's words:

> The nursing profession has many interested and grateful friends who appreciate the service which it renders, and it is quite right and just that they, in addition to the provincial and city government boards, and boards of hospitals and public health and welfare associations, should now be asked as individuals to contribute to the support of nursing education (1 December 1932).

Support was also to be solicited from foundations, businesses, and corporations; however, the appeals to these organizations failed and the response was a great disappointment. "All was not lost, however, for the appeal to Canadian nurses did not go unheard and 'miraculously the money poured in. Within two months, more than $5,000 in cash was on hand and over $12,000 pledged'" (Tunis, 1966, p. 56).

The role of alumnae groups all over the country in ensuring the survival of the McGill School for Graduate Nurses was the critical factor in the resolution of the financial crisis that spanned more than a decade. In the process, the stature of nurses and nursing was raised, as nurses demonstrated a single-minded commitment to continuing the good work that had been started at McGill. The documents that pertain to the crisis also indicate an element of surprise on the part of McGill administrators that nurse alumnae members and others would have sufficient interest or strength of purpose to donate funds so generously. Although the total amount raised never reached the goal of $40,000, about $20,000 was raised, which was applied directly to the operating costs of the school on an annual basis.

The fact that $20,000 was sufficient to see the school through 10 difficult years was attributed to strict control over spending by school administrators (Tunis, 1966). An example of the nature of the commitment and dedication to the school is found in Miss Harmer's report (1933) to the principal on the results of the first, and possibly the most important, phase of the campaign:

> I am enclosing a statement showing results of the efforts of nurses to raise $40,000 to endow the School for the next five years. As it seemed hopeless, however, under present conditions, to raise this sum, efforts were concentrated on raising $8,000 in

the hope that better times would enable us to raise an endowment later. Deducting my salary, (my services were offered at the end of the year when it seemed the only hope of saving the School) left $5,000 as the objective. As the enclosed statement shows we have pledges for $5,597 for the next year, and $6,355.52 toward the next four years (1 May 1933).

In addition, many special lecturers who gave series of lectures in courses in the program accepted reduced fees for their services or waived them altogether. Operating costs were lowered further when faculty members bought books for the library and supplies out of their own pockets (Tunis, 1966). Sir Arthur Currie's announcement (1933) that sufficient funds had been received in the first five months of the fund-raising campaign to continue the school for one more year was a cause for rejoicing among faculty, alumnae, and friends of the school:

> On the understanding that the Budget for the next year does not exceed the year just closing, and relying on the pledges outlined in your letter of May first, 1933, I shall recommend to the Board of Governors that the School for Graduate Nurses be continued for another year, that is, until June 30, 1934. (Currie, 12 May 1933).

The struggle was to be long, however, and neither Miss Harmer nor Sir Arthur Currie would live to see to its conclusion. After Miss Harmer's resignation and death in 1934, the continuing struggle for existence was carried on under the direction of Marion Lindeburgh as Acting Director until 1939 and as Director thereafter. The stringent economies that were practised required that fewer courses be taught and that the two-year diploma programs initiated by Miss Harmer be dropped in favour of the one-year certificate programs (Tunis, 1966). The degree program had to be postponed until much later because, for many years, program development priorities had to focus on retaining the programs that remained operational.

THE DEVELOPMENT OF AN EXPERIMENTAL SCHOOL
OF NURSING AT TORONTO

It is ironic that at the very moment that the McGill School for Graduate Nurses was served with notice of intent to terminate its programs by its administration, the University of Toronto School of Nursing received financial and philosophic encouragement to continue the innovative experimentation with basic curriculum design that had begun in 1926, a program that was the vision of Edith Kathleen Russell. However, this event had been preceded by many years of groundwork by Kathleen Russell and the grant was not the first the School had been awarded by the Rockefeller Foundation for the development of its program.

The program established in 1926 and the improved one begun in 1933 were diploma rather than degree programs. Their importance for Canadian nursing was that they were radical departures from existing philosophy in university education for nurses. These events took place at a time when the content and form of university nursing programs and courses were somewhat fluid and undefined, and when nurses in many other university centres were constantly trying to justify their existence to skeptical and budget-minded administrators.

Miss Russell, who came to the University very early in the development of higher education in nursing nationally, was blessed with good health, a sound mind, and rare qualities of leadership. She had time to establish herself at the University and to think critically, thus developing her ideas about the pursuit of knowledge and truth as applied to nursing in the university setting. The credibility of the work at the university School of Nursing and Kathleen Russell's unique capabilities for leadership were remarkable. Ultimately, these factors augured well for the University of Toronto because, as Carpenter has indicated, "In the 30-year period ending in 1953, the Foundation supported the development of nursing education in 48 countries. The University of Toronto was the only Canadian university to receive this support" (1970, p. 94).

The proposal for the 1933 program, which also established the School of Nursing as an autonomous unit within the administrative framework of the University and provided it with a status that would allow it to participate fully in University governance, was first submitted to the Rockefeller Foundation in 1929. The Foundation agreed to support the project if support was also obtained from the University and the Ontario government; those guarantees were subsequently provided.

The major feature of this 39-month program, which was unique from a developmental standpoint and made this curriculum model stand apart from the nonintegrated curriculum pattern, was the principle that the faculty of the school would assume total responsibility for the education of the student. Because the School was administratively independent from the hospital, new value was placed on clinical teaching. Student learning needs would no longer be put aside in favour of pressing hospital nursing service demands because students were not utilized in "staff" positions. They were viewed as learners, with the rights and responsibilities that accompany that role; the role of the faculty member in the clinical settings was one that was critical in facilitating the integration of theory and practice and fostering creative thinking and a questioning attitude (Carpenter, 1982). The function of the university school, as conceived by Miss Russell, was as follows:

> The intention of the University School of Nursing is to prepare professional women who, through studies in the humanities and social sciences, will grow in understanding and wisdom; with this education in the realm of human values they may approach with some degree of safety the work which is awaiting them (1956, p. 35).

UNIVERSITY SCHOOLS IN THE DEPRESSION YEARS

The 1930s were extremely difficult years for Canadian universities, and the annual reports of presidents of the major institutions of higher education through these years are replete with accounts of the impact of the economic situation, which produced conditions that were unfamiliar to the universities. The 1920s had been productive years, during which adequate financial support had been available to support programs and for expansion into new fields. During this period nursing had entered the university scene in Canada, with development of programs in six universities. However, growth and expansion in these institutions after 1929 was limited because of the general lack of economic resources. There are frequent references to salary cuts that professors accepted rather than see colleagues lose their positions because of financial constraints. Evidence of the lack of growth in the decade after the stock market collapse was observed in all institutions, but particularly those in Western Canada.

During the 1920s, several new five-year, non-integrated degree programs were initiated at Canadian universities, similar to the 1919 degree program established at the University of British Columbia. The second degree program was established at the University of Western Ontario in 1924, followed in 1925 by one at the University of Alberta and in 1926 by a program at l'Institut Marguerite d'Youville. The University of Toronto experimented throughout the 1920s and 1930s with a new model of a diploma program that would evolve into the integrated degree program, while McGill was involved in a difficult struggle to maintain its certificate programs in the 1930s.

The religious order associated with the University of Ottawa initiated what was essentially a hospital diploma program in 1933. Only three degree programs were initiated during that decade, and then only during the later years. The University of Saskatchewan and the University of Ottawa introduced degree programs in 1938; St. Francis Xavier University began a program in 1939. Thus by the end of the third decade in the history of university nursing education in Canada, five degree programs were operational and two other universities offered diploma or certificate programs.

NEW INITIATIVES AND INCENTIVES IN UNIVERSITY NURSING EDUCATION BETWEEN 1940 AND 1955

In 1940, as Canada became involved in World War II, the sluggish national economy improved because of the need for manufactured goods. The war also affected higher education. Education in the health sciences became a priority; the nation quickly recognized the need for health professionals to care for military personnel and the civilian population and placed a new value on services provided by practitioners in these professions.

In the nursing profession, pressures arose from the conditions of returning prosperity in 1940; as these mounted, the balance between supply and demand reversed abruptly from what it had been during the 1930s. Where there had been oversupply, there was now a distinct shortage. With increasing prosperity, the return of the demand for private duty nurses in both hospitals and homes was partially responsible for this turn of events, which placed the profession and health services in general in a tight squeeze. The economic conditions of the 1930s had forced many small hospitals to close their schools of nursing and hire from the large pool of unemployed nurses who would work for very low wages. By the end of the decade, general staff nursing in hospitals had become a major form of employment among nurses (Allemang, 1974). This contrasted sharply with the previous decade, in which there were few staff nurse positions in hospitals and graduate nurses generally sought employment as independent practitioners whose services were retained by families to care for ill family members in hospitals and homes.

Other factors that contributed to the development of the shortage included the wartime demands on a profession with a contribution to make:

> Nursing administrators, supervisors, head nurses, teachers and public health nurses left their civilian positions for those of military service. These were key people in providing quality in nursing services and nursing education. Since bedside nursing care accompanied by supervision and ward teaching was considered the core of the curriculum, their loss was deeply felt (Allemang, 1974, p. 211).

Nurses were also needed in wartime industries, which generally offered better salaries and working conditions. For the most part, the shortages were most acute in rural areas for hospital and public health positions, as well as in special areas, such as tuberculosis sanatoria, isolation hospitals, and psychiatric institutions, where nurses were badly needed. In fact, the needs became so great and the possibilities for meeting them were so limited that a new category of health worker was created to fill the gap—the certified or registered nursing assistant or licensed practical nurse. Although some consideration was given to shortening nursing programs in Canada to meet specific needs related to war, this development never occurred because enough nurses volunteered for the armed services. (Lindeburgh, 1942).

University schools of nursing soon began to reap benefits from federal interest in higher education, both from subsidizing the operations of the institutions and from its considerable response to the assistance requested by the professional organizations. Federal funds for nursing education, distributed through the Canadian Nurses Association (CNA) to the schools, amounted to $150,000 in 1942 and $250,000 each in 1943 and 1944. The program was maintained until the end of the war. Funds were then awarded through the provincial nurses' associations to the diploma and university schools of the provinces. In addition, the W.K. Kellogg Foundation initiated a program of fellowships in nursing and, between 1941 and 1959, granted $11,680 to institutions and agencies to be awarded to Canadian nurses for additional study. The university schools of nursing received the greater part of these funds so that they could upgrade the academic qualifications of their faculties. The fellowships were tenable in the United States and, during that period, there were no master's programs for nurses in Canada. The new funds, most of which were provided between 1941 and 1945, provided a stimulus to nursing education at a time when it was needed.

The W.K. Kellogg Foundation also made scholarship and loan funds available, for students in programs at five universities between 1942 and 1944. Under this program, McGill University, l'Université de Montréal, the University of Toronto, and the University of Western Ontario each received $4000, and Laval University received $6000. The Victorian Order of Nurses, a national agency, which needed nurses with specific preparation in public health nursing, reactivated the bursary program, initiated during the 1920s and discontinued in 1933;

for students seeking certificate or baccalaureate preparation. The Canadian Red Cross Society also made scholarships in public health nursing available (Tunis, 1966).

An awakened interest in nursing and nursing education in the post-war period, evidenced by the availability of extrauniversity funding, appears to have been a prime factor not only in consolidation and growth of existing schools but also in the founding of new programs in nursing in several universities. Queens University (1941) and McMaster University (1941) initiated programs early in the decade, the University of Manitoba in 1943, Mount St. Vincent University in 1947, and Dalhousie University in 1949. Clearly, federal funds made available for schools and fellowship and bursary programs under the auspices of private foundations and agencies played an important role in the new developments that occurred. As in 1920, universities became aware of potential benefits to their institutions from the sponsorship of nursing programs.

At McGill, the influx of additional funds was considerable and continuous. The courage and perseverance of those faculty, alumnae, and friends who had held out for the retention of the School through the long Depression and war years were rewarded; their steadfast conviction that the School had a significant and critical function to fulfil at McGill was vindicated. The funds provided to the McGill School from the federal grant program administered by the CNA included: "$2,100 [in 1942] an amount that was increased to $6,000 in 1943, and which by 1945 totalled $27,750" (Tunis, 1966, p. 73). The impact on programs has been described as follows:

> Conditions at the Schools were affected with startling rapidity. For the first time since the crisis of 1932, a programme of expansion could be considered. Two four-month courses were undertaken in 1942, one in administration and supervision in public health nursing, the other in clinical supervision, in an effort to meet war-time demands for trained personnel. These courses, which were offered annually until the autumn of 1945, could be used as credits toward the 1-year certificate course (Tunis, 1966, p. 73).

Nursing faculty at McGill were again able to entertain the idea of a degree program. Preparations began in 1941 for a five-year nonintegrated degree course, the proposal for which was subsequently approved; the first students were accepted in 1944. In 1945 the alumnae of the School disbanded their Special Finance Committee, which had served the School so well during the Depression and war years, but simultaneously revitalized earlier efforts to establish a Flora Madeline Shaw Endowment Fund to establish a Chair in nursing (Tunis, 1966).

DIPLOMA TO DEGREE: THE INCEPTION OF THE BASIC DEGREE PROGRAM AT THE UNIVERSITY OF TORONTO

The development of curricula in baccalaureate education for nursing has not been without difficulties. These difficulties have centred largely around contractual agreements between the university schools of nursing and hospitals and other agencies used for clinical experience. In her postwar report on the state of nursing education, Esther Lucile Brown (1948) defined the responsibility of the university school:

> One general principle, however, must be kept clearly in mind. The university school should enter into relations with other institutions exclusively to obtain necessary clinical laboratories, not to help provide nursing service for patients. Regrettably some university schools find themselves in the same situations as most hospital schools, where students are expected to supply nursing care at the expense of the educational process (1948, p. 157).

Brown (1948) cited two reasons to explain why these issues arose as major problems: the traditional outlook of the hospital viewing nursing education as service and the meagre financial resources of many university schools and students.

Probably the most influential event in the history of Canadian degree programs was the introduction of the basic degree program at the University of Toronto in 1942. This was not an isolated event, but one step in a process that began some 16 years earlier. It provided an alternative to the existing pattern of baccalaureate nursing education. In this integrated program, studies in the arts and sciences were combined with the nursing component. Courses were carefully planned and sequenced so that individual student development would be enhanced. The departure from the previously established pattern was striking:

> It is of particular interest that for the first time in a nursing undergraduate degree programme full authority and responsibility for the teaching of nursing rested in the university. The nursing courses were planned, taught, and evaluated by full-time university teaching staff. This simple fact, nonetheless, was a radical departure from existing degree programmes, the roots of which, by this time had been firmly established in both Canada and the United States (King, 1970, p. 72).

It is always difficult to break with tradition, and in nursing, the nonintegrated degree pattern had established its stepladder approach to nursing education well over 20 years before. In addition, the hospital programs on which this approach leaned had been entrenched for an even greater number of years. Effecting a change that made the basic degree program stand apart from its nonintegrated counterpart required a great leader and, as previously noted, Edith Kathleen Russell was such an individual. In instituting this change, she exerted a profound influence on the thinking of her colleagues in nursing, and she was able to enlist the moral support of the Faculty of Medicine and the President of the University of Toronto, as well as the financial support of the Rockefeller Foundation. In regard to her influence, Emory (1964) notes: "It has been said that greatness is attained through changing the course of events and changing them for always. If this be true, then in retrospect there can be detected in Edith Kathleen Russell's professional life and work an element of true greatness" (1964, p. 7).

A SECOND BASIC DEGREE PROGRAM BEGINS

Bonin, who studied basic degree programs in Canada, said: "The most salient driving forces which spurred the establishment of basic degree programs are key persons, especially Kathleen Russell and Gladys Sharpe, in two pioneering universities" (1976, p. 178). Four years after the introduction of the University of Toronto basic degree program, a second basic degree program was developed at McMaster University under the direction of Miss Gladys Sharpe, who was largely responsible for phasing out the early degree and diploma program called "Arts and Nursing," which had begun in 1941 at McMaster, and introducing a new basic degree program. At McMaster, the initiative of the Hamilton General Hospital had been important in developing the earlier affiliation between the Hospital and the University, and the Hospital continued to support the new program and its Director. Support from an associated hospital, while not always forthcoming, occurred in 1919 with the establishment of the University of British Columbia School of Nursing. It was also evident that there was an extremely close working relationship between the Toronto General Hospital and the School of Nursing at the University of Toronto. In the early 1930s, consideration was given to combining the Toronto General nursing program with that of the University of Toronto (Carpenter, 1970).

SURVEYS OF NURSING EDUCATION

In the history of Canadian nursing education, periodic surveys have been undertaken by professional organizations and government to assess the prevailing situation and aid in making improvements in areas where weaknesses were demonstrated. Miss Kathleen Russell carried out a survey in New Brunswick that addressed the whole gamut of issues in nursing education in that province and had considerable impact on the thinking of nursing educators. The establishment of the School of Nursing at the University of New Brunswick in 1959 was a direct result of her conclusions and recommendations about higher education in nursing in New Brunswick (Russell, 1956). Soon afterward, the CNA, under the direction of Dr. Helen K. Mussallem, launched the Pilot Project for Evaluation of Schools of Nursing. This study, designed to determine the feasibility of and issues associated with a system of accreditation of schools of nursing in Canada, was published in 1960.

One of the recommendations from the Mussallem study (1960) was: "1. That a re-examination and study of the whole field of nursing education be undertaken" (1960, p. vii). This recommendation was implemented within a very short time; a Royal Commission was appointed by the Federal Government to investigate the problems and issues related to all aspects of the delivery of health services in Canada. The report of that Commission recommended that 10 more university nursing programs, under administratively autonomous schools of nursing, be established in Canada as soon as possible (Royal Commission on Health Services, 1964). It also recommended elimination of nonintegrated basic programs at a time when admissions were 22% higher than admissions to integrated programs. The impact of this report was impressive; only four years later "admissions to integrated programmes constituted ninety-seven percent of all admissions to baccalaureate programmes" (King, 1970, pp. 178-79). In addition, the number of candidates seeking postbasic degrees after graduation from hospital or college programs doubled during the same period. Because there is normally a limitation on enrolment in schools of nursing due to the constraints imposed by available clinical facilities, schools of nursing began to make concerted efforts to increase their maximum enrolment levels in response to the Royal Commission recommendation:

> It is of the utmost importance that these schools be expanded in number to enable them to prepare approximately one-fourth of the total recruits to the nursing force. It is from this pool that the instructors, supervisors, administrators and other leaders in the profession must come (1964, p. 67).

Since 1965, the ratio of diploma-to-baccalaureate-prepared nurses has increased to approximately 1 in 10 nationally. In addition, all of the 10 new university schools recommended by the Royal Commission were established. However, enrolments in university schools are still very low in comparison with those in diploma programs. In Chapter 24, questions pertaining to entry to practice are considered.

CONCLUSION

This chapter has identified and documented events and trends of major significance to university nursing education. The enterprise began with informal and on-the-job training. Hospital schools of nursing began to develop after 1874 and university schools after 1919. Community college nursing education programs, which began to appear in the 1960s, also offered diploma preparation. Today in Canada, nursing education is offered under the auspices of the three types of schools. However, the profession's entry to practice position has led to a drive for expansion of university programs at both the basic and post-RN levels. Contemporary approaches to educational issues of importance are discussed in other chapters.

REFERENCES

Allemang, M.M. (1974). *Nursing education in the United States and Canada, 1873-1950: Leading figures, forces, views on education.* Unpublished Ph.D. dissertation, Seattle: University of Washington.

Bonin, M.A. (1976). *Trends in integrated basic degree nursing programs in Canada: 1942-1972.* Unpublished Ph.D. dissertation, Ottawa: University of Ottawa.

Brown, E.L. (1948). *Nursing for the future.* New York: Russell Sage Foundation.

Canadian Nurses Association. (1968). *The leaf and the lamp.* Ottawa: Author.

Carpenter, H.M. (1970). The University of Toronto School of Nursing: An agent of change. In M.Q. Innis (Ed.), *Nursing education in a changing society,* (pp. 86-108). Toronto: University of Toronto Press.

Carpenter, H.M. (1982). *Divine discontent: Edith Kathleen Russell—Reforming educator.* Toronto: Faculty of Nursing, The University of Toronto.

Currie, Sir Arthur W. Letter to Bertha Harmer, 12 May 1933. Acc. 2432, File. "Financial crisis: 1933 to 1943," McGill University Archive, Montreal, Quebec.

Currie, Sir Arthur W. Letter to Dr. Helen R.Y. Reid, 27 June 1932. Acc. 2432, File. "Financial crisis: 1933 to 1943." McGill University Archive, Montreal, Quebec.

Emory, F. (1964). *Edith Kathleen Russell: An appreciation of her professional life and work.* 6 March. Acc. A-73011 Mimeographed Faculty of Nursing, University of Toronto.

Gibbon, J.M. and Mathewson, M.S. (1947). *Three centuries of Canadian nursing.* Toronto: Macmillan.

Gunn, J.I. (1933). Educational adjustments recommended by the survey. *The Canadian Nurse,* 29(3), 139-145.

Harmer, B. Letter to Dr. C.F. Martin, 6 May 1929. Acc. 2432, File "Financial crisis: 1933 to 1943," McGill University Archive, Montreal, Quebec.

Harmer, B. Letter to presidents of provincial nursing associations, 1 December 1932. Acc. 2432, File. "Financial crisis: 1933 to 1943," McGill University Archive, Montreal, Quebec.

Harmer, B. Letter to Sir Arthur W. Currie, 1 May 1933. Acc. 2432, File. "Financial crisis: 1933 to 1943," McGill University Archive, Montreal, Quebec.

King, M.K. (1970). The development of university nursing education. In M.Q. Innis (Ed.), *Nursing education in a changing society,* (pp. 67-85). Toronto: University of Toronto Press.

Lindeburgh, M. (1942). Important emergency measures. *The Canadian Nurse,* 38(12), 925-926.

MacMurchy, H. (1918). University training for the nursing profession. *The Canadian Nurse,* 14(9), 1284-1285.

Mussallem, H.K. (1960). *Spotlight on nursing education: The report of a pilot project for the evaluation of schools of nursing in Canada.* Ottawa: The Canadian Nurses Association.

Royal Commission on Health Services. (1964). Vol. I. Ottawa: Queens Printer.

Russell, E.K. (1956). *The report of the study of nursing education in New Brunswick.* Fredericton: Government of the province of New Brunswick.

Tunis, B.L. (1966). *In caps and gowns.* Montreal: McGill University Press.

CHAPTER TWENTY FOUR

Entry to Practice: Striving for the Baccalaureate Standard

JANET ROSS KERR

T he baccalaureate degree as the minimum educational qualification for entry to the practice of nursing is undoubtedly the most controversial and hotly debated contemporary issue in the nursing profession. Besharah has called it "the most contentious issue in the history of nursing in this country" (1981, p. 6). Cool heads must prevail when considering the position, the rationale given for it, and the potential implications of implementation for the profession. Discussion of such questions is bound to generate strong emotions because implementing such a change involves restructuring the educational system in nursing.

Some feel threatened by the possibility of change in the traditional system because it may imply a loss of identity derived from association with particular programs and patterns of nursing education. Many may also worry that perhaps ties with their roots would be changed in some permanent and irrevocable way. Still others may believe that the methods and content of the past are appropriate for modern nursing education. Some have reacted to the possibility of change by blaming certain sectors of the profession. Who is to blame—nursing administrators, educators, practitioners, or researchers? Scapegoating is not constructive and is essentially a negative response to an issue that is increasingly seen in a very positive light. Further, it is important to recognize and respect all of those who contribute to the profession in a meaningful way; that is, those in practice, education, administration, and research. The contributions of the practising nurses of today and yesterday to the promotion, maintenance, and restoration of health have made the nursing profession one that is esteemed by the public today. Those contributions have also moved nursing to the threshold of the university because of the complexity of knowledge and skills required, and the fact that the educational process must transmit the latter to nursing students. It is necessary and important to understand and appreciate nursing as a complex, multifaceted process embracing many roles and functions.

262

ENTRY TO PRACTICE: THE POSITION, ITS DEVELOPMENT AND RATIONALE

The entry to practice position is often misunderstood. It refers to all those graduating from schools of nursing and entering the practice of nursing in the year 2000. These graduates and those in subsequent years would require the baccalaureate qualification in nursing to practise nursing. Thus those who graduated from diploma nursing programs in the year 1999 or before would not require the baccalaureate credential. This approach, often termed "grandparenting," means that the new standard is phased in gradually, allowing ample time to make changes and adjustments in systems and resources. This approach also ensures that those already in the profession are not jeopardized in terms of their right to practise their profession.

More than a decade has passed since the first statement of the entry to practice position by the Alberta Task Force on Nursing Education (1975). Since then much change in thinking has occurred about the possibility of such a position so that now it has become a major focus of discussion and dialogue about the nursing profession. Strategies to facilitate implementation of the position are being developed at both provincial and national levels by professional associations. There has also been a concomitant increase in the demand for post-RN baccalaureate education by members of the profession qualified at the diploma level. Many of these nurses recognize a personal need for additional preparation as well as the inescapable fact that additional study may improve an individual's competitive position in relationship to available positions, particularly those at a leadership level.

When discussing educational opportunities for registered nurse (RN) students, it is important to remember that the entry to practice position does not refer to RNs, however important it may be to make baccalaureate preparation available to those in this group who desire it. It is a position that applies to those entering the profession in the year 2000 and thereafter. The accomplishment of such a goal is itself a monumental undertaking because of the number of students who will need to receive at least part of their education under the auspices of the university.

The voice of the profession on this matter has become an increasingly united one, as one professional association after another has espoused commitment to the position that all nurses entering the profession should be qualified at the baccalaureate level by the year 2000. Initial leadership came, however, neither from the profession nor from university faculties of nursing, but from a government-appointed committee established to study needs in relation to nursing education in the Province of Alberta, the Alberta Task Force on Nursing Education. Although the Alberta government subsequently issued a denunciation of its Committee's recommendation, stating that it did "not agree with making the baccalaureate degree a mandatory requirement for practice," the matter was not allowed to rest there (Government of Alberta, 1977, p. 6).

Discussion of the controversial document ensued among all interested parties immediately after its publication. The Alberta Association of Registered

Nurses (AARN) issued a response to the Task Force report shortly thereafter (Alberta Association of Registered Nurses [AARN], 1976), endorsing the position put forward, but at the same time recommending the year 2000 as a more realistic date than the 1995 goal suggested by the Task Force. At the 1980 Biennial Convention of the Canadian Nurses Association (CNA) in Vancouver, delegates found themselves debating a resolution to establish the development of a statement on the minimum educational qualification needed to enter the profession as a priority for the coming biennium. Momentum began to grow with the establishment of a committee to study the issue, and articles began to appear in *The Canadian Nurse* debating both sides of the question (Kerr, 1982; Rajabally, 1982). The decision to endorse the baccalaureate standard was taken by the Board of Directors of the CNA in February 1982, when the Report of the Committee was presented. Support was high and the motion was carried unanimously. Delegates to the 1982 Biennial Convention in Newfoundland added further strength to the position by adopting a motion of support.

Since that time, support of the position has been growing within the profession as the issues have been debated in provinces that had not already adopted a position on the matter; and province by province, positions in support of the baccalaureate standard have been taken. The enthusiasm and eagerness to reach the goal by the year 2000 is evident as nurses from one end of the country to the other identify and develop mechanisms to ensure that logical, well-articulated, reasonable plans are made for its achievement. If they are to be successful, such plans must result in public policy commitments to the baccalaureate standard as it is clear that additional years of university-level nursing education for students will require the redistribution of existing resources or, alternatively, the infusion of new ones.

Why are more nurses advocating the baccalaureate standard? The reason can only be found in the changing nature of practice and the knowledge necessary to engage in practice. Attempting to raise professional status through higher educational standards does not constitute good and sufficient reason for implementing the baccalaureate standard for entry to practice. A decade ago, there were five or six distinct areas of hospital and community-based practice; today there are upwards of 30 or 40 different clinical nursing areas, each requiring mastery of a unique and specialized knowledge base. The era of specialization in nursing is here. No longer is it possible, if in fact it ever was, to graduate finished products. It is now recognized that today's graduate is a beginning practitioner and that registered nurses must be lifelong learners. There is no way one can be master of all, either within the context of a program of basic nursing education or after graduation when concentrating on a field of practice. The rapid rate with which care based on new knowledge is integrated into practice makes continuing education an individual, organizational, and professional responsibility to ensure that practitioners remain abreast of new developments in their areas of practice.

Advances in the health sciences have meant that today's programs of basic nursing education are hard-pressed to offer curricula that address the depth and breadth of theoretical content and related clinical experience for safe and effective practice. The impact of technology and changing roles requires the acquisition of appropriate knowledge and the development of new skills. The expansion of the knowledge required for competent practice and the range of responsibilities expected of the nurse at all levels provide substantial rationale for an increase in the length of the basic nursing program and for the standard of educational preparation offered at a baccalaureate level.

STANDARDS OF NURSING EDUCATION: A HISTORICAL PERSPECTIVE

Florence Nightingale founded the first modern school of nursing in 1860 in conjunction with St. Thomas' Hospital in London. The idea was novel and soon became the model for the establishment of hospital training schools throughout Europe and America. Nightingale's reputation from her service in the Crimea was such that her idea for a school of nursing was taken up readily and the nurses she prepared in her school were widely sought to lead new developments elsewhere.

Standards of education have historically been a concern of the nursing profession. There is considerable evidence that the quality of nursing education was one of the early concerns of professional organizations. During the 1920s and 1930s, after the successful resolution of the struggle to achieve nursing registration in each province, the profession became concerned with achieving higher educational standards through development and adoption of a standard curriculum for schools of nursing. Undoubtedly these efforts, headed by the CNA, did much to raise educational standards in schools of nursing (Weir, 1932). Although today the idea of a national standard curriculum may seem somewhat strange and rather prescriptive, undoubtedly there was a need for this kind of guidance as educational standards were described as deplorable by many observers.

With the initiation of the first university degree program in Canada for nurses at the University of British Columbia in 1919, a new era in nursing education began. Red Cross funding to six Canadian universities after World War I encouraged the establishment and development of a variety of nursing programs in each institution. Most began as certificate programs and all eventually developed into degree programs. The first degree programs were based on the prevailing American model and were termed nonintegrated programs. In such programs, the principle of university control over university courses and hospital control over the clinical nursing part of the program became firmly entrenched (Kerr, 1978).

In 1926, dissatisfied with the results of "an ill-arranged program of studies," Miss E. Kathleen Russell, Director of the Department of Public Health Nursing at the University of Toronto, set out to demonstrate that a nurse could be prepared in a much more effective and educationally sound manner by establishing the principle of university direction and control over all courses in the program (Russell, 1932, p. 87). Close cooperation with health care agencies was maintained, but faculty who were responsible for clinical nursing education were employed by the university. A substantial Rockefeller Foundation grant was obtained to fund this innovative experiment in basic degree nursing education, resulting in 1942 in the first integrated program in Canada at the University of Toronto. McMaster University followed with a similar program in 1946.

In the formative years between 1940 and 1955, university schools of nursing became firmly established and began to accommodate ever increasing numbers of students and administer increasingly large budgets. It is interesting that until 1965, no additional integrated degree programs were established in any Canadian university. However, the Report of the Royal Commission on Health Services (1964) was to change university nursing education dramatically and rapidly, with recommendations that were highly critical of the existing system. These recommendations were that 10 more university nursing programs under administratively autonomous schools of nursing be established in Canada as soon as possible and that nonintegrated basic programs in universities be eliminated at a time when admissions were 22% higher than admissions to integrated programs. The impact of this report was impressive; only four years later "admissions to integrated programmes constituted ninety-seven percent of all admissions to baccalaureate programs" (King, 1970, pp. 78-79). The Royal Commission also recommended that baccalaureate programs "be expanded in number to enable them to prepare approximately one-fourth of the total recruits to the nursing force" (*Report of the Royal Commission on Health Services*, 1964, p. 67).

MOVING TOWARD THE YEAR 2000

Although we have been dealing with questions involving standards of education in nursing since nursing became formally established in this country, the issues of today are quite different; everything has changed—the settings, conditions of practice, health needs and problems, beliefs about individual responsibility in health care, and performance expectations for nurses in all settings. Change is the inexorable reality of our existence. The choices involve ways of influencing the direction of change in the manner most appropriate for the service rendered. At the individual level, making an effort to understand all sides of the question is a responsible course of action, enabling one to exercise freedom of choice—in this case to discover the alternatives and to attempt to influence change, with the health care consumers of the future firmly in mind. Questions of "how" and "when" in relation to the baccalaureate standard for initial entry to practice, although some of these apply to the next century, are important issues to consider today.

The educational and service sectors must be prepared to cope with the changes that will result. Collaboration between diploma and degree programs to produce a baccalaureate-level practitioner must be facilitated. Creative new nursing education program models must be developed to facilitate the baccalaureate standard. Hospitals and other health agencies, colleges, and universities must become partners in planning and promoting an integrated system of nursing education that will benefit the health-care consumers of the next century.

The respective roles of the provincial and national nursing associations in the process of encouraging the implementation of the baccalaureate standard will undoubtedly continue to be the critical factors in influencing opinion and action in both the health-care and public sectors. After the adoption of the entry to practice resolution by the Board of Directors, the CNA quickly moved to adopt a proactive stance on the issue. They appointed committees to develop long-term goals and plans, developed discussion papers and annotated bibliographies on the subject, developed strategies to achieve goals, and encouraged member associations to develop specific plans for their provinces. A new five-year National Plan for Entry to Practice was adopted by the CNA in March 1989. Professional nursing associations in all provinces except Ontario are charged with legislative authority for the registration and discipline of nurses (see Chapter 26). In Ontario, the College of Nurses carries out regulatory functions for the profession. Except in Alberta, Ontario, and Quebec, the provincial nursing associations have statutory responsibilities for nursing education (see Chapter 26); all are committed to improving standards of nursing education. The "grass roots," found at the provincial level, is where the campaign to implement the baccalaureate standard will be carried out. Since the provincial ministries of education and health must make decisions about allocation of budgets for postsecondary education and for nursing service, the question of implementation of the entry to practice position is of vital concern.

Because of the complexity of determining costs of student education, conclusions based on inadequate information or comparisons may lead to assumption of exorbitant costs associated with implementation of the baccalaureate standard, a conclusion the CNA has termed "unclear, unfounded, unwise and unwarranted" (Canadian Nurses Association [CNA], 1984, p. 1). It is suggested that there are no well-designed studies of the cost of nursing education in Canada and that "institutional costs per 'student year' or per 'student credit hour' or per 'student years of future graduates' may well be lower in universities than in other institutions" (CNA, 1984, p. 1). Thus the conclusion that a baccalaureate nursing program is more expensive than other types of nursing programs has no basis in fact, and the actual situation may be quite the reverse.

Nursing faculty in universities have been articulate proponents of the baccalaureate standard for entry to nursing practice; however, academic units in nursing in universities are likely to sustain extensive change as a result of the tremendous impact of implementation. Also, other sectors of the nursing education enterprise would undoubtedly be dramatically affected by adoption of the baccalaureate standard. Questions that arise immediately pertain to recruitment of qualified faculty. Most deans of university faculties of nursing already spend a good deal of time trying to recruit suitably qualified faculty. It is evident that the preparation of faculty is a critical issue in relation to the baccalaureate standard. Therefore, graduate programs strong in clinical and research preparation are key elements in expanding the ranks of well-prepared nursing faculty in universities. The development and expansion of university programs in nursing at the baccalaureate level cannot be accomplished without the infusion of considerable numbers of faculty prepared at the master's and doctoral levels. Although master's programs are available in most regions of the country, the development of doctoral programs in nursing has been very slow and is just on the horizon. Expansion of programs at the graduate level will be needed, as will fellowships for students and special funding to expand programs. Strong and productive graduate programs will be essential in all approaches to implementing the entry to practice position.

The impact of program expansion on health care agencies will be considerable. A key factor will be partnership in the process. It will be essential for universities to ensure that there is effective participation by health care agencies in the plans for development of new goals, program changes, and in the teaching and learning process itself. There are many ways in which working together can be fostered, including the use of joint appointments, secondment arrangements, shared projects, and organizational structural changes to foster partnership for mutual benefit.

There is evidence that students are enroling in existing baccalaureate programs at increased rates. From 1985 to 1988, admissions to basic baccalaureate programs climbed 31%. In the same period, full-time enrolment in post-RN baccalaureate programs decreased by 0.6%, while part-time enrolment rose by 24.4% (CNA, 1989). Also, collaborative models for new baccalaureate programs are taking shape. The announcement that the Vancouver General Hospital planned to make a transition from diploma nursing education to baccalaureate nursing education through a collaborative effort with the University of British Columbia and would enrol the first class in the newly structured program in September 1989 was the first of many such joint ventures at the discussion and approval stages to be implemented (CNA Connection, 1989a). An innovative arrangement between the University of Alberta Faculty of Nursing and Red Deer College saw a collaborative model for an initial program of nursing education, leading to a baccalaureate degree in nursing implemented between a community college and a university. Enrolment of the first students in the program took place in September 1990, and all courses throughout the four-year program are offered on the Red Deer site. Finally, the announcement in 1988 of the decision by the government of Prince Edward Island to "phase out diploma education in favour of a degree program" (CNA Connection, 1989b) was the culmination of many years of effort on the part of nurses in Prince Edward Island to secure a baccalaureate program of nursing in their province. An additional collaborative model between a large diploma school of nursing at the University of Alberta Hospitals and the University of Alberta Faculty of Nursing has been in the planning stages for several years and is expected to be approved for admission of the first students in September 1991. This effort is unique in that all other diploma schools of nursing in Edmonton, including Grant MacEwan College Department of Nursing, the Misericordia Hospital School of Nursing and the Royal Alexandra Hospital School of Nursing, have been part of this collaborative effort from the outset and all except Grant MacEwan College are planning to admit students to the program in the fall of 1991.

The tasks ahead are difficult and challenging. However, a cursory glance through the pages of nursing history confirms that the road has never been easy, and nursing is at this educational crossroads today because there have been leaders with vision and courage who developed and found support for wise initiatives. Unity of purpose and action is needed now as never before. The rationale for implementation of the baccalaureate standard can only be understood and accepted on the basis of the nature and range of knowledge and skills required to practise nursing and the right of the health-care consumer to receive care from a well-prepared professional nurse. There are roles for all nurses as the debate on the questions heats up; and explanation, demonstration, candour, and persuasion will be needed in large measure to secure the public policy commitments needed to make baccalaureate preparation for entry to the practice of nursing a reality.

REFERENCES

Alberta Association of Registered Nurses. (1976). *The response of the Alberta Association of Registered Nurses to the Government of Alberta's Position Paper on Nursing Education.* Edmonton: Author.

Alberta Task Force on Education. (1977). *Position paper on nursing education: Principles and issues.* Edmonton: Author

Besharah, A. (1981). When will the shouting start? *The Canadian Nurse, 77*(3), 6.

Canadian Nurses Association. (1984). *Entry to practice bulletin.* Ottawa: Author.

Canadian Nurses Association. (1989). *Entry to practice newsletter, 5*(3), 1, 3.

CNA Connection. (1989a). VGH School joins UBC. *The Canadian Nurse, 85*(2), 12.

CNA Connection. (1989b). Baccalaureate education comes to PEI. *The Canadian Nurse, 85*(3), 10.

Government of Alberta. (1975). *Report of the Alberta Task Force on Nursing Education.* Edmonton: Author.

Kerr, J.C. (1978). *Financing university nursing education in Canada from 1919 to 1976.* Unpublished Ph.D. Dissertation, Ann Arbor, MI: The University of Michigan.

Kerr, J.C. (1982). The shouting starts. *The Canadian Nurse, 78*(2): 42-43.

King, M.K. (1970). The development of university nursing education. In M.Q. Innis (Ed.), *Nursing education in a changing society,* (pp. 67-85). Toronto: University of Toronto Press.

Rajabally, M. (1982). We have seen the enemy. *The Canadian Nurse, 78*(2), 40-42.

Royal Commission on Health Services Report, Vol. 1. (1964). Ottawa: Queen's Printer

Russell, E.K. (1932). The teaching of public health nursing in the University of Toronto. In *Methods and problems of medical education,* (pp. 82-88). New York: The Rockefeller Foundation.

Weir, G.M. (1932). *Survey of nursing education in Canada.* Toronto: University of Toronto Press.

CHAPTER TWENTY FIVE

Collaboration Between Nursing Education and Nursing Practice for Quality Nursing Care

JANNETTA MacPHAIL

I nadequacies in relationships between nursing education and nursing service have been recognized increasingly as a major issue in Canada and the United States, particularly in the 1970s and 1980s. The risks and benefits pertaining to this issue have been identified in the literature and at national and international conferences by the proponents of unifying nursing education and nursing practice through a number of mechanisms and strategies. The benefits pertain to the recipients of care and the nursing staff in health-care agencies, as well as to the students and faculty involved in education, practice, and research.

HISTORICAL INFLUENCES ON SEPARATION BETWEEN EDUCATION AND SERVICE

Historically, nursing education was developed within hospital training schools in Canada and the United States. Training schools were developed to staff the hospitals regardless of hospital's size. Until the late 1930s and even into the 1940s in some hospitals, nursing care was provided primarily by nursing students; the only registered nurses were the superintendents of nurses, supervisors, and perhaps head nurses. Thus the hospitals were dependent on students to staff them around the clock and throughout the year. One of the unfortunate consequences of this arrangement was that the need for students to provide care or service needs usually took precedence over educational or learning needs of the students. Until the middle of this century, students were exploited to meet service needs, without regard for learning needs (Schlotfeldt and MacPhail, 1969a). Although nurse writers may not have identified this problem directly, the

270

history of hospitals in both countries records this method of staffing. Moreover, many retired and older nurses, educated before the middle of the century, can attest to the fact. One of the consequences of this situation was that nurse educators became increasingly frustrated because of their lack of control over the learning opportunities provided students and the planning of students' time. Their solution was to separate the school of nursing from the hospital nursing service, although both were under the same administration, board, and budget.

Another factor that influenced the separation between service and education was the development of nursing programs in universities and later in community colleges that had no clear delineation of relationship to service. Although the first university school of nursing was established in Canada in 1919 at the University of British Columbia, the early university programs did not promote separation because they were not designed as separate entities. The first university nursing programs were five years in length, with students enroling for one year in liberal arts courses, then entering a hospital school of nursing for three years, and returning to the university for the fifth year in which they specialized in either teaching and supervision in nursing or public health nursing. Programs of this design have been referred to as *sandwich* baccalaureate programs because the nursing component, which was not under the control of the university, was *sandwiched* between two years in the university. Such programs continued in many parts of Canada into the 1960s. In 1933, Kathleen Russell, a visionary and effective leader, developed the first integrated baccalaureate program, with nursing courses and liberal arts courses integrated throughout, at the University of Toronto. It was five years in length. Although this type of program was much sounder educationally, it resulted in a clear separation between education and service, as did the nursing programs developed later in colleges. Faculty in such programs became "guests" in the clinical agencies where they placed students for practice and supervised them in practice. They did not have, and in most cases still do not have, any control over the practice environment and the role models involved in practice. Their *modus operandi* became one of persuasion and compromise, which was sometimes to the detriment of learning opportunities provided to students.

Another factor influencing the separation between education and service was the tendency of instructors in educational institutions to separate themselves from practice. This was evidenced by their withdrawal from the practice setting except to supervise students. In some cases, they chose to wear a lab coat instead of a uniform to differentiate themselves from the staff. This served as an additional impediment in relationships between educators and staff, since attire tends to be a status symbol and an important means of identifying people in hospital settings. In some cases, instructors were perceived by staff as having chosen teaching to escape from practice. In fact, they were allowed limited involvement in practice by the nursing education administrators. One consequence was that there were often negative attitudes toward the faculty and students. In many cases, learning opportunities were inadequate because of lack of staff support and interest in facilitating students' learning. Another outcome was the tendency to "label" each other, with the result that a lack of respect and trust developed between nursing educators and nursing service personnel.

Consequences of the situation were limited communication between the two groups and sometimes open conflict and negative controls.

Clearly, the organization and structure of nursing school/faculties had no relationship to health-care agencies, even in academic health centres. Chater (1983, p. 59) states "University-owned and university-affiliated hospitals became part of academic health centers so that medical schools could have control over the environments for patient care and guaranteed access to the mix of patients required for the clinical programs." Have nursing schools/faculties obtained the same control and access as the medical schools/faculties in Canada and the United States?

THEORETICAL FRAMEWORK

Organizational theorists have identified factors that contribute to separation between organizations and factors that promote interaction (Blau, 1975; Stinchcombe, 1968; Ullrich and Wieland, 1980). Batey (1983, p. 3) applies this theoretical knowledge to nursing, showing how structure influences interaction between persons in an organization. She defines structure as: "A network of relationships among social positions that effects differences in role relations and social integration." One would expect more interaction among members of like groups than among members of different groups. It is also known that status differences influence interaction. One of the outcomes of interaction in an organization is for members to develop shared values. If interaction is limited, there is less opportunity to develop shared values; there may even be conflicts among different groups (Batey, 1983).

To what extent have such outcomes occurred in nursing? One need only reflect on some of the differences in values that can be found between education and service, such as the importance of research; conceptualizations of practice; priorities for care; and theoretical foundations of practice. Given the differences between faculty and nursing staff in health-care agencies on such variables as education, work setting, autonomy and status, clearly "the structured forces against integration are stronger than the forces for it" (Batey, 1983, p. 5). Although it is important to recognize differences, it is equally important to take steps to reduce them and increase interaction in order to strengthen values and to work together to overcome deterrents to the common goals of nursing: quality care, quality education, and quality research.

MEANS OF OVERCOMING DETERRENTS

One means of overcoming deterrents to interaction is to develop a collaboration or unification model, such as those developed at a few universities in the United States and Canada. The first such model was developed in 1959 at the University of Florida by Dorothy Smith, then Dean of the College of Nursing (Smith, 1959; Smith, 1965). Although this model did not survive, it made an important contribution to promoting collaboration. Smith later acknowledged that her model had not been based on organizational theory, nor had it used role theory; she perceived that these factors contributed to its demise. Such theories were considered carefully and used in developing subsequent models. The next application of an interorganizational model was at Case Western Reserve University and University Hospitals of Cleveland in the 1960s under the direction of Schlotfeldt and MacPhail (MacPhail, 1972, 1975, 1980, 1983; Schlotfeldt, 1980; Schlotfeldt and MacPhail, 1969a, 1969b, 1969c). Other examples are the application of a unification model, beginning in 1972 at the University of Rochester and Rush University in Chicago. Subsequently, a "contractual agreement approach" was developed at Rutgers University (Joel, 1985); a "partnership plan" was developed at the University of Pennsylvania (Fagin, 1985); and a "partnership model" was designed and tested at the University of South Carolina (Baker et al, 1989a; Baker et al, 1989b). Although all were designed to promote and facilitate interinstitutional collaboration, each was a different model, on a different scale, designed to fit a particular situation. This is an important concept to consider when making an effort to foster collaboration. Although several Canadian universities have developed joint appointments, which is another approach to promoting interaction between nursing service and nursing education, only McMaster University has developed an organization based on a collaboration model.

Despite these efforts, most university nursing schools in Canada and the United States are still separated organizationally and structurally from the health-care agencies in which nursing students practise. The schism between education and service in nursing was one means of overcoming exploitation of students and of preventing faculty from gaining control of all learning opportunities for students. Have these goals not been attained sufficiently to decrease the separation and work toward overcoming deterrents to collaboration and promoting interaction and the development of shared values?

COLLABORATION/UNIFICATION MODELS

The two best known organizations based on unification models in existence today are at the University of Rochester and Rush University in the United States, both of which were initiated in 1972. While there are differences in position titles and roles, their basic structures are similar. Figure 25.1 shows the structure for the University of Rochester model, which reflects one chief executive officer for nursing, encompassing the positions of the dean and director of nursing, with much of the responsibility for service delegated to the associate dean of nursing practice and considerable responsibility for nursing education delegated to the two associate deans (undergraduate and graduate). Clinical nursing chiefs are responsible for practice, education, and research in their respective clinical specialties; and they share in policy development and planning that affect all clinical areas. There is commitment to involvement in teaching, practice, and research at the level of the clinical nursing chief, the faculty, and nursing staff.

Faculty who also hold Clinician II appointments teach; maintain their competence in practice; and use their practice to generate research, improve care,

FIGURE 25.1 A model organization chart from the University of Rochester School of Nursing.

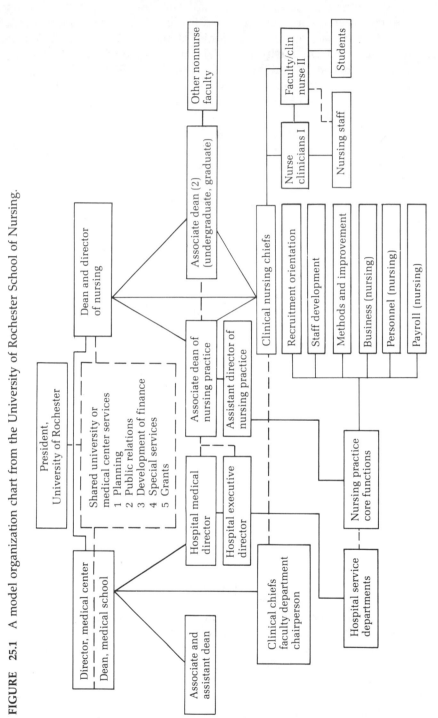

Modified from Ford, L.C. (1980a). Creating a center for excellence in nursing. In Aiken, L.H., (Eds). Health policy and nursing practice. New York: McGraw-Hill.

serve as role models for students, and develop collegial and team relationships with other health professionals, especially physicians (Ford, 1980a). Persons with Clinician I appointments are baccalaureate prepared, are responsible for patient care on a 24-bed unit, and provide clinical leadership in helping to plan student programs. Faculty-Clinician II appointees hold master's degrees and are clinical specialists, who serve as consultants to the Clinician I and staff nurses and provide clinical supervision and classroom instruction for students. In the Rochester model, Ford (1980a, p. 257) states: "The practice component contributes to education, the education component to practice, and research draws from each and contributes to the advancement of both." The Rush University model is similar to the Rochester model in terms of having one board of trustees, one administrator for nursing, and one budget with nursing education and service unified. The teacher/practitioner in the Rush University model is similar to the Faculty-Clinician II appointee of the Rochester model (Christman, 1979).

The model discussed previously is different from the Case Western Reserve University/University Hospitals of Cleveland interorganizational model, which involves two private, independent organizations, each with its own board, budget, and administration. Mechanisms and strategies were developed to facilitate and ensure collaboration between the two organizations. Figure 25.2 shows the model or organizational scheme for interinstitutional relationships developed in that setting to achieve shared goals.

Leadership in the school and in the department of nursing of the hospital is believed to require the full-time involvement of an administrator, and the chief executive officer in each organization is expected to have cooperative relationships. The clinical directors, who also serve as chairs of the faculty groups, are similar to the clinical nursing chiefs in the Rochester model. To facilitate and promote interaction and opportunities to develop shared values, three types of joint appointments were developed: shared cost, clinical, and associate. The shared cost appointments are similar to the Faculty-Clinician II appointments in the Rochester model. Cost sharing may be on different percentage bases (50%-50%; 75%-25%, or 80%-20%), depending on the needs of the two organizations. Clinical appointees are nurses with master's preparation who hold leadership positions in the hospital or other health-care agency and a clinical appointment in the school of nursing. Associate appointees are faculty who hold an associate in nursing appointment in a health care agency. There is no cost sharing for these two types, but there is sharing of time and talents to contribute to the other organization.

Although these three models differ in specific structures, roles, and titles, all contain an organizational structure that facilitates and ensures interaction and communication between education and service and the opportunity to develop shared values. All are directed toward the same goals: (1) improving the quality of nursing care through research and strong clinical leadership; (2) enhancing the learning climate and learning opportunities for nursing students and nursing staff; (3) promoting nursing research and use of valid and reliable research findings; (4) fostering interprofessional collaboration, particularly between nurses and physicians; and (5) using human and material resources cost-effectively.

FIGURE 25.2 Organizational scheme for interinstitutional relationships necessary to achieve shared goals: Case Western Reserve University and University Hospital of Cleveland.

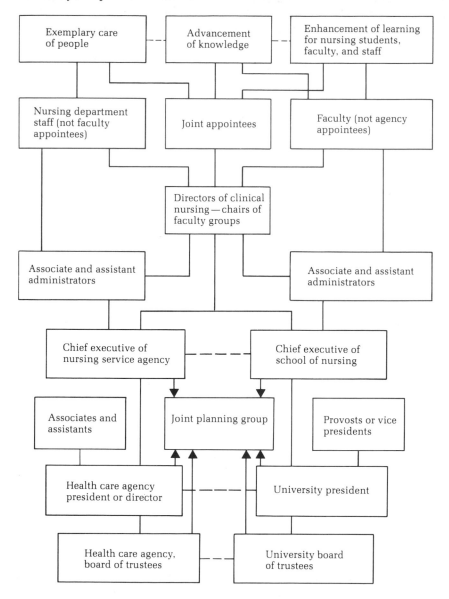

Modified form Schlotfeldt, R.M. The development of a model for verifying nursing practice and nursing education. In Aiken, L.H., (Ed.). Health policy and nursing practice. New York: McGraw-Hill.

THEORETICAL BASES AND OUTCOMES OF THE MODELS

The development of organizational structures that are based on these models has required major changes in organizations and in the relationships between organizations. The structures were based on organizational theories and theories of planned change. Changes in roles and relations were based on role theory, emphasizing the importance of the five factors known to influence role development: education; experience to reinforce the education; reference group identification or role modelling; the status system in the organization; and the incentive system of the organization. All of the models have involved decentralizing authority and responsibility within nursing service; restructuring within each organization and between organizations; redefining roles and role relations; changing expectations for role incumbents by those with whom they interact, including nurses, physicians, and patients; developing strong leadership in nursing; and increasing involvement of faculty in practice.

Outcomes of these models have been development of strong leadership within the educational institution and the health-care agency; attraction of faculty and clinical specialists to the settings; increased attraction and retention of nursing staff in the health-care agencies; and increased resources and expertise available to both organizations, with sharing of resources between service and education. A major consequence experienced by all involved in those settings has been increased interaction between the incumbents of roles in both education and service, with the opportunity to develop trust and respect for each other, and shared values.

CRITICISM OF COLLABORATION/UNIFICATION MODELS

There has been criticism of the existing collaboration/unification models for increasing workloads and contributing to burnout (Blazek et al, 1982; Ford, 1980b; Powers, 1976; Sovie, 1981b; Spero, 1980). These problems have occurred in some settings; however, one can learn from the mistakes of others and try to avoid such pitfalls. The administrators who develop the model must set reasonable expectations and provide guidance and flexibility to joint appointees to try to prevent them from attempting to assume two full-time jobs. This hazard applies particularly to persons in shared-cost appointments.

The models have also been criticized for decreasing research productivity and publication; however, most models have facilitated and ultimately increased scholarly endeavours. Problems tend to arise if the nurse administrator in each institution is not familiar with the expectations held for the joint appointees in the other institution and if guidance and incentives are not provided for role incumbents to meet all expectations to a reasonable degree. For example, one cannot expect a joint appointee in a 50%-50% position to maintain the same teaching responsibilities in the school of nursing or to have the same involvement in agency programs as the person who does not hold such an appointment.

All collaboration/unification models have contributed to enhancing the learning environment for students by virtue of the improved quality of care, exemplary role models, and the supportive learning climate provided by staff. The old *we-they* concept no longer exists, as all are collaborating in developing shared values and pursuing common goals. Head nurses and staff nurses are helped to see their importance in students' learning and are used to advantage rather than being ignored. The latter tends to create negative attitudes in staff who feel excluded.

FACULTY PRACTICE

Over the past two decades, increasing attention has been given to "faculty practice," particularly as an integral part of collaboration/unification models. Unfortunately, the schism between nursing education and nursing practice resulted in many nursing faculty failing to maintain involvement in practice and not being perceived as role models by either nursing students or nursing staff. Much of the impetus for the focus on faculty practice derived from the publication of a "Statement of Belief Regarding Faculty Practice" (1979), written by 13 nursing leaders in the United States who were highly committed to collaboration and keenly aware of the difficulty many faculty were experiencing in incorporating practice into their role. The statement called for legitimizing nursing practice as an integral part of the faculty role; developing incentives to promote and reward practice as a means of enhancing practice, education and research; and adapting organizational structures and policies to facilitate faculty practice. The American Academy of Nursing sponsored four annual symposia from 1983 to 1986, the first three of which were partially funded by the Robert Wood Johnson Foundation, a philanthropic organization strongly committed to promoting faculty practice to improve patient care (Barnard, 1983; Barnard and Smith, 1985).

Several definitions of faculty practice can be found in the literature. Ford (1983, pp. 13-14) defines it as "activities related to the care of patients which must meet two criteria: (1) Be scholarly in orientation with associated scholarship outcomes; and (2) Have the care of patients or clients as the central focus." Faculty practice may involve any roles that faculty members play in service agencies that meet the criteria. These include activities in the direct and indirect care of patients and participation in programs, such as staff development, quality assurance, clinical advancement, and administrative and committee assignments (Ford, 1983). Other definitions (Algase, 1986; Anderson and Pierson, 1983) exclude indirect care activities and limit faculty practice to direct care of patients/clients. Faculty practice is perceived as quality care through which clinical judgement is enhanced. It has the potential for enriching teaching; generating credibility in students, nursing staff, and colleagues in other disciplines; influencing the selection of research problems to be investigated and the methods of inquiry used; promoting application of research findings in practice; sensitizing nurse educators to nursing service issues and problems; increasing the testing of theory in practice; and enhancing the quality of care provided patients/clients and education of students. Faculty practice is an integral part of collaboration/unification models.

DETERRENTS TO COLLABORATION BETWEEN SERVICE AND EDUCATION

If collaboration between service and education, of which faculty practice is an integral part, is possible and can accomplish the objectives stated previously, one may ask why more such models are not developed. Some of the factors identified to date are lack of interest by either faculty or nursing service personnel; skepticism by faculty or nursing leaders who seem to have difficulty believing that the system can work; fear of heavy work load, leading to burnout; faculty role strain and role conflict (Barger and Bridges, 1987); limited access to practice sites due to inflexible policies that permit practice on a limited basis (Millonig, 1986); failure to adapt criteria for promotion and tenure to recognize and reward faculty practice; and lack of organizational support through formalized practice policies, expectations, or remuneration mechanisms to promote and facilitate faculty practice (Lambert and Lambert, 1988). Additional factors are insufficient clinical expertise of faculty who are threatened by the expectations required in the clinical settings, and an inadequate number of risk takers in nursing. Other possible deterrents to promoting collaboration are insufficient communication and interaction between nurses in education and service to develop shared values and common goals; fears of faculty that research productivity will be decreased because of additional commitment to practice; and obvious differences in values, status, and education between the stakeholders in nursing education and those in nursing service.

JOINT APPOINTMENTS AS FACILITATORS OF INTERACTION

A collaboration/unification model is not feasible in all settings. Another means of facilitating collaboration and achieving at least some of the goals of collaboration is developing joint appointments between nursing education and the health-care agencies, in which students practise and in which research is conducted by faculty and students. Joint appointments are designed to increase interaction; nurture shared values; and promote a sense of joint accountability for quality nursing practice, quality education, and quality research. Various types of joint appointments have been developed in a number of Canadian universities, including Alberta, Calgary, British Columbia, McGill, Toronto, and Dalhousie.

The system of joint appointments at the University of Alberta was designed in the 1982–1983 academic year through a group effort involving representatives from four health-care agencies and three representatives from the Faculty of Nursing. Two types of joint appointments exist: *Faculty-Agency,* with the primary appointment in the faculty; and *Agency-Faculty,* with the primary appointment in the health-care agency. There may or may not be sharing of costs in these two types; however, most do not involve cost sharing. In a cost sharing appointment, the incumbent must hold a primary appointment in either the educational institution or the health-care agency, and the other institution is billed for its share of salary and fringe benefits, as mutually agreed. The privileges and responsibilities entailed in the two types of appointments have been specified; they serve as a guide for incumbents of the joint appointments and provide a basis for writing an annual report on an individual's participation in the other organization. It is vitally important to have reasonable expectations in both organizations and to have flexibility in evolvement of the role. Some cost-shared appointments are faculty who serve as clinical nurse researchers for a portion of their time in a health-care agency, which may be on a 50%-50%, 30%-70%, or 20%-80% basis. Others are clinical nurse specialists in a health-care agency with an appointment in the Faculty of Nursing or a master's prepared unit supervisor (head nurse) who provides clinical supervision for students placed on the unit.

The privileges and responsibilities of the two types of joint appointments have been developed with careful attention to balance or equality in each of the items (Faculty of Nursing, 1983). For example, an individual from a health-care agency who holds an Associate Faculty appointment is listed in the Faculty of Nursing Calendar, obtains a library card, and has opportunity to participate in faculty meetings with voice, but not vote. The person has access to faculty development programs and opportunity to gain knowledge of and contribute to the development of curricula. There may also be opportunities to serve as preceptor for students or teach in courses related to expertise and to increase research competence through research and use of consultation resources.

In a similar vein, a faculty member who holds an Associate in Nursing appointment in a health-care agency may participate in administrative or clinical meetings and contribute to staff development programs in the agency. The person has opportunity to gain knowledge of and contribute to nursing practice and program development in the agency. There are opportunities to practise or conduct research in the agency, although ethical clearance must be obtained for this to do research. Faculty who hold such an appointment may use it to assist staff in research development and contribute to staff development. The individual may choose to contract to practise a certain proportion of time weekly, serve as consultant to staff, or be involved in several activities.

All privileges and responsibilities are negotiated with the person responsible for programs in the other organization. Negotiation is logical since persons in leadership positions have knowledge of the programs and know what would be appropriate and needs involvement. In addition, they are the individuals ultimately responsible for evaluating the performance of the joint appointee and deciding whether the appointment will be continued.

EVALUATION OF OUTCOMES

One criticism of the collaboration/unification models and of joint appointments has been insufficient effort to evaluate outcomes to demonstrate benefits. Admittedly, in the early collaboration models, much effort went into developing the models, with less attention devoted to evaluation of outcomes. In addition, some of the outcome measures used by proponents of the models to demonstrate results have involved inconclusive data because of the nature of the phenomena being evaluated.

A major objective of joint endeavours is to improve nursing practice. Such improvement is evident in the amount of research conducted and the extent to which research findings are applied in practice. Neither of these aspects have as yet been documented systematically, but they could be in future models or joint appointments. If one believes that research is necessary to improve practice and that it is through research that knowledge is advanced and practice improved, this would seem to be a logical means of evaluation.

Documenting the initiation of new programs of care by experts who have been attracted to leadership positions in these collaboration models is often used as evidence of improvement in care. To have such systematic documentation, it is necessary to obtain baseline data about the programs of care before a model is implemented, which in most cases has not been feasible. Nonetheless, one can reflect on the nature of programs of care at the outset and document progressive programs that have been implemented. Some examples in maternity nursing might include preparation for childbearing, support of parents having such preparation by staff, and father and sibling visitation programs. Other examples would be parent participation in child care and educational programs for patients and families pertaining to particular kinds of health problems.

Patient satisfaction studies are another method of evaluating care. These have been used to some extent, although the validity and reliability of these instruments have presented problems in such studies over the years. Sovie (1981a) notes that care in the Rochester model was evaluated as excellent by patients and families, physicians, and staff. Similar outcomes are reported by MacPhail (1972) in relation to the Case Western Reserve University/University Hospitals of Cleveland model. Sovie (1981a) also identifies excellent patient and family teaching programs and materials as an outcome of the Rochester model. Another mechanism that verifies improvement of care is the accreditation report, through which written and verbal comments are received about the quality of nursing care and the extent to which standards are met and surpassed (Sovie, 1981a). Some nursing service leaders refer to the outcomes measured by quality assurance indicators; however, others are reluctant to use such indicators because of problems with the validity and reliability of some of the quality assurance indicators.

Another outcome is enhancement of the learning climate and learning opportunities for students and staff. This is evidenced by reports of changes in access to patients by faculty, improvements in student learning, changes in attitude of staff toward learners, types of learning experiences made available to students through collaborative efforts and sharing of information, and improved role models for students. It is logical to want a clinical setting in which students gain experience to be characterized by high quality of care. It has been clear to observers that this has been an outcome of collaborative efforts in all three models previously described due to joint decision-making at the clinical leadership level.

Another objective of collaboration pertains to the promotion and facilitation of research endeavours. This can be documented by collecting data about the number and nature of studies conducted over time and about efforts to apply research findings in practice. Data reflecting these efforts include conferences and research rounds to share research findings and assist staff nurses in applying them, as well as the actual application of findings in specific situations. Other indications include publications, presentation of papers, and active research promotion activities in both nursing education and nursing service, such as research day or research week as an annual activity in a health-care agency, and evidence of attention to research in internal nursing newsletters.

Another objective is to enhance interprofessional collaboration. This can be documented by change in the number and nature of joint meetings and collaborative or interdisciplinary endeavours. Changes in joint planning on hospital units and joint educational efforts between and among educational programs would also indicate success in meeting this objective. Sovie (1981b) refers to collaboration between nursing and medicine in designing innovative approaches to the organization and delivery of ambulatory care. Other measures of success would be respect and recognition between the professions and the position of influence and power obtained by nursing through such a joint endeavour. Reference has been made to these outcomes by Sovie (1981b) and MacPhail (1972).

Results of changes in the organizational structure to facilitate interaction and development of shared values can provide powerful and persuasive evidence of movement toward goals. Such evidence can be documented in terms of joint meetings, collaborative endeavours, new programs developed jointly, and the extent to which values are shared versus differences emphasized on a long-term basis.

In her review of nursing research on faculty practice, Chicadonz (1987) included research on collaboration/unification models of which faculty practice is an integral part. She found a dearth of published research, with only six studies that are "descriptive in nature and barely begin to address the questions related to faculty practice and unification models" (Chicadonz, 1987, p. 145). She emphasizes the need for more research and identifies the lack of theoretical conceptualizations as a problem in developing future investigations. Chicadonz (1987, p. 145) presents five areas for future research: "the expansion of faculty practice, case studies of unification models, impact studies, social context studies, and studies on faculty who practice."

RECEPTIVITY TO COLLABORATION BETWEEN NURSING EDUCATION AND NURSING SERVICE

Whether nurse educators and nursing service leaders are receptive to the introduction of joint appointments or a collaboration/unification model may be influenced by perception of the benefits and risks involved. Yarcheski and Mahon (1985) conducted a study of receptivity to a theoretical proposal for a unification model among nurse educators in the United States. The three status groups studied were deans, tenured faculty, and nontenured faculty. All perceived "moderately high benefits accruing to their statuses and thus moderately high receptivity to unification, which was further substantiated by the strong positive relationship found between these two variables in the sample as a whole" (Yarcheski and Mahon, 1985, p. 125). Although predicted differences for both receptivity and level of perceived risk were not found, Yarcheski and Mahon (1985) stated that the status-risk theory of receptivity could be used effectively to study receptivity in different status groups of nurse educators during the actual implementation of a collaboration/ unification model.

CONCLUSION

There are undoubtedly other ways to promote collaboration between nursing education and service and overcome barriers between them. Study of organizational theories and structure leads one to conclude that structures are required to promote and facilitate interaction and communication between education and service that is needed to develop shared values and goals. In addition, there is need for carefully designed strategies to promote and facilitate collaboration using existing knowledge of planned change, role development, and other organizational concepts that enter into such a collaborative endeavour. Educators and practitioners need to respect and trust, not blame. To achieve this goal requires good communication; interaction; openness; objectivity; readiness to examine beliefs, attitudes, and values; and willingness to recognize that compromises are needed to move toward the goal of collaboration and joint accountability for practice, education, and research. Together, educators and service leaders can develop the quality of nursing practice to which nurses in general aspire, as well as an exemplary learning environment for both nursing students and staff. Creating a supportive research environment will help improve the quality of practice through research and encourage application of research findings for the benefit of consumers of nursing care and nurses.

REFERENCES

Algase, D. (1986). Faculty practice: A means to advance the discipline of nursing. *J Nurs Educ* 25. 74-76.

Anderson, E.R. and Pierson, P. (1983). An exploratory study of faculty practice: Views of those faculty engaged in practice who teach in an NLN-accredited baccalaureate program. *Western J Nurs Res 5.* 129-143.

Baker, C.M. et al. (1989a). Interinstitutional collaboration for nursing excellence: Part 1, Creating the partnership. *J Nurs Admin 19(2).* 8-12.

Baker, C.M. et al. (1989b). Interinstitutional collaboration for nursing excellence: Part 2, Testing the model. *J Nurs Admin 19(3).* 8-13.

Barger, S.E. and Bridges, W.C. (1987). Nursing faculty practice: Institutional and individual facilitators and inhibitors. *J Prof Nurs 3(6).* 338-346.

Barnard, K. (1983). Preface. In K. Barnard, (Ed.). *Structure to outcome: Making it work.* Kansas City, MO: American Academy of Nursing.

Barnard, K. and Smith, G. (Ed.). *(1985). Faculty practice in action.* Kansas City, MO: American Academy of Nursing.

Batey, M. (1983). Structural consideration for the social integration of nursing. In K. Barnard (Ed.). *Structure to outcome: Making it work.* Kansas City, MO: American Academy of Nursing.

Blau, P.M. (1975). *Parameters of social structure: Approaches to the study of social structure.* New York: Free Press.

Blazek, A.M. et al. (1982). Unification: nursing education and practice. *Nursing Health Care 3(1).* 18-25.

Chater, S. (1983). Faculty practice considerations in academic health centers' schools of nursing. In K. Barnard (Ed.). *Structure to outcome: Making it work.* Kansas City, MO: American Academy of Nursing.

Chicadonz, G.H. (1987). Faculty practice. In J.J. Fitzpatrick and R.L. Taunton (Eds.). *Annual review nursing research* (vol. 5). New York: Springer.

Christman, L.B. (1979). The practitioner-teacher. *Nurse Educator 4(2).* 8-11.

Faculty of Nursing, University of Alberta. (1983). *Joint appointments: terms of reference.* Unpublished statement of definition, policies and procedures, role expectations and privileges. Edmonton: University of Alberta.

Fagin, C. (1985). Institutionalizing practice: historical and future perspectives. In K. Barnard and G. Smith (Ed.). *Faculty practice in action.* Kansas City, MO: American Academy of Nursing.

Ford, L.C. (1980a). Creating a center for excellence in nursing. In L.H. Aiken (Ed.). Health policy and nursing practice. New York: McGraw-Hill.

Ford, L.C. (1980b). Unification of nursing practice, education and research. *Intern Nurs Rev 27(6).* 178-183, 192.

Ford, L.C. (1983). Organizational perspectives on faculty practice: issues and challenges. In K. Barnard (Ed.). *Structure to outcome: making it work.* Kansas City, MO: American Academy of Nursing.

Joel, L. (1985). The Rutgers experience: One perspective on service-education collaboration. *Nursing Outlook 33(5).* 220-224.

Lambert, C.E. and Lambert, V.A. (1988). Faculty practice: unifier of nursing education and nursing service? *J Prof Nurs 4(5).* 345-355.

MacPhail, J. (1972). *An experiment in nursing: Planning, implementing, and assessing planned change.* Cleveland: Case Western Reserve University.

MacPhail, J. (1975). Promoting collaboration between education and service, *The Canadian Nurse 71(5).* 32-34.

MacPhail, J. (1980). Implementation and evaluation of the Case Western Reserve University unification model. In L.H. Aiken (Ed.). *Health policy and nursing practice.* New York: McGraw-Hill.

MacPhail, J. (1983). Collaboration/unification models for nursing education and nursing service. In N.L. Chaska (Ed.). *The nursing profession: A time to speak.* New York: McGraw-Hill.

Millonig, V. (1959). Faculty practice: A view of its development, current benefits, and barriers. *J Prof Nurs 2(3).* 166-172.

Powers, M. (1976). The unification model in nursing, *Nursing Outlook 24(8).* 482-487.

Schlotfeldt, R.M. (1980). The development of a model for unifying nursing practice and nursing education, In L.H. Aiken (Ed.). *Health policy and nursing practice.* New York: McGraw-Hill Inc.

Schlotfeldt, R.M. and MacPhail, J. (1969a) An experiment in nursing: rationale and characteristics. *AJN 69(5).* 1018-1023.

Schlotfeldt, R.M. and MacPhail, J. (1969b). An experiment in nursing: Introducing planned change. *AJN 69(6).* 1247-1251.

Schlotfeldt, R.M. and MacPhail, J. (1969c). An experiment in nursing: Implementing planned change. *AJN 69(7).* 1475-1480.

Smith, D.M. (1959). Practice: A part of teaching. *Nursing Outlook 7(3).* 134-135.

Smith, D.M. (1965). Education and service under one administration. *Nursing Outlook 13(2).* 54-56.

Sovie, M.D. (1981a). Unifying education and practice: one medical center's design. I. *J Nurs Admin 11(1).* 41-49.

Sovie, M.D. (1981b). Unifying education and practice: one medical center's design. II. *J Nurs Admin 11(2).* 30-32.

Spero, J. (1980). *Faculty practice as one component of the faculty role.* New York: National League for Nursing.

Statement of belief regarding faculty practice. *Nursing Outlook 27(3).* 158.

Stinchcombe, A.L. (1968). Constructing social theories. New York: Harcourt, Brace & World.

Ullrich, R.A. and Wieland, G.F. (1980). *Organization theory and design.* Homewood, Ill: Richard D. Irwin.

Yarcheski, A. and Mahon, N. (1985). The unification model in nursing: a study of receptivity among nurse educators in the United States. *Nurs Res 34(2).* 120-125.

CHAPTER TWENTY SIX

Monitoring Standards in Nursing Education

JANNETTA MacPHAIL

N ursing education programs in Canada were originally developed in hospital schools of nursing, primarily for the purpose of staffing the hospitals. This was the pattern for staffing, regardless of the size of the hospital. Indeed, some admitted as few as 10 to 12 students per year even in the 1950s. The only registered nurses in the hospitals were the head nurses, supervisors, and the director of nursing. Nursing students received instruction from a few nurses, who taught such courses as anatomy and physiology and nursing arts (basic procedures) in the classroom, and from physicians, who taught courses about diseases and medical or surgical treatments. The only clinical supervision was provided by head nurses and supervisors.

Schools of this nature proliferated in the early part of the twentieth century and continued into the 1940s and early 1950s, despite the recommendation of the Weir Report in 1932 that nursing education be organized and administered separately from the hospitals, which was the independent pattern of organization promoted by Florence Nightingale in the nineteenth century. Nursing leaders, such as Isabel Hampton Robb and Mary Adelaide Nutting, recognized the need for a system to monitor standards of education and worked for nurses within the professional nursing organizations to assume this role. Their goal was to devise a system requiring approval for new nursing programs, standards for existing schools of nursing that were equal to the new schools, and regular inspection of all programs to ensure that standards continued to be met.

NURSING EDUCATION STANDARDS

Standards in nursing education are delineated by knowledgeable nurse educators who have expertise in the practice of nursing and in methods of education. Standards range from minimal to ideal, depending on the purpose for which they are defined. There are two basic mechanisms for monitoring educational programs: approval and accreditation. Approval is a process used to designate an educational institution's competence to prepare practitioners for entry to nursing practice, that is, permission to operate a nursing program (Committee on Credentialing, 1979). The standards set by the monitoring body are usually minimal, whereas the standards established for accreditation of programs are intended to promote quality. "Accreditation is a process whereby institutions or programs are assessed and measured using a set of predetermined criteria which, if met, connote a basic level of quality" (Committee on Credentialing, 1979, p. 33).

Approval is a mandatory process, and minimal standards are established by a body authorized by provincial legislation or regulations pursuant to that legislation. Accreditation, voluntary and national in scope, measures institutions against criteria established by the accrediting body to promote quality. Accreditation of educational programs exists in many professions, but approval and monitoring of programs are unique to nursing. No other profession is governed by legislation that regulates the conduct of educational programs; however, nursing is the only profession that does not require university-level preparation for entry to practice. Because diploma-level education continues to exist in nursing, there is a potential for wide variability in standards; hence, the monitoring mechanism of approval is considered essential.

The purpose of any credentialing mechanism is to protect the public and ensure accountability to consumers. In nursing education programs, the consumers are the students, although patients or clients are the ultimate consumers of the services provided by nursing students and by graduates of nursing programs. Because any system of credentialing also benefits those who are credentialed, whether institutions or individuals, a system of checks and balances within the credentialing mechanism is necessary to ensure that the public is protected. In approval and accreditation, standards provide the checks and balances that ensure that the practitioners prepared in nursing education programs are competent to enter the practice of professional nursing.

APPROVAL OF PROGRAMS IN NURSING EDUCATION

In Canada, constitutional responsibility for education and health care rests with the provinces. Consequently, policies and mechanisms for monitoring standards in nursing education are defined by each province. This responsibility is delineated in legislation that regulates the conduct of educational programs, whether conducted in universities, colleges, or hospital schools of nursing. In all provinces except Alberta, Ontario, and Quebec, the responsibility for defining and monitoring standards in nursing education is assumed by the provincial nursing association. Although specific mechanisms for defining standards and the process for approval of basic nursing programs may vary among provinces, the profession controls the educational standards for the admission of new practitioners to the profession (see Chapter 3).

In Alberta, responsibility for approval of nursing programs is delegated in the Universities' Coordinating Council (UCC), which, under the terms of the Universities' Act, has ultimate responsibility for defining and monitoring standards for all postsecondary education in the province. The responsibility for regulating and monitoring nursing education is delegated by UCC to a Committee on Nursing Education, which is responsible to UCC and includes five representatives: two from college programs, two from hospital nursing programs, and one from university nursing programs. This Committee sets standards and approves functions for the seven diploma programs located in community colleges and the four hospital schools of nursing (Nursing Education Committee, 1982). Because the two basic baccalaureate degree programs (Alberta and Calgary) must meet the standards and obtain approval within each university, as designated by UCC for all university programs, they are not monitored and approved by the Nursing Education Committee.

In Ontario, the Health Disciplines Act was enacted in 1974 to "govern nursing as well as dental, medical, optometric and pharmaceutical practitioners, a unique approach to nursing legislation in Canada" (Prowse, 1983 p. 20). The College of Nurses of Ontario (CNO), responsible to the Minister of Health, fulfils the registration and discipline functions for registered nurses and registered nursing assistants in that province. Monitoring and approval of nursing education programs for 22 diploma programs, that are located in community colleges is conducted by the CNO, which has a contractual arrangement with the Ministry of Colleges and Universities for this purpose. The standards of the CNO were originally delineated through the Provincial Advisory Council on Nursing Education, which was later dissolved. The responsibility for standards was transferred to the Council of Regents, advisory to the Minister of Colleges and Universities, and in 1989 to the Ministry of Colleges and Universities (J. Legg [personal communication, April 17, 1990]). One exception to this approval mechanism is the diploma program at Ryerson Polytechnical Institute, where the Academic Council is authorized for the monitoring and approval functions. This exception may be explained by the fact that Ryerson has degree-granting privileges and grants a degree in nursing. Monitoring and approval of the nine basic baccalaureate degree programs located in universities is accomplished by the Ontario Region Chapter of the Canadian Association of University Schools of Nursing (ORCAUSN), whose Accreditation Committee defined the standards and approval process. Since the accreditation program was implemented by the Canadian Association of University Schools of Nursing (CAUSN) in 1987, ORCAUSN has accepted accreditation of a baccalaureate degree program by CAUSN in place of its approval (J. Legg [personal communication, April 17, 1990]). This may explain why five of the eight universities that have been reviewed or are scheduled for review in 1990 are in Ontario. It is expected that this arrangement will eliminate the need for an approval program in the ORCAUSN (S. Cameron [personal communication, May 1, 1990]).

In Quebec, all postsecondary education, including nursing programs, is governed by the Ministry of Higher Education and Science. There has been no mechanism for approval of nursing programs, but a mechanism for approval is being developed for the diploma programs of the Collèges d'Enseignement Généraux et Professionnels (CEGEP). University nursing programs are subject to the approval process required of all educational programs in their respective universities. The Ministry of Higher Education and Science, a ministry established in

1985, studied nursing manpower needs and diploma programs and decided that an approval and monitoring system is needed to ensure that standards are maintained. An approval program was tested, and implemented in 1988 as a five-year monitoring process. The standards were developed with advice from the Ordre des Infirmières et Infirmiers du Québec (L. Michon [personal communication, July 23, 1987]).

Thus primary responsibility for approval of nursing education programs is delegated to the provincial nursing association in all provinces except those previously mentioned. One can expect considerable differences in the systems for regulation and monitoring because of the variety and number of nursing education programs. All provinces have university nursing programs, with the exception of Prince Edward Island, which has only a diploma program; however, "On November 9, 1988, a provincial government decision to phase out diploma nursing education in favour of a degree program was announced — a move supported by the professional nursing association, nurses' unions, employers and educators alike" (CNA Connection, 1989 p. 10). Their goal is to recruit a dean/director by mid 1990. They were successful in recruiting a director to lead the development of the program, recruit faculty and determine whether the program should be established as a faculty or school within the university structure. When the transition is complete, Prince Edward Island will be the first province in Canada to achieve the goal of a baccalaureate degree as the minimal entry level into nursing.

Nursing education programs in colleges exist in all provinces except Newfoundland, New Brunswick, Nova Scotia, and Prince Edward Island. Hospital schools of nursing, which were initially the only type of nursing education program in all provinces, no longer exist in Ontario, Quebec or Saskatchewan. The governments in those three provinces phased out hospital schools of nursing and transferred the responsibility for diploma-level education to the college system. At present, there are 22 basic baccalaureate level programs and 110 diploma programs, 27 in hospital/independent schools of nursing and 83 in colleges (Statistics Canada, 1990). In the near future, two of the hospital schools will be phased out in deference to the decision made in Prince Edward Island and the decision of the Vancouver General Hospital (VGH) to convert its school of nursing from a diploma to a baccalaureate degree program by joining forces with the University of British Columbia (UBC) in September 1989. The students entering were required to meet UBC admission standards and were enroled as UBC students. "They will take the same 5-year program as students who enter the UBC program. The current VGH program will be merged with the UBC program with VGH becoming a major clinical practice and research facility for the UBC nursing programs" (CNA News, 1989, p. 12).

The standards for nursing education programs in each province cover areas such as administration and general organization, philosophy and objectives; faculty; students; curriculum; educational resources and facilities, records, and reports; and evaluation. Approval must be obtained to establish a new program in nursing, and monitoring for continued approval occurs at five-year intervals. Approval must also be obtained to eliminate a nursing program. The approval process involves submitting a report before a visit by persons designated by the authorized body to assume this responsibility. These individuals are normally qualified registered nurses who report their recommendations to the appropriate body. In most provinces, nursing education programs in universities are required to meet the standards defined by the university according to an Act governing the universities; it is not usually necessary for these programs to participate in the approval process defined for the diploma programs located in colleges and hospital schools of nursing.

Although the approval mechanism in all provinces is designed to ensure compliance with minimal standards, it is important that the standards and the process by which they are implemented ensure that nursing students are adequately prepared to enter practice. Delineating adequate preparation for entry is the subject of much debate and has always been a major issue in nursing education. In the days when almost all nursing students were prepared in hospital schools of nursing and each hospital recruited its own graduates, few questions were asked about the adequacy of preparation. The inbreeding that resulted from this system may have fostered obedience and strict adherence to the status quo. At that time, the emphasis was on procedures and technical preparation as opposed to the broader education that was encouraged after the initiation of university nursing programs. It has been difficult for some nurses in practice settings to accept the fact that graduating students are novices, not expert practitioners, which tended to be the perception of new graduates in the past. However, such an attitude was unrealistic because new graduates, even then, had much to learn. No other profession expects expert performance from newly graduated practitioners.

Another issue in the approval process pertains to the delineation of minimal standards. Who decides what minimal is and what standards are considered more than minimal? It is important that standards be defined by well-prepared, competent nurses. Definition is possible within the professional associations and also in Alberta by the Committee on Nursing Education that is responsible to the UCC. In Alberta, when the Nursing Profession Act of 1984 was being formulated, the professional association's goal was to transfer responsibility for the approval process to the professional association from the UCC. Because the Alberta Government demanded conditions the profession could not accept the price for such a change, and thus there was danger of losing the new act and responsibility was left with the UCC. Although the responsibility for delineating standards and the approval mechanism remains with professional nurses, there is no doubt that the ideal in all provinces is to have this important regulatory mechanism remain with the professional associations. One exception may be Ontario, where the Registered Nurses Association of Ontario (RNAO) does not have responsibility for registration or discipline because the CNO has this authority.

The question of whether all programs should be under the same approval mechanism will continue as long as there is more than one program for preparation for entry to nursing practice. This will no longer be an issue when the goal of the baccalaureate for entry to practice is attained, we hope, by the year 2000. Nurses in all provinces are working diligently to attain the goal even though they are fully aware of the barriers to be overcome and the resistance raised by nurses who feel threatened in spite of a grandparenting clause that would apply for those graduating before the year 2000. There is also some opposition to the position from outside the profession.

Another problem that is prevalent in imposing regulatory mechanisms is avoiding rigidity in the standards and allowing for flexibility within the system. It is important that standards be defined broadly enough to allow for differences and creative approaches while maintaining basic accountability to the public and to the consumers of nursing education, the students.

ACCREDITATION

No system for accreditation of nursing education programs was present in Canada until 1986, when CAUSN approved the establishment of a program for university nursing programs after devoting 12 years to the development of an accreditation program. The major impetus for the program was that nursing was one of the few health sciences educational programs that did not have a system for accreditation (Joint Working Group, 1977). French states:

> In 1972 CAUSN was designated as the accrediting agency for university programs in nursing. In 1974 CAUSN established a committee on accreditation to develop a program of accreditation for university based programs in nursing. Recognizing the need for a method to stimulate the development of educational programs that are responsive to societal needs, and the dangers inherent in the accreditation process, CAUSN demanded a program that would support and promote change. The criteria on which the accreditation process was to be based had to reflect attributes of change and development. The major objective of the program of accreditation was to ensure that the educational programs were preparing the quality of practitioner required to deal effectively with existing and future health problems. Through the process of accreditation, institutions would be encouraged to engage in a process of self-evaluation, i.e., to study the goals of its educational program(s) and the means of attaining those goals (1982, p. 2).

From 1974 to 1984, the CAUSN Committee on Accreditation examined existing programs of accreditation, including the National League for Nursing accreditation program in the United States, which had existed since 1952. Three major qualities were proposed by Allen (1977) and adopted by CAUSN as the criteria by which programs would be evaluated. These qualities were: (1) relevance to the trends in society that have an impact on the health needs of the community; (2) accountability, defined as the extent to which the program teaches students that the primary responsibility in nursing is to the client; and (3) relatedness or the extent to which parts of the program support and build on other parts, thereby promoting the achievement of goals. Subsequently, a fourth criterion, uniqueness, was adopted. It was defined as "the extent to which a program capitalizes on the resources within its particular setting" (Canadian Association of University Schools of Nursing [CAUSN], 1978 p. 3).

The CAUSN Committee on Accreditation developed procedures for applying these criteria in the process of accreditation. A number of university nursing programs across Canada were involved as test sites in developing standards and instruments. Thus, the program of accreditation for university-based nursing programs evolved over 12 years before being accepted for general implementation by CAUSN Council in June, 1986.

CAUSN implements its accreditation function through a Board of Accreditation, that includes six members appointed by CAUSN Council who function within the policies and guidelines established by the Association. To date the Board has reviewed 8 of the 27 university nursing programs and accepted 4 more requests for review by 1994 (CAUSN Newsletter, 1990). Three more programs are scheduled for review in 1990. The new baccalaureate degree program at Ryerson Polytechnical Institute was reviewed for candidacy in 1990; this is an option for new programs that do not wish to apply for full accreditation while still in developmental stage (CAUSN Newsletter, 1989).

Within CAUSN's framework, "accreditation has two main purposes: (1) the support and improvement of standards of baccalaureate and graduate nursing programs in CAUSN member institutions; and (2) the recognition of programs that have been reviewed and have met specific standards" (CAUSN Newsletter, 1989, p. 1). CAUSN's policy is "that once a member unit has received notice from the Board of Accreditation concerning its accreditation status, and has had opportunity to respond, and if no appeal is pending, then it becomes public information and it will be published in the CAUSN Newsletter" (CAUSN Council, 1989). Thus accreditation status will become known to recipients of the CAUSN Newsletter, including all 27 member institutions and all individual members of the four regional chapters of CAUSN: Atlantic Region (ARCAUSN), Quebec Region (QRCAUSN), Ontario Region (ORCAUSN), and Western Region (WRCAUSN). Until now there has been no stated means of providing information about accreditation status to prospective students, to guidance counsellors, or to nurses who are interested in earning a baccalaureate or master's degree in nursing; however, the CAUSN Council has made a decision that such information is in the public domain, and steps will be taken to make this known to the groups mentioned (J. Bouchard [personal communication, April 25, 1990]).

In the United States, where the National League for Nursing (NLN) has been responsible for accreditation of all nursing programs since 1952, the listing of accredited programs appears regularly in the official journal of NLN and is published annually in booklet form. However, it includes only accredited programs and does not provide information as to whether programs not listed have failed to meet required standards or simply did not seek accreditation, which is a voluntary process. McCloskey (1985) and others question whether the concept of public accountability is actually fulfilled when accreditation bodies publicize only programs that have been accredited and do not release information about those that have not.

Financing the accreditation program has been a major concern. In 1977, CAUSN submitted a proposal to the WK Kellogg Foundation for possible funding; however, support was not obtained. The foundation was approached again in 1979, but by 1980 there were strong indications that support would not be forthcoming. Consequently, CAUSN proceeded with plans for implementing the program and a special annual fee, assessed to all university nursing programs, was kept in reserve to support the accreditation program. This fee, $1000 per school per year initially, was reduced to $500 in 1981. When the accreditation program was implemented in 1987, completing a review of the first program to seek accreditation, a specific fee for the review had not been established; a fee was charged based on the amount of involvement with each program (J. Bouchard [personal communication, April 25, 1990]). However, it became obvious that additional funding was needed. In November 1989, CAUSN Council approved a fee of $3000 to be instituted in the 1989 to 1990 academic year and increased to $4500 for 1990 to 1991 and 1991 to 1992, and also stated that the accreditation program become cost-recovery over the next five to seven years (CAUSN Council, 1989).

The cost of the program includes fiscal costs and costs related to the development of graduate programs, including implementation of doctoral programs in nursing, which are nonexistent in Canada; development of research in nursing, particularly in university nursing schools, to advance nursing knowledge and improve practice; and development of exemplary nursing practice in settings where students learn to nurse and faculty continue to practice and conduct research. The problem here is the amount of time required for a faculty or school to conduct a self-study and for faculty participation in the visitation and review processes for programs other than their own. Time thus expended is not available to pursue other goals. French (1984) states:

> A program of accreditation had to facilitate, not impede the achievement of these goals. Accreditation was to be conducted with a minimum of effort, cost and time. It was to promote the interest of the educational consumers and the portability of educational qualification were identified as basic objectives of accreditation.

The 20 programs that have not yet sought accreditation will have to decide if they will do so; the $3000 fee for 1989 to 1990 will be increased to $4500 for 1990 to 1991. Their decisions may be based on the availability of financial resources and time to do the self-study, or on other factors, such as the benefits of having accreditation status within the system of higher education. There is no doubt that an accreditation system encourages self-study and peer review by faculty and staff of an institution. This goal can be achieved through internal review, which is a common practice in most universities across Canada. In fact, internal reviews may be conducted every five years; in these cases, thought must be given to the number of times the self-study process and the review procedure can be carried out in an academic unit.

The major issue pertaining to the CAUSN accreditation program is whether 27 university nursing education units in Canada can support such a program with annual membership fees plus a special accreditation fee and still obtain services from CAUSN. In 1985, the basic annual membership fee was increased from $1000 to $1500, plus the established fee of $3.00 per full-time (FTE) student, which could amount to a total annual fee of $4000 for schools with large enrollments. In 1988, the basic annual fee was increased by 15% to $1750 plus the same per FTE student fee; however, this fee structure was still not adequate for CAUSN to fulfil its goals. Consequently, in November 1989, CAUSN Council voted in a new fee structure, to be implemented in the 1990 to 1991 academic year. It is based on the number of FTE students enroled in a faculty/school of nursing, using the FTE formula (3.5 part-time students = 1 FTE) used by Statistics Canada. The range of annual membership fees will be: $3000 for 1 to 99 FTE students, $3500 for 100 to 199, $4000 for 200 to 299, $4500 for 300 to 399, $5000 for 400 to 499, and $5500 for more than 500 (CAUSN Council, 1989). Based on current enrolments, this fee structure could generate an annual income of $115,000. Whether this amount plus the special accreditation fee will be enough to support all CAUSN programs has not been determined. Nor is it known whether they will be able to afford the time required for the actual process if they seek accreditation and if faculty choose to be involved in the peer review process of accreditation in other institutions.

Many issues other than cost are related to accreditation in general and to accreditation in nursing education. One benefit purported by accreditation's supporters is that it facilitates transfer of students from one institution to another. This may be true in the United States where there are thousands of colleges and universities, including private ones; but it may not be true in Canada. Knowledge of accredited programs may help a student select a transfer institution, but transferability of courses depends on the equivalence of courses in the institutions and the student's achievement in these courses. In Canada, the low number of private institutions and the geography of the country discourage frequent transfer.

McCloskey (1985) questions the extent to which accreditation helps prospective students decide which institution to attend. She notes that most students are unaware of accreditation status and that it is doubtful that guidance counsellors in high schools use this information. Whereas accreditation status may have relevance for prospective students in the United States, where there are approximately 500 accredited baccalaureate nursing programs from which to choose, it is questionable if this would apply in Canada, where 22 basic bacalaureate degree programs are located in public universities and are required to give preference to residents from their own provinces. Substantial provincial support for higher education has been responsible for this preference although provisions of the Canadian Charter of Rights may soon eliminate such policies. The range of choices in Canada is limited, with only 22 basic baccalaureate nursing programs scattered across the country. Geographic factors alone raise the issue of cost.

One of the stated goals of CAUSN's accreditation program is to raise the standards of nursing education in Canada. The question of whether accreditation promotes quality is difficult to answer because of problems in measuring quality. Young states: "Accreditation has never defined 'quality of education' except in terms of numbers of Ph.D.'s produced, books published, grants received, and the like; the validity of these criteria has never been demonstrated" (1976, p.622). Although CAUSN is attempting to address the validity of the four criteria selected, the validity and the reliability of the instruments must continue to be addressed by other programs.

An important question that is often raised is the effect of accreditation on research, which is important in university nursing programs. Faculty in these

programs have devoted more attention to teaching and curriculum development than to research. Unless the criteria emphasize and require research, the
process of accreditation may not help promote it, as evidenced by events in the
United States for many years. In fact, U.S. participants in accreditation have
reported that the time and effort devoted to accreditation impeded the progress
of research. The problems are the amount of time required by the self-study and
visitation processes, and the time required for faculty to serve as visitors and
review board members. This time could have been devoted to research. What
can accreditation do to promote research? If it does not promote research and
the application of research findings in teaching and practice, can one say that it
is promoting quality in nursing education?

Another question to be addressed is whether accreditation will help programs obtain what they need. This is considered a potential benefit by some
proponents of accreditation who assume that if the accreditors note a deficiency
and the recommended action to correct it requires infusion of resources, this will
influence the administration to grant funding. Although this may occur in some
cases, in times of financial constraint it may not. Only experience can answer this
question.

Whether the accreditation program will be or should be extended to involve
graduate education in nursing, as well as baccalaureate education, is another
issue that should be addressed. This is the case at the master's level in the United
States, although nursing education administrators and nursing faculty involved
in doctoral education in the United States have strongly resisted any extension
of accreditation at the doctoral level. To date, their resistance has been effective
in preventing movement in this direction.

CONCLUSION

It is important to have standards for nursing education and a system to
monitor the achievement of standards and promote quality in nursing education. The question in Canada is whether the 27 university nursing education
units that comprise the membership of CAUSN can afford to support and be
involved in several systems of monitoring, the approval process in provinces
where university programs are monitored, intrainstitutional evaluation programs where they exist, and the accreditation process. To advance nursing
knowledge, improve practice, and gain acceptance of nursing as an equal and
legitimate participant in universities, research must be advanced and made an
integral part of the faculty role for all faculty in tenured/tenurable appointments.

The goal of accreditation, to promote excellence, depends on the extent to
which the process influences standards of education. One of the hazards, as
identified in the Study of Credentialing in Nursing, is that "continual upgrading
or revision of standards, however, can sometimes create unrealistic movement
away from the concurrent goals of society, as can static standards impede
progress and innovation" (Committee on Credentialing, 1979, p. 34). There is
need to focus on student outcome criteria as a more valid index of educational
quality because the criteria have tended to be structure-process oriented, dealing

more with the teaching-learning environment than with the actual learning that takes place (Committee on Credentialing, 1979).

Accountability to the public is of vital importance in any credentialing mechanism. This involves the development and maintenance of programs that the public expects will prepare practitioners who can deliver a high level of care. In addition, accountability involves the credentialing body. This organization must be willing "to assure that the standards, criteria, and process through which credentials are conferred and retained are valid and reliable measures of the quality of expertise or service associated with the credential" (Committee on Credentialing, 1979, p. 45). If the public is to be served, there must be a means to maintain standards and to demonstrate and assess the accountability factor.

REFERENCES

Allen, M. (1977). *Evaluation of educational programmes in nursing.* Geneva: World Health Organization.

Canadian Association of University Schools of Nursing. (1978). *Development of a method to promote growth and change in university schools of nursing and in nursing in general.* Ottawa: The Association.

Canadian Association of University Schools of Nursing Council. *Minutes of meeting of November 17, 1989.*

Canadian Association of University Schools of Nursing. *CAUSN Newsletter:* September, 1989.

Canadian Association of University Schools of Nursing. *CAUSN Newsletter:* June, 1990.

CNA Connection. (1989). Baccalaureate education comes to PEI. *The Canadian Nurse, 85*(3), 10.

CNA News. (1989). VGH school joins UBC. *The Canadian Nurse, 85*(2), 12.

Committee on Accreditation. (1985). *Accreditation: Criteria and process for baccalaureate program in nursing.* Book I. Canadian Association of University Schools of Nursing.

Committee on Credentialing. (1979). *The study of credentialing in nursing: A new approach.* Volume 1. The report of the committee. Kansas City, MO: American Nurses Association.

French, S. (1982). Design for accreditation of educational programs in nursing. In M.S. Henderson (Ed.), *Recent advances in nursing no. 4: Nursing education* (pp. 81-102). London: Churchill Livingstone.

French, S. (1984). *The development of an accreditation program for university programs in nursing in Canada.* Document submitted to Canadian Association of University Schools of Nursing.

Joint Working Group of the Association of Universities and Colleges of Canada and the Association of Community Colleges in Canada. (1977). *Report of the Joint Working Group on Coordination of Accreditation of health, sciences, educational programs,* Ottawa: The Association.

McCloskey, J.C. (1985). Accreditation of nursing education: An overview and issues. In J.C. McCloskey and H.K. Grace (Eds.). *Current issues in nursing,* (2nd ed.). London: Blackwell Scientific Publications.

Nursing Education Committee, Universities' Coordinating Council: *Regulations governing nursing education programs in the Province of Alberta leading to nursing registration.* Edmonton: Alberta, The Committee.

Prowse, J.A. (1983). *Nursing legislation in Canada: An overview for health services administration.* Unpublished master's paper. The University of Alberta. Edmonton, Alberta: Department of Health Services Administration.

Statistics Canada. (1990). Nursing in Canada 1988, (Catalogue 83-226). Ottawa: Statistics Canada.

Young, K.E. (1976). Issues in accreditation. *Nursing Outlook, 24*(10), 622-624.

CHAPTER TWENTY SEVEN

Credentialing in Nursing

JANET ROSS KERR

T he study of credentialing in nursing is illuminating, for it draws attention to the growth and development of nursing as a profession. Its relation to professionalization can be seen in what has been referred to as "the natural history of professionalization" (Moloney, 1986, p. 23). Wilensky has asserted that this is recognizable and sequential in nature:

> There is a typical process by which the established professions have arrived; . . . begin doing the work fulltime and stake out a jurisdiction; the early masters of the technique or adherents of the movement become concerned about standards of training and practice and set up a training school, which, if not lodged in universities at the start, makes academic connections within two or three decades; the teachers and activists then achieve success in promoting effective organization, first local, then national. . . . Toward the end, legal protection appears; at the end, a formal code of ethics is adopted (1964, p. 144).

The presence of a specialized knowledge base is fundamental to the processes and mechanisms of credentialing in nursing. Goode (1960) noted that the perception of the defining characteristics of this knowledge determines identification and acceptance of a field as a profession. These may be briefly summarized as follows: whether the knowledge and skills are abstract and consist of principles considered relevant to everyday situations, belief that the specialized knowledge will produce positive results when applied to real problems, involvement of those in the profession in developing and applying the knowledge base and providing expert opinion in contentious cases, and complexity of the knowledge and skills and the fact that only a few have the ability to acquire them (Goode, 1960).

In a historical sense, Canadian nurses recognized early in this century that the knowledge and skills fundamental to the profession were important and that unqualified and unskilled practitioners could harm patients for whom they cared. It was concluded that not only was it important to ensure that nurses were graduates of recognized schools of nursing, but also that professional standards were needed to regulate nursing education and practice. Hospitals did not need to be encouraged to establish schools of nursing in the late nineteenth and early twentieth centuries in Canada; they all sought to emulate the successful Nightingale model in Britain and gain an assured, qualified, and inexpensive staff. However, this was the antithesis of what Nightingale intended, as her school was supported by the Nightingale endowment and was financially and administratively independent. Evidence of graduation from a school of nursing was the earliest form of credentialing. The period during which this occurred was also characterized by a concerted drive by nursing leaders to secure legislation for registration of nurses to ensure that the educated would be differentiated from the uneducated for the protection of the public.

In a general sense, credentialing issues are similar today, although the nature and extent of knowledge and skills that must be acquired to practise nursing have changed. The need for recognizing standards in programs, knowing the meaning of a certificate, securing qualified staff for many areas of specialization, establishing standards at the national level, and ensuring that practitioners update knowledge and maintain competence throughout their careers are important areas for discussion and study. However, questions pertaining to protection of the public from unscrupulous, unqualified and unskilled practitioners are fundamental to credentialing processes and mechanisms.

CREDENTIALING MECHANISMS

The Canadian Nurses Association (CNA) has described credentialing as "a term used to refer to all those processes by which individuals or institutions (or one or more of their programs) are designated as having met established standards at a specified point in time, by an agent recognized as qualified to do so" (Canadian Nurses Association [CNA], 1982, p. 5), which means recognizing the individuals who have met the established standards in particular areas by awarding credentials. Thus, individuals with knowledge and skills in a certain area are distinguished from those who do not have such skills. Describing credentialing as a system of checks and balances seems appropriate. Nursing has two main credentialing mechanisms: professional and educational. In the professional side, registration and licensure are awarded to individuals for practice of the profession.

THE MOVEMENT TO SECURE LEGISLATION FOR REGISTRATION

The drive for registration of nurses occurred early in the development of the profession in Canada. This was the issue that brought nurses together in professional organizations. The formation of the first national/international organization in 1893, the American Society of Superintendents of Training Schools for Nursing of the United States and Canada, was followed by the Associated Alumnae of the United States and Canada in 1896. The purpose of the new organization was "to secure legislation to differentiate the trained from the untrained" (CNA, 1968, p. 35). Both organizations were initially headed by one of the most important nursing leaders of the time, Isabel Hampton Robb, a Canadian nurse from Ontario who was the first superintendent of nurses of Johns Hopkins Hospital in Baltimore, Maryland. These groups stimulated the formation of many other professional nursing groups at the local, regional, and national levels in the United States and Canada, all of which worked to complete the groundwork necessary for the passage of legislation to regulate nursing in the provinces. The publication of the *American Journal of Nursing* in 1900 and the *Canadian Nurse* in 1905 helped the cause.

The American and Canadian groups separated as activity intensified, and it was evident that the battle had to be fought regionally. In Canada, it was fought in the provinces because the British North America Act of 1867 provided that the legislatures of each province be given exclusive right to make laws in relation to health and education. The Canadian Society of Superintendents of Training Schools for Nurses emerged in 1907, followed by the Provisional Society of the Canadian Nurses Association of Trained Nurses in 1908. The first president of both groups was Mary Agnes Snively, a graduate of Bellevue Hospital in New York who had headed the School of Nursing at Toronto General Hospital since 1884. (CNA, 1968).

From the beginning, there have been valid reasons for requiring registration. Professional registration/licensure makes the benefits that accrue from the services of a highly skilled group available to society and protects society from those who are not highly skilled, as well as from those who might knowingly misuse their knowledge and skills to the disadvantage of the populace. In each province in Canada, local graduate nurse groups joined forces to become provincial nurses' associations and sought legislation for registration of nurses. Nurses believed that registration acts that set standards for training schools would also improve quality of care.

Two powerful social forces influenced the drive for legislation for the registration of nurses. The first was consciousness-raising, in terms of the rights of women, which was part of the movement for the enfranchisement of women. The second was that nurses' services were valued during World War I when many nurses served with dedication and valour. The passage of legislation in every province over a 12-year period may have been facilitated by these factors and general recognition of the need for a system to ensure that nurses were qualified.

There was considerable activity for a number of years before legislation was first passed in 1910, when Nova Scotia passed an act that made registration voluntary and allowed nongraduate nurses to register. Succeeding acts in other provinces were more restrictive in terms of the standards incorporated into the legislation. Minimum standards for admission and curricula in schools of nursing were set, as were rules governing registration and discipline of practising nurses. Ontario was the last province to achieve legislation for nursing due to a lobby against the legislation by hospitals fearing that educational standards for maintaining schools could not be met. There was also opposition from nurses who felt they could not meet the qualifications. The objections were overcome or overruled, and legislation was passed in that province in 1922 (Sabin, Price, & Sellers, 1973).

In all provinces, the initial legislation gave the provincial nursing association the responsibility for administering the legislation. In Alberta, the Registered Nurses Act was passed in 1916, and uniform registration examinations

TABLE 27.1 Chronology of Legislation Regulating Nursing in the Ten Canadian Provinces

Province	Date Legislation First Enacted	Current Status of Legislation		Date Mandatory Legislation First Enacted
		Mandatory	Permissive	
British Columbia	1918		x	—
Alberta	1916	x		1983
Saskatchewan	1917		x	—
Manitoba	1913		x	—
Ontario	1922		x	—
Quebec	1920		x	1964
New Brunswick	1916	x		1984
Nova Scotia	1910	x		1985
Prince Edward Island	1922	x		1969
Newfoundland	1931	x		1953

From Good & Kerr, 1973, p. 189; Prowse, 1983, pp. 10-28; 36-41.

were instituted in 1919. This statute was unusual because it placed nursing education under the aegis of the Senate of the University of Alberta. A chronology documenting the process of securing registration in each of the provinces is presented in Table 27.1.

THE CASE FOR MANDATORY LICENSURE

Licensure laws were designed to protect the public from unethical and incompetent practitioners, not to protect the nursing profession from competition. The only justifiable reason for legislation to guarantee professionals such a right is protection of the public against unqualified and incompetent practice; it cannot and must not bestow a special benefit on people who have completed a certain educational program and demonstrated certain qualifications. In recent years, there has been public concern about self-rule by professional groups, the fear being that power may be exercised in the interest of the profession. The thrust of the consumer movement is presenting challenges in areas where the consumer interest may not be protected (International Council of Nurses, 1986). The health-care field is no exception in such efforts. This phenomenon and the fact that it is not easy to make changes in existing legislation that governs professional groups explain why only six provinces have replaced their original permissive legislation with a mandatory statute. However, the provinces that have achieved mandatory licensure have done so by emphasizing the need to assure the public that licensed nurses have met an appropriate standard of practice, as determined by the profession.

The provinces that have mandatory statutes are Newfoundland (1953), Quebec (1964), Prince Edward Island (1969), Alberta (1983), New Brunswick (1984), and Nova Scotia (1985). The Northwest Territories passed an ordinance requiring mandatory licensure in 1973. The presence of a statutory definition of the scope of nursing practice is an important feature of legislature in jurisdictions with mandatory licensure. The permissive Manitoba statute also contains a definition of practice; however, the Manitoba legislation places the onus on the employer to hire only registered nurses to perform functions incorporated in the definition of nursing. Nurses' functions are delineated more explicitly when a definition of nursing practice is incorporated into the statute. The potential for overlap with functions performed by other health workers that exists in mandatory jurisdictions may be addressed through specific exemptions or by extending rights only to health-care workers practising by virtue of other statutes (Prowse, 1983).

Registration and licensure ensure a minimum level of safe practice at the time of initial registration. Those registered are eligible for reregistration annually if practice requirements are met and there is no evidence of unsafe practice. New knowledge is continually introduced to the field, and the individual must maintain and extend competence in the changing requirements. The nursing profession has wrestled with the problem of maintaining competence in an effort to demonstrate public accountability. As Prowse has noted: "As a peer review mechanism, the registration/licensure provisions of Canadian nursing statutes have . . . an explicit or implicit capacity for assuring the continued competence, capability and good conduct of nursing practitioners (1983, p. 65)." Mandatory versus permissive continuing education programs have been debated at length. In most provinces, mandatory continuing education has been rejected in favour of maintaining a certain number of days of employment within a specified time period and a record of satisfactory practice as evidence of current knowledge and skills. The move toward refresher courses for those who have been out of practice, upgrading programs, and opportunities for continuing education has become an integral and essential part of the nursing education system, as the practice of a profession must incorporate a commitment to lifelong learning.

REGISTRATION AND LICENSURE

Registration is an official roster of member nurses that is maintained by the profession. A nurse must be a member in good standing of the organization incorporating the statutory responsibility for registration to be named on a register. In the provinces that still have permissive registration, the legislation protects only the title of the registered nurse; that is, a person may practise nursing without being registered, but may not use the initials R.N. In acts that provide for mandatory registration, the nature of the service provided by the profession is defined. This means that those who do not meet the requirements of the legislation may not practise the profession. Title is protected, as in permissive acts, but the definition of nursing and the restriction of practice as it applies to registered nurses are the critical features that differentiate the two forms of legislation. Requirements for initial registration are similar in all provinces. An applicant must be a graduate of an approved school of nursing;

minimum standards for nursing education are established by an approval body. In all provinces except Alberta and Ontario, the approval body is the professional association. In Alberta, the Nursing Profession Act established the Universities' Coordinating Council as the approval body; in Ontario, the Health Disciplines Act gives authority for approving programs to the College of Nurses of Ontario.

The terms registration and licensure have different meanings, although they are used interchangeably in some situations. As previously noted, registration refers to the listing of a member in good standing of an organization on the roster of members. Licensure refers to granting of exclusive right to practise nursing to a member in good standing by a government body. In provinces where registration is mandatory, the same process may also be described as licensure. Practice of the profession by any person who has not been granted such a right is prohibited and punishable by law.

SPECIALIZATION IN NURSING

The tremendous change in the nature and scope of nursing practice in Canada in this century has taken place almost imperceptibly, but it has been an evolution with profound impact on health care and society. It has become increasingly difficult to master the knowledge required for practice in every area in which nurses function. The burgeoning increases in knowledge in the health-care field have led to specialization in nursing, which has raised questions about ensuring competence in those practising in specialized areas.

The medical profession itself is highly specialized. The movement toward specialization in medicine has been strong and, to a certain extent, has influenced nursing. Although there has been an attempt to place more value on the role of the general practitioner in medicine, more physicians are specializing. Given the tremendous increase in medical knowledge, this trend is not surprising. Nursing is influenced by many of the factors that have led to more specialization in medicine, and the outcome has been the development of discrete and increasingly complex nursing specialties.

Transfer of functions from medicine to nursing is also of interest; many functions that were previously restricted exclusively to medical practice have been redefined as nursing responsibilities. Although this is primarily a task oriented approach to practice in an area where functions overlap, it is important, as the changes in medical practice that produce the changes are immediately apparent. It is also important to recognize that (1) transfer of functions between the health professions is an ongoing process, and (2) there will always be overlap of functions between professions. With increases in knowledge, skills, and functions, the nurse is in a pivotal position in the delivery of health care. The nurse of today assumes roles and functions that were expected of the general medical practitioner of yesterday. In fact, the general practitioner of yesterday might be overwhelmed at the complexity of nursing roles today!

The reasons for the trend toward specialization in the nursing profession are increasing knowledge and the corresponding increase in skill needed for judgement and decision making. There is an almost constant demand for nurses who have expertise in highly specialized areas, so nurses must recognize the specialized skills and value the knowledge they require.

RECOGNITION OF SPECIALIZATION

To minimize confusion, the CNA has provided an interpretation of the term specialty: "A specifically defined area of clinical and functional nursing with a narrowed, in-depth focus, necessary for the safe delivery of the full range of services required in that area of nursing" (CNA, 1982, p. 25). Specialization has become an important phenomenon in nursing practice. Canadian nurses have sought certification from programs in the United States to demonstrate knowledge in their areas of practice. However, the situation in the United States developed rapidly, and many organizations set themselves up as certification bodies from the outset. The American Nurses Association (ANA) developed some certification programs, but entered the scene somewhat later than the majority of organizations. Because of the number of organizations that initiated certification programs in the United States, the ANA and the National League for Nursing (NLN) sponsored a credentialing study that recommended a centre for coordinating all programs. However, no action was taken on this recommendation (Committee for the Study of Credentialing in Nursing, 1979).

Because of problems of quality control, Canadians have not wanted to emulate the U.S. system. At the June, 1980 Biennial Convention of the CNA in Vancouver the CNA Board passed a resolution to study the feasibility of developing certification examinations in major nursing specialties. Consideration of the issues involved led the CNA to develop a policy statement on credentialing in nursing and to make a commitment to facilitate the development of certification in nursing specialties (CNA, 1982). Guidelines for a certification mechanism were adopted, and a certification program was designed (CNA, 1986a). The process involved designation of a specialty for certification, development of a certification examination by the Canadian Nurses Association Testing Services (CNATS), and certification of individuals. The CNA differentiated those acquiring certification in this manner from the clinical nurse specialist, who is designated as a nurse with advanced preparation in a clinical area at the master's level (CNA, 1986b).

The response of the national association to the issues presented by specialization and certification has been positive and is likely to augur well for future developments. Although it is important for the provinces to consider these matters, this is an area for the national association to provide leadership, for membership in specialty groups tends to be small. It is unlikely that the cost of developing a quality program could be borne by the province, and reciprocity would be an issue if different programs were developed in each province. Because specialization and certification are not part of basic preparation for practice (regulated by provincial legislation pursuant to the jurisdiction of provinces as designated in the Constitution Act), development of programs at the national level appears to be the most appropriate and reasonable course of action.

The development of a CNA Advisory Council "to provide a forum for discussions between the Council and the CNA board of directors on health and nursing issues" (CNA Connection, 1989b, p. 10) has enabled special interest groups to address the CNA. The approach to the certification process taken by the CNA is broad: "The designation process applies to an area of nursing rather than to a group or an association, and the process may be initiated by any group of nurses that is able to provide evidence that a specific nursing area meets the required criteria" (CNA Connection, 1989b). A discussion paper produced by the Canadian Association of University Schools of Nursing (CAUSN), *Specialization in Nursing and Nursing Education* (1989), stimulated a rebuttal by the CNA; it interpreted the paper as criticism of the specialty designation and certification processes (Canadian Association of University Schools of Nursing, 1989). The CNA expressed the view that CAUSN's view of specialization was "technologically-oriented and therefore, narrow, regarding skills and knowledge base", whereas its own view emphasized "Nurses' knowledge of illness patterns and therapies, patterns of response in certain situations, including physical and psychosocial aspects" (CNA Connection, 1989b).

In 1981, the CNA agreed to develop a certification examination for the Occupational Health Nurses, who had received a grant to develop this program. They hired the CNATS to develop the examination. Consultation services relative to the development of the examination were offered "on the understanding they would join the CNA certification program when it became a reality" (CNA Connection, 1989a). However, the disappointing announcement was made that "Following discussion and correspondence between CNA and the Canadian Council of Occupational Health Nurses Inc., the process of integrating the occupational health nursing examination into the CNA certification program has been suspended" because the occupational health nurses "would like more time to consider integration criteria, and has suggested waiting until at least 1991 to begin the process" (CNA Connection, 1990, p. 14). Furthermore, the CNA decided that groups that had been scheduled to enter the certification program after the Occupational Health Nurses would be accommodated first (CNA Connection, 1990). Although the development of its certification program has taken time and has had its share of challenges, the CNA has successfully brought special interest groups into the mainstream of professional association activities by establishing the process, developing an Advisory Council of representatives from specialty associations, and creating a position on the CNA board of directors for a representative from this group. The profession has been strengthened by these initiatives and it is likely that this will continue as more specialty groups become part of the certification program.

REFERENCES

Canadian Association of University Schools of Nursing. (1989). *Specialization in nursing and nursing education*. Ottawa: Author.

Canadian Nurses Association. (1968). *The leaf and the lamp*. Ottawa: Author.

Canadian Nurses Association. (1982). *Credentialing in nursing: Policy statement and background paper*. Ottawa: Author.

Canadian Nurses Association. (1986a). *CNA's certification program: An information booklet*. Ottawa: Author.

Canadian Nurses Association. (1986b). *Statement on the clinical nurse specialist*. Ottawa: Author.

CNA Connection. (1989a). *The Canadian Nurse, 85*(1), 7.

CNA Connection. (1989b). *The Canadian Nurse, 85*(9), 10.

CNA Connection. (1990). *The Canadian Nurse, 86*(1), 14.

Committee for the Study of Credentialing in Nursing. (1979). Credentialing in nursing: A new approach, *American Journal of Nursing, 19*(4), 674-683.

Good, S.R. and Kerr, J.C. (Eds.) (1973). *Contemporary issues in Canadian law for nurses*. Toronto: Holt, Rinehart & Winston of Canada, Ltd.

Goode, W.J. (1960). Encroachment, charlatanism, and the emerging professions: Psychology, sociology and medicine. *American Sociological Review, 25*, 903.

International Council of Nurses. (1986). *Report on the regulation of nursing: A report on the present, a position for the future*. Geneva: Author.

Moloney, M.M. (1986). *Professionalization of nursing: Current issues and trends*. Philadelphia: J.B. Lippincott Company.

Prowse, A.J. (1983). *Nursing legislation in Canada: An overview for health services administrators*. Unpublished master's paper. Edmonton: The University of Alberta.

Sabin, H., Price, D., and Sellers, B. (1973). Nursing: What it is and what it is not. In Good, S., & Kerr, J. (Eds.), *Contemporary issues in Canadian law for nurses*, (pp. 63-82). Toronto: Holt, Rinehart & Winston of Canada, Ltd.

Wilensky, H.L. (1964). The professionalization of everyone. *American Journal of Sociology, 70*(2), 143-144.

CHAPTER TWENTY EIGHT

Developing Specialty Certificate Programs With Credit Toward the Baccalaureate Degree in Nursing

JANET ROSS KERR

In the seventh decade of its growth and development in Canada, bacca-laureate degree education in nursing centres on generalist rather than specialist preparation. Due to the amount of essential clinical knowledge that must be taught in a basic program; theory and practice in specialty clinical areas cannot be included. Diploma programs in nursing must adequately cover basic material and associated clinical experience in a shorter time than the university degree programs in nursing. A problem for nursing administrators responsible for ensuring that specialty practice areas are staffed with suitably qualified staff is that few professional nurses with the necessary preparation to practise in these particular areas are available. Most staff nurses working in specialty clinical areas have had on-the-job training because there has been no integrated system of specialty courses or programs creditable to baccalaureate degree programs.

When nursing programs first appeared in Canadian universities, they offered preparation in special areas: first in public health, beginning in 1920, and later in nursing education and nursing administration. In the 1960s and 1970s, prepara-tion for public health nursing was phased into basic and post-RN baccalaureate programs, and certificate courses in teaching and administration were discontin-ued to allow institution of baccalaureate programs. Many programs, however, allowed the student to select courses in these subjects within degree programs. Until recently, most Canadian universities have not offered certificate programs in clinical nursing areas of specialty. The most notable exceptions were the

Certificate Program in Advanced Practical Obstetrics offered by the University of Alberta, from 1944 to 1984, when it was phased into the Master's Degree Program as a midwifery option, and the two-year Certificate Program in Outpost Nursing offered by Dalhousie University beginning in 1967.

Hospitals that operate schools of nursing have offered postgraduate programs in a number of specialty clinical nursing fields including, operating room; emergency; orthopaedic; neurosurgical; psychiatric; rehabilitation; eye, ear, nose, and throat; neonatal intensive care; and critical care. The last two programs have been common since the early 1970s, after the widespread introduction of intensive care units in hospitals. Community college nursing programs, instituted in the 1950s, also offer continuing education programs in a more narrow range of clinical specialty areas, principally critical care, long term care, mental health, and occupational health. In recent years hospitals have reduced the number and range of programs offered, and many have withdrawn them almost entirely. These programs involve enormous costs, and when hospital budgets are closely monitored by provincial governments, it is difficult to justify the expenditures. Until recently, few of the postgraduate courses offered by hospitals offered credit toward baccalaureate degree programs. Community colleges, on the other hand, have added some specialty clinical courses, and a few universities have offered new certificate programs in clinical nursing specialties. Some of the community college offerings have recently been approved for transfer credit to certain university degree programs, and several university courses have become creditable to degree programs. Since the 1960s, there has been an increase in the numbers of post-RN students entering university degree programs in nursing, which has increased the demand for clinical specialty courses and programs with degree credit.

Courses offered at the baccalaureate level in areas called specialty areas do not necessarily produce specialists. Any area could be considered a specialty area; nurses develop areas of concentration or focus in health care. Specialization is a confusing term, for it means only certain designated clinical areas to some, knowledge and skills to others, and educational programs to still others. This chapter assumes that preparation of a specialist in clinical nursing involves study at the master's level, however, although there is also room for education in these areas at the baccalaureate level.

PROFESSIONAL INTEREST IN SPECIALIZATION

The increase in the range and depth of knowledge in clinical fields has generated interest in specialization in professional nursing organizations. Since the 1970s, it has become necessary for every nurse to specialize in an area of practice after completing a program of basic nursing education. There has been concern about the competence of graduate nurses to function in the specialty areas without additional education. The safety question has prompted many tertiary care institutions to provide intensive and substantive courses specific to areas of specialty, in orientation for new staff. The cost of these programs and the fact that hospitals are service not, educational agencies have led nursing service administrators to promote developing specialty programs with the educational institutions.

Nurses have expressed doubt about whether an individual can function effectively when transferred from one hospital unit to another by nursing managers in the interest of maximum workload efficiency. The need for a complex array of skills and good judgement based on knowledge in a particular specialty have led to questions about the wisdom of short term transfers of staff and using the traditional float pool to cover shortages. Nursing unions have included these questions in contract negotiations, supported by members who are concerned about the professional issues involved. The opposite issue is the cost of not using these techniques in management, for the bottom line of the budget is maximum use of the health-care dollar. It is evident that special preparation in clinical specialty areas is a prerequisite for safe and competent practice (Woodrow and Bell, 1979) and that educational institutions have a major role in ensuring the provision of these programs.

The Canadian Nurses Association (CNA) has assumed a leadership role in developing initiatives for certification programs in various nursing specialties, spurred on by the situation in the United States, where many organizations are involved in credentialing and certification in nursing specialties and there is considerable variation in quality (Erickson, 1979; McCarty, 1979). With the lessons learned from the United States, the CNA's intent is that the process in Canada be rational and that quality be an important consideration for all specialty groups (Porter-O'Grady, 1985).

Most certification programs determine how knowledge is acquired by the candidate through examination. Some gain knowledge by practising in a specific area, attending workshops and reading, whereas others enrol in short- or long-term courses in the specialty. There must be a means of acquiring the knowledge unique to an area to have safe and competent practice. It is probable that the most efficient way to learn is to enrol in programs that offer courses taught by experts and that include supervised clinical practice.

Further to a resolution passed at the 1980 CNA Convention in Vancouver that the CNA "study the feasibility of developing certification examinations in various nursing specialties," (Canadian Nurses Association [CNA], 1986, p. 1) the CNA Board launched an examination of credentialing and developing certification examinations. The Policy Statement and Background Paper on Credentialing that resulted from this initiative is an important work that documents processes and designations that are relevant to nursing education of all types in Canada (CNA, 1982). The statement was adopted by the CNA Board, which directed that an initiative be launched to establish guidelines for a credentialing mechanism. Three committees were established to study questions on specialization and certification, and a program was designed at the conclusion of this study. The CNA notes that the program is not "carved in stone"; it must evolve over time, and flexibility is needed to ensure that this can happen.

Recognizing that certification is a voluntary process, which requires periodic updating, the CNA identified three purposes of a certification mechanism: "1) to provide an opportunity for practitioners to validate their expertise in a specialty; 2) to promote high standards of nursing practice in order to provide quality nursing care to the people of Canada; and 3) to identify, through a recognized credential, those nurses who have met the specialty standards" (CNA, 1986, p. 2).

Three additional phases have been identified as part of the CNA certification process. Phase One is designation of a specialty for certification based on six criteria that are applied to determine eligibility of a group: knowledge, standards, practitioner role descriptions, and uniqueness of the specialty, and ability of the group to support the certification process. Because of the costs involved, the CNA reserves the right to terminate a certification program. Phase Two, development of a certification examination, involves a process similar to that used for development of registration examinations. Experts in the specialty determine the content of the examination; test plans and objectives are developed; and the examination is written, tested, and revised. The principle of cost recovery is applied in setting fees for the examination. Phase Three involves certification of individuals; criteria are used to determine eligibility for the examinations: registration status, experiential background in the field of specialty, and a satisfactory performance record, as verified by a colleague and a supervisor/consultant in the specialty. Recertification criteria are similar. The CNA Committee on Certification is responsible for applying and implementing CNA certification policy. The CNA states that the product of this process should be distinguished from the clinical nurse specialist who is prepared at the master's degree level in nursing (CNA, 1986).

ORGANIZING CERTIFICATE COURSES/PROGRAMS IN SPECIALITY CLINICAL AREAS FOR CREDIT TOWARD A BACCALAUREATE DEGREE

University nursing education administrators are often asked, by registered nurses enroled in undergraduate degree programs in nursing, for advanced degree credit for postgraduate clinical courses and certificate courses offered by other agencies. Most universities have been reluctant to award credit for work not completed under the auspices of a university, although some have recently recommended certain courses for credit. Because very few universities have been involved in offering certificate programs in nursing until recently, the issue of credit toward the bachelor's degree for these programs is relatively new. It seems that registered nurses attending universities to earn credentials related to their clinical areas of specialty want such programs to apply toward the baccalaureate degree.

Preparation for specialty practice concerns hospital departments of nursing service because of the increasing complexity of care and wide use of specialty units. Staff shortages continue to be serious concerns for nursing service administrators. Recently, universities and hospitals have been collaborating to establish high-quality nursing certificate programs. Programs have been designed to enable nurses to gain university credit toward a degree and, at the same time, meet the agencies' needs for nurses who are prepared to assume complex responsibilities in specialty areas.

The Certificate Program in Outpost Nursing by Dalhousie University, developed under a grant from Health and Welfare Canada in 1967, prepares nurses for the primary care challenges of nursing in the Canadian North. Although it initially provided no credit toward the baccalaureate degree, beginning in the fall of 1986, students have earned 20 to 22 credit hours, over two academic years, toward a 77 credit hour BScN degree program for work completed. The remainder of the program requires approximately 16 months for completion. Studies in midwifery are part of the program, and prenatal assessment was emphasized as a result of the 1979 revision of the program. Students gain experience in the management of labour and delivery by performing 10 to 20 deliveries during their clinical experience in the program. The program is funded by the Department of Supply and Services, and approximately 12 students per year are admitted (R. May [personal communication, May 14, 1987).

Memorial University of Newfoundland also developed an Outpost Nursing program in 1978. The program was a two-year diploma program, consisting of six full semesters. A 1982 revision separated the Outpost Program into two distinct components: Diploma in Nurse Midwifery and Community and Primary Care Nursing. These may be taken separately or together, as the Diploma in Outpost Nursing Program. Partial program funding has come from the International Grenfell Association, and nursing stations of the Grenfell Regional Health Services are used for clinical experiences in the program. The midwifery component of the program is composed completely of nursing courses; whereas the community and primary care component includes courses in transcultural health care, health assessment, clinical management, community health, biology, sociology of the family, and developmental psychology. The program has provided full credit toward the baccalaureate degree for work completed since it was initiated. (S. Solberg [personal communication, May 14-15, 1987]).

The University of Alberta joined with the University of Alberta Hospitals in 1982 in a certificate program in neonatal intensive care nursing. The program was designed as a part-time program so that nurses specializing in this area at several Edmonton hospitals could participate. The three courses in the program incorporating theory and practice in the specialty were approved as University of Alberta courses and provided course credit toward the BScN degree. The cost of employing a faculty member to teach the program was borne jointly by the Faculty of Nursing and the University of Alberta Hospitals. The Faculty of Nursing soon realized that the program was popular with nurses working in this area; after completing the certificate program, many of them entered the post-RN baccalaureate program.

The success of the venture in neonatal nursing resulted in another joint effort, which involved the Faculty of Nursing, the University of Alberta, and the Misericordia Hospital School of Nursing, in emergency/intensive care nursing. This program, which began in September 1985, offered two courses on a full-time basis over four months. The two courses in this program were also established as Faculty of Nursing courses and were creditable toward the post-RN degree. In 1986, the University of Alberta Hospitals joined in the collaborative effort, making it a three-way arrangement. The Royal Alexandra and Grey Nuns Hospitals were to join later and the name of the program was changed to Certificate Program in Critical Care Nursing. External funding to support the cost of the master's prepared nurses engaged to teach the courses was sought and received. However, students were responsible for tuition, subsistence expenses, cost of books, and other incidental educational expenses. A similar arrangement was developed between the University of Manitoba School of Nursing and the Manitoba Health Sciences Centre for the critical care certificate program offered by that hospital.

In 1986, the Faculty of Nursing responded positively to a request from nursing service administrators to develop a certificate program in nephrology nursing, based on part-time study and designed for students with a special interest in this area. Physicians supported this program, and a funded position for an instructor was made available (from the University of Alberta Hospitals) through their efforts.

In Toronto, a collaborative certificate program in critical care nursing was developed between Ryerson Polytechnical Institute and Toronto General Hospital in 1984. The program was initially financed by the Ministry of Health of Ontario as a research project and offered direct funding of full-time students. Over time, the program has expanded to include more students and is now a collaborative venture, with six hospitals providing clinical settings for practice. Although Toronto General continues to be the key health-care agency, other hospitals involved include St. Michael's, Toronto Western, Wellesley, St. Joseph's Health Centre, and Women's College Hospital. Up to 300 students per year are prepared in the initial part of this program. The program consists of seven courses, three of which are taught in the first seven weeks of full-time study and constitute the core program. Students become eligible for the certificate if they complete four other courses: two advanced nursing courses, one course in nursing theory or communication and teaching, and one liberal arts elective. The latter two courses in the certificate program provide credit toward the BScN degree. Currently, Ryerson provides funding for instruction, and the hospitals where the students are employed provide student funding. Reports of program outcomes indicate a high degree of satisfaction for the students and institutions. Although not all students complete the certificate, the opportunity is there for those who wish to take advantage of it.

The community colleges will probably continue to play a significant role in preparation for specialty practice in nursing. Many clinical specialty programs offered by these institutions across the country meet the needs of practitioners and agencies for nurses prepared in certain areas. Some universities are now giving partial credit for courses completed, but this is not universal. The possibility that college courses and programs will provide full credit toward university degrees is minimal given the questions about the quality and level of instruction, as well as standards for the programs.

Some hospitals continue to offer postgraduate programs, but as previously noted, the number has declined since the mid-1960s. Tight budgets and a mandate to provide service rather than sophisticated educational programs, will inhibit further expansion of the educational enterprise in hospitals. It is also unlikely that universities can meet all of the needs for specialty programs because of budget restraints and their efforts to expand programs at the baccalaureate and master's levels and to initiate doctoral programs to support practice and research initiatives.

ISSUES FOR THE FUTURE

That some university schools and faculties of nursing are considering involvement in certificate programs comprised of courses that meet baccalaureate degree requirements may be a sign of their maturation. Nursing has entered the age of specialization, and given the increasing complexity of knowledge in health care and the performance expectations of nursing service administrators for registered nurses with expertise in clinical specialty nursing, there can be no retreat.

It is important, however, to note the changing philosophy of program models from the 1950s and 1960s to the present. In the past, specialty programs were offered primarily by hospitals and tended to be organized on an apprenticeship basis, with more emphasis on clinical practice, often unsupervised, than on theoretical knowledge in the field. Also, the instructional component tended to be provided by faculty members who had minimal preparation in nursing and would not qualify for faculty appointments in universities. Students in these programs were paid salaries because of the amount of service they provided, but these salaries were considerably lower than those paid to registered nurses. Often, no tuition charges were made. Students were not supernumerary to the unit, and they replaced higher cost staff members; thus the hospital gained financially and programs were self-sustaining. In many instances, programs were revenue-generating. The issues here are the same as those raised to support the transfer of the basic nursing educational enterprise to the general educational system.

The new programs tend to be organized on a sound educational basis. Faculty are expected to have suitable academic qualifications for their positions, including considerable clinical expertise. The quality of faculty is important in universities where the maintenance of standards must be justified. Clinical experience is a significant part of the program and is carefully supervised. Programs will probably be financed in the usual manner, and students will not be expected to subsidize the cost of the program through service to the hospital. For this reason, the new certificate programs in clinical specialty areas cannot be compared with those that existed in earlier decades. Moreover, the increased complexity of nursing knowledge in all areas and the need for knowledgeable and competent practitioners in clinical specialities, with education beyond the basic level, makes education in specialty areas a professional necessity.

REFERENCES

Canadian Nurses Association. (1982). *Credentialing in nursing: Policy statement and background paper.* Ottawa: Author.

Canadian Nurses Association. (1986). *CNA's certification program: An information booklet.* Ottawa: Author.

Erickson, E.H. (1979). ANA's program of certification in nursing administration, *Journal of Nursing Administration, 9*(9), 32-33.

McCarty, P. (1979). Certification process: Complex but rewarding. *The American Nurse, 11, 47.*

Porter-O'Grady, T. (1985). Credentialing, privileging, and nursing bylaws: Assuring accountability. *Journal of Nursing Administration, 15*(12), 23-27.

Woodrow, M. and Bell, J.A. (1979). Clinical specialization: Conflict between reality and theory. *Journal of Nursing Administration, 1*(6), 73-78.

CHAPTER TWENTY NINE

Distance Education in Nursing: Increasing Accessibility of Baccalaureate Education in Nursing

JANET ROSS KERR

T he entry to practice position, adopted and actively promoted by the Canadian Nurses Association (CNA) and the provincial professional associations,
has many implications for the profession. Although the position addresses only
graduates of nursing programs entering practice in the year 2000 and after, it
implies that the profession is anticipating baccalaureate for all at some time after
the year 2000. Nurses qualified at the diploma level before the year 2000 will
retire or otherwise cease to practise, and the baccalaureate standard will be
implemented in its entirety.

Based on the direction the profession has taken, it is important that diploma-
prepared nurses who wish to study for a baccalaureate degree are able to do so.
Off-campus programs using distance education and outreach methods make it
possible for university schools and faculties of nursing to extend their range and
offer courses, even degree programs, to a greater geographic area than would
otherwise be possible. These programs enhance and support the entry to practice position because they are accessible to those whose place of domicile might
preclude enrolment in a baccalaureate degree program in nursing in large urban
centres. Canada's universities, a number of which are large and highly diversi-
fied "multiversities," are primarily located in these areas.

Ideas are needed to design BScN programs with greater accessibility. The
size of the nation, some 5,000 thousand miles from east to west, makes it the
second largest nation on earth. Also, the variation in terrain, from rugged
mountain ranges to bald prairie to impassable muskeg, with bitter winter

weather conditions in many areas, presents a unique geographic and mete-orologic picture. A relatively small population is scattered across this vast expanse of land, and there are challenges in transportation and communication. Canadian history is replete with examples of people working together to over-come the obstacles of distance, geography, and climate to build a modern indus-trialized society. Much progress has been made in transportation since the last spike for the Canadian Pacific Railway was driven at Craigellachie in 1885, uniting East and West with a single transportation system for the first time. Today, there is a choice of transport, and travel is faster and more efficient than ever before. After Sir Alexander Graham Bell's invention of the telephone, advances in technology were steady until, in the past two decades, a virtual explosion of developments took place. Sophisticated means of communication are available from one corner of the globe to another. Decreases in the price of new instruments and machines in the communications area have made them affordable.

It is interesting that the entry to practice goal has surfaced at a time of major technologic advance. Universities are being challenged to make the new tech-nology accessible and available to everyone. Definitions of potential students at universities have also changed, and the character of the student population has expanded to include an increasing proportion of returning adults. The resolve of the nursing profession in Canada to achieve the entry to practice goal by the turn of the century heralds a new and important phase in the evolution of the profession. However, this development is predicated on a commitment to searching for the answers to nursing questions through research and a contin-uous redefinition of the nature and scope of nursing.

CHARACTERISTICS OF SUCCESSFUL OFF-CAMPUS PROGRAMS

The practical issues that arise in overcoming the barriers of distance in taking educational programming at the baccalaureate level to locations beyond the universities may seem formidable. However, a positive approach, commitment to achieving the entry to practice goal, and institutional support can facilitate program development. Many institutions have initiated a program by using outreach (in person) methods in off-campus locations exclusively. The ineffi-ciency and cost, human and monetary terms, of these methods promote consid-eration of distance education methods, which include both interactive and noninteractive teaching methods.

STRUCTURE AND ORGANIZATION FOR LEARNING

Structure and organization for learning are the key processes in establishing a successful off-campus program in nursing. When students are scattered across a wide geographic area, in locations remote from faculty members responsible for course instruction, these processes assume major importance, both at the course or program level and at the individual level. It is wise to define institu-tional intentions, in terms of courses and programs to be offered, at the outset. Students considering enrolment in a baccalaureate program in nursing need to know which courses will be offered in subsequent semesters, whether the entire program can be completed in distance mode, and if not, what the possibilities are for transfer of credit for successfully completed courses. An outline of courses to be offered during the time period allotted for the program and any special requirements should be available to students from the outset to facilitate individual planning and commitment. Also, course content and expectations should be fully delineated at an individual course level so that students are aware of requirements and make an informed commitment to the course.

It may be wise to give a faculty member responsibility for day-to-day planning, coordination, and administration of the off-campus program. This person can work with students and other faculty members to ensure that planning is appropriate and that there is ongoing communication of information about course and program activities. Academic advisement for off-campus students can also be provided by this individual, who becomes the students' link to the university faculty of nursing. The person who fulfils this role must have excellent communication skills, commitment to the off-campus endeavour, and sensitivity to students' needs. If all requirements are met, the incumbent will serve as a stabilizing and unifying force, facilitating and enhancing the success of the program.

Designated opportunities for students to discuss questions with the professors teaching off campus courses are important. Planning for this at a group or individual level can occur in a teleconference session or through long-distance telephone communication. Financing of the particular program and location of the student may affect times and methods of communication between faculty member and student.

Variety in instruction is as important for traditional programs as it is for those in long-distance mode. Faculty members in traditional settings who think about and plan learning experiences frequently achieve success in terms of learning outcomes and student perceptions of the learning experience. Varied educational methods and experiences in off-campus courses are also important; they tend to help the learner view the subject in more depth and from a number of perspectives. In an off-campus mode, adjuncts to teaching, such as graphics, visual enhancements, outlines and handouts, are essential for successful programs. Again, time and planning are necessary for optimum results.

THE HUMAN ELEMENT

Important questions about off-campus programs address that elusive area known as "the human element," that is, an expectation by the student that the professor demonstrates human qualities of thinking, reasoning, and competence in the subject and is interested in the student's learning needs, problems, and achievements. This may be an area where concerns are expressed in traditional and nontraditional programs and may be related to many factors, including class size and the workload of the particular faculty member. The quality of communication between student and faculty member is at issue here, as well as the level of mutual understanding achieved. Ensuring that human feeling characterizes the learning encounter requires slightly different approaches in off-campus programs. In addition, student-to-student interactions and relationships constitute part of the human element in teaching-learning situations, for students learn from each other. Depending on the particular situation, the latter may be achieved in many different ways in off-campus programs.

COLLABORATION

Cooperation and collaboration with other institutions has been a necessary and important defining characteristic of Canadian distance education programs in nursing. Because of the unique nature and extent of the arrangements required to offer off-campus courses and programs, it is unlikely that any one institution can "go it alone," without help from other organizations. There is usually a need to negotiate arrangements with agencies for computer space and classes offered via teleconference or videoconference methods. These agencies include community colleges, continuing education centres, hospitals, facilities of educational consortia, and public libraries.

Other educational institutions may be an integral part of the program through the provision of courses, either onsite in community colleges, or by other universities in distance format, using interactive or noninteractive methods. Athabasca University, situated in Athabasca, Alberta, is a postsecondary institution established with a mandate to develop distance learning programs. The majority of courses offered consist of learning packages of printed materials, although audiocassettes, videocassettes, tutorials by telephone or in person in some regional settings, and teleconference sessions are used in some courses. Since the major thrust of this institution is in the arts and science fields, Athabasca courses can potentially provide the backbone of the liberal arts and science component of a baccalaureate program in nursing offered on an off-campus basis. Because the technology used in most of its courses is kept simple, it is possible to enrol in Athabasca courses from any location with postal service. Growth in this sector of educational activity in the 1980s and the potential for the future make it likely that other postsecondary institutions with distance education mandates will develop, and that existing universities will redirect their traditional focus to include the distance mode. This will facilitate the development of baccalaureate degree programs in nursing offered to off-campus students.

THE CLINICAL COMPONENT

The clinical component in nursing programs sets them apart from other university programs in traditional and nontraditional settings. A commitment to providing clinical instruction of high quality in regional and rural settings may seem to present insurmountable difficulties in developing off-campus programs in nursing. However, this is not necessarily true, as a variety of arrangements are possible for supervision of clinical learning experiences. These include use of preceptors in some areas, telephone or teleconference communication with faculty members on the main campus, hiring suitably qualified faculty members in off-campus locations, and sending faculty members to off-campus sites to supervise clinical learning. A program may be strengthened by seeking clinical practice arrangements beyond the walls of large tertiary health-care institutions in urban areas; such arrangements are now occurring in traditional programs. Community general hospitals offer important clinical learning opportunities that can enhance programs. In addition, the health units, home care programs, and other health-care agencies serving largely rural populations can offer a range and depth of experiences appropriate for baccalaureate courses in nursing. Many new ways of approaching arrangements for clinical practice in the context of baccalaureate-level programming will be formulated and explored in the future.

TECHNOLOGY

The increasingly widespread availability and use of technology has begun to revolutionize higher education. For off-campus programs in nursing, technology can be very helpful, making possible interactive teacher-student communication and instructional enhancement of various kinds. The School of Nursing at the University of Victoria has pioneered the use of learning packages in nursing courses for off-campus students in their post-RN baccalaureate program. These involve various modes of instruction, including printed materials, audiocassettes, and videocassettes. Through satellite transmission, nursing courses presented via television have been accessible to registered nurse students residing in the "footprint" region of Western Canada. Questions telephoned in while the instructor is on the air allow for two-way interaction between students and the faculty member. The facilities of the "Knowledge Network," a public television broadcast station, and the Opening Learning Institute, which provides liberal arts courses via printed learning packages, both created by the British Columbia government, have been used by both of the university schools of nursing in that province for courses offered to students in off-campus locations. The School of Nursing at the University of Victoria has been a pioneer in distance education for nursing. Efforts have focused on developing multimedia learning packages for students who work on them at their own pace to fulfil course requirements. Use of the Knowledge Network, with simultaneous teleconferencing in some courses, has allowed for interactive learning in designated courses. In 1986, the University of Victoria announced that all courses in its degree program could be pursued on an off-campus basis, and they began to market their courses on a widespread basis (Collins, 1987). For many nurses, the availability of these courses with emphasis on independent learning, allowed study toward a degree not previously attainable. The University of British Columbia has also made considerable progress toward implementing a distance model for its post-RN baccalaureate program; by the spring of 1991, all of its courses will be available in distance format, using print, video, and teleconferencing methods.

In Ontario, the University of Ottawa initiated a teleconferencing distance education program during the 1982 to 1983 academic year, with a "satellite" course in Cornwall, Ontario (DuGas, 1985; Styran, 1985). The teleconference sessions were part of the regular instructional program, specifically courses being offered in the post-RN baccalaureate program in the evening. By 1984 to

1985, students in four other centres — Brockville, Pembroke, Peterborough, and the Ottawa Civic Hospital — were permitted to enrol in the courses being offered in the evening program. In 1983 to 1984, an electronic blackboard was purchased to enhance the instructional component (DuGas, 1985; DuGas & Casey, 1987, Styran, 1985). Dalhousie University in Nova Scotia, the University of Western Ontario, and other universities have also been working toward making the baccalaureate degree more accessible to registered nurses (Hart, Crawford, & Hicks, 1985).

In Alberta, the University of Calgary Faculty of Nursing decided to phase its existing post-RN baccalaureate program into one that would be offered only in distance methods. Implemented in 1989 to 1990, this program provides access to baccalaureate nursing education via distance delivery in the southern half of Alberta. (The northern half has been served by the University of Alberta Faculty of Nursing's distance delivery program since 1984.) In 1989, the Alberta government provided funding to Athabasca University to establish a post-RN baccalaureate program in nursing in Alberta.

AN EXAMPLE OF A MODEL OF DISTANCE EDUCATION AT ONE UNIVERSITY

The University of Alberta in Edmonton has, since 1985, offered the entire post-RN degree program on an off-campus basis (Kerr, 1985; Kerr, 1987). At the time, it was the only university in Canada to offer an entire BScN degree program off campus. The University of Alberta first began to consider off-campus programming in 1978 with the submission of a proposal to the Alberta government for expansion of the post-RN baccalaureate program. The expansion was funded in 1979, and enrolment doubled; half of the expansion enrolment was reserved for off-campus students.

At the outset, outreach methods used to provide courses were primarily traditional classroom methods and instructors went from the main campus to certain designated centres to offer courses on a weekly or biweekly basis. Teleconferencing was introduced in the fall of 1984. The program was initially conceived as a three-year one that required one year of full-time study on the main campus of the University of Alberta in Edmonton. This period was reduced to one term in 1982 – 1983, and was eliminated altogether for those centres beginning the program in 1985, when teleconferencing became the primary mode of instruction for courses. Residence requirements at the University of Alberta refer primarily to full-time study requirements on the campus; the campus is wherever University of Alberta faculty are providing courses. Residence requirements for undergraduate programs in the Faculty of Nursing were also eliminated in 1983, so students could study on a part-time basis, provided that the post-RN program was completed within five years. Today the program is offered to off-campus students on a part-time basis over four years.

Teleconferencing was the technology that revolutionized the off campus program at the University of Alberta. Equipment was purchased, a Darome bridge was rented through the Alberta Hospital Association (AHA), and long distance telephone charges were assumed by the faculty. In many instances, students used convenors and microphones owned by local hospitals, and hospital FX lines (flat rate for long distance use) were made available for use in the evening program sessions. Use of the AHA bridge continued for two years but was discontinued because of expensive rental charges. Alternatives were explored, and the University of Alberta purchased a Confertech full-duplex bridge of its own in the spring of 1986. Six faculties of the University, committed to the need for this bridge, were able to raise sufficient funds to purchase it. Through the cooperative organization of educational agencies using teleconferencing in the province, the Alberta government made its government RITE-line system (provincial telephone exchange operated by the Alberta government) available to the institutions, for educational purposes, at no cost after 4:30 P.M. Thus the Faculty of Nursing could offer programming in centres throughout Alberta, served by the RITE-line system, without incurring long distance telephone charges.

The Faculty of Nursing obtained a grant from the University to finance the purchase of three "Telewriter II" units for use in the off-campus program. The Telewriter system is a software package that allows production and storage of graphic materials for transmission during teleconference sessions. The associated modem allows two-way transmission of data over one telephone line. The system was implemented in September 1986, and an educational assistant with computer expertise was engaged in October to prepare graphics for faculty and ensure that technical arrangements for teleconference sessions were managed. Since several courses are ongoing at any one time, a competent individual must assume responsibility for details. In 1987, three more systems were purchased for use in off-campus centres and the "Telewriter II" software was upgraded to "Telewriter III"; the new software and additional equipment, such as graphics boards in the computers and use of a video camera, allow for transmission of video images to and from the off-campus sites.

A cooperative approach among faculties at the University and the efforts of the Distance Education Group have encouraged sharing of facilities and expertise. The intent of the Group is to place "Telewriter" systems in several locations in the province to which the University of Alberta delivers programs to facilitate programming by all academic units. Cooperation with other universities and postsecondary institutions will also enhance the possibilities.

Other instructional methods involving technology, used in regular and off-campus post-RN program at the University of Alberta, include computer-assisted learning and computer-managed learning. In 1981, a health assessment course was developed in this format and implemented in the program. The program was adapted from the PLATO format for use on an IBM computer, with provision for communication via modem and the TINA network (a provincial system for lowering long distance telephone charges for computer use), and was used by instructors in the Faculty of Nursing. Thus it was only necessary to hold the laboratory sessions for practice in regional centres.

Although to date, all distance education programming at the University of Alberta Faculty of Nursing has been at the post-RN baccalaureate level, plans have been announced for a collaborative degree model with Red Deer College to offer a basic degree in nursing on the Red Deer site. Government funding for the program was approved and the program was initiated in September 1990. Distance delivery methods, an important part of this collaborative model, use the expertise of faculty members in courses offered from Edmonton. Distance delivery of graduate courses and programs has not yet begun, but the issue has been raised as an important one for the future.

CONCLUSION

Higher education in this country is undergoing a technologic revolution, that is rapidly changing the character of instruction in traditional settings and in centres outside main university campuses. Students will benefit from these changes and from the fact that a growing number of institutions will be making efforts to make programming available to adult students in nontraditional settings. University libraries are rapidly achieving success in placing their information on computers, and the ability to search the catalogue will soon be available to any individual who owns a computer terminal and modem and is allowed access to the university computer system.

The technology for distance learning is not really foreign to most people. It is as available as the communication devices used in everyday living. The technology does not need to be highly sophisticated, although the use of two way videoconferencing via satellite could be incorporated into existing systems of distance delivery if the cost were not so high. The telephone is the mainstay of most current distance programs. Its potential significance in distance education has not always been universally appreciated, but the success of programs, particularly those involving computers along with video enhancements, has consolidated its place in the system.

The effort to develop off-campus programs at the undergraduate-degree level in nursing, although challenging, has become an important one in Canada. It requires the effort and commitment of many people, and the pooled resources of educational institutions and health-care agencies. There is a new appreciation of the vital role that technology has in extensive programs of distance offerings to students in remote locations. Achievement of the entry to practice goal of the profession will be facilitated by extending the campus and offering baccalaureate-degree programs in other than traditional university settings.

REFERENCES

Collins, F. (1987). Update on distance education at the University of Victoria. *The Canadian Nurse, 83*(2), 10-11.

DuGas, B.W. (1985). Baccalaureate entry for practice: A challenge that universities must meet. *The Canadian Nurse, 81*(5), 17-19.

DuGas, B.W., and Casey, A.M. (1987). Teleconferencing. *The Canadian Nurse, 83*(5), 22-25.

Hart, G., Crawford, T., and Hicks, B. (1985). RN to BN: Building on education and experience. *The Canadian Nurse, 81*(5), 22-23.

Kerr, J.C. (1985). Taking the campus to the student. *The Canadian Nurse, 81*(5), 30-31.

Kerr, J.C. (1987). History of off-campus programs and distance education at the University of Alberta. *AARN Newsletter, 43*(3), 19-20.

Styran, P. (1985). Winds of change. *The Canadian Nurse, 81*(5), 20-21.

CHAPTER THIRTY

Primary Health Care: The Means for Reaching Nursing's Potential in Achieving Health for All

JANNETTA MacPHAIL

Primary health care has been purported by the World Health Organization (WHO) as the means for promoting and maintaining the health of nations around the world. What is the meaning of the concept of primary health care? Why is it endorsed and proclaimed as the solution to many ills in existing health care systems? Is it a feasible goal for Canada? What reforms will be required in Canada's health-care system to implement the concept? Does the profession of nursing support the concept? Are nursing students being educated to function effectively in a primary care system? These questions are addressed as the meaning and significance of primary health care are explored.

HEALTH FOR ALL BY THE YEAR 2000

The goal of Health for All by the Year 2000 was established in 1978 at an international meeting held at Alma-Ata in Kazakh Republic of the Soviet Union, under the auspices of the World Health Organization (WHO) and the United Nations International Children's Emergency Fund (UNICEF) (World Health Organization [WHO], 1978a). The meeting, attended by representatives of 127 nations and 72 international organizations, was to promote the concept of primary health care as the only viable means of attaining equitable distribution of health resources to enable people to attain "a level of health that will permit them to lead a socially and economically productive life" (WHO, 1978b, p. 429). The report of the conference challenges all countries and governments of the world to employ a primary health-care approach with emphasis on the development of their health services. The approach is "based on practical, scientifically sound, and socially acceptable methods and technology made universally accessible to individuals and families in the community through their full participation and at a cost that the community and country can afford" (WHO, 1978b). The International Council of Nurses (ICN) pledged its full support to making primary health care a reality in all countries of the world. Recognizing that most health care in the world is delivered by nursing personnel, ICN encouraged nurses in each country to participate in developing a primary health-care system that is relevant to the country's needs and uses nurses effectively in its implementation (WHO, 1978b, p. 429).

Commitment to t e goal of Health for All by the Year 2000 led to another conference, held in Ottawa, Canada in November 1986, which was jointly organized by WHO, Health and Welfare Canada, and the Canadian Public Health Association (CPHA). It was attended by 212 participants from 38 countries who met to exchange experiences, share knowledge, and develop a plan of action to achieve the goal. Those attending the meeting were representative of a wide range of governmental, voluntary, and community organizations, as well as active practitioners and academics. The three main aims of the conference were to promote:

> ... *visibility:* to encourage and enhance health promotion development by assessing past and current achievements;
> *sharing:* to put people in contact with each other, sharing examples of success and failure; and
> *consensus:* to develop through the active participation of conference members a conference statement on the future development of health promotion (Nutbeam and Lawrence, 1987, p.1).

The conference was primarily a response to growing expectations for a new public health movement around the world. It was built around five major issues, which participants discussed in workshops conducted over a one-week period. The issues were building healthy public policy, creating supportive environments, strengthening community action, personal skills, and reorienting health services (Nutbeam and Lawrence, 1987). One outcome of the conference was the publication of the "Ottawa Charter for Health Promotion," which identifies three elements basic to health promotion: advocating health, enabling people to achieve their fullest health potential, and mediating differing interests for the pursuit of health (Nutbeam and Lawrence, 1987).

The Honourable Jake Epp, Minister of National Health and Welfare Canada, chose the occasion of the conference to launch the Canadian Government strategy document, "Achieving Health for All: A Framework for Health Promotion." He emphasized that the purpose in releasing the document was to promote dialogue among Canadians interested in health and to achieve better health for ourselves and contribute to better health for the people of the world. His goal was to move health promotion from the periphery of the health field to a central position (Nutbeam and Lawrence, 1987).

THE CANADIAN APPROACH TO ACHIEVING HEALTH FOR ALL

The Canadian approach to achieving health for all is to focus on health promotion, which is perceived as the best strategy. Figure 30.1 identifies the

FIGURE 30.1   A framework for health promotion.

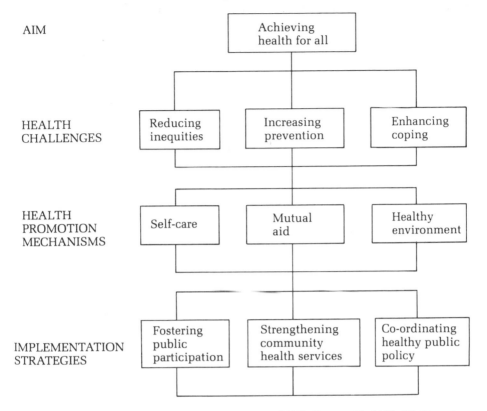

AIM

Achieving
health for all

HEALTH
CHALLENGES

Reducing
inequities

Increasing
prevention

Enhancing
coping

HEALTH
PROMOTION
MECHANISMS

Self-care

Mutual
aid

Healthy
environment

IMPLEMENTATION
STRATEGIES

Fostering
public
participation

Strengthening
community
health services

Co-ordinating
healthy public
policy

Modified from Ottawa Charter for Health Promotion. (1986). Ottawa: World Health Organization, Health and Welfare Canada, and the Canadian Public Health Organization.

overall aim, health challenges, health promotion mechanisms, and implementation strategies.

Self-care, a mechanism supported by nurses, is defined in the document as
the decisions and actions individuals take in the interest of their own health.
This concept supports nursing's goal of helping people to become increasingly
responsible for their own health. However, creating conditions and surround-
ings conducive to health, which is implied in creating healthy environments,
goes beyond the individual and requires community action. One example of this
philosophy is creating a smoke-free environment, which cannot be accomplished by an individual; there must be agreement by groups, such as health-
care institutions and educational institutions. Today, there is a definite trend to
promote smoke-free environments because of the harmfulness of smoke to
nonsmokers, who should not have to suffer from the poor health habits practised by smokers.

Achieving healthy environments will require developing the political will "to
overcome likely conflicts between public health interests and commercial and
other vested interests" (Nutbeam and Lawrence, 1987, p. 2). This offers a real

challenge to governments in relation to creating a smoke-free environment. They must provide alternatives for farmers who have made a living for many years by growing tobacco and deal with animosity and resistance from tobacco companies who have made millions producing products that are harmful to the health of smokers and those exposed to secondhand smoke, including the unborn fetus, who is more likely to be premature if the mother smokes during pregnancy. Achieving the goal of health for all will require governments to take unpopular stands, which could jeopardize the party in power in an election. Those committed to promoting the public's health must remain firm and serve as role models for others in promoting healthy behaviours. This has implications for the positions taken by associations of health professionals and for the education of health professionals.

Reorienting health services to focus on health rather than illness presents another challenge to health professionals and governments. One of the major objectives is to effect change in the roles of health professionals, which may necessitate the development of new skills and expertise and require moving away from intervening to "do what we consider best for patients" to a mediating role for health professionals. The Ottawa Charter for Health Promotion states:

> The prerequisites and prospects for health cannot be ensured by the health sector alone. More importantly, health promotion demands coordinated action by all concerned: by governments, by health and other social and economic sectors, by non-governmental and voluntary organizations, by local authorities, by industry and by the media. People in all walks of life are involved as individuals, families and communities. Professional and social groups and health personnel have a major responsibility to mediate between differing interests in society for the pursuit of health (1986, p.1).

At present, government funding of health services in Canada strongly favours cure and sickness care, with a minor proportion of the health-care dollar going to support health promotion and prevention of illness. Change in financial incentives will be needed to support health promotion activities. Similarly, changes will be needed in the initial and continuing education of health professionals to change their focus and priorities to primary health care and prepare them to help people achieve their fullest health potential and make decisions about matters that affect their health and well-being.

Maglacas, chief scientist for nursing with WHO, points out that although the aim of the Health for All movement has been interpreted by many as making health services available to everyone, the actual goal is to have all people in all countries achieve at least a level of health that allows them to work productively and participate actively in the social life of the community in which they live (CNA Connection, 1988). In 1987, almost 10 years after the WHO declaration at Alma-Ata, Maglacas assessed nursing's response to the Health for All challenge as "fragmented, sporadic, unplanned, and uncoordinated, and [as involving] few, if any, other disciplines or sectors" (1988, p. 67). Primary health care, as envisioned by Maglacas and other nursing leaders, is perceived as the way to achieve the goal.

PRIMARY HEALTH CARE

Primary health care has been confused with primary medical care and primary nursing, but it is distinctly different from both. In the United States and in some parts of Canada, the concept of primary health care is limited and tends to be equated with the nurse practitioner role. It is portrayed as a nurse, practising in an ambulatory setting or a remote site, who assesses the health and illness status of clients through "health history, physical examination, and diagnostic tests; develops and implements therapeutic plans; [and] engages in appropriate referrals, health counselling, and collaboration with other health care providers" (Ulin, 1982, p. 532). It is much like primary medical care, and seems to be so when comparing nurse practitioner and physician practice in ambulatory care, such as that reported by Diers, Hamman, and Molde (1986). Studies of nurse practitioner effectiveness, as compiled by Feldman, Ventura, and Crosby (1987) and as reviewed by Molde and Diers (1985), lend credence to this evaluation of the nurse practitioner role by Ulin.

Initial efforts to expand the role of the nurse in Canada in primary health care followed the pattern of two types of practice, as identified by Allen (1977). The first type of practice is the assistant to the physician, which involves performing tasks delegated by the physician and is seen most commonly in physicians' offices and family practice units. The second type is replacement of the physician, which signifies that the nurse performs the same tasks as the physician, although not those of the specialist, such as a surgeon. This type of practice is prevalent in remote areas in the North; in private practice, by nurses serving such populations as psychiatric patients; and in family practice units, where patients are allocated randomly to physicians and nurses depending on the availability of staff. Some nurses support the perspective of nurses replacing or substituting for physicians, as practised in the United States and carried out at McMaster University in the 1970s (Spitzer et al, 1975).

In 1972, the Boudreau Committee, which was established to address a gap in health-care services in Canada, recommended that short-term practitioner programs be developed in selected Canadian universities to prepare nurse practitioners to practise in remote sites, such as the Far North, where physicians did not wish to reside and practise (Report of the Committee on Nurse Practioners, 1972). Such programs were established, and all but one have been phased out. The remaining program is at Dalhousie University, which has continued because it includes a nurse-midwifery component that meets a need in outlying areas in the Atlantic region. The intent was to incorporate primary health-care concepts and physical assessment and history-taking skills into basic baccalaureate programs so that this essential content would be an integral part of the preparation of all nurses graduating from baccalaureate degree programs. This has been achieved, but the baccalaureate programs do not include preparation for the "physician substitute" skills that were included in some of the Canadian nurse practitioner programs to prepare them to practise in remote areas, where consultation was provided by physicians by telephone. Some of the nurse practitioners have practised in urban areas, usually in central city underserved areas, where the poor, the unemployed, and the indigent seek health-care services from clinics. With the rapid expansion of knowledge and the knowledge base and skills needed to make clinical decisions, it is recognized that short-term programs are not adequate to prepare nurses to practise in relatively independent, autonomous roles in which they actually substitute for physicians in remote areas.

The concept of primary health care envisaged by WHO is "essential health care made universally acceptable to individuals and families in the community by means acceptable to them, through their full participation and at a cost the community and country can afford" (Mahler, 1981, p. 5). It includes four major facets: health promotion; illness prevention; illness care; and rehabilitation at individual, family, and community levels (Canadian Nurses Association [CNA], September, 1988). Thus, the concept is much broader than primary medical care and health promotion, although health promotion is the central focus, designed primarily to improve health potential and thereby maintain balance or stability. To achieve this goal "the focus in nursing must be moved to health and actions must move beyond the health sector and must involve the people themselves" (Maglacas, 1988, p. 67).

The key role for health professionals in this concept of primary health care is "empowering people to improve their lives and life styles, develop self-reliance and self-determination and take control of their health actions" (CNA Connection, 1988, p. 14). Fundamental changes in structure, roles, and relationships will be required to move from the present health-care system, which is increasingly expensive and emphasizes high technologies aimed at curing the few, to a very different and more widely available service built around health needs, with individuals, families, and communities taking increased responsibility for their own health. The focus would be on community health and social centres in the community rather than a system centred in acute care hospitals, for which 95% of the health-care dollar is now expended (Weller, 1980),

NURSING'S RESPONSE TO THE CHALLENGE

Are organized nursing in Canada and Canadian nurses prepared to support the changes needed to move to such a system of primary health care? In the past few years, the Canadian Nurses Association (CNA) has given high priority to considering the possibility and accepting the challenge. In September 1988, the CNA published a major document, *Health for all Canadians: A call for health care reform*, which provides an analysis of inadequacies in the existing health-care system and a vision of the changes needed and strategies to effect them to move to a system based on the philosophy and principles of primary health care. The CNA supports individuals, families, and communities being active partners in their health care and recognizes the need for a major reorientation of health-care policies and health-care professionals to meet the challenges of the future.

In March 1989, the CNA Board of Directors approved a five-year plan aimed at implementing this vision of primary health care in Canada. It includes steps to define and clarify the roles of nurses in primary health care, to establish stable and adequate funding to facilitate demonstration projects, to examine the implications for educational programs in nursing, and to establish a lobbying campaign to expedite the development of primary health care. "The major goals of the plan are to provide support for member associations to adopt and implement primary health care and to communicate the primary health care position at the national level" (CNA Connection, 1989). In March 1989, the CNA published a *Position Statement on the Nurses' role in Primary Health Care*. Nurses are portrayed as having a key role, which has four main aspects: "direct care provider; teacher and educator of health personnel and the public; supervisor and manager of primary health care services; and researcher and evaluator of health care" (CNA, 1989).

Nursing already has a number of examples of their participation in primary health care on which to build. Nurses practising in remote parts of Canada integrate principles of primary health care, in varying degrees, in their daily practice (Chamberlain and Beckingham, 1987). In addition to the replacement model of practice seen in remote areas, Allen (1977) identified a complemental model. It differs from that of other health professionals, yet is complementary, so the client is provided with a more complete range of health-care services by experts. Allen developed such a practice in a "Health Workshop" staffed by faculty and students of the McGill University School of Nursing. The workshop, or health centre, was located in two middle-income suburban communities, selected as representative of persons who consume large proportions of expensive medical services for life-style-related difficulties. They were also selected because existing models for improving health care were based largely on information from medically indigent populations and because families with young children tend to predominate in such suburban communities (Allen, 1981). The centre gave nurses the opportunity to help families "to examine their health habits and strategies for coping with life, practise new health behaviours, and search out healthy ways of living" (Warner, 1981, p. 34). The model was evaluated by Allen, who reported that 83.2% of the persons brought health situations and 16.8% brought illness problems. "Approximately half the health contacts related to life-style and health behaviour, 20% to adaptation and management of illness, and 23% to changes in the family and interpersonal relationships combined" (Allen, 1983, p. 55). Although the model demonstrated that the health-care services provided were not available elsewhere and were needed, it did not continue because there was no mechanism for reimbursement of services through the existing health-care system. A need for change is indicated when a model that helped people become more self-reliant about their health and reduced the use of costly medical care services could not be supported and financed.

Increasing evidence suggests that alternative models for primary health care are cost-effective and enhance the quality of care. For example, home visits by public health nurses in Ottawa resulted in greater mobility and higher morale among the elderly and fewer admissions to hospital (Flett et al, 1980). In Manitoba, Ramsay et al (1982) reported that patients who attended a clinic staffed by nurses achieved a greater decrease in blood pressure and greater weight loss than the patients attending a physician-staffed clinic. Similarly, persons in Newfoundland who received primary health care delivered by nurses had a decrease in admission to acute care hospitals, whereas those receiving traditional, physician-based care had a 39% increase in use of acute care hospitals (Denton et al, 1982). The length of hospital stay was shortened for patients who had members of the Victorian Order of Nurses (VON) involved in their discharge planning and follow-up care; and physical, social, and emotional outcomes were improved for these patients, in comparison to patients who did not have VON nurses' care (Chambers and West, 1978). In a comparative study of the health behaviours of mothers in three primary care settings in Quebec—hospital clinic, private physician's office, and community health centre—nurses' care made a difference in the health behaviours of the mothers and the health status of children under five years of age (Thibaudeau and Reidy, 1977). Other examples have been cited in the literature, but they have not had a systematic evaluation component to assess outcomes. Hence, there is need for designing and testing more primary health care models, in which nurses are the primary caregivers, and incorporating a sound evaluation component.

Approximately 40 government-funded community health centres have been developed in Ontario since 1973. It is estimated that there are also 160 in Quebec, 29 in the Atlantic provinces and 35 in the Prairie Provinces and British Columbia. They use a multidisciplinary approach, employing a variety of health professionals, such as community, home care and palliative care nurses, nurse practitioners, nutritionists, physicians, physiotherapists and chiropodists, and nonprofessional staff to meet identified needs. Ontario's centres are reported to have reduced costs; the persons using them have had 16.7% fewer hospital days than those using the services of physicians in private practice. There is reported to be low turnover and increased accountability and commitment among nursing staff. While these centres are not the primary health-care model envisioned under nurse leadership, they have facilitated community outreach and provided opportunity for collaborative research, which is critical for health-care programming and evaluation (Innes, 1987).

The Association of Registered Nurses of Newfoundland, in collaboration with the Danish Nurses Organization, has embarked on such a demonstration project, which will continue until 1991. Primary health care is being practised by nurses in selected communities in Newfoundland, and outcomes are being evaluated in terms of measurable improvement in health status of individuals and families and in health-directed life-styles. The communities are to be involved in all aspects of program planning, implementation and evaluation, which is an important concept in primary health care. A major objective is to demonstrate that nurses can provide safe and effective primary health-care services in an affordable and cost-effective manner, and to develop a prototype of primary health care that could be tested in other communities in Newfoundland, in other provinces, and worldwide (Association of Registered Nurses of Newfoundland, 1987).

OPPORTUNITIES FOR NURSING LEADERSHIP
IN PRIMARY HEALTH CARE

The development of other demonstration projects, with an evaluation component designed by experts, is of crucial importance to obtaining data to convince the policy makers and the public in all provinces that a community-focused primary health-care system with nurses as leaders is the way for the future in Canada. The CNA Board of Directors has emphasized their strong commitment to the concept of primary health care and has established a plan to work toward that goal and lobby to influence and change health policy in Canada. Similar evidence of commitment to the cause is needed in the provinces and territories, where both health-care policy and educational policy are determined. To facilitate changes in the health-care system and in nursing education, both must be changed to enable nurses to provide leadership and function effectively.

To achieve this goal, nurses must be prepared to accept shared responsibility with people for their own health, rather than use the traditional, authoritative approach as providers of care. Nurses must be willing to support communities in addressing matters concerning their health, life-styles and well-being. They must develop new skills in enabling people to increase control over and improve their health; in empowering people for self-care, self-help, and environmental improvement; and in promoting healthy coping strategies to maintain health (Maglacas, 1988).

Nursing educators must examine curricula to ensure that they are teaching the concept of primary health care as previously interpreted. This is particularly important if the findings of a study of nursing education programs, as reported by Edwards and Craig (1987), are representative of all programs in Canada. The purposes of their study were to determine: (1) the primary health-care concepts in Canadian nursing curricula, (2) faculty's familiarity with primary health-care concepts, (3) the perceived importance of a primary health-care focus in various settings, and (4) the extent to which primary health-care concepts are taught by nursing educators. Their findings revealed that 31.4% of the respondents were aware of the Alma-Ata Declaration and 19.6% had read the ICN statement on primary health care. Approximately 88% were unaware of the Canadian government's position on primary health care. Responses indicated poor differentiation between the concepts of primary care, primary nursing, and primary health care. The inclusion of primary health-care knowledge and skills was minimal and significantly less than expected.

THE QUESTION OF NURSE MIDWIFERY IN CANADA

A current issue related to primary health care is the status of nurse-midwifery in Canada. Currently, Canada is one of the eight WHO countries that do not recognize midwifery as a profession. The other seven are "Venezuela, Panama, New Hebrides, El Salvador, Dominican Republic, Colombia, and Burundi" (McCourt, 1986, p. 285).

Over the past four decades, the public has had increasing influence on the delivery of maternal and infant care. Since the days of the introduction of natural childbirth by Dr. Grantly Dick Read in England, young parents have sought to have more control over the type of care for pregnancy and childbirth and have demanded more participation in decision making. Although some childbearing families in Canada and the United States have been allowed more control over the process of childbirth since the early 1950s, changes of this nature have been slow in developing. In fact, some parents believe that medical technology has been allowed to advance at the expense of their rightful control over a normal physiologic process. As a result, some have opted for home birth attended by a practising midwife or occasionally a physician. The hazards of home birth are well known and midwives who provide such care are practising illegally. Young people are likely to continue to pursue this option if not given more voice in the type of care available.

Despite the lack of legal recognition of midwives in Canada, some continue to practise in almost all provinces. In 1987, it was estimated that "approximately 50 midwives were practising in Ontario outside the official health care system" (Task Force on the Implementation of Midwifery in Ontario, 1987). The number practising in other provinces has not been documented, although the Canadian Confederation of Midwives Newsletters (1988 and 1989) include reports from provinces that indicate strong support from midwives across the country to have midwifery recognized legally as a separate profession. Some of these midwives are practising midwifery, whereas others are practising as nurses in obstetric units in hospitals, particularly in labour and delivery units. It is not known what proportion are lay midwives without formal training, nurse midwives, or nonnurse midwives who have earned their credentials to practise midwifery in other countries through approved educational programs. In countries such as Great Britain and the United States, only nurses are admissible to midwifery programs, whereas preparation as a nurse is not an admission requirement in many European countries, including Germany, Denmark, Switzerland, and the Netherlands. Nurses employed by the federal government in Canada in nursing stations/outposts provide comprehensive care to women living in remote areas during the prenatal and postpartal periods and may give emergency labour and birth care when it is not possible to fly a woman to a hospital. Although some of these nurses have had midwifery training in another country, which is considered invaluable, they are not recognized as midwives.

The viability of nurse-midwifery has been demonstrated in the hospital setting in three pilot projects: namely, the Grace Hospital Nurse-Midwifery Project in Vancouver (Weatherston, et al, 1985), The Chedoke-McMaster Hospitals Nurse-Midwifery Project in Hamilton (Task Force on the Implementation of Midwifery in Ontario, 1987), and The Misericordia Hospital Pilot Project in Edmonton (Marcos, 1983). In these projects, the nurses function under the aegis of delegated medical functions, which means that ultimate responsibility resides with the physicians who are available for consultation and referral. The Grace Hospital Project was the first to use nurses, trained as midwives in other countries, in a primary health care role. It was the result of a collaborative effort by a team of obstetricians and nursing instructors who organized a joint practice. A total of 61 families were cared for in the low-risk clinic, which was a small portion of the families who applied for the service. The approach to care supported the principles of health promotion and primary health care as stated in the Canada Charter. Self-responsibility for care was encouraged, and the care provided a great deal of support and teaching. The parents were active participants during labour and delivery, and the midwife was responsible for delivery of the baby. Midwives made postpartum physical assessments of mother and baby, provided emotional support when necessary and taught maternal self-care, care of the baby, and breastfeeding. They were on call to the mother for six weeks after the birth and checked the mother at two weeks and six weeks postpartum. Weatherston et al conclude:

> The way the health care system provides for the needs of childbearing women is a major women's health issue. The low-risk clinic provided a different approach to meet the health care needs of women in the perinatal period. Pregnancy and birth were viewed as normal processes and routine medical interventions were avoided. Women were involved in their own care; there was an emphasis on teaching and self-responsibility. The families involved were all extremely positive about the project and the approach taken to providing care. The midwifery approach provided safety as well as recognition of the broader significance of the event in the women's lives and those of their families (1985, p. 37).

Although all of the pilot projects used nurse-midwives or nurses who had considerable experience and skill in maternity nursing, active support has developed across Canada for legalizing midwifery separately from nursing so that it will be an autonomous profession. Midwifery associations have been established to head this movement in all provinces except New Brunswick and Prince Edward Island. In addition, the Canadian Confederation of Midwives (CCM) serves as a mechanism for communication and coordination of efforts. The trend to organize and license midwifery separately from nursing has been opposed by the provincial nursing associations in Ontario, Alberta, British Columbia and Saskatchewan and the CNA, whose position is that registration as a nurse should be a prerequisite for admission to a midwifery program and that nurse-midwifery should be a nursing specialty. This position is adamantly opposed by the proponents of midwifery as a separate profession, some of whom have been quoted by the press as stating: "Nurses look after sick people, midwives look after well people. Nurses do things that are designed to cure, which presupposes a person is unwell. Midwives act more as supports, and as preventers of illness" and "A nurse is an adjunct to medicine and as in the medical model, is treating sick people. We don't want to practise medicine. We don't want to care for sick people. We are not nurses. The nurse-midwife is a creation of doctors, a physician extender" (Prokaska, 1985, p. C1). Such perceptions of nursing practice are antithetical to those purported by CNA and the provincial nursing associations and certainly to the concept of primary health care described here. Both of the persons quoted were trained in another country (Elizabeth McDonald in Australia and Rena Pourteous in Scotland), and it is possible that their concepts of nursing differ from the roles of nurses, as practised in Canada and as envisioned for the future, applying concepts of primary health care.

The greatest progress in the current midwifery movement has occurred in Ontario, where the Minister of Health announced in 1986 "the government's intention to establish midwifery as a recognized part of the Ontario health care system and that midwifery would become a regulated health profession" (Task Force on the Implementation of Midwifery in Ontario, 1987, p. 7). Several factors are reported to have led to the decision to give legal recognition to midwifery: (1) public support from women who wanted more holistic care than that provided by physicians and more participation in decision-making about their care, (2) an increasing number of practising midwives who were increasingly effective in communicating their case for recognition to the government and the public, and (3) the death of an infant delivered by a midwife which resulted in the coroner's jury recommending that midwifery be granted legal recognition and become incorporated into the health care system (Task Force on the Implementation of Midwifery in Ontario, 1987). An omnibus bill to make midwifery 1 of 24 health professions has been drafted and is to be tabled soon. It proposes that a College of Midwives be established within the Ontario Ministry of Health, through which midwives will be licensed/registered, regulated and disciplined, as are other health professionals, including nursing through the College of Nurses. An interim regulatory council has been appointed to prepare drafts of standards of practice and criteria for eligibility to practise. In addition, a curriculum blueprint for midwifery education is being prepared, including a proposal for the level of education to be required. The Task Force report (1987) favoured a four-year university program, leading to a baccalaureate degree in midwifery, for students with no previous relevant postsecondary education, and a 12 to 18 month option for nurses with university level education who wish to become midwives. There is evidence of support from the Ontario Medical Association and the Ontario College of Family Practice. Hence, there no longer seems to be a question of whether midwifery will be established as a separate, autonomous profession in Ontario, but rather when and how it will be implemented (K. Kaufman [personal communication, April 16, 1990]).

The Midwives Association of British Columbia (MABC) has been actively involved in efforts to have midwifery recognized as a separate and autonomous profession in that province. They also provided testimony for a coroner's inquest into the death of a baby, of which the outcome was "strong recommendations to the Ministry of Health, Grace Hospital, and [the MABC] to legalize autonomous midwifery into the health services of British Columbia and to establish a college of midwives to regulate education and practice" (Scriver, 1989, p. 6). The MABC reports that they have established good professional relationships with both the Registered Nurses Association of British Columbia (RNABC) and the Ministry of Health. They are able to discuss differences with RNABC, but that has not changed the position of RNABC that midwifery should be a nursing specialty and not a separate, autonomous profession that admits persons without nursing preparation to its educational programs. To date, no midwifery proposal has been produced, but an internal working paper is reported to have been drafted (K. Kaufman, [personal communication, April 16, 1990]).

In Alberta, the movement toward recognition of midwifery as a separate and autonomous profession is slowly gaining momentum. It began in 1980 when "the Domiciliary Midwives Council of Alberta presented a brief to the Health Occupations Board for registration as a licensed body as their members were engaged in home delivery. There was strong consumer support for this move, but it was not granted because the domiciliary midwives were viewed as a sub-occupational group" (Brief to the Premier's Commission on Future Health Care for Albertans, 1988, p.1). The Alberta Association of Midwives (AAM) was established in 1986, which includes nurses with midwifery training and empirically trained midwives who are practising in Alberta. Their position is the same as those taken in Ontario and British Columbia, and they are opposed by the Alberta Association of Registered Nurses and the Alberta Medical Association, both of whom support nurse-midwifery but not direct entry into midwifery without prior education as a nurse. Field and Campbell (1986) believe that midwifery will need its own professional act if it is to be accepted as part of the health-care system in Alberta. Both are nurse-midwives with advanced education in nursing, but regard it inappropriate to consider only nurse-midwifery and to consider midwifery as a specialty of nursing. They raise many issues that need to be discussed, such as how midwives will work with their colleagues in nursing, the most appropriate method for educating midwives, how midwives will be financed and insured, and whether they will increase or decrease the costs of the system. Field is in charge of the certificate program in nurse-midwifery implemented by the University of Alberta Faculty of Nursing in 1987, which may be taken only in conjunction with the Master of Nursing Program. The Faculty of Medicine has collaborated in the development of the certificate program, as they did in the operation of the Advanced Practical Obstetrics program offered by the Faculty of Nursing from 1944 to 1984. It was designed to better prepare nurses for practice in remote areas and for delivering babies in the absence of a physician. Since midwifery practice is not yet legalized in Canada, the graduate students enroling in this program will be well prepared for leadership roles in maternity nursing and for teaching in universities, but they will not be able to continue to practise nurse-midwifery, which is essential to maintaining clinical competence to teach and guide others in practice. The AAM had defined standards of midwifery practice and prepared a position paper on the scope of midwifery practice. In 1988, they presented a brief on the need for midwives in Alberta and documented ideas about role and functions, educational preparation, licensure, liability insurance, and costs to the Premier's Commission on Future Health Care for Albertans. The AAM has collaborated with the Alberta Task Force on Midwifery, which was established for publicity and lobbying purposes, in designing materials for educating the public and politicians about the need for and potential of legalized midwifery practice in Alberta. In 1989, the AAM was encouraged, by the government department responsible for professional legislation, to target legislation in 1990 (Scriver, 1989).

It is evident that the leaders in midwifery in Canada are networking and helping and supporting each other in their attempt to have midwifery recognized as a separate, autonomous profession in Canada, and that they do not wish to be another nursing specialty or limit their ranks to nurses only, although they support and apply the principles of primary health care in their practice.

CONCLUSION

The opportunities for nurses to practise primary health care as envisioned by the CNA, Maglacas, and other nursing leaders, are unlimited if they believe in the concept and accept the challenge to work with communities and help them assume responsibility for their own health and well-being. The vision of primary health care is relevant for midwifery practice and would respond well to the wishes of childbearing families to have more control over this important event in their lives. If ever there was a need for unity in nursing, this is the time, as we move forward into the twenty-first century, to advance the cause of primary health care. To attain nursing's goals and achieve Health for All by the year 2000, will require changes in the health-care system and reorientation of perceptions of nursing and the education needed to function effectively in the primary health-care system. As nurses, why not join forces with the public and work toward these goals?

REFERENCES

Alberta Association of Midwives. (1988, June 30). *Brief on the need for Midwives in Alberta to the Premier's Commission of Future Health Care for Albertans.* Unpublished manuscript.

Allen, M. (1977). Comparative theories of the expanded role and implications for nursing practice. *Nursing Papers, 9*(2), 38-45.

Allen, M. (1981). The health dimension in nursing practice: Notes on nursing and primary health care. *Journal of Advanced Nursing, 6*(3), 63-64.

Allen, M. (1983). Primary care nursing: Research in action. In L. Hockey (Ed.), *Primary care nursing,* (pp. 32-77). Edinburgh: Churchill Livingstone.

Association of Registered Nurses of Newfoundland. (1987). *Primary health care: A nursing model: An overview.* St. John's, Nfld: The Association.

Canadian Nurses Association. (1988, September). *Health for all Canadians; A call for health care reform.* Ottawa: The Association.

Canadian Nurses Association. (1989, March). *Position statement on the nurse's role in primary health care.* Ottawa: The Association.

Chamberlain, M.C. and Beckingham, A.C. (1987). Primary health care in Canada: In praise of the nurse? *International Nursing Review, 34*(6), 158-160.

Chambers, L.W. and West, A.E. (1978). The St. John's randomized trial of the family practice nurse: Health outcomes of patients, *International Journal of Epidemiology, 7*(2), 153-161.

CNA Connection. (1988). Keynote speaker: Empowerment key role says Maglacas. *The Canadian Nurse, 84*(8), 14-15.

CNA Connection. (1989). CNA board endorses primary health care. *The Canadian Nurse, 85*(5), 8.

Denton, F., Gafini, D., Spencer, B., and Stoddart, G. (1982). *Potential savings from the adoption of nurse practitioner technology in the Canadian health care system,* Hamilton, Ontario: McMaster University.

Diers, D., Hamman, A., and Molde, S. (1986). Complexity of ambulatory care: Nurse practitioners and physician caseloads. *Nursing Research, 35*(5), 310-314.

Edwards, N.C. and Craig, H. (1987). *Does nursing education reflect the goals of primary health care?* Hamilton, Ontario: McMaster University.

Feldman, M.J., Ventura, M.R., and Crosby, F. (1987). Studies of nurse practitioner effectiveness. *Nursing Research, 36*(5), 303-308.

Field, P.A. and Campbell, J. (1986). An opinion: midwifery in Alberta. *AARN Newsletter, 42*(7), 17-18.

Flett, J.E., Last, J.M., and Lynch, G.U. (1980). Evaluation of the public health nurse as primary health care provider for elderly people. In V. Marshall, (Ed.). *Aging in Canada: Social perspectives.* (pp. 177-188). Don Mills, Ontario, Fitzhenry and Whiteside.

Innes, J. (1987). Health care reform: Sketching the future. *AARN Newsletter, 43*(8), 1, 5-6.

Maglacas, A.M. (1988). Health for all: Nursing's role. *Nursing Outlook, 36*(2), 66-71.

Mahler, H. (1981). The meaning of health for all by the year 2000. *World Health Forum, 2*(1), 5-22.

Marcos, F. (1983). *Obstetricians and nurse-midwives: An "inquiry" into a team approach.* Unpublished manuscript. Edmonton, Alberta, Misericordia Hospital.

McCourt, C. (1986). Legalization of midwifery and the issue of home births. *Canadian Medical Association Journal, 135*(4), 285-288.

Molde, S. and Diers, D. (1985). Nurse practitioner review: Selected literature review and research agenda. *Nursing Research, 34*(6), 362-367.

Nurse-Midwifery Program of Chedoke-McMaster Hospitals. (1986). *Brief to the Task Force on the Implementation of Midwifery in Ontario.* Unpublished manuscript.

Nutbeam, D. and Lawrence, J. (1987). *Positive health: An update on health promotion in action: A charter for action.* Cardiff: Institute for Health Promotion, College of Medicine, University of Wales.

Ottawa Charter for Health Promotion. (1986). Ottawa: World Health Organization, Health and Welfare Canada, and the Canadian Public Health Association.

Prokaska, L. (1985, August 8). New approach to midwifery at Mac. *The Hamilton Spectator,* p. C1.

Ramsay, J., McKenzie, J.K., and Fish, D.G. (1982). Physicians and nurse practitioners: Do they provide equivalent care? *American Journal of Public Health, 72*(4), 55-57.

Report of the Committee on Nurse Practitioners. (1972). Ottawa: Department of National Health and Welfare. The Committee.

Scriver, B. (ed.) (Summer 1988). *Canadian Confederation of Midwives Newsletter, 2*(1): Calgary, Alberta.

Scriver, B. (1989, Summer). *Canadian Confederation of Midwives Newsletter, 2*(2): (CCM Coordinator, Station G, 50 Couture, Sherbrooke, Quebec. J1H 5M4).

Spitzer, W., Kergin, D.J., and Yoshida, M.A. (1975). Nurse practitioners in primary care: The Southern Ontario randomized trial. In Leininger, M. (Ed.), *Health care dimensions.* Philadelphia: F.A. Davis Co.

Task Force on the Implementation of Midwifery in Ontario. (1987). *Report of the task force: Executive summary and summary of recommendations.* Toronto: Ontario Ministry of Health.

Thibaudeau, M.F. and Reidy, M.M. (1977). Nursing makes a difference: A comparative study of the health behaviours of mothers in three primary care agencies. *International Journal of Nursing Studies, 14,* 97-107.

Ulin, P.R. (1982). International nursing challenge. *Nursing Outlook, 30*(6), 531- 535.

Warner, M. (1981). The health workshop: A nursing model of primary health care in a rural community. *The Canadian Nurse, 77*(1), 34-36.

Weatherston, L., Carty, E., Rice, A., and Tier, D. (1985). Hospital-based midwifery: Meeting the needs of childbearing women. *The Can Nurse, 81*(1), 35-37.

Weller, G.R. (1980, Fall). The determinants of Canadian health policy. *Journal of Health Politics, Policy and Law, 5.* 408-409.

World Health Organization. (1978a). *Report of the International Conference on Primary Health Care:* Alma-Ata, USSR, Geneva, September 6-12, 1978.

World Health Organization. (1978b). The Alma-Ata Conference on Primary Health Care. *WHO Chronicle, 32* (11), 409-430.

CHAPTER THIRTY ONE

The Growth of Graduate Education in Nursing in Canada

JANET ROSS KERR

T he first half-century of university education in nursing in Canada might be termed the era of the undergraduate basic degree program. The development of graduate education has become an identifiable thrust in recent years, with master's degree programs only recently available in sufficient numbers to ensure broader access, and with doctoral programs still on the horizon (Fig. 31.1). Increased research activity in nursing has occurred gradually as a result of a slowly increasing pool of nurses with preparation in research. This development goes hand-in-hand with, and is a necessary condition for, establishment of graduate education in nursing. Most of the research in any field takes place in university settings, and teaching research methods is an important facet of graduate education. Approval of new programs by universities is unlikely without evidence of substantial research activity and the doctoral degree as a standard qualification for faculty appointment.

Although the primary educational problems confronting the profession in the 1940s and 1950s centred around issues of quality in baccalaureate and diploma nursing education, the critical need for nursing leaders prepared at the master's and doctoral levels was beginning to be recognized. In her study of the needs and resources for graduate nursing education in Canada, Hart observed that:

> . . . an increasing number of Canadian nurses recognized that graduate education was necessary to qualify for other specialized functions besides teaching. Canadian nurses had enroled in programs leading to the master's degree to prepare for positions such as administration, supervision and consultation. Canadian nurses secured preparation for the specialized functions in nursing education as well as in nursing service in hospitals and health agencies. In spite of increasing demands for graduate education, by the time the study was undertaken there was still no provision for graduate study in nursing in Canada (1962, p. 51).

FIGURE 31.1   Chronology of the growth and development of university degree
programs in nursing in Canada.

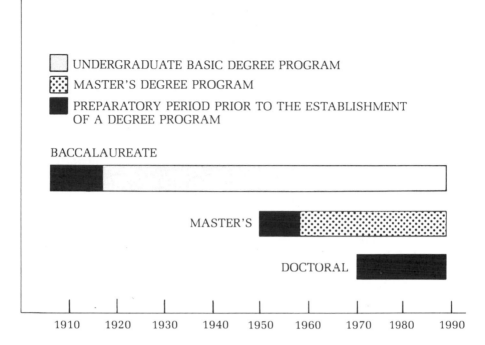

Hart (1962) concluded that the need to leave the country to pursue graduate
study meant that relatively few Canadian nurses were qualified for leadership
positions. Good concurred with this assessment ten years later: "Canadian
nurses too have followed the pattern of study abroad for graduate education.
The country of focus was, and still is, the United States of America" (1969, pp.
3-4).

The Canadian Nurses Association (CNA) was in the forefront of developments and strongly supported the call for graduate programs in nursing. Its
Committee on Nursing Affairs reported to the 31st Biennial Convention in 1962:

> We should promote immediately an assessment of present facilities, both university
> and clinical, in order to ascertain what is needed by way of the expansion of univer-
> sity nursing education ... On the principle that one can never go wrong with an
> investment in human beings, a crash program for the development of qualified
> faculty for Canadian schools of nursing should be undertaken by CNA ... CNA might
> also interest itself in giving some leadership to the development of graduate pro-
> grams in nursing education, especially in terms of the pooling of university resources
> in particular specialties. (Canadian Nurses Association [CNA], 1962, pp. 23-25)

The Committee on Nursing Education also recommended that:

> Programs in nursing at the baccalaureate level should be expanded.

The director of the school of nursing should be a nurse with preparation at a master's level and should have the necessary qualifications to assume the responsibility for administration of the school.

All nurses responsible for teaching nursing students should have professional and academic preparation at least at the baccalaureate level and have demonstrated professional competence.

Programs should be developed at the master's and doctoral level to prepare nurses who will be qualified as nursing specialists and for administration, consultation, research and teaching (CNA, 1962, p. 46).

Thus the focus of the profession was broadened to include graduate education as a necessary adjunct in the quest for quality in basic professional education.

As was the case when baccalaureate programs were in their incipient stages, the first thrust was to be the development of fellowship programs to prepare nurse faculty to take on the responsibilities associated with graduate education. Hart reported that in 1957:

> . . . a few unrestricted scholarships and fellowships were found to be available for graduate study in Canadian colleges and universities. Some scholarships were available specifically for nurses and other members of the health professions . . . If programs for graduate study were available in Canada, it is likely that students in the nursing field would utilize such scholarship and fellowship aid (1962, p. 47).

However, the Kellogg Foundation fellowship program, which spanned two decades, provided a much needed source of funds for graduate students who had to incur the expenses associated with taking up residence in a foreign country to find appropriate educational opportunities at the graduate level (Table 31.1). In 1962 the Canadian Nurses Foundation (CNF) was formed with the assistance of a grant of $136,639 from the Kellogg Foundation for the establishment of a fellowship program for study at the master's and doctoral levels and for research assistance for nurses. The CNF completed its first mandate admirably, with a total of 310 graduate fellowships awarded between 1962 and 1986: 244 for study at the master's level and 66 for doctoral work (E. Mountain [personal communication, April 21, 1978]; B.A. Smith [personal communication, April 23, 1987]). A summary of the number and amounts of awards for graduate study from 1962 to 1987 is presented in Table 31.2. Due to problems in maintaining the size of the fund, the Research Committee of the CNF "formulated plans for developing nursing research in Canada but unfortunately, due to lack of funds, these could not be implemented" (Imai, 1971, p. 90). The CNF later initiated a program of research grants. The first such grant was one given to the Canadian Association of University Schools of Nursing (CAUSN) for a research project on accreditation of university schools of nursing. With the establishment of an Ad Hoc Research Committee in 1983, the CNF Board of Directors initiated a program of research grants, which, although small, has been important in encouraging nurses to undertake research.

TABLE 31.1 Kellogg Foundation Grants to Canadian University Schools of Nursing and Selected Other Agencies, 1940 to 1960

			Amount of Grant
Alberta			
University of Alberta, Edmonton	Fellowships in nursing	1949 to 1954	$ 10,862
British Columbia			
University of British Columbia, Vancouver	To aid in establishing nursing education curricula leading to registered nurse licensure, baccalaureate, master's and doctoral degrees	1974 to 1977	333,225
	Fellowships in nursing	1940 to 1953	18,032
Vancouver Metropolitan Health Department	Fellowships in nursing	1946	675
Manitoba			
University of Manitoba, Winnipeg	Fellowships in nursing	1941 to 1949	2,815
New Brunswick			
New Brunswick Association for Registered Nurses, Fredericton	Fellowships in nursing	1953	715
University of New Brunswick, Fredericton	To aid in establishing a degree program in basic nursing	1958 to 1965	198,857
	To help establish a program of continuing education in nursing	1958 to 1961	17,504
Ontario			
Canadian Nurses Association, Ottawa (for Province of Ontario)	Fellowships in nursing	1950	1,493
McMaster University, Hamilton	Fellowships in nursing	1948 to 1954	19,787
	To help establish a graduate education curriculum in nursing	1973 to 1978	290,935

TABLE 31.2 Canadian Nurses Foundation Fellowship Awards, 1962 to 1987

Awards Given In	Number of Master's Awards	Number of Doctoral Awards	Total Amount Awarded
1962 to 1963	9	1	$ 11,700
1963 to 1964	12	—	31,000
1964 to 1965	8	3	35,700
1965 to 1966	6	2	27,250
1966 to 1967	11	3	37,175
1967 to 1968	11	2	36,700
1968 to 1969	15	2	52,550
1969 to 1970	16	1	42,100
1970 to 1971	14	5	56,537
1971 to 1972	11	2	32,500
1972 to 1973	12	2	36,200
1973 to 1974	9	1	31,000
1974 to 1975	3	1	13,500
1975 to 1976	5	1	17,900
1976 to 1977	8	0	21,900
1977 to 1978	12	2	35,500
1978 to 1979	12	2	37,800
1979 to 1980	9	4	61,500
1980 to 1981	5	5	34,000
1981 to 1982	4	3	15,000
1982 to 1983	15	6	37,208
1983 to 1984	12	5	37,700
1984 to 1985	9	6	32,500
1985 to 1986	9	2	36,000
1986 to 1987	7	5	44,000
TOTAL	244	66	$854,920

From personal communication with Eileen Mountain, Assistant to the Secretary-Treasurer, Canadian Nurses Foundation, 21 April 1978; and Bette Ann Smith, Assistant Secretary-Treasurer, 23 April and 15 May 1987.

ESTABLISHMENT OF MASTER'S DEGREE PROGRAMS

The efforts of the University of Western Ontario (UWO) to develop a one-year diploma program in nursing service administration led to the establishment of a master's level program in that area, a program that became the first graduate program in nursing in Canada (Overduin, 1970). In 1957, when the President of the University, Dr. G.E. Hall, applied for Kellogg funding to implement the diploma program that had received the approval of the University Senate as early as 1956, he:

> ... requested $100,000 from the Foundation ... $50,000 of which was slated for the 'intensive development' of the new DNSA program—the Foundation indicated its

willingness to support the school of nursing in its educational efforts in nursing administration. It supported the development of a master's program in Canada, to be supported by the Foundation over a five-year period just as it had done earlier in American universities (Overduin, 1970, p. 84).

A brief was prepared and submitted to the Kellogg Foundation.

> [It] showed that Western met all the requirements set by the Foundation, described in detail the programs and courses offered by the school of nursing, and a projected budget for a five-year period indicating the cost of five major areas which would be supported by the Foundation: the master's program, and project of case-writing in administration, two fellowships per year to be granted during each year of the grant — each fellow to receive $2,000 per year for each year of her two-year program, an annual seminar for senior nursing executives, and continuing education for faculty (Overduin, 1970, p. 84).

Although it is reported that $142,000 was awarded by the Foundation for the establishment of this program (Overduin, 1970; University of Western Ontario [UWO] School of Nursing, 1967 to 1968), Kellogg records indicate that $128,618 was in fact expended between 1959 and 1965 "to help establish a program of graduate education in nursing service administration" (WK Kellogg Foundation. Cited in Kerr, 1978, p. 261) (Table 31.1). Planning for the implementation of the new program began in March of 1959, and "On October 30, 1959, the Senate approved the first year of the program, and the entrance requirements" (Overduin, 1970, p. 85). Of note was the recognition that "the great need for research, especially research in appraising nursing care and service, was instrumental in the decision that a student would be required to produce a thesis" (Overduin, 1970, p. 85).

At McGill University, much progress had occurred since 1944, when the baccalaureate degree program was established. The transition to the integrated program occurred in 1957; however, planning for a master's level program began even earlier:

> Research in nursing at McGill had been urged in Miss Green's report of 1953. The following year students in the second year degree programme undertook small research projects under the direction of staff members. Miss Chittick began to press for the creation of a Master's programme in nursing at the School for Graduate Nurses (Tunis, 1966, p. 11).

After a resolution was passed at the 1958 CNA convention, expressing the need for opportunities for graduate study in nursing in Canadian universities, "at McGill a two-year programme leading to a degree of M.Sc. (Applied) was drawn up for approval by the Faculty of Graduate Studies and Research" (Tunis, 1966, p. 112). Senate approval, in principle, was received in September 1959, and again the Kellogg Foundation provided financial support to operationalize the program plans with a grant of $195,000 over five years (Tunis, 1966). This brought the total amount of Kellogg Foundation assistance to McGill, between 1946 and 1967, for the development of curricula to $221,252 (Tables 31.1 and 31.3). Once again in the vanguard of developments in university nursing education in Canada, the WK Kellogg Foundation expressed its rationale for

TABLE 31.3 Kellogg Foundation Support for Development of Master's Degree Programs in Nursing in Canada*

	Univ. of B.C.	Univ. of West. Ont.	McMaster Univ.	Univ. of Toronto	McGill Univ.	CNA	TOTAL
1959		19,233					19,233
1960		24,453					24,453
1961		25,406			48,159		73,565
1962		24,427			22,812	13,920	61,159
1963		25,948			28,209	27,717	81,874
1964		17,985			26,672	27,837	72,494
1965					14,567	69,668	84,235
1966					21,425		21,425
1967					18,499		18,499
1968				34,852			34,852
1969				28,159			28,159
1970							0
1971				72,006			72,006
1972				28,968			28,968
1973			135,143				135,143
1974	76,838		79,798	8,738			165,374
1975	131,316			75,436			206,752
1976	84,337		46,984				131,321
TOTAL	292,491	137,452	261,925	248,159	180,343	139,142	1,259,512

From Annual Reports of the WK Kellogg Foundation from 1959 to 1976.
*Since 1982 no grants have been made for Canadian health projects, as new guidelines have restricted grants outside the United States to Latin America and Southern Africa.

the assistance: "graduate programs in Canadian universities are greatly needed. Better teachers of nursing produce better practitioners and, hence, improve patient care" (WK Kellogg Foundation, 1966, p. 56).

There was a considerable lapse of time after the early activity in the establishment of master's programs at UWO and McGill University sponsored by the Kellogg Foundation grants. However, demonstrations had begun and it was up to the institutions to obtain their own resources if they wished to initiate graduate programs in nursing. Given the historical reluctance of university administrators and academics to approve the development of new and costly graduate programs, which required a commitment to ongoing and increasing operating expenditures, it is not surprising, particularly in the absence of financial inducements to cover the early years, that five years passed before another program was established. The year 1966 witnessed the inception of the graduate program at l'université de Montréal, the first master's program in the French language in the world, and in 1968, a program was developed at the University of British Columbia (Good, 1971).

The WK Kellogg Foundation again offered support for development in master's programs, with an award of $178,000 to the Faculty of Nursing at the University of Toronto "to establish a graduate program to prepare clinical nurse specialists" (WK Kellogg Foundation, 1971, p. 28). In her annual report to the President, Dean Helen Carpenter describes the nature of the program in its first year of operation:

> The Master's Degree programme embodies specialization, mastery in depth of a specific area of knowledge, independent and critical study, and research. The purposes of the course are to make available advanced preparation for leadership roles in selected areas of nursing, and to advance nursing knowledge and skills through analytical study and investigation. Opportunity is provided for the students to acquire knowledge from nursing and the related sciences to provide the rationale for the management of complex health problems. (1970, p. 74)

Another indication of interest in innovative developments in nursing curricula in Canada is the Foundation support, granted in 1973 for a five-year period, to the School of Nursing at McMaster University for an "interdisciplinary graduate program to prepare clinical nurse specialists in primary and ambulatory care" (WK Kellogg Foundation, 1975, p. 19). This program award was for $290,196. An excerpt from the Foundation's *Annual Report* discusses the nature of this unique program.

> Foundation funds are helping the Division of Health Sciences of McMaster University, Hamilton, Ontario, develop an interdisciplinary graduate program to prepare nurses for advanced clinical practice in primary and ambulatory care. Students may choose clinical practice in maternal child health, family practice, or rehabilitation. Every attempt is made to include a true interdisciplinary experience, with members of several health professions learning together about issues in the delivery and management of health care. Nursing students will work with a physician preceptor during their clinical experience. The physician preceptor will also work with medical residents and will relate to both groups toward effective interdisciplinary clinical practice (1974, pp. 10-11).

Although the master's program at the University of Alberta, established in 1975, did not receive external funding, it derived substantial benefit from the development of the Master's in Health Services Administration program in 1968. This program was initiated under the auspices of the Western Canadian Council on Education of Health Personnel, with a Kellogg Foundation grant of $212,250 for a five-year period (WK Kellogg Foundation, 1970). This program incorporated a stream for nursing administrators and paved the way for the 1975 development of the Master of Nursing program by providing for a joint appointment between the Division of Health Services Administration and the Faculty of Nursing and by developing a strong research thrust in the program. Both developments were assets to the Faculty of Nursing and facilitated the development of its master's program in 1975.

At the University of British Columbia (UBC), the initiation of the master's program took place initially without external funding. However, five years later, a large W.K. Kellogg Foundation grant was awarded to the School of Nursing "to aid in establishing nursing education curricula leading to registered nurse licensure, baccalaureate, master's and doctoral degrees" (WK Kellogg Foundation. Cited in Kerr, 1978, p. 259) (Table 31.1). Although the basic elements of such a "ladder system" approach were developed before the termination of the grant in 1977, the doctoral part of the program was not established during the five-year time frame, and to date no Canadian institution has developed such a program. Noteworthy, too, is the fact that UBC dropped the "ladder" concept before the end of the decade to concentrate on its basic and post-RN baccalaureate and master's programs. Another development in the availability of master's programs was the establishment of the first program in the Atlantic area at Dalhousie University in 1975.

Documentation of Kellogg Foundation support for the initiation of graduate programs on an annual basis between 1959 and 1986 provides a clear picture of financial resources expended by the Foundation in the first phase in the development of graduate education in nursing in Canada (Table 31.1). The resources, which were awarded to the CNA for the establishment of the CNF and are also included as CNF awards for graduate study, were a critical factor in the development of the faculty resources needed to offer graduate programs in Canada. Total support from 1959 to 1976 amounted to $461,812, with an average award of $2730 in any one year. Awards were made to five universities for this purpose. All awards, with the exception of the 1974 award to the UBC, were designed to assist with the establishment of new master's degree programs in nursing. In the case of UBC, support was designated for an articulated nursing program from baccalaureate through doctoral levels, although, as previously noted, this program did not materialize. Support was awarded for a five-year period, after which the institution assumed full responsibility for all operating costs of continuing programs. Kellogg Foundation funding is no longer available for Canadian health projects, as "programming guidelines since 1982 have restricted grants outside the United States to Latin America and our beginning efforts in southern Africa" (Grace [personal communication, May 14, 1987]).

ANALYSIS OF ENROLMENT TRENDS IN MASTER'S PROGRAMS

Considerable growth has occurred in master's programs since 1959 when the total enrolment at the UWO was two students (Overduin, 1970) or since the 1960 to 1961 academic year when the combined enrolment at UWO and McGill University was 16. During the five-year interval between 1960 to 1961 and 1965 to 1966, when there were still only two programs in operation, total enrolment grew by 56%. In the next five-year interval, three more programs were established and there was an increase of 675 in total enrolment (see Table 31.4). During this time, programs that offered study in a clinical content area were developed, beginning with the program at l'université de Montréal in 1966. An analysis of early trends in the development of graduate education in nursing prompted one author to speculate on the reasons why Canadian nurses were still travelling to the United States for graduate study instead of enroling in the new Canadian programs:

TABLE 31.4 Enrolment Changes in Master's Programs in Canadian Universities, 1965 to 1966 and 1986 to 1987

Year	Total Enrolment	Percentage Change in Enrolment From Year to Year
1965 to 1966	37	Base Year
1966 to 1967	51	+28
1967 to 1968	56	+9
1968 to 1969	79	+29
1969 to 1970	73	−8
1970 to 1971	112	+35
1971 to 1972	151	+26
1972 to 1973	159	+5
1973 to 1974	172	+8
1974 to 1975	177	+3
1975 to 1976	203	+13
1976 to 1977	244	+17
1977 to 1978	278	+12
1978 to 1979	263	−6
1979 to 1980	304	+13
1980 to 1981	345	+12
1981 to 1982	381	+9
1982 to 1983	381	0
1983 to 1984	526	+28
1984 to 1985	524	0
1985 to 1986	699	+25

From Canadian Association of University Schools of Nursing Statistics 1975 to 1979; Canadian Nurses Association and Statistics Canada, 1985; *Nursing in Canada,* 1984.

1. Historical precedent
2. More and better qualified nurse faculty
3. Greater variety in programming

In the latter instance, US universities offer advanced study in five to eight clinical content areas, as well as in the functional specialties. At present, only one Canadian master's program offers study in a clinical area; all offer functional specialization. (Good, 1969, p. 7).

In the period between 1970–1971 and 1975–1976, three more new master's programs were initiated, and total enrolment grew by 47%. No new programs began between 1975–1976 and 1980–1981, as the impact of the slow growth and retrenchment of the early 1970s began to take hold; however, three new master's programs were initiated in the next five-year period at the University of Calgary (1981), the University of Manitoba (1982), and Memorial University of Newfoundland (1984). In 1986–1987, another new master's program was initiated in the West, at the University of Saskatchewan.

Also interesting are enrolment trends since 1965. Erratic changes characterize the first five-year period, probably due to the smaller aggregate numbers on which the calculations are based, and to the beginnings of retrenchment, as growth was replaced by shortfalls in enrolments nationally. The year 1969–1970, when four programs were operational, was the only one of the decade in which there was a decrease in enrolment over the previous year. The next year saw a 35% increase, and a 26% increase occurred in 1971–1972.

For the academic years from 1971 through 1975, enrolment increases were lower, ranging from 3% to 8%, representing a slow but steady increase in student numbers and increased access to programs made possible by the addition of two programs after 1969–1970. In 1975–1976 there was a larger overall increase — about 13% — in the total enrolment figures. The new programs accounted for the larger percentage increase. Exponential increases occurred over the next decade with the addition of new programs and increases in the size of existing ones. Demand was apparent as more students applied for admission than could be accommodated in programs.

DEVELOPING THE FACULTY RESOURCES FOR GRADUATE PROGRAMS

The element that constitutes the most essential resource in successfully operating a graduate program is its faculty. Securing faculty members with the requisite skills to offer such a program is the most critical and difficult task. This was recognized earlier by Kathleen Russell as she laid the foundations of the basic baccalaureate degree program at the University of Toronto:

> Among the criteria established for faculty positions were: the capacity for independent and creative thought and critical analysis, a broad concept of nursing, a university degree representing sound, general education in the humanities, and preparation for teaching. As nurses with these qualifications were difficult to find, fellowships were secured to assist those selected to undertake additional study and to broaden their understanding of nursing through travel and observation in other countries (Carpenter, 1970, p. 93).

Although skills such as creative thinking and critical analysis, complemented by a broad knowledge of nursing and research skills, can be learned in other than formal university settings, Stinson observed the following about the development of research skills: "One must consider the point that a great deal about research can be learned from participating in increasingly more complex projects" (1977, p. 29). However, she also notes that "it is only in the rare instance that sound research preparation and high research productivity can occur in the absence of substantial amounts and kinds of formalized instruction" (1977, p. 29).

University nursing administrators have experienced difficulty in securing suitably qualified faculty for teaching in university programs. This was a major concern during the formative years in the establishment of baccalaureate programs, and there were times when schools were forced to operate with fewer staff than was desirable because of unfilled faculty positions. Supply and demand questions aside, there is still the leadership connection; that is, whether or not administrators of university schools were sufficiently perceptive and aggressive in recognizing the necessary skills and in encouraging their development in faculty members who showed promise.

Fellowship programs for faculty development have been available since the 1920s. In the early years these were, for the most part, under the sponsorship of private foundations and were earmarked for faculty development. They were also often awarded directly to the institutions to offer to suitable candidates. However, in the late 1950s, public funds became available from federal sources administered through the provinces. With the establishment of the CNF, fellowship funds for graduate study also became available from that source. Although they have been used to a great extent for faculty development, the new funds were not specifically earmarked for this purpose and have also been used for graduate preparation of nurses for practice, educational, and administrative settings.

The dearth of prepared faculty prompted Good to conclude in 1969 that "the void in qualified nurse faculty in Canada has deterred development of Canadian graduate nurse education, and subsequent nursing research." The situation in 1960–1961, shortly after master's programs were first initiated, was that among faculty teaching in university schools, 58% held baccalaureate and 38% held master's degrees (Mussallem, 1965). Mussallem noted that:

> ... although the academic qualifications of faculty in university schools of nursing are higher than those for hospital schools, it should be recognized that university instructors are teaching at the baccalaureate level and their preparation should be beyond that of their students (1965, p. 84).

The situation changed slowly throughout the next decade as more master's programs became available, and by 1970–1971, 1.43% of faculty in university programs held doctoral degrees, 44% held master's degrees, and 49% held baccalaureate degrees (CNA, 1971). In the five-year period ending in 1975 to 1976, there was evidence of additional progress, as 3.74% now held doctoral degrees, 31.28% held master's degrees, and 58.02% held the baccalaureate qualification (Statistics Canada, 1976). In 1980, Larsen and Stinson conducted a national survey to learn the number of nurses holding doctoral degrees. Of the 81 qualified at the doctoral level, 69% were employed in universities (Larsen and Stinson, 1980). A 1982 update of these statistics indicated 124 now hold doctoral degrees; of these, 73% were employed in universities (Stinson, Larsen, and MacPhail, 1984). Stinson, MacPhail, and Larsen did a further update of the doctoral statistics, and will be published by the CNA.

PREPARING TO ESTABLISH DOCTORAL PROGRAMS IN NURSING

In 1975, at the Fourth National Nursing Research Conference held in Edmonton, Alberta, a group of participants interested in facilitating the establishment of doctoral programs in the country held an informal meeting to discuss how this might be accomplished. Other discussions were held at national nursing meetings, and, in 1976, a resolution passed at the CNA Biennial Convention directed the Association to provide leadership in the quest to establish doctoral education in Canada. Through a joint initiative of the CNA, CNF, and CAUSN, a national seminar on doctoral education in nursing was convened in 1978. The W.K. Kellogg Foundation provided funding for the seminar, which brought together deans/directors of university schools of nursing and deans of graduate studies at those institutions to consider issues in planning for the establishment of doctoral education in Canada. The meeting produced a commitment to establishing one or more PhD programs in nursing (Zilm, Larose, and Stinson, 1979). This was the first public recognition of the need to develop one or more programs in this country. As had happened when access to baccalaureate and later master's programs was limited, Canadian nurses emigrated to the United States to take advantage of the educational programs there. Some never returned to Canada, as they were offered attractive positions in the United States.

Another initiative at the national level was the establishment of the Working Group on Nursing Research in 1982, by the Medical Research Council (MRC). The council was the result of efforts by the CNA to document the low level of nursing research funding provided by the national granting councils. Although the smallest funding body, the National Health Research and Development Program, provided limited funding, funds were not specifically designated for nursing; and many other disciplines depended on it for the major share of their funding. Also, although both the MRC and the Social Sciences and Humanities Research Council stated that nursing was included among the disciplines that could be funded, nurses had difficulty getting either council to review nursing proposals. Consequently, few nursing proposals had been funded by either body. The Working Group was created to address these difficulties. Final recommendations in the Report of the Working Group in 1985 addressed the need to assist in creating opportunities for the establishment of PhD in Nursing programs. Also addressed was the need to designate nursing research for funding within the MRC (Medical Research Council of Canada, 1985). A special initiative to support nursing research was established in 1988 jointly by the MRC and the National Health Research Development Program (NHRDP) but meager results have emerged from this venture thus far.

After the Kellogg National Seminar in 1978, McGill University and l'université de Montréal prepared a joint submission for a cooperative, bilingual PhD program; but several factors prevented the approval of the program when it was proposed in 1980. The University of Toronto developed an arrangement with the Institute of Medicine whereby nurses could be admitted to the PhD program offered by that unit to pursue studies in nursing. This arrangement included some Faculty of Nursing input in the program and allowed nurses to take a program more closely related to their own discipline. In 1980, the Council of the Faculty of Nursing of the University of Alberta approved the development of a proposal for a PhD program. Consequently, a proposal was developed and approved by that Faculty Council by 1985 and was approved by the Board of Governors of the University in 1986. The program is currently awaiting funding by the Department of Advanced Education although there are indications that it may be funded shortly. Also in 1980, the University of Toronto approved in principle the development of the PhD in Nursing program. In June 1984, a program for a special case doctoral student in nursing was approved at McGill University. L'Université de Montréal currently is working toward approval of a doctoral program in nursing at that university.

It is startling to realize that more than 10 years after the Kellogg Foundation seminar, no PhD in Nursing program has emerged in any university in the country. In contrast to the American effort, the lack of progress in Canada is striking; in 1975, there were 10 programs in the United States, today there are about 40. Nurses are entering PhD programs in other disciplines in the absence of the opportunity to study nursing in Canada. Many are also enroling in doctoral programs in the United States and the United Kingdom. It is hoped that the era of doctoral education in nursing in Canada is about to begin, and one or more PhD in Nursing programs will appear in the near future.

REFERENCES

Canadian Nurses Association. (1962). *Folio of reports 1962*. Ottawa: Author.

Canadian Nurses Association. (1971). *Countdown 1971*. Ottawa: Author.

Carpenter, H.M. (1970). The University of Toronto School of Nursing: An agent of change. In M.Q. Innes (Ed.), *Nursing education in a changing society*, (pp. 86-108). Toronto: University of Toronto Press.

Good, S.R. (1969). *Submission to the study of support of research in universities for the Science Secretariat of the Privy Council*. Ottawa: Canadian Nurses Association and Canadian Nurses Foundation.

Good, S.R. (1971). *Submission to the Association of Universities and Colleges of Canada*. Calgary: University of Calgary.

Hart, M.E. (1962). *Needs and resources for graduate education in nursing in Canada*. Unpublished doctoral dissertation. New York: Teacher's College, Columbia University.

Imai, H.R. (1971). Professional associations and research activities in nursing in Canada. In *National Conference on Research in Nursing Practice*. Ottawa: School of Nursing, The University of British Columbia.

Kerr, J.C.R. (1978). *Financing university nursing education in Canada: 1919-1976*. Ph.D. dissertation. Ann Arbor, MI: The University of Michigan.

Larsen, J. and Stinson, S.M. (1980). *Canadian nursing doctoral statistics*. Ottawa: Canadian Nurses Association.

Medical Research Council of Canada. (1985). *Report to the Medical Research Council of Canada by the Working Group on Nursing Research*. Ottawa: Author.

National Conference of Canadian Universities. (1944). *Proceedings*. Ottawa: Author.

Overduin, H. (1970). *People and ideas: Nursing at Western 1920-1970*. London, Ontario: The University of Western Ontario.

Statistics Canada. (1976). *Nursing in Canada: Canadian nursing statistics, 1976*. Ottawa: Author.

Stinson, S.M. (1977). Central issues in Canadian nursing research. In B. LaSor and M.R. Elliott (Eds.), *Issues in Canadian nursing*, (pp. 3-42). Scarborough, Ontario: Prentice-Hall of Canada Ltd.

Stinson, S.M., Larsen, J., and MacPhail, J. (1984). *Canadian nursing doctoral statistics: 1982 update*. Ottawa: Canadian Nurses Association.

Tunis, B. (1966). *In caps and gowns*. Montreal: McGill University Press.

University of Western Ontario. (1967-68). *Calendar*. London, Ontario: Author.

W.K. Kellogg Foundation. (1966; 1970; 1971; 1974; 1975). *Annual Report*. Battle Creek, MI: Author.

Zilm, G., Larose, O., and Stinson, S. (1979). *Ph.D. (nursing)*. Ottawa: Canadian Nurses Association.

PART V

The View Beyond

CHAPTER THIRTY TWO

International Nursing: Looking Beyond Our Borders

RICHARD SPLANE AND VERNA HUFFMAN SPLANE

This chapter identifies issues relating to the complex and challenging field of international nursing. Although these issues are important to nurses everywhere, they are reviewed from a Canadian perspective.

Although the topic is approached developmentally, touching on international nursing's evolution and giving recognition to nurses who have played a role in its progress, most attention focuses on what now occupies the central stage—Health for All by the Year 2000, proclaimed by the United Nations. Through its unanimous adoption, all member nations, including Canada, have committed themselves to achieving that far-reaching objective.

The policy base for the Health for All goal was laid at the historic conference in Alma Ata, Union of Soviet Socialist Republic, in 1978. The conference, jointly sponsored by two of the United Nations' specialized agencies, the World Health Organization (WHO) and the United Nations Childrens' Emergency Fund (UNICEF), identified primary health care as the major strategy for achieving universal health and constituted the centrepiece of the Declaration of Alma-Ata.

One of the ten points that outline the scope and implications of the Declaration provides the core of its definition of primary health care as:

> ... essential health care based on practical, scientifically sound and socially acceptable methods and technology made universally accessible to individuals and families in the community through their full participation and at a cost that the community and country can afford to maintain at every stage of their development in the spirit of self reliance and self determination (World Health Organization [WHO], 1978. p. 3).

The definition also states that primary health care "forms an integral part both of the country's health system, of which it is the central function and main

Dr. Richard Splane is Professor Emeritus, School of Social Work, University of British Columbia and a Consultant in Social Policy for Splane Associates. Verna Huffman Splane is Associate Professor, Associate Faculty, Faculty of Nursing, University of Alberta and Nursing Consultant in International Health Policy for Splane Associates.

focus, and of the overall social and economic development of the community" (WHO, 1978).

Advance notice of how the term *primary health care* is being defined throughout the chapter is one reason for this preface. A second is to provide an early indication of what will likely emerge as major international nursing issues of our time and of the foreseeable future. A third is to give visibility and emphasis to principles and strategies of the Alma-Ata Declaration that should be part of the catechism of the well-informed nurse.

STRUCTURES AND INSTITUTIONS: NONGOVERNMENTAL ORGANIZATIONS

Nongovernmental organizations (NGOs) include the International Council of Nurses (ICN) and other organizations, some of which involve nurses only and others in which nursing plays a role within a multidisciplinary or multipurpose structure. They include agencies functioning under religious auspices, universities, and other educational and research institutes and ad hoc bodies that may convene a conference or address some problem that nurses from more than one country wish to explore.

The International Council of Nurses

Primary attention is focused on the ICN because of its central importance to world nursing. It is a remarkable organization in many respects. It was founded in 1899, less than 40 years after the first Nightingale nursing program was established, and to which the beginning of modern professional nursing is frequently ascribed. Although the ICN began with only three national associations, it had the distinction of being the first international professional organization in the health field. It attracted the attention of nurses everywhere who were struggling in their local settings with issues of nursing standards, training, status, recognition, and interdisciplinary relationships. In country after country, specialized nursing groups and local and provincial groups recognized the opportunity the ICN provided for them to become members of a world family of nurses. To accomplish this goal they needed to form national associations, and membership in the ICN constituted a strong force for the development of national nursing associations. This was true in Canada where, in 1908, 16 nursing groups from across the country formed the national organization (destined to become the Canadian Nurses Association [CNA]) that sought and secured membership in the ICN the next year. The CNA became the seventh member of ICN, which by 1990 had 102 national member associations and one million nurses.

It is individual nurses on whom the entire structure of nursing depends, a structure that extends, in Canada, from the local chapter through the provincial association and through the CNA to the ICN. Every nurse who is a member of a provincial or national organization should take pride in the vital part she or he plays in the endeavours of the global organization.

The ICN has served as the official voice of nursing throughout this century. As an independent professional body and through its consultative status with the United Nations, it represents the nursing profession in the international community. It has a twofold objective: the development and enhancement of strong national professional associations capable of providing the nursing component in national health-care systems, and the promotion of favourable conditions of life and work for its members. It maintains a continuous review of its standards and guidelines for nursing education, practice, research, and ethics.

The policies of the ICN are determined by a Council of National Representatives composed of the presidents of the national nursing associations. The Council meets every two years, and every four years convenes an international congress open to all nurses. At each Congress a board of directors, a president, and three vice presidents are elected. The Nineteenth Congress, held in Seoul, Korea in 1989, emphasized long-term planning for the nursing profession. The Tenth Congress, held in Montreal in 1969 and attended by over 10,000 nurses, was notable for two associated events. One was a meeting in Ottawa of chief nursing officers in national ministries of health from some 30 countries—a meeting that recognized the important role that senior nurses play in the formulation and implementation of national health policy. The second historic event was the inaugural meeting of the Commonwealth Nurses' Federation.

The presidents of the ICN, for much of its history, were drawn from developed countries, but those elected in the quadrennial congresses in the 1980s have been from developing countries: Eunice Muringo Kiereini from Kenya, in 1981; Nelly Garzon, from Colombia, in 1985; and Mo-Im-Kim, from Korea, in 1989. The emergence of strong leadership from developing countries gave evidence of the worldwide range of the organization and of its capacity to address environmental and socioeconomic problems of global dimensions that are critical to the Health for All objective.

Since 1981, the secretariat of the ICN, located in Geneva, Switzerland, has been led by Constance Holleran, an American nurse with extensive experience in influencing governmental policy on nursing. She has developed close working relationships with WHO and other United Nations agencies, with NGOs having related socioeconomic concerns and with international foundations.

Canadian nurses have played major roles in the ICN from its inception. Mary Agnes Snively, the first President of the CNA, served as Honourary Treasurer early in the century and Alice Girard, an inspiring nursing leader, was President from 1965 to 1969. There have been three Canadian vice presidents: Grace Fairley, 1949 to 1953; Verna Huffman Splane, 1973 to 1981; and Helen Glass, 1985 to 1989. Other Canadian nurses have served as members of the Board of Directors, the Council of National Representatives, and the Professional Services Committee and have been presenters at quadrennial congresses and key figures involving ICN collaboration with other international bodies. Joan McNeil is currently involved in a major cooperative endeavour involving the national nursing associations of eight African countries seeking to work together to combat the epidemic of acquired immune deficiency syndrome (AIDS).

It is predictable that, as the ICN responds to the challenges of the Alma-Ata Declaration during the rest of the century, Canadian nurses will continue to assume leading and supporting roles.

The Canadian Nurses Association

More important, perhaps, than the support given to the ICN by individual Canadian nurses has been the strong role that CNA has played in international nursing, as a member of the parent organization and through channels other than the ICN. The CNA has extensive networks of nurses throughout the world who look to it for professional help in strengthening their capacity to serve the nursing needs of their countries. From the mid-1960s to the mid-1980s, requests for assistance of this kind increased dramatically, prompting the Board of Directors in 1984 to establish an International Affairs Department charged with the review, coordination, and evaluation of international proposals and projects. The Government of Canada, through its Canadian International Development Agency (CIDA), has encouraged and promoted this development through funding, consultation, and collaboration. In 1987 the CNA was actively engaged in a number of projects in South America, the Caribbean, Africa, Southeast Asia, and the People's Republic of China.

National nursing associations and nursing schools in developing countries have high praise for the help they have received from the CNA. Much of the credit for this international thrust in Canadian nursing is due to the leadership of the CNAs executive directors, notably Ginette Rodger during most of the 1980s and her predecessor, Helen Mussallem, who served through a lengthy period during which Canadian nurses became increasingly aware of the obligations and opportunities for service beyond Canadian borders.

Educational Institutions

The interest in international nursing expressed by the university schools of nursing and other educational institutions for nurses in Canada has varied over the years. A current international study, which involves interviews with nurses who have held senior government posts in the past 60 years, has revealed the historically important role played by the nursing schools of the universities of Toronto, McGill, and Montreal. There are frequent references to the directors and faculty by members of what might be called the "international circuit" of nursing leaders and educators in the prewar and early postwar periods. That group included Eli Magnussen of Denmark, Majsa Andrell of Sweden, Yvonne Henstch of Switzerland, Fernada Alves Diniz of Portugal, Kathleen Raven and Phyllis Friend of Britain, Tehmi Adranvala of India, Nita Barrow of Barbados, Antonia Sernandez of Venezuela, Leman Virol of Turkey, and Matsu Kameko of Japan.

In more recent years, nurses have demonstrated a growing interest in international affairs. Numerous connections have been formed between Canadian educational institutions and agencies with those in other countries, including faculty exchanges, consultations, and the external examination of student papers and the student grading process.

Many international meetings and conferences have been held under educational sponsorship. A tour of five noted authorities in 1979 gave university and college campuses across Canada their first in-depth exposition of primary health care. Especially notable was the International Nursing Research Conference held in Edmonton in 1986, which gave prominence to the extent and quality of existing nursing research and impetus to the measures needed for its support and expansion. Other meetings involving international nursing participation were the Conference on Distance Learning in Victoria in 1986, the Second International Symposium of Clinical Research and the Child and Family in 1987 in Montreal and, in the same year, the International Conference on Aspects of Nursing Diagnosis held at the University of Calgary.

Intercountry study of health care and nursing is assisted by travel grants and fellowships from organizations such as WHO, the Commonwealth Foundation, the International Development Research Centre, the Association of Universities and Colleges of Canada, and the Canadian Public Health Association. The Educational Institution Program of the CIDA supports linkages with counterpart universities in developing countries.

Of special importance to student nurses is the International Health Exchange Program (IHEP) of the Canadian Society for International Health. The growing interest of nursing students in work or travel abroad and concern about international affairs has led to the formation of linkages with students in all health disciplines across the country and to requests for international health and nursing courses in their curricula. The number of nursing programs in Canada offering such courses is expected to expand in the 1990s.

Religious Auspices

International nursing under religious auspices has a long history. Nursing was brought to French Canada by religious orders in the seventeenth century. One of these served under the lay direction of Jeanne Mance, the first European woman to arrive in Montreal. This importation of European nurses within religious sisterhoods was complemented, over the years, by an outflow of Canadian nurses to countries in many parts of the world. From the later years of the nineteenth century the Protestant denominations sent nurses with missionary callings to numerous countries in Latin America, Asia, and Africa. Their work in improving health services and in developing nursing training programs constitutes a fascinating story.

The work of religious bodies in the health field has been greatly enhanced by the work of the World Council of Churches, based in Geneva, and composed of 300 churches from 115 countries. Through its Christian Medical Commission, it plays an active role in upgrading and monitoring church-related health services around the world. It influences the policies of the individual denominations in their recruitment and deployment of nursing and other personnel; but the recruitment and utilization of health-care personnel in the missions remain the responsibility of the denominations. The Council's Medical Commission was headed for a number of years by Nita Barrow, an outstanding nurse and world leader in many fields who added significantly to the visibility of international nursing and reinforced the Council's commitment to primary health care involving interdisciplinary collaboration.

Other Nongovernmental Organizations

Much of the work in the field of international health previously carried out under religious auspices is now performed by numerous nongovernmental agencies that deal with disaster relief, refugees, and populations with differing forms of handicaps or vulnerability. The International Red Cross stands out in this regard; within it, for many years, the League of Red Cross Societies has played direct and catalytic roles in nursing and nursing education. Variants of the nongovernmental organizations that focus on existing problems of health and deprivation are those oriented toward longer term social and microeconomic development.

A Canadian NGO that is making an outstanding contribution to Health for All is the Canadian Public Health Association. Its role in international immunization and contagious disease control involves nursing in many countries and reflects the leadership of the nurses in its key positions, notably Karen Mills, Sandra McKenzie, Helen Mussallem, Margaret Hilson, and Anne Wieler.

GOVERNMENTAL INSTITUTIONS

The focus now shifts to the governmental sector, the importance of which cannot be overstated. Here the reference is to national governments (though some provincial governments in Canada have significant international programs); to regional government structures, notably the European Economic Community; and to world government, as represented by the United Nations and its specialized agencies. Among these are the Food and Agriculture Organization (FAO), the United Nations High Commission for Refugees (UNHCR), UNICEF, the International Labour Organization (ILO), and WHO, which is the one of greatest relevance to nurses and nursing.

AGENCIES OF THE NATIONAL GOVERNMENT: HEALTH AND WELFARE CANADA AND THE CANADIAN INTERNATIONAL DEVELOPMENT AGENCY

National governments express their commitments to international health in many ways. In Canada, the Department of National Health and Welfare plays a number of international roles concerned with health protection and promotion and with Canada's obligations under resolutions of the United Nations, including working to advance the goal of Health for All by the Year 2000 through primary health care and related strategies. Matters related to nursing, both nationally and internationally, are the concern of the Principal Nursing Officer, Dr. Josephine Flaherty, who, in her official role, advises the Minister on how nursing can be most effectively used at home and abroad.

The CIDA, a crown corporation of the government, expresses Canada's commitment to helping the countries of the developing world to improve their social and economic conditions. Over 100 countries have received aid through

ZCIDA's multilateral and bilateral programs, many of which have to do with Canada's support and sponsorship of resolutions adopted by the General Assembly of the United Nations. Frequently, CIDA's aid is in support of initiatives that are also being promoted by the specialized agencies, notably WHO. CIDA directly recruits and funds individuals, including nurses, to assist in developmental projects when developing countries request such professional and technical help.

Increasingly, however, CIDA has turned to Canada's NGOs, including professional associations, for the skills needed to meet the wide variety of requests from countries seeking help with their health and other social and economic needs. Among the NGOs who have enlisted nurses, usually young nurses, for overseas assignments are the Canadian University Service Overseas (CUSO) and the World University Service of Canada. CIDA has also supported the CNA in many of the international projects referred to previously, most of which assist nurses in developing their associations and improving nursing's role in national health systems. CIDA has also collaborated with Canadian universities, including schools and faculties of nursing, as they have taken on projects to assist in education and training in developing countries.

REGIONAL GOVERNMENT: THE EUROPEAN ECONOMIC COMMUNITY

Governments of countries in parts of the world that have structures to deal with common interests frequently are concerned with health and personnel issues that crucially affect nursing. One regional governmental structure where this has emerged in a formal and highly significant way is the European Economic Community (EEC), which now consists of 12 European countries. The EEC aims to integrate the countries' economies, coordinate social developments, and create a common labour market. To achieve the goal of labour mobility without endangering the public, the EEC has had to establish standards of qualification. For nurses, the EEC has passed legislation in the European Parliament to document, with some precision, the levels of education and training that are needed for a nurse to assume professional nursing positions in the member states. The enactment of the legislation was preceded by difficult negotiations by nursing associations, and its implementation is monitored by a standing committee of nursing representatives from the member states. The EEC legislation has had an important impact on the education and movement of nurses in Europe, and its influence is likely to affect the intense debate on nursing standards that is taking place in Northern European countries, three of which (Norway, Sweden and Finland) are not members of the EEC. It will also provide guidelines for advances in nursing in the countries of Eastern Europe that broke through the ideologic and military barriers separating them from the West at the end of 1989.

The EEC is the most advanced of the regional groupings of governments. Nurses in other parts of the world need to be aware of the stake they have in the formation and the policies of comparable regional structures in their areas.

WORLD GOVERNMENT: THE WORLD HEALTH ORGANIZATION

The organization within the structure of world government that plays the largest role in international nursing is the WHO, founded by the United Nations soon after its creation at the end of World War II. Building on the work of its international and regional predecessors, WHO established a highly creditable record in promoting world health, with particularly impressive successes in the control and elimination of communicable diseases.

Nursing was given a high priority in the early years of WHO. In the first sessions of the World Health Assembly the shortage of health personnel was identified as a major problem, particularly in developing countries, and measures were taken to deal with it. Recognizing the central role of nursing in health services, WHO set up a nursing unit directed by a chief nursing officer at headquarters in 1949 and thereafter established nursing officer positions in the six WHO regions. Experienced and well-qualified nurses were recruited from many nursing specializations and from many countries to provide consultation, conduct and promote studies and research, and perform direct nursing services in demonstration projects.

The work of the nursing components of WHO at its headquarters and in the regions has transformed nursing throughout the world and has contributed immeasurably to WHO's objectives, including that of extending unequivocal support to Health for All, largely through the primary health-care strategy.

Nursing in WHO, however, had a serious setback in the early 1970s when the nursing unit and the position of chief nursing officer were abolished and the nurses were transferred to the Organization's functional units. There were also reductions in the complement of nurses in the regions.

In succeeding years, extending into the 1980s, the role of nursing in advancing the Health for All goal was not adequately recognized or provided for. Those years were referred to in 1985 by Dr. Halfdan Mahler (the Director-General from 1973 to 1988), as "the years of doubt." The doubt was in the minds of those controlling WHO's policies, including Dr. Mahler, and the doubt was about nurses capability of assuming roles other than "resources to physicians" (WHO, 1985a).

The Director-General's dramatic reappraisal of nursing was a result of his review of the extent to which the health professions were making the changes needed for the implementation of the primary health-care strategy. Noting that "the nursing profession was infinitely more ready for change than other professional groups", he stated that "it was now time that nurses were brought in much more than hitherto . . . as leaders and managers in the primary health care/Health for All team" (WHO, 1985b). Referring to nurses worldwide "as a powerhouse for change," he called for the optimal use of nurses in program planning and evaluation and in senior management, policy development and decision making.

What was not acknowledged by Dr. Mahler was that WHO's action in abolishing the chief nursing officer position and the associated nursing unit in the early 1970s had not only reduced the effectiveness of WHO itself but constituted a damaging precedent for similar action in national ministries of health in many parts of the world. On the advice of WHO, numerous chief nursing positions had been initially established. Accordingly, WHO's seeming repudiation of that model strengthened the hands of those in national ministries of health who wished to take similar action to remove nurses from senior positions in policy development and management. The loss of chief nursing officer positions in many national ministries of health since 1970 may be attributable to many factors, not the least of which is the example set by WHO.

It is ironic that the Director-General's call in 1985 for the training of an adequate number of nurses "to assume a greater managerial role and to participate in developing policy with assurance and confidence" (WHO, 1985a) was made after the key positions where such roles could be creatively managed in national ministries had been lost, probably irretrievably, through actions by governments that were following WHO's own ill-advised action in the early 1970s.

The gradual rebuilding of the influence of nursing within WHO is associated with the one designated nursing position established at the Geneva headquarters after the abolition of the nursing unit. The position, ultimately designated a Chief Scientist for Nursing, was held for 14 years by Amelia Mangay Maglacas, a nurse from the Philippines with extensive experience in international nursing, teaching, administration, and research. The functions of the position were expanded over the years and as its role as the focal point for nursing affairs in the Organization was creatively used by Dr. Maglacas, its status and influence grew.

The means used to strengthen global nursing included actions relating to the implementation of regulations of WHO's General Assembly, the convening of expert committees on nursing, measures to promote improved education and training of nurses, the continued use of experienced nurses as consultants to the member countries, the provision of WHO educational fellowships and close collaboration with nursing leaders and associations, most notably with the ICN.

Specific initiatives taken with the support of Dr. Mahler included the convening of a high-level invitational meeting in Tokyo, Japan in April 1986 on Leadership in Nursing for Health for All. Of great long-term significance was the unveiling, also in 1986, of the plan to establish a worldwide chain of Collaborating Centres for International Nursing Development. The first Centre was launched at the College of Nursing, University of Illinois in Chicago. By the end of the decade there were 12 centres in 9 countries in 4 of the 6 WHO regions, and negotiations were proceeding on the establishment of a centre in Canada.

In 1988, Dr. Mahler was succeeded as Director-General by Dr. Hiroshi Nakajima of Japan and in 1989 Amelia Mangay Maglacas was succeeded by a nursing leader of comparable qualifications and experience, Miriam Hirschfeld of Israel. Dr. Nakajima's message to the Nineteenth Congress of ICN in Seoul in 1989 appeared to indicate that he appreciated the potential of nursing and the roles nurses have in meeting the contemporary range of health needs and issues, and this found some expression in his appointment at headquarters in 1989 and 1990 of two nurses to the global AIDS program.

There is, however, a continuing lack of evidence that WHO's managers are providing sufficient nursing resources either at headquarters or in the regions for nurses to make their optimal contribution to the Health for All objective.

The contributions of Canadian nurses to WHO are noteworthy.This was especially true of the work of Lyle Creelman, the chief nurse from 1952 to 1968, a period of remarkable growth and achievement. Lily Turnbull, her successor from 1968 to 1972, was also Canadian, and there were senior nurses in all six WHO regions at various times. Examples are Margaret Cammaert, the Chief Nursing Officer in the Pan American Health Organization, the WHO regional office for the Americas, and Dorothy Hall, who served as Regional Nursing Officer both in Southeast Asia and in Europe. Over the entire history of WHO, scores of Canadian nurses have held positions as consultants, project leaders on both long-term and short-term assignments and on WHO committees. To the extent that well-prepared nurses are cognizant of and committed to the principles of the Alma-Ata Declaration, they will continue to have opportunities to participate in the global endeavours of WHO.

ISSUES WITH INTERNATIONAL DIMENSIONS

Nursing issues with international dimensions are evident now and are likely to be prevalent during the remainder of the century. Two categories of issues are identified: one has to do with the capacity and willingness of nurses to retain strong national and international organizations based on the firm commitment to general nursing that is needed if nurses and their professional organizations are to play effective roles nationally and internationally; the second has to do with the issues associated with the Health for All objective and the primary health-care strategy required for its achievement. Three or four subordinate but important issues fall within this second category.

GENERAL NURSING AND THE INTEGRITY OF THE PROFESSION

Nursing, through its professional associations provincially, nationally, and internationally, has demonstrated that it is strong and influential, both in reality and potential. Its present and future strength, however, depends on three associated conditions: (1) that nurses receive sound education in general nursing, (2) that they maintain an enduring commitment to the general nursing core of the profession, and (3) that the professional associations created to represent the interests and reflect the concerns of general nursing continue to honour that commitment.

The issue of the threat to the general nursing core comes essentially from two rather divergent sources. One is the tendency that derives from a misapplication of the managerial concepts of efficiency and effectiveness, which seeks to shorten the duration and restrict the content of basic general nursing programs. It comes from the expanding demand for personnel with skills in the increasingly technical procedures in modern hospitals and clinics and results in pressure to channel nursing students prematurely into one or another of nursing's more technical or complex specializations.

This trend is affecting the reciprocal recognition of nurses between some European countries where the country of migration does not accept those certified in the country of graduation, where the latter has reduced the duration and the quality of its basic general nursing certificate. Those opposing this trend believe that if it is not arrested and reversed, it will destroy nursing and the nursing profession. The pressure to reduce basic general nursing education continues to be strong, however, and comes both from health-system managers and from governments seeking to reduce costs. They tend to ignore or reject the case for broad general nursing as having enduring value for the health-care system and as forming the foundation for the profession of nursing.

The other source of threat to general nursing comes from the special-interest groups in nursing. These groups are to be welcomed for their commitment to attaining the highest levels of knowledge and performance in their specific areas of interest. What is *not* to be welcomed is their tendency to separate from the general nursing profession and to form autonomous, sometimes competitive, organizations. The CNA's approach to arrest that type of development through providing a process for linkages within its structure may prove to be a model for countries where there is still time to prevent nurses from abandoning their general nursing affiliation. The importance of such action can hardly be over-stressed. It is only through strong and united national organizations capable of supporting a strong international professional association, the ICN, that the nurses of the world can speak with one voice on the great issues that are linked to the goal of Health for All.

NURSING AND PRIMARY HEALTH CARE

Since 1979, nurses around the world have been exploring the meaning and implications of the Alma-Ata Declaration. Presented here are some succinct comments on three aspects of the question: attitudinal, educational, and political.

ATTITUDINAL ISSUES

The Alma-Ata Declaration presents a sweeping and comprehensive challenge. It challenges people to think of their health and its preservation and restoration in ways that are radically different from the accustomed norms. It also challenges governments and especially health providers, who are called on to question and to change the prevailing values that constitute the existing systems of health care and the even more basic social, cultural, and economic systems within which the health system is situated. That challenge requires profound attitudinal changes, individually and collectively. None of the health professions will change their attitudes without stress and trauma. As noted earlier, the former Director-General of WHO has described the nursing profession "as infinitely more ready for change than other professional groups" (WHO, 1985b). That is heartening. Time will test its validity.

EDUCATIONAL ISSUES

The most promising and fruitful modality for attitudinal change is education; in this case, the professional education of nurses. The implication of the Alma-Ata Declaration is that the education of nurses become "international." The objective of Health for All calls for a world view of nursing.

Few of the existing curricula in programs of nursing education show a recognition that international nursing constitutes a field of study. That situation and a meaningful acceptance of the Alma-Ata Declaration cannot co-exist. It is not sufficient for international nursing to be an elective in a few postbasic nursing programs. The Health for All objective calls for international health and nursing to be part of nursing education, basic and postbasic, everywhere.

POLITICAL ISSUES

The achievement of health for all requires political decisions at every level of government. The decisions to be made extend beyond the health care system as it is usually defined. They extend to the range of policies that determine, in the words of the Alma-Ata definition, a country's "overall social and economic development" (WHO, 1978). Health for All cannot be achieved for people who are homeless, are without income for necessities, and without other services and facilities needed for their inclusion in the normal life of the community. Few countries can claim to meet these preconditions for Health for All.

Nurses and other human service workers see the impact on the lives of people of social and economic policies that fail to provide the preconditions to good health. What they see and know entails a moral imperative to political action at the community, provincial, national, and international levels.

Action begins at the grassroots level in conveying the principles and providing the aid needed to enhance self-help and individual responsibility. It extends to reformulating the policies and changing the practices over the entire range of the social services. It focuses on governments, provincial and national, with jurisdictional responsibility for social services, income support, income redistribution, and the economy in general. Finally, it must reach those international bodies where macropolicies are made and macroresources are deployed: the World Bank, the International Monetary Fund, the United Nations, and all its specialized agencies.

This action carries nurses and nursing organizations beyond their accustomed fields of political concern and action, but nurses have met formidable political challenges in the past in many jurisdictions around the world. The Alma-Ata Declaration calls for more sustained action, but action that is carefully planned and implemented in concert with other agencies and organizations working for peace, social development, and human well-being. It can be undertaken in the faith that what *must* be done *can* be done to achieve Health for All in this century.

REFERENCES

Abou Youssef, E. (1989). *Health for all: Where are we today and where do we need to go?* Paper presented at the Pre-Congress Conference of the WHO Collaborating Centre for International Nursing Development in Primary Health Care, Seoul, Korea, May 26-27.

Association of Universities and Colleges of Canada. (1990). *Synergy,* 2(1), Spring.

Baumgart, A.J., and Larsen, J. (Eds.) (1988). *Canadian nursing faces the future: development and change.* St. Louis: The CV Mosby Co.

Canadian Nurses Association. (1989). *Annual reports: 1975-90.* Ottawa: The Association.

Canadian Public Health Association. (1989a). *A miracle in the making: Canada's international immunization program.* Ottawa: The Association.

Canadian Public Health Association. (1989b). *Partners around the world: Newsletter of international health secretariat.* Ottawa: The Association.

Cox, C. (1989). *Forging nursing's future: A sociopolitical perspective.* Proceedings the 19th Quadrennial Congress of the International Council of Nurses. Geneva: International Council of Nurses.

Epp, J. (1986) *Achieving health for all: A framework for health promotion.* Paper presented at the International Conference on Health Promotion, Ottawa, November 1986, Health and Welfare Canada.

Fulop, T. and Roemer, M. (1982). *International development of health manpower policy.* Geneva: World Health Organization. (WHO Offset Publication No. 61).

Government of Canada. (1988). *Annual reports 1975-88.* Ottawa: Government of Canada.

International Council of Nurses. (1974). The special ICN 75th anniversary issue, May/June, July/August 1974. *The International Nursing Review.* 21(3-4), 1-27.

International Council of Nurses. (1989). *Biennial reports of the executive director to the Council of National Representatives. 1973-89.* Geneva: The Council.

Kiereini, E.M. (1989). *Health policy: Barriers and means of achieving health for all by the year 2000.* Paper presented at the Pre-Congress Conference of the WHO Collaborating Centre for International Nursing Development in Primary Health Care, Seoul, Korea, May 26-27, 1989. Korea: Yonsei University.

Maglacas, A. (1986). *Proposals for networking of WHO Collaborating Centres in nursing.* Proceedings of the (ECHO) Conference, August 27-29, 1986. Chicago: University of Chicago, College of Nursing.

Mahler, H. (1986). *Why leadership for health for all.* Proceedings of the WHO Conference, International Encounter on Leadership in Nursing, Health for All. Geneva: World Health Organization.

Miller, T. (1989). *Health for all: Where are we today and where do we need to go.* Paper presented at the ICN Pre-Congress Conference of the WHO Collaborating Centre for International Nursing Development in Primary Health Care, Seoul, Korea, May 26-27, 1989. Korea: Yonsei University.

Quinn, S. (1989). *ICN: Past and present.* Geneva: International Council of Nurses.

Rodger, G. (1989). *Public policy considerations.* Paper presented at the ICN Pre-Congress Conference of the WHO Collaborating Centre for International Nursing Development in Primary Health Care, Seoul, Korea, May 26-27, 1989. Korea: Yonsei University.

Styles, M.M. (1986). *The regulation of nursing.* Geneva: International Council of Nurses.

University of Illinois at Chicago. (1990). *International network news: 1986-1990.* Chicago: University of Illinois at Chicago.

World Health Organization. (1978). *Primary health care: report on the International Conference on Primary Health Care. Alma Ata, USSR. 6-12 September 1978.* Geneva: WHO.

World Health Organization. (1982). *Nursing in support of the goal for health for all by the year 2000.* Geneva: WHO.

World Health Organization. (1985). *Nurses lead the way.* WHO Features. June 1985a No. 97. Geneva: Who.

World Health Organization. (1985). WHO Press, January 14, 1985b. Geneva: WHO.

World Health Organization. (1987). *The work of WHO in the Western Pacific region: Biennial report of the regional director, 1 July 1985 - 30 June 1987.* Manila: WHO.

World Health Organization. (1989). *The work of WHO: Biennial reports of the director-general (1948-1989).* Geneva: WHO.

World Health Organization. Regional Office for Europe. (1986). *A simplified guide to nursing in WHO.* Copenhagen: WHO, Regional Office for Europe.

World Health Organization. Regional Office for Europe. (1990). *Nursing/midwifery in Europe.* 6(3), Winter 1989-1990.

Yule, B.M.G. (1983). *Red Cross nursing: Impact on health care.* London and Geneva: International Red Cross.

CHAPTER THIRTY THREE

Looking Ahead

JANNETTA MacPHAIL
AND JANET ROSS KERR

M any issues of importance to the nursing profession have been discussed in this book. Traversing nursing practice, education, administration, and research, current issues in nursing have been presented from a Canadian perspective. It is essential for every nurse to develop an awareness of matters of professional significance, for these affect everyday practice, and knowledge and understanding can significantly improve approaches to practice. The future depends on nurses entering practice today and tomorrow and the profession's ability to attract and retain a cadre of intellectually able and visionary risk takers to provide future leadership. It is the same professional practitioner who will have the ability to understand the concept of primary health care as the way to empower and enable Canadians to assume increasing responsibility for their own health, and to press for changes in the health-care system to incorporate a focus on primary health care.

The story of the nursing profession in Canada is ongoing. Three-and-a-half centuries of rich tradition have provided a wonderful and distinguished background from which to move forward. Nursing was an integral part of the early settlements along the shores of the St. Lawrence, and health-care facilities established and operated by nurses were available before the arrival of most settlers. As founder of the city of Montreal, Jeanne Mance, along with Paul de Chomédy, Sieur de Maisonneuve, and a small company, laid the foundations for the nursing service that would meet the needs of the struggling colony for many years. In later years, the importance of establishing educational programs for nurses was recognized, as was the need to develop legislation to differentiate between qualified and unqualified practitioners. Succeeding years brought important advances in health-care knowledge and technology and new issues and problems.

The challenges are clear: developing and extending of nursing knowledge through research; the provision of opportunities for nurses to study at the doctoral level in nursing in Canada; extending educational opportunities in nursing at the master's level; preparing practitioners at the baccalaureate level for practice; and restructuring the health-care system to allow nurses to function in the roles for which they are prepared. All these challenges are aimed at achieving Health for All by the year 2000. These are all major thrusts of the profession and represent challenges that require careful thought and concerted action by politically astute leaders, supported by the majority of the professional membership. The nursing profession has accomplished a great deal in its three-and-a-half centuries in Canada; there is no doubt that more accomplishments will follow.

Index